DRIVEN TO CRIME

'There are only three sports: bullfighting, motor racing, and mountaineering; all the rest are merely games.'

Ernest Hemingway

'Like any sport, motor racing can boast its share of shady individuals. Whispers and rumours are as far as it gets in many cases but sometimes the facts are incontrovertible and occasionally sensational.'

Gordon Cruickshank

DRIVEN TO CRIME

TRUE STORIES OF WRONGDOING IN MOTOR RACING

EVRO
PUBLISHING

CRISPIAN BESLEY

For Hugo and Charlie
With all my love
Daddy

Published October 2022

ISBN: 978-1-910505-70-0

Edited by Mark Hughes
Designed by Richard Parsons
Front cover artwork by Giuseppe Camuncoli

Printed and bound in Malta

Note to the reader

Most of the chapters in this book concern perpetrators
of crime in motor racing but some are about victims
who have been associated with the sport.

Author's acknowledgements

Of all the many people who have helped me research this book, I would especially like to thank former Grand Prix driver Howden Ganley with whom I first discussed the project over dinner at the Teretonga circuit in New Zealand where I was racing in 2017. Although I had already started my research, it was he who persuaded me to put pen to paper and has encouraged me ever since. Of the many others, two who stand out are veteran motorsport journalist and broadcaster Andrew Marriott and journalist and circuit commentator Ian Titchmarsh, both of whom have been incredibly generous with their time and in sharing their encyclopaedic knowledge with me, for which I am most grateful. I have also had wonderful support from my family but the biggest thanks go to my editor Mark Hughes who has helped me at every stage and modelled my verbosity into a book that I hope is both readable and enjoyable, even to those who may have just a passing interest in the sport.

My thanks also go to the following: Wil Arif, Trevor Baines, Jonathan Baker, John Bartlett, Martin Braybrook, Lord Charles Brocket, Charlie Campbell, Richard Chetwode, Michael Clark, Gordon Cruickshank, Robin Donovan, Mike Doodson, Roger Earl, John Fitzpatrick, Howden Ganley, Chris Goodwin, Tony Goodwin, Geoff Green, Ben Horton, Martin Laubert, Vic Lee, Chris Locke, Calum Lockie, Doug Nye, Richard Page, Jonathan Palmer, Ian Phillips, Jessica Pratt, Marcus Pye, Duncan Rabagliati, Graham Rabagliati, Tom Rubython, Richard Smeeton, Tony Southgate, Charles Stevens, John Swift and David Tremayne.

CONTENTS

INTRODUCTION

I have had a lifelong love affair with the motor car and a special passion for motor racing, where I have been fortunate enough to have enjoyed a modicum of success at a non-professional level. I have always been captivated by what motivates other people to participate in motor racing, which, unlike most other sports, can cost not only the wealth, homes, sanity and relationships of participants but also sometimes their health and even their lives.

My professional background in investment banking has also helped to add to my fascination with the commercial aspects of motor racing at every level and the lengths to which some people will go to fund their involvement, especially as I went through the process of raising sponsorship to pay for my own early forays in the sport as a teenager. There are a lucky few who will find support from family or inherited wealth, or the businesses of family, friends or associates, but for most it is a matter of sheer hard graft. However, there is also a small minority who finance their aspirations by turning to crime, and over several decades of following motor racing as an avid enthusiast I have always been intrigued by those who did just that and invariably became unstuck.

That was the genesis of this book, the title of which seemed to choose itself but at the same time is somewhat misleading. The more I investigated characters who resorted to illegal activities to fund their racing and often to further enrich themselves, the more I noticed and uncovered other instances of criminal activity surrounding the sport less directly. Hence this book includes chapters not only about perpetrators who have been 'driven to crime' but also about victims of crime who have been involved in racing.

Dishonesty in sport, of course, is most certainly not confined to motor racing. The great chronicler of English life, George Orwell, famously observed: 'Serious sport has nothing to do with fair play. It is bound up with hatred, jealousy, boastfulness, disregard of all rules and sadistic pleasure in violence.' The temptation to cheat is human and most sports are no stranger to corruption, cheating and scandal, fragilities of human nature that have been with us since time immemorial.

Throughout top-level sport, the stakes have become so high that one could write about criminality in almost any realm of sporting endeavour. Some misdemeanours in sport, indeed, have reached worldwide levels of publicity beyond anything crooked that has occurred in motor racing. Perhaps the most notorious example is cyclist Lance Armstrong's use of performance-enhancing drugs that led to him being stripped of his seven consecutive Tour de France victories along with an Olympic medal. The infamous murder trials involving American footballer O.J. Simpson and South African Paralympian Oscar Pistorius were also reported all over the world.

Betting is one element of criminality endemic in various sports, whether in the obvious field of horse racing, or match-fixing in cricket and football, or gambling on outcomes in one-to-one contests such as professional boxing. Research carried out in 2014 by the International Centre for Sport Security in conjunction with Sorbonne University in Paris revealed that 80 percent of global betting on sport is illegally transacted and therefore invisible to regulators and investigators.

In other instances, crime in sport may just be for glory, affirmation and feeding of ego. Tonya Harding was so desperate to win a gold medal for figure skating at the 1994 Winter Olympics that she and her husband hired thugs to 'take care of' her principal rival's knee. A contrasting example at amateur level was Rosie Ruiz, who was foolish enough to try to claim victory in the women's Boston Marathon of 1979 by taking the subway to the final half-mile of the course and joining the proceedings before the genuine winner came into view.

But back to motor racing. The very broad variety of wrongdoing described in this book embraces embezzlement, robbery, fraud, espionage, murder, smuggling, Ponzi schemes, money laundering, drug trafficking and race fixing. It catalogues criminal activity in all tiers of the sport from Formula 1 down to club-level motor racing. It covers entrants, drivers, team owners, mechanics, sponsors, race promoters, circuit owners, spectators, fantasists and even protestors. And it tells of the double lives that often accompany deception.

Unlike most sports, motor racing requires exceptionally expensive equipment as well being among the most dangerous and egotistical of all sporting arenas. Perhaps this element of excess and risk explains some of its captivation to those who involve themselves in it, especially as drivers. By its nature, motor racing is a world made up of extreme personalities, some of whom can be aggressively competitive beyond the norm, to the point of dishonesty. It is also a sport that has always had more than its fair share of sometimes dysfunctional rogues among its numbers, often inextricably linked to each other at any given time.

For those whose interest may be more focused on the crimes themselves rather than motor racing, it is important to understand how deeply addictive this sport can be and what seduces people into participating in it and sometimes going on to commit crime to enable them to do so. Of course, competitors in all sports want to win, but rarely does this urge turn into the compulsive addiction so often found in motor racing, where huge egos lie behind the ambition to be the very best with the accompanying lust for bigger, better, faster and more powerful machinery.

Adrenaline is a very powerful hormone that can produce extreme emotions and motor racing is fuelled by it. The allure of the sport encompasses fast cars, romance, glamour, beautiful people and speed, together with escapism, excitement and inherent danger in a highly charged theatre of competition. All this adds up to an intoxicating combination that is powerfully addictive and has always attracted self-obsessed characters who are often motivated by the fear of losing. It is a sport where money talks louder than any other commodity and because it is beyond the reach of all but a very few it can lead some people to resort to unorthodox and illegal means of bankrolling their dreams.

Where there's crime there's money, and money truly makes the wheels go round in a sport like motor racing. An old adage that holds true is that if you want to make a small fortune, start with a large one and then go motor racing. The sport is fuelled by and consumes a prodigious amount of money and so crime has always been one way to finance it.

Motor racing also provides an ideal platform for certain forms of crime, two of which stand out. Firstly, money laundering — the process by which large amounts of money generated by criminal activity can be made to appear to come from a legitimate source — is an area of illegality that motor racing readily suits with all its expensive equipment. Secondly, drug smuggling can be that much easier for criminals to conduct when engaged in frequent international travel with sophisticated racing transporters packed with masses of equipment.

Robin Herd, formerly the co-owner of March Engineering, once told the journalist Mike Lawrence: 'It's a funny thing, but when you get criminals in motor racing, they tend to play by the rules. Within the sport they are absolutely straight as though they are trying to do something right in their lives.'

Wherever there is a crime, there is always a victim and I do not seek to trivialise any of the crimes reported nor the suffering endured by victims. Neither have I made any attempt to glorify the miscreants involved or to be judgemental. I have tried simply to report what happened and what is in the public domain.

Some of the crimes covered in this book may be known to *aficionados* of the sport but most of them should be new to even the most knowledgeable enthusiasts. A few readers may feel that 'he's left out so-and-so' but a line had to be drawn somewhere and I do not believe there are any significant omissions. Assembling the evidence and piecing together all these tales has been a fascinating exercise for me over many years and I hope you will find it both enjoyable and instructive to read them.

Crispian Besley
August 2022

CHAPTER 1

AKIRA AKAGI
Eastern promise

This highly successful
Japanese property developer
was the title sponsor of the
revitalised March Formula 1
team in the late 1980s and
briefly took ownership before
becoming embroiled in the
biggest financial scandal in
Japanese history.

After studying business administration at university, Akira Akagi joined his father's property development company, Kenzai, in 1966 and after taking control built it up into a hugely successful business. In 1981, he moved Kenzai under the umbrella of a holding company he created called Marusho Kosan, which was involved in real-estate sales, leasing and management. The Japanese property market was booming at the time and on the back of this, in 1984, he decided to create a lifestyle brand, similar in concept to the business model of British tycoon Richard Branson and the Virgin Group. At one stage he had lived in England, in the East London district of Leyton, and decided to incorporate this into the name of his newly expanded empire. The Leyton House Group evolved to operate 21 companies with interests as diverse as travel, retail, sportswear, hotels, restaurants and clubs.

The strength of the Japanese property market reflected the surging economy that took the country's stock market to its highest level in history at the end of 1989. This led to a flurry of Japanese companies jumping on a bandwagon of involvement in Formula 1 to increase their global exposure.

Akagi was an extrovert and enthusiastic man who not only owned a large collection of classic road cars but was also very keen on motor racing, having competed in rallycross in his youth. After meeting a promising young racing driver, Akira Hagiwara, he declared that his company would take him all the way to Formula 1. So it was that the first Leyton House-branded racing car was a Mercedes 190E 2.3-16V touring car entered in Japan's national series, while a season in Japan's Formula 2 championship was also planned using a March-Yamaha 86J. Tragically, Hagiwara was killed very early in the exercise, in April 1986, when he crashed the Mercedes while testing at the Sugo circuit in Miyagi.

Chastened but undeterred, and still keen to use motor racing as a platform to promote his group of companies, Akagi backed the Japanese-entered, TOM'S-run, Toyota-powered Dome in the Le Mans 24 Hours. Still seeking a replacement driver for his Formula 2 plans, he stayed on in Europe afterwards to attend a Formula 3000 race at Imola the following weekend. While there, he was introduced to a young Italian driver, Ivan Capelli, who was struggling to fund his own season. The two reached an agreement whereby Capelli would race the Formula 2 March in Japan in return for a healthy percentage of the generous prize money on offer and would also carry allegiance to Akagi's company on his Formula 3000 car in Europe. Wearing the vivid turquoise corporate livery of Leyton House on his Genoa Racing March-Cosworth 86B in the International Formula 3000 Championship, Capelli became champion.

Although Capelli's talents had already earned him a handful of uncompetitive Formula 1 outings with Tyrrell and AGS, his success in Formula 3000 was sufficiently impressive to encourage Akagi to sponsor him to the tune of $4 million in Formula 1 in the returning March team for 1987. With the development costs of running turbocharged engines having spiralled out of control at this time, the FIA had recently announced that turbos were to be banned in Formula 1 for 1989, with naturally aspirated engines being phased back in during 1987 and '88. The timing of this presented the ideal opportunity for March to make a return to Grand Prix racing after an absence of four years. For Capelli and his team owner Cesare Gariboldi, who was also the Italian importer for March customer cars, this was an obvious fit.

The revived March team, managed by former journalist Ian Phillips, modified its Formula 3000 chassis to accept the Cosworth DFZ V8, with engine preparation entrusted to Heini Mader. Although results in 1987 were hindered by poor engine reliability, Capelli's performances showed

Akira Akagi's brief ownership of the March Formula 1 team, which he renamed Leyton House, ended with his arrest in September 1991 for his part in a big financial scandal in Japan.

The name of Akagi's organisation was prominently displayed on his team's distinctively coloured cars. Lead driver Ivan Capelli scored Leyton House Racing's best result with second place in the 1990 French Grand Prix.

promise. In 1988, the small team secured the supply of a new engine built by John Judd and adapted from a powerplant derived from a Honda design. Of greater significance, March reached agreement with Adrian Newey — a highly skilled aerodynamicist who would go on to become arguably the most successful Formula 1 designer of all time — to return from America, where he had been race-engineering Mario Andretti's March Indycar, and design a new car. Towards the end of the 1988 season, Capelli and his March-Judd 881 showed flashes of brilliance, with third place in Belgium and second place in Portugal. Continuing with the car for the first few races of 1989, Capelli's team-mate, Maurício Gugelmin, added another third place in Brazil.

The car that replaced the 881, the CG891, was less successful due to over-ambitious aspects of its design and inaccurate readings obtained from sessions in the wind tunnel at Southampton University. Neither driver scored a single point in it, adding up to a terrible 1989 season that had already started badly for Capelli with the death of his mentor and close friend Gariboldi in a car crash.

Meanwhile, Akagi's company moved from being just March's Formula 1 title sponsor to becoming the team's owner. He also acquired from March the production rights to manufacture customer Formula 3000 cars, which necessitated rapid expansion and put unnecessary extra pressure on the Formula 1 team. By 1990, the operation, now renamed Leyton House with no reference to March, had dramatically increased its headcount from 19 people to 120. Newey produced a new design, the Judd-powered Leyton House CG901, with help from Gustav Brunner.

The 1990 season brought highs and lows. Neither car qualified for the races in Brazil and Mexico, but then came a remarkable turnaround. Just two weeks after the Mexican Grand Prix, Capelli led the French Grand Prix for 45 laps, with Gugelmin holding second place behind him for a while, and was only passed by Alain Prost's Ferrari three laps from the end. It was a sensational result that Leyton House Racing was never able to repeat. Thereafter, the team's fortunes unravelled with team boss Phillips already sidelined by a severe bout of meningitis that knocked him out for the rest of the season. Leadership of the beleaguered outfit was taken over by an accountant, Simon Keeble, but by this time the beginning of the end was in sight for the struggling team, which was having to endure continual reductions in budget by the team owner, who was running into severe financial difficulties. Keeble, in his invidious position of finance director, had to juggle priorities.

'Akagi was starting to struggle,' stated Newey. 'He borrowed heavily against the banks but had to be seen to be still in F1, because if he pulled out, the banks would have wondered why. He was playing a poker game on the minimum cost possible, so he was reducing the budget.'

One of the top names in Japanese banking, the Sumitomo Bank, disclosed in 1990 that one of its officials had arranged illegal loans for an indicted stock manipulator. Many observers simply attributed the wrongdoing to an aggressive profit-driven culture, and even when Fuji Bank admitted that an executive had forged nearly $2 billion worth of deposit receipts in a loan scheme, some shrugged it off as just another part of a dash for growth. However, these revelations proved to be the tip of an iceberg, for Japan found itself engulfed in an unprecedented series of financial scandals. They involved several banks and included similar alleged fraud cases at both Tokai Bank and Saitama Bank.

In a separate controversy, Fuji Bank had dismissed four employees in connection with $1.92 billion of questionable loans that the bank had made and the alleged use of falsified deposit certificates. Fuji Bank was Japan's fifth-largest general bank with deposits totalling nearly $292 billion and police were quick to arrest two of the disgraced employees just a month after the scandal erupted. As matters unfolded, it became clear that this pair had issued fake deposit receipts to 23 of the bank's clients, for use as collateral for loans.

To the great consternation of everyone at Leyton House, in September 1991 police in Japan arrested Akira Akagi and Masato Yajima, respectively president and managing director of Marusho Kosan, because they were implicated in the fraud and forgery of some documentation. The turmoil had far-reaching consequences for the health of Japan's economy and also propelled the country's banking into a crisis that led to numerous high-profile resignations and ultimately the downfall of Fuji Bank, as well as a major crash of the Japanese stock market. The country's speculative bubble had well and truly burst by 1991.

When it was proven that Akagi had been the beneficiary of illegal loans, the 46-year-old was jailed. His Formula 1 team struggled on for the rest of the 1991 season before being sold to a consortium that returned it to its original name of March before folding completely in 1993. On his release from jail, the team's former patron went back into business but died suddenly after returning from an overseas trip in August 2018 aged 74.

CHAPTER 2
KANKAMOL ALBON
Mother's pride

Seven years before Anglo-Thai racing driver Alex
Albon reached Formula 1, his mother made headlines
when she was convicted and jailed for large-scale VAT
evasion and for operating a fraudulent pyramid scheme
involving prestige cars that swindled investors out of
£7.5 million. As a result, 16-year-old Alex was left in
the role of head of the family looking after his younger
siblings while simultaneously trying to pursue his
aspirations in the sport.

Kankamol Ansusinha arrived in Britain from Thailand as a teenager in
1984 and married British racing driver Nigel Albon. Their first child,
Alexander, was born in London in 1996, by which time Nigel had been
racing for three years, initially in the Renault Clio Cup before moving on to
the British Touring Car Championship for 1994, running a Renault 19 with
Harlow Motorsport. With bookkeeping help from Kankamol, he built up a
successful high-end car dealership, the NA Carriage Company, and by 2000
the young family was living in the bucolic surroundings of Bures, Suffolk in
Smallbridge Hall, a magnificent 14th-century moated 10-bedroom house.

With motorsport in his blood, Alex began racing karts at the age of
eight and became a prolific winner, claiming the European and World
Championships in the KF3 class in 2010. He attracted the attention of Red
Bull, which supported him through its junior driver programme and financed
his switch to cars in 2012 to race in the Formula Renault Eurocup series.
Lack of success led Red Bull to drop him at the end of the year but two more
seasons at that level proved to be a solid grounding for his progression to

European Formula 3, where he scored four rookie-class wins in 2015. The following season he moved to the GP3 championship where four victories put him runner-up to Charles Leclerc in the final standings. His ART team promoted him to a FIA Formula 2 campaign in 2017 for his rookie year in the category before he switched to the rival DAMS team in 2018. Despite the insecurity of initially competing on a budget-restricted race-by-race basis, Alex took three wins and finished third in the championship behind the highly rated George Russell and Lando Norris. While both of his rivals were rewarded with Formula 1 drives for 2019, Alex signed a deal to compete in Formula E with the Nissan e.dams operation. However, in a surprise move, Red Bull decided that it wanted him back under its wings, quickly bought out his contract and placed him in its second-string Toro Rosso Formula 1 team alongside Russian Daniil Kvyat.

When Alex made his Formula 1 début in Australia at the start of the 2019 season, racing under the Thai flag, he became his country's first Grand Prix driver of the modern era, following on from Prince Birabongse of the Siamese royal family who competed before and after the Second World War under the name 'B. Bira'. Alex hit the ground running and in only his second race claimed his first points with ninth place in Bahrain and then continued to make a good impression by recording more points finishes in China, Monaco, Germany and Hungary. Over the summer break, his meteoric career moved up another gear when Red Bull's team management decided to swap him with under-performing Frenchman Pierre Gasly, thereby putting Albon in the senior Red Bull alongside the prodigiously talented Max Verstappen for the season's remaining nine races. The continuation of his eye-catching form led to top-six finishes at every round except Brazil, where he was heading for his maiden podium before being punted off by reigning World Champion Lewis Hamilton in the closing stages.

Albon's first podium finishes arrived during pandemic-afflicted 2020 with third places in the Tuscan Grand Prix at Mugello and the late-season Bahrain Grand Prix. Despite the promise he had shown over two seasons, Red Bull then demoted him to the role of test driver for 2021 before placing him at Williams in 2022.

By 2004, when Alex was eight, his parents had separated. Records at Company House show that Kankamol, more often known as 'Minky', had taken over both the NA Carriage Company and Smallbridge Hall from her estranged husband and continued to sell luxury cars. To her friends and network of wealthy clients, she appeared to be a charming and highly successful businesswoman who displayed all the trappings of success. Despite now being a single parent, she was able to afford expensive holidays as well as the cost of private education for her two sons and three daughters.

But the opulent lifestyle was built on a pyramid scheme in which she conned wealthy individuals into handing over huge sums of money to pay upfront for prestige cars including Ferraris, Maseratis and Bugattis, although most never received them. The scam centred around promising her victims that she was able to buy the cars at good discounts and immediately resell them for significant gains. In profit-sharing agreements, 'clients' would then be persuaded to roll over the hypothetical proceeds, adding to the illusion that she was running a genuine and highly profitable business. In reality, she was living a life of luxury using customers' money, with income from new investors also being used to pay off earlier investors when they became disgruntled, accelerating her increasingly desperate need to raise further capital by inducing ever more new customers to invest money that was rarely, if ever, repaid.

In August 2008, the burden of repayments spiralled out of control, causing the edifice to collapse. The police, who caught up with her when a victim launched a civil case to recover money, initially focused on her

Kankamol Albon, mother of Alex Albon, was arrested in February 2009 for fraudulent trading in expensive cars and sentenced to six years in prison. At the time of his mother's arrest, Alex Albon was making his name as a 12-year-old in karting and eventually reached Formula 1 in 2019.

allegation that she had been blackmailed into selling hundreds of cars for less than their market value, but it was soon established that this was simply a smokescreen for criminal acts and she was arrested in February 2009. After a lengthy investigation by Suffolk Constabulary, she was discovered to have committed fraudulent offences totalling £7.5 million.

When the case went to court in 2012, the jury heard that, between July 2007 and August 2008, Albon had generated a very high turnover in expensive cars but had sold them for less than she had paid and was therefore operating at a loss, which was compounded by her withdrawal of £580,000 from the enterprise in this 14-month period. The prosecution told the court that most customers never received their cars and that she had even sold one vehicle twice to different people. It was also revealed that out of 122 vehicles Albon claimed to have bought, 107 of the deals were fictitious and she had used bogus documents to support her claims.

It transpired that, even while she was on bail during police investigations in 2010 and 2011, the mother of five had also been fiddling the taxman. After Her Majesty's Revenue & Customs conducted its own investigations into VAT that she had claimed back under the pretence of selling vehicles overseas, it discovered that these cars had never actually been purchased and nor was there any evidence of exports. This led to a second court case in which HMRC pursued an action for further fraud of £1.8 million.

Kankamol Albon pleaded guilty to seven offences of dishonestly making a gain by false representation, participating in a fraudulent business and cheating the public purse. In sentencing her to six years' imprisonment at Ipswich Crown Court in October 2012, Judge Rupert Overbury called her crimes a 'massive, greed-driven fraud'.

Smallbridge Hall was repossessed and police officers from the Economic Crime Unit seized quantities of her designer handbags and shoes that were subsequently auctioned off under the Proceeds of Crime Act and recouped more than £60,000. Her extravagant existence had largely been funded by using the millions of pounds of proceeds from her crimes, with the car dealership doubling as a front for the VAT fraud. After serving three years of her sentence, she was released in 2015, thus relieving her eldest son from the responsibilities of being primary carer for his younger siblings.

In her role as his proud mother, she was then seen regularly supporting Alex in the Formula 1 paddock, including during his time as Red Bull team-mate to Max Verstappen, who coincidentally also has a parent with criminal convictions (see Chapter 59). She told Netflix that she felt she had paid for her crime and that her racing driver son had forgiven her.

CHAPTER 3
GIOVANNA AMATI
Miss Fortune

By default, Giovanna Amati chose the hardest-possible way to seal her place in motor racing's history books when in 1992 she became the fifth — and most recent — woman to attempt to qualify for a Formula 1 Grand Prix. Despite this achievement, she's more often remembered for an earlier episode in her life, as a victim of a terrible crime. In what could have been a plot from a film shown in one of her father's many cinemas, she was kidnapped as an 18-year-old by a serial criminal who, it was claimed, then became emotionally attached to his captive.

Born in Rome in July 1959, Giovanna Amati came from an extremely privileged background. Her millionaire father was Giovanni Amati, who worked his way up from being a butcher to becoming, in the post-war years, an extremely successful entrepreneur and the owner of a chain of more than 50 cinemas in Rome. Her mother, the actress Anna Maria Pancani, was 30 years younger than her father, and appeared in several high-profile Italian films, and was known as much for her volatile character as for her work.

Although Giovanna led a sheltered home life, she had a rebellious, tomboy streak and developed a strong interest in motorsport from an early age. She drove anything she could lay her hands on, starting with a tractor at the family's country house at the age of nine. Pursuing her passion for speed, she used her allowance to buy a Honda 500cc motorcycle when she was 15 and managed to hide it from her parents for two years, taking it out at night to ride secretly around the city streets despite not being old enough to hold a licence.

The similarly affluent family of Elio de Angelis, then an up-and-coming racing driver, was friendly with the Amatis and he used to accompany her while she was practising for her driving test, often on the way to school. Elio was a big influence upon her decision to try her hand at motor racing in 1980, by which time he had reached Formula 1 and was driving for Team Lotus. Unbeknown to her parents, de Angelis encouraged the 21-year-old to attend the Henry Morrogh Racing School at the nearby Vallelunga circuit to learn her craft and qualify for a racing licence. As soon as she was able to, she began competing in the newly created Formula Abarth Championship, run for cars with tubular-framed chassis fitted with 2-litre Lancia engines. With an average entry of 60 cars per meeting, this was the Italian junior single-seater race series of the time and the perfect training ground for her.

Her results in Formula Abarth were competent rather than astounding but she did win a few races over four seasons before feeling able to progress to Italian Formula 3 in 1985 with a Ravarotto Racing Ralt RT30. In her second year at that level she improved steadily and managed to win a race in a Volkswagen-engined Dallara 386 run by the Prema Racing/Forti team. Despite her lack of any major success, this was enough to persuade her to move onwards and upwards to International Formula 3000, a category below Formula 1 using the Cosworth V8 engines that had once dominated Grand Prix racing.

Unfortunately, she found herself completely out of her depth in five seasons of Formula 3000. In 1987, having put together sponsorship for just four races in a British-entered BS Automotive Lola T87/50, she managed to qualify for only one of them, at Donington Park, where she finished 16th. For 1988, she joined Colt Racing, this time qualifying for four of eight races entered and earning more respect from her peers. She finished two races that year, at Jerez and Monza, both in 10th place. At Monza, she was able to hold off future Ferrari Formula 1 star Jean Alesi, who was most upset about being beaten by a woman and got pretty vocal with his team about it.

She did more Formula 3000 in 1989 but now tried her luck in the Japanese domestic series only to find that her efforts were in vain because the level of competition there was also extremely high. Back in Europe for 1990, she again struggled and only qualified for two races from ten attempts, in 26th place on the grid on both occasions, despite switching between teams several times. During that season, she displayed her mother's renowned volatility and fiery Latin temperament by forcing British driver Phil Andrews off the road at a test session at Oulton Park in what appeared to be a deliberate act of retribution for a perceived wrongdoing at the previous race at Hockenheim. This certainly wasn't her finest hour and Andrews's car went flying through the air at 160mph into an impact of aircraft-like proportions that the bemused driver was lucky to survive let alone walk away from, especially as he struck his head on his steering wheel.

After four years in Formula 3000, her 1991 season really had to be make or break. Now, finally confident at this level, she managed to make the grid for seven of ten races with a GJ Motorsport Reynard 91D and recorded an encouraging best-ever finish of seventh from penultimate position on the grid at the Le Mans Bugatti circuit in France. This result, and another reasonably respectable performance that produced ninth place at Oulton Park, led Benetton Formula 1 team boss Flavio Briatore, recognising her undoubted publicity value, to offer her a 30-lap test at Donington Park, but no lap times were ever issued and nothing more came of it. Given Briatore's reputation as a flamboyant playboy, it was widely reported that the two were romantically involved but it was all speculation and the rumours were never substantiated.

In the days when experience counted more than race results, Amati had, in the eyes of the sport's governing body, FISA, done enough to be granted the requisite 'superlicence' to enable her to compete in Formula 1. Although it seemed highly unlikely that a suitable race seat would become available, one did, against all predictions.

Unlike almost all other sports, women must generally compete in motor racing on equal terms with men, but plucky females have been trying to do just that ever since the birth of the motor car. As for Formula 1, however, only two women drivers have ever raced in Grands Prix since the birth of the World Championship in 1950. By far the more notable of these was Maria Teresa de Filippis, who took part in three Formula 1 World Championship races in 1958.

The youngest of five children, Maria Teresa was the second daughter of the wealthy Italian Count of Serina and his Spanish wife, and had shown great skill on horseback, having taken up equestrian sports from an early age. Two of her brothers, Giuseppe and Antonio, were much more interested in fast cars and after taking part in some events they challenged their little sister to a bet that she couldn't compete in motorsport with the same level of success she had achieved on horses. This spurred the 22-year-old to enter a local hill climb in her tiny Fiat Topolino in 1948. Much to their surprise and chagrin, she showed immediate talent and won not only her class but also a 'silver steering wheel award' for her outstanding performance first time out.

After lots more racing, Maserati engaged her as an occasional works driver in sports cars and eventually, in 1958, she tried Formula 1. Her first race with her own Maserati 250F — the model in which Juan Manuel Fangio had just won his fifth World Championship title — was the non-championship Syracuse Grand Prix in Sicily and she finished fifth. Just four weeks later, in Monaco, she became the first woman to enter a World Championship Grand Prix, as one of 31 entrants battling for a place on the 16-car starting grid at the tight street circuit, but she narrowly failed to make the cut. However, at the next race, the Belgian Grand Prix, she did manage to qualify and finished 10th, but her two other outings of the year, in Portugal and Italy, ended in retirements.

The tragedies of racing affected her deeply. At the 1958 French Grand Prix, where the race director had prevented her from taking part, her former fiancé Luigi Musso was killed in his Ferrari. The following year, she had occasional drives for close friend Jean Behra's team and was present at the German Grand Prix on Berlin's AVUS circuit when Behra lost his life driving a Porsche in the supporting sports car race. Aged 33, she retired from the sport with immediate effect.

Nearly a generation later, another Italian racer, Lella Lombardi, followed in Maria Teresa's footsteps and became the only female driver ever to complete a World Championship Grand Prix in a points-scoring position. Driving a March 751 as team-mate to fellow Italian Vittorio Brambilla, she finished sixth in the 1975 Spanish Grand Prix at Montjuich in Barcelona. However, the race was stopped prematurely after a tragic accident in which Rolf Stommelen's Hill GH1 lost its rear wing, causing the car to fly over a crash barrier into the crowd, killing four people. As less than half of the race had been run, only half points were awarded — so Lella got half a point.

Within a few years, two more women attempted unsuccessfully to compete in World Championship Formula 1 races. British former Olympic skier Divina Galica tried three times, at the British Grand Prix in 1976 with a Surtees TS16 run by Nick Whiting (see Chapter 62) and in Argentina and Brazil in 1978 for Lord Hesketh's Olympus-backed team in a Hesketh 308E. South African Desiré Wilson's big season was 1980, when she not only won a round of the Aurora AFX British Formula 1 Championship at Brands Hatch driving a Theodore Racing Wolf WR4 but also enjoyed two victories in world championship sports car races with Alain de Cadenet, at Silverstone and Monza. Although she failed to qualify her Williams FW07 for the British Grand Prix that year, she did compete for the Tyrrell team in the 1981 South African Grand Prix, a race that was subsequently stripped of its World Championship status.

More recently, several female drivers, notably Susie Wolff and the late María de Villota, have held test-driving roles with Formula 1 teams.

The Brabham Formula 1 team, despite an illustrious history, was a shadow of its former self by 1992 and facing increasingly serious financial difficulties. That season, the team's first choice of driver was 1988 Japanese Formula 3 Champion and Formula 3000 race winner Akihiko Nakaya as he had both the required money and talent, but FISA rejected his application for a superlicence, determining that those Japanese championships weren't a recognisable stepping stone to Formula 1. The fact that Amati, whose Formula 3000 record had been underwhelming, did qualify for a superlicence was illogical, but it opered up an unexpected opportunity of a lifetime for her. When she received a call-up from Brabham team manager Dennis Nursey in January 1992, she had been contemplating a move to the US to compete in Indycar, where female drivers like Janet Guthrie and Desiré Wilson had proved that women could compete on a more equal footing with their male counterparts.

While Brabham recognised the marketing value of having a woman driver and saw her signing as a commercial exercise, she was still required to bring funding to the team, reported at the time to have been $3 million although it's doubtful that the true figure would have been anywhere near that amount. So far her family wealth had backed her career but now she needed help. Although her father was no longer alive, one of his old friends, Giulio Andreotti, had recently become prime minister of Italy and at the 11th hour made the requisite introductions that helped her find the budget she needed. Less than two weeks before the first race, she was duly signed to drive alongside the Belgian Eric van de Poele, who had decidedly better credentials.

She turned up at Kyalami in South Africa hoping to make her Grand Prix début despite having had no opportunity to familiarise herself with the hastily cobbled-together Brabham-Judd BT60B. When she arrived at the circuit, her car was still being built up by overworked mechanics, who struggled even to mould a proper seat for her due to the inevitable call on her time as the centre of attention for journalists and photographers. If she had any reservations about driving Brabham #8, knowing that this was also the race number of the Brabham in which her childhood friend Elio de Angelis had been killed nearly six years earlier, they didn't show, for she appeared totally at ease about the magnitude of the challenge that lay ahead.

The first of Giovanna Amati's three unsuccessful attempts to qualify for a Formula 1 Grand Prix in 1992 came at Kyalami in South Africa, where she is pictured after a spin in practice.

Despite her confidence, these weren't the best circumstances in which to make a Grand Prix début. Even allowing for gear-selection problems and lack of experience with carbon-fibre brakes, her efforts were punctuated by multiple spins in the practice and qualifying sessions, and at one point her progress was slowed when she had to switch to Brabham's spare chassis after a fuel-pressure problem on her car. Her best lap time was nearly four seconds slower than her team-mate's and nearly nine seconds behind Nigel Mansell on pole position in his Williams-Renault FW14B. It was hardly surprising that she came nowhere near making the grid.

Her second attempt to qualify for a Grand Prix came in Mexico three weeks later. Her car suffered from a multitude of mechanical woes that prevented her from making any mark and led to a change of engine. Although she did manage to reduce the deficit to her team-mate's time to three seconds, she was still 8.5 seconds away from pole-sitting Mansell, with whom she made herself extremely unpopular by holding him up on one of his flying laps. Her third and final opportunity to qualify came in Brazil, where Mansell scored his third consecutive pole position but Amati now found herself a massive 11 seconds off his pace.

Had Giovanna been a man, her less-than-stellar track record wouldn't have got her anywhere near a seat in a Grand Prix team, even one as beleaguered and short of money as Brabham at that time. However, desperate times call for desperate measures: the once-great team was struggling for survival and its new signing came with a bag full of much-needed Italian *Lire* and plenty of publicity value. The exercise did neither party any good but while the media spotlight shone squarely on the driver, who made an easy scapegoat, the reality was that she was never given a proper chance because the team was unable to provide the necessary resources and support to either of its inexperienced drivers. Van de Poele also struggled to qualify: although he just scraped onto the grid in South Africa, 26th and last, he wasn't able to do so in Mexico and Brazil. Not only was the BT60B hopelessly uncompetitive but it was also, like all contemporary Formula 1 machinery, extremely physical to drive because driver aids like power steering and paddle-shift gear changes were still years away. This was inevitably an additional handicap for a female driver.

When Giovanna's backers defaulted on sponsorship payments, Brabham wasted no time in firing her after those three outings. Her replacement was Damon Hill, who was much more experienced thanks to his role as Williams test driver. Nonetheless, even he needed five attempts before he finally managed to qualify the recalcitrant and outdated BT60B — in front of his home crowd at the British Grand Prix — and he only made the grid twice in eight outings that season. Despite this shaky start, he went on to become Formula 1 World Champion in 1996.

Giovanna continued to race for several more years in a variety of sports car arenas, including the Porsche Supercup, the European Ferrari Challenge and the FIA International Sports Racing Series, before moving on to television and print journalism. Although she never showed exceptional speed, she can be proud that she got as far as she did in the sport. She remains the last woman to have attempted to qualify for a Formula 1 Grand Prix.

Before she had even taken her first steps in motorsport, Giovanna Amati's name was already familiar in Italy thanks to widespread media coverage of an ordeal she had experienced 14 years earlier. On the evening of 12th February 1978, the 18-year-old had spent the evening at a nightclub with two friends and was sitting with them in her parked car outside her family's luxurious villa in Rome in the early hours of the morning. Suddenly, three masked gangsters forcibly removed her from the car and manhandled her into a van.

The ringleader was Jean Daniel Nieto, a notorious expatriate French criminal of Corsican origin, well known to the authorities after his escape from a French prison two years earlier. Not only was he the head of the clan of the Marseillais, a coalition of French and Italian mafia involved in drug trafficking and extortion, but he was also a member of the powerful 'Tre B' gang, which took its initials from founders Albert Bergamelli, Maffeo Bellicini and Jacques Berenguer. At a time when politically related violence and lawlessness was rife in Italy, Giovanna was an obvious target for kidnappers due to her high profile and wealthy background.

She was initially held captive in a property only a short distance from her home, although she had no idea where her abductors had taken her, and police came very close to finding her quite quickly, to the point of ringing the doorbell on several occasions. Her captors soon moved her to an apartment in a more remote location where she was held for 75 days, until the end of April, while her 72-year-old father negotiated a ransom for her safe return. During most of this time she was either wrapped in polythene sheets or incarcerated and chained up in a coffin-sized wooden crate where she suffered a terrifying cocktail of appalling mental cruelty and physical abuse that allegedly included rape by more than one member of the gang. The kidnappers tormented their victim mercilessly. 'In the beginning she spat in their faces,' said Giovanna's older sister Vittoria. 'They hit her with wet towels and kicked her when the ransom negotiations didn't go the way they wanted. One day they would threaten to cut off an ear, another day a finger.'

Her father eventually persuaded the kidnappers to accept 800 million *Lire*, which was half the sum that had originally been demanded and amounted to nearly $1 million dollars. As abductions of wealthy people and high-profile politicians were commonplace in Italy at the time, the authorities were desperately trying to put a halt to what was becoming an epidemic and a judge had therefore frozen the assets and bank accounts of Giovanna's parents in the hope that this would prevent them from paying the ransom. However, her determined and resourceful mother Anna Maria scraped some of the money together by selling and pawning her jewellery and raised more by persuading servants to lend their own savings. Most of the ransom money, however, was obtained by her father Giovanni, who secretly managed to circumvent the judge's instructions and divert box office takings from his chain of cinemas, notably from the success of the first *Star Wars* film.

Giovanna was returned safely after her father arranged delivery of the ransom money to Maurizio Massaria's tobacconist's shop. Very shortly afterwards, police raided Massaria's apartment and arrested seven of the suspected kidnappers, but Nieto managed to evade them.

During Giovanna's captivity, 31-year-old Nieto had developed a strange bond of affection and empathy for her. This became clear to her family when, within weeks of her release, Giovanna began to receive red roses and love letters that were apparently signed 'S.D.G.', which stood for '*Scarpe Da Ginnastica*' ('Gym Shoes') and referred to his favoured footwear. Then she started getting phone calls from him at her sister's apartment, rekindling a bizarre relationship. It transpired that the gang leader had apparently shown Giovanna some kindness throughout her ordeal and tried to protect her from further suffering at the hands of his associates. It was reported that he had comforted her and looked after her, bringing her pasta and magazines every Sunday as well as playing disco music to her.

'Often he confided in me and told me of his life,' she is said to have told her family after her release. 'Sometimes when I cried he came near me and caressed my head softly.'

Her mother's retort was more cynical and forceful. In her customary style, Anna Maria would give theatrical interviews to the press outside her house during which she repeatedly said of her daughter, as quoted by *People* magazine: 'She left home a virgin and came home raped — a mother can tell.'

When police learned that Nieto was communicating with Giovanna after her release, they persuaded her to cooperate and help them capture him. Had she refused to do so, there was a possibility of her being arrested as an accessory to her own kidnapping and the extortion that followed. With the police listening in, she agreed in a phone call to meet Nieto on the Via Veneto in Rome. When she arrived on her red Honda 500cc motorcycle, the *Carabinieri* surrounded the gangster as he waited for her on a street corner, holding a bouquet of roses. When he drew a gun, the officers fired warning shots at his feet, forcing him to drop it. When they seized him and hauled him away, a hysterical Giovanna apparently followed, screaming, weeping and begging for the forgiveness and release of the man whom she said had done nothing wrong, telling reporters afterwards that she felt 'like Judas' now that he faced incarceration because of her.

Contrary to that alleged reaction, she subsequently protested that rumours of any romantic involvement were just salacious gossip on the part of the newspapers and that she wanted each and every member of the gang caught and imprisoned. This simply fuelled the media hysteria and encouraged journalists to feed the public's appetite for more details about the unconventional relationship between a low-life gangster from Marseille and the glamorous daughter of a prominent Italian millionaire. This shook the resilience of her family, who refused to believe any feelings could have existed between their daughter and her captor. Anyway, even if there had been, falling in love is not a criminal offence but any subsequent aiding or abetting of a criminal most certainly would have been.

Nieto, who styled himself '*Il Bandito Gentiluomo*' ('The Gentleman Bandit'), was sentenced to 18 years for kidnapping and rape. He was incarcerated in the high-security prison at Volterra in Tuscany from where he managed to escape while on temporary release on licence in 1989. Having been involved in another kidnapping, this time of a policeman, he was soon tracked down in Paris with an accomplice while trying to negotiate the sale of stolen jewels after a robbery in Belgium. He escaped and remained a fugitive for 20 years.

By April 2010, Nieto was a 63-year-old married father of two sons with five grandchildren living quietly in Cadolive, France. Quite by chance, an eagle-eyed ticket inspector on the Milan–Ventimiglia train in northern Italy saw a well-dressed man pick up his ticket from the floor after dropping it. As the man bent down, the ticket inspector noticed on his neck a tattoo of a green and black gecko with five dots along its back and recognised this as an emblem commonly associated with prisoners from the 1970s and 1980s. When Nieto was arrested, he offered no resistance and, as he extended his wrists to be handcuffed, remarked: 'It took you 20 years to find me and here I am. Be quiet. Now I'm old. Once, it would have been different.' Twelve hours after his identity had been formally confirmed, he was transferred to Marassi prison in Genoa and ordered by the General Attorney at the *Court d'Appelo di Roma* to serve an additional 10-year sentence.

Much maligned and often written off as the rich girl who should never have got near a Formula 1 car, Giovanna Amati nonetheless demonstrated immense resilience in her racing career with burning ambition to succeed in what was an uphill struggle. In an interview with the BBC in 2015, she agreed that the incredibly traumatic ordeal she had suffered as a teenager contributed immeasurably to the strength and stubbornness required to fight the adversity that she encountered, including prejudice and lurid rumours about alleged relationships with important men in the sport. Without such intense determination, she almost certainly wouldn't have got as far in the sport as she did.

In 1988, two years after his son Elio's death, Giulio de Angelis was also abducted. The wealthy 56-year-old building contractor, himself a former championship-winning powerboat racer, was taken from his luxury beach house in Sardinia in the middle of the night by four armed bandits and had his earlobe amputated before his release was negotiated by Don Sergio Mantovani, the parish priest of Modena. The priest became a hostage himself for several hours while the kidnappers counted the cash and made sure none of the notes were marked.

COLIN VANDERVELL
Bearing up

Another talented racing driver who was abducted as a teenager was Colin Vandervell, the son of multi-millionaire industrialist and engine-bearing magnate Tony Vandervell, the man behind the Formula 1 Vanwalls raced with great success by Stirling Moss and Tony Brooks. Colin attended Stowe School, not far from Silverstone, and regularly escaped to sneak into the circuit to watch the action, while during school holidays he was a regular at Grands Prix watching his father's cars do battle. He hit the headlines aged 16 when he was snatched from Stowe School. On the evening of 4th February 1962, the kidnappers bundled him into a car and bound, gagged and drugged him before being dumped in a field about 20 miles away. He managed to escape and went to a nearby house from where he was returned to the school.

Colin was desperate to become a racing driver but his father had seen too many of his friends lose their lives and vetoed it. Only after his father's death in 1967 did Colin get his chance and he was able to prove himself naturally gifted, winning 29 races on his way to a Formula Ford title in 1970. More success followed in Formula 3, where he beat future World Champions, and Formula Atlantic, where he won the 1973 British series. His versatility was such that he even took part in the 1974 RAC Rally in a Ford Escort.

A chip off the old block, he cut a slightly eccentric figure who often wore green corduroy trousers beneath his overalls and invariably his old school socks complete with the name tags in them. He eventually lost interest in the sport and after two seasons racing a Ford Capri in touring cars, in which he scored three victories, he decamped to live in Monaco.

CHAPTER 4
FRANCO AMBROSIO
Not a grain of truth

This multi-millionaire Italian industrialist's involvement in Formula 1 came initially through his enthusiastic sponsorship of the Shadow team and then his early bankrolling of the new Arrows operation. The success of the high-profile and well-connected businessman led to him being affectionately dubbed 'The King of Grain' but his fame and notoriety came far more from his fall from grace — fraud and financial irregularities led to multiple convictions and several jail terms — and ultimately his gruesome death.

Renzo Zorzi was a little-known Italian racing driver who in his day job was an engineer and tyre test and development driver at Pirelli. Intimate knowledge of tyre technology and his connections helped him break into motor racing and an undistinguished record in the Italian and European Formula 3 series followed. This was capped with a surprising and fortuitous first-ever victory in the prestigious support race at the 1975 Monaco Grand Prix, where he benefited from a chaotic final in which the cars ahead of him either collided with each other or were disqualified. This result provided enough momentum for him to secure sponsorship from a wealthy backer, Franco Ambrosio, who was present that day.

Ambrosio's support led to a couple of unremarkable outings at the back of the grid in cars run by Frank Williams before Zorzi was elevated in 1977 to a seat alongside the highly talented Tom Pryce at Shadow, where Ambrosio had become the primary sponsor. The high point of Zorzi's Grand Prix career came when he scored a solitary championship point with sixth place in Brazil. However, this was immediately followed by the lowest of low points in the South African Grand Prix at Kyalami when he became far better known for his unwitting involvement in the awful tragedy of Pryce's death.

While Zorzi was running near the tail of the field, a fuel leak caused him to roll to a halt on the left-hand verge of the start/finish straight. He scrambled out of the cockpit as flames licked around the back of his car but he had activated the onboard fire extinguisher system and it quickly doused the fire. However, two well-meaning marshals armed with hand-held extinguishers had already started running across the track to assist him. The location of the incident was a short distance beyond a blind brow and, just after the marshals started their run, Pryce's Shadow appeared at top speed. It hit one of the men, Frederik Jansen van Vuuren, and his heavy extinguisher struck the driver's head. Pryce and van Vuuren were both killed instantly.

Unjustly shouldering some of the blame for an accident in which he was entirely innocent, poor Zorzi lasted just two more races before his Italian sponsor decided to replace him with his latest protégé without thinking of telling him. Indeed, the first Zorzi knew about it was when he arrived in Monaco, the scene of his greatest triumph two years earlier, only to find the name of another Ambrosio protégé, Riccardo Patrese, emblazoned on the cockpit of his car. This marked the end of Zorzi's top-line career after just seven races.

Pryce's replacement at Shadow was Alan Jones, who went on to score the Shadow team's one and only World Championship Formula 1 victory later that season, in Austria. Photos of the winning car appeared in the press all over the world but Ambrosio's name wasn't on it. He never got on with Shadow's enigmatic, eccentric and mysterious American owner, Don Nichols (see Chapter 44), and by this time had neglected to pay some of his bills, prompting Nichols to have the Ambrosio identity removed from the team's cars for the Austrian race, to which the enraged sponsor responded by instructing Patrese not to drive.

In the midst of this, Jackie Oliver, Nichols's right-hand man and long-time former driver, had decided that he wanted to form his own team and within a few weeks of the success in Austria he left with a breakaway group of disaffected employees, all of whom had become disgruntled about the way Shadow was heading under Nichols, with the team seemingly starved of funds. For Oliver, it was quite a break because he had been a very capable driver for Shadow almost since the beginning, first in Can-Am from 1971 (becoming champion in 1974), then in Formula 1 from

1973, before stepping down from driving to become Nichols's lieutenant in running the operation.

The new team's name, Arrows, was derived from the surnames of its founders, the 'A' standing for Ambrosio, who had provided a significant proportion of the funding. Just as Nichols used his initials, DN, to designate his Shadows, the first Arrows was called the FA1 in recognition of its benefactor. However, before the FA1 ever raced, Ambrosio ran into trouble with the Italian authorities over financial irregularities and was arrested, leaving Arrows having to seek new sponsorship in a hurry. The car that was named in his honour never actually displayed his name at a Grand Prix.

Francesco 'Franco' Ambrosio was born in 1932 and at the age of 18 began employment at a wheat-milling business near Naples. Ten years later, he was running the grain company and had renamed it Italgrani. Under his leadership, the enterprise expanded massively and became a multinational conglomerate of businesses. Through the 1970s, Ambrosio created a holding company that was made up of almost 50 separate business entities and the group established a strong position in the American milling industry with the construction of the New England Milling Co (NEMCO) and US Durum Milling Inc. The conglomerate was involved in the import and export of a range of commodities across several continents. At its peak, his empire had a turnover equivalent to €1.2 billion and was a major company employing a large workforce in southern Italy in grain storage, pasta production and wheat milling, all of which gave rise to him being accorded the soubriquet 'The King of Grain'.

The wrongdoing that came to light during the Arrows team's gestation concerned a fraud scheme involving the Banco di Roma, resulting in Ambrosio receiving a five-year prison sentence in 1980. Despite two unsuccessful escape attempts, one of which involved bribing a guard and hiding in a refuse bin, he was released two years early, in February 1983.

Into the 1990s, Ambrosio's group of businesses gradually unravelled as his involvement in a succession of further financial scandals was uncovered. These included collusion with politicians who approved large bank loans in return for backhanders and donations to their campaigns. *Mani pulite*, meaning 'clean hands', was the label given to the government initiative that spawned a nationwide investigation into the endemic and widespread political corruption prevalent in Italy. Crime after crime was exposed and the value of bribes paid by companies bidding for large public contracts

Franco Ambrosio's Formula 1 involvement, first with Shadow, then with Arrows, ended with his arrest and subsequent imprisonment for fraud. Many years later he was murdered.

Ambrosio's name graced the side of Shadow's cars for most of the 1977 season, including here at Kyalami in South Africa where team leader Tom Pryce tragically lost his life.

extended to many billions of dollars. The investigation resulted in the disappearance of several groups that had been masquerading as legitimate political parties and led to the demise and in some cases even suicide of industry leaders and politicians. Reports suggested that almost half of the members of the Italian Parliament ended up under indictment and several thousand other high-profile figures came under suspicion.

Ambrosio's part in all this centred on the Enimont corruption scandal, in which Enimont, a large chemical company, was found to have bribed politicians in return for tax relief. Ambrosio was jailed for a second time in October 1993 after being found guilty of money laundering and receiving stolen goods. He was arrested again in June 1994 on allegations of attempted bribery and defrauding the European Union by claiming $32 million of subsidies for non-existent export shipments of durum wheat to Algeria. Only a year later year, in 1995, he was back in the limelight and under intense public scrutiny after being arrested yet again for allegedly collecting kickbacks on behalf of his friend Paolo Cirino Pomicino, a former Christian Democrat minister.

Through all of this, Ambrosio's industrial empire gradually crumbled and Italgrani finally collapsed into bankruptcy in 1999. He was arrested yet again on suspicion of fraud and false accounting in January 2001, leading to a further conviction for fraudulent bankruptcy and a nine-year sentence.

On the morning of 15th April 2009, one of Ambrosio's sons found him and his wife Giovanna Sacco dead in their seaside villa in the exclusive Naples district of Posillipo. He was lying in a pool of blood in the kitchen while she was in a study. Both were in their night clothes and had been bludgeoned to death, seemingly with blows to their heads from a steel bar. Whilst it is more than likely that Ambrosio would have accumulated his fair share of enemies over the years, many of whom might have had good reason to wish him harm, it appeared that he and his wife were simply victims of a violent robbery that went wrong. Entry to the house had been via a smashed window on the terrace, various possessions were found scattered and valuables were missing.

The police immediately focused their investigations on gangs of Albanians and Romanians who had been responsible for a spate of robberies at villas in the Naples area and the following day three Romanian immigrants, including one who had worked as a gardener at the house, were arrested and charged with the murders. At the time of his death, Ambrosio was once again due to appear in court to appeal against his sentence for false accounting when declaring the bankruptcy of Italgrani.

CHAPTER 5

SIMON ATKINSON
Cooped up

A hard-working and prosperous owner
of an abattoir chose to fund his expensive
hobby of racing GT cars in European
championships by systematically
defrauding the British taxpayer rather
than paying for his hobby out of the
wealth he had accumulated from his
successful multi-million-pound
family-owned business.

Simon Atkinson raced sporadically in Britain and across mainland Europe between 2010 and 2017, taking in rounds of the Britcar MSA Endurance and British GT Championships as well as the GT division of the Dutch-organised Supercar Challenge, a series that appears to have been his main focus. Long-distance racing was clearly a branch of the sport that appealed to him and he competed in at least one 24-hour race most years, starting at Silverstone in 2010 driving a BMW M3 and concluding at Paul Ricard in 2017 in a Lotus Evora GT4, with other 'enduros' along the way at Zandvoort in the Netherlands, Catalunya in Spain and Portimão in Portugal, the latter an event that lasted 32 hours.

However, most of the races in which Atkinson participated were shorter ones, usually with one of the powerful, exotic Lamborghini Gallardo models run for him by Mark Hosken and his team at Milton Keynes-based Backdraft Motorsport but also occasionally entered by the prophetically named Panic Racing Team. In Britcar events, he found himself up against stiff competition from some of the top GT drivers on the British scene such as Chris Goodwin and Andrew Kirkaldy, and occasionally he competed against the top professionals from the world of touring cars, including Andrew Jordan, Gordon Shedden and Anthony Reid. In two-driver races he also partnered some very experienced names, one being Dutch Le Mans driver Cor Euser, and such experts helped to ensure that the amateur driver didn't disgrace himself.

As a middle-aged 'journeyman' driver who had started racing GT cars relatively late in life, Atkinson achieved respectable rather than outstanding results that included some class wins and several podium positions.

Racing high-performance sports cars at this level against such exalted company was an extremely expensive commitment for a provincial chicken farmer from Hertfordshire but that didn't matter to him as he was 'living the dream' and doing so without actually having to pay for his exploits. It wasn't as if he couldn't afford to fund his sport, had he been able to persuade the other stakeholders in the generations-old family business to agree to it, but he just decided that he didn't need to bother with that because he had come up with an easier and far more creative 'sponsorship' solution.

Long-established Bell Farm Poultry at Bovingdon, Hertfordshire was a business of significant size that had been trading as IHP (Imran Halal Poultry) since 2007 and slaughtered approximately 300,000 chickens each week, equating to a staggering 15.5 million birds annually. In September 2013, in his capacity as IHP's managing director, Simon Atkinson proudly announced that the company — one of the largest halal abattoirs in the UK — had become the first such poultry-processing facility to be certified and monitored by the Sharia Halal Board.

Unfortunately for him, the company was already under investigation by HM Revenue & Customs for failing to comply with government anti-money laundering regulations. HMRC officers had stumbled across a £450,000 tax fraud.

While scrutinising the company's records, HMRC discovered that Atkinson had been regularly falsifying invoices, by instructing various suppliers to invoice the company for his personal motor racing expenses as bona fide business costs. Quantities of such invoices dated between 2011 and 2015 were found under spurious headings such as 'transportation' and 'engineering services'. In reality, these bills were for preparation and maintenance of his expensive racing cars together with all the associated costs of the transport and logistics involved in getting them to and from

Simon Atkinson funded
his GT racing by
cheating HM Revenue
& Customs, including
fraudulently purchasing
a Lamborghini
Gallardo GT3 in
racing specification.

race meetings. One invoice even related to the acquisition of a Lamborghini
Gallardo GT3 in full racing specification ordered from the factory in
Bologna in 2011, its cost justified as a legitimate business expense and
noted in the company's accounts under the heading 'machinery and capital
goods expenditure'. Once the fraud was unravelled, it became clear that
the businessman had been funding his motor racing adventures by fiddling
his tax returns and fraudulently claiming all the related operating costs as
business expenses, through which he received £112,186 in VAT repayments
and evaded £338,630 in income tax.

At Luton Crown Court on 20th July 2018, Atkinson pleaded guilty to
two counts of failing to comply with money-laundering regulations and two
of cheating the public revenue. Although the 54-year-old then paid back
most of the stolen money, at a subsequent court appearance in Luton on
17th December he was sentenced to three years four months in prison, and
also ordered to repay the remaining balance of £30,125 within 42 days as
well as £1,901 in costs. In addition, IHP Ltd, where he had remained a

company director until May of that year, was fined £20,000 and ordered to pay £1,000 in costs after also pleading guilty of failing to comply with money-laundering regulations.

No doubt enjoying the satisfaction of a successful conviction, Kath Doyle, assistant director of HRMC's Fraud Investigation Service, used a string of suitable clichés in her description of the wrongdoing: 'Atkinson was thinking only of himself as he stole from the taxpayer to fuel a life in the fast lane — money that should have been going into our vital public services. His scam has well and truly hit the skids and not only has he been put behind bars, he also has to pay back all the stolen money. It proves tax crime doesn't pay.'

Her words were designed to send out a very clear message, namely that if you're going to indulge in such an expensive hobby then it's probably best to stick to the established business model of paying for it yourself, rather than attempting to get the taxpayer to fund it for you. Atkinson's battle with the tax authorities was one contest that he was never destined to win.

CHAPTER 6

TREVOR BAINES

Jet set to debt set

**Socially well-connected with high-rolling
European friends, this Manx millionaire
and financial tycoon at one stage appeared
on 'The Sunday Times Rich List'. He was
a daredevil with a passion for adrenaline
that encompassed motor racing, flying and
riding the notorious Cresta Run, but all that
came to a halt when he served time in the
only jail on the Isle of Man.**

B orn in 1939, Trevor Baines gained his full private pilot's licence before
his 20th birthday and became a skilled and experienced aviator who
owned a succession of light aircraft. In 1977, at the relatively late age of
38, he became a member of the St Moritz Toboggan Club (SMTC), which
organises the somewhat eccentric sport, established 135 years ago, of riding
the notorious Cresta Run on a 'skeleton' toboggan. Three-quarters of a mile
long, the Cresta Run involves lying head-first on a toboggan and racing
at frighteningly high speeds — up to 80mph — just a few inches from the
ground. So talented was Baines as a rider and competitor that for many
years, in his official capacity as 'guru', he patiently imparted his advice and
instructed novices — including the author — on the techniques and dangers
of riding the treacherously steep ribbon of sheet ice at this millionaire's
playground in Switzerland. The club became a major part of his life.

The Cresta shares obvious similarities with motor racing in terms of
speed, adrenaline and danger, so there are more than a few SMTC members
who also race cars, and Baines was one of them. An engaging and colourful

character with plenty of high-profile friends, he owned a variety of Jaguars, including Mark 1 and Mark 2 saloons and a fixed-head E-type with the number plate 'HOT 12', and enthusiastically raced some of them in Jaguar club events, winning numerous trophies and awards. His most recent track exploits were in an X-type saloon that he bought new before stripping it out and converting it for racing. He had great success with the sinister-looking black machine, which sported allegiance to his beloved SMTC — through the creative number plate 'B1 5MTC' — and to the Dracula Club, a St Moritz nightclub that has been a favourite haunt for generations of Cresta riders. Also showing allegiance to the nightclub, one of his Mark 2s carried a mock number plate reading 'DRAK 1'.

Baines was an engaging and colourful character who lived on the Isle of Man. In the world of motorsport, the island is best known for the Tourist Trophy motorcycle races that have taken place for over 100 years and are revered by enthusiasts all over the world. Tens of thousands of fans make the annual pilgrimage every summer for the festival of speed and danger when the island turns into motorcycle nirvana as some of the world's greatest road racers test themselves on the infamous 'Mountain Course', a terrifying and dangerous 37.7-mile circuit using public roads closed for the occasion and featuring 264 corners. As for the Isle of Man itself, it's classed as a crown possession rather than being part of the United Kingdom and therefore enjoys considerable autonomy. In the past, its detractors used to say that every £1 on the Isle of Man was on the run from somewhere, but it's now regarded as **a properly regulated tax haven** with established finance and offshore banking sectors.

From his home on the island, Africa House, a grand Victorian villa, Baines and his wife Wendy ran several companies, including his trading and banking operation. The bulk of his fortune had been built up from a property portfolio and other business interests and included an investment in the 'Miss World' beauty pageant. He had certainly been successful but not to the extent that *The Sunday Times* suggested in 2008 when the newspaper included him in its annual 'Rich List' with an optimistic and unlikely estimate of wealth of £130 million, alongside musicians Eric Clapton and Phil Collins.

Only a year later, however, Baines was convicted of false accounting and laundering criminal money around banks on the Isle of Man after he and his wife had become embroiled in a complex share scam. A Greek Cypriot businessman, Roys Poyiadjis, was a major shareholder and joint chief executive of an American software firm, AremisSoft, and had amassed funds

Trevor Baines raced a variety of Jaguars, including this Mark 2 saloon
bearing the identity 'DRAK 1' in homage to the Dracula Club,
a St Moritz nightclub beloved of Cresta Run riders.

of $175 million by artificially inflating the company's stock-market value
through fraudulently overstating the value of contracts. This dishonesty had
caused the share price of AremisSoft to rocket on Wall Street, netting him a
vast and ill-gotten fortune when he sold shares and secreted the proceeds in
Swiss bank accounts. Some of this money found its way into an investment
fund in which Baines was intimately involved.

In November 2009, the Douglas Court House on the Isle of Man
heard from the prosecution that Baines was one of three trustees who had
administered a fund for a US investor and was aware of the provenance
of the money that had been obtained dishonestly. Although Baines didn't
benefit directly from the fund itself, his company received fees for the
administration of the fund. Although he vehemently denied any knowledge
that the money had been obtained fraudulently, the court didn't believe
him. In one of the largest cases of money laundering ever seen on the Isle of
Man, the court determined that it would make an example of him in order
to protect the island's international reputation. Baines was sentenced to six
years of incarceration in the island's only prison while his 50-year-old wife
Wendy received a suspended nine-month sentence for her part in the scam.
The outcome was such a shock to Baines that he collapsed in the dock.

The husband-and-wife team appeared in court again at the beginning of

KAYE DON
Red mist

The Isle of Man was also the scene of an accident involving pre-war racing driver Kaye Don that resulted in his conviction for manslaughter and imprisonment.

Don began his career racing motorcycles but switched to cars, achieving great success at Brooklands in an ex-Malcolm Campbell Grand Prix Sunbeam between 1926 and 1928, when he also won the first-ever Ulster Tourist Trophy race at the wheel of a Lea-Francis. A multi-faceted and skilled racer, he had already made attempts on the land speed record and had also taken part in powerboat racing, where he set four world water speed records culminating in 119.81mph on Loch Lomond in Lord Wakefield's *Miss England III* in 1932.

Back in cars, he entered the 1934 Mannin Moar race held on closed public roads on the Isle of Man. During practice, he told his mechanic Francis Tayler that he wasn't happy with the brakes on his MG Magnette and asked him to try to adjust them. That evening, Tayler reported back that he thought he had managed to make some improvement, so Don foolishly took the MG out on the circuit to test the brakes with Tayler as a passenger, even though it was dark and the car had no lights, and the roads were once again open to the public. Don crashed into a taxi, fortunately without harming any of its occupants, but the MG lost a wheel and overturned. Both men were injured and Tayler died seven hours later. At the subsequent hearing at the Coroner's Court, it was found that the mechanic's death had been due to Don's negligence and at the subsequent trial he was convicted of manslaughter. Despite several appeals by Don's defence, which included the fact that a riding mechanic was aware of the occupational dangers, the racing driver was sentenced to four months in prison.

2011. This time Baines was sentenced to an additional two and a half years in prison after being found guilty of 'borrowing' nearly £600,000 from a friend's trust fund and his wife to 18 months for obtaining £400,000 by deception. The court heard that the pair had stolen money from Hermitage Securities Limited Trust, a fund they had managed as corporate service providers, in order to pay off legal fees incurred in their previous trial.

In what appeared to be a harsh injustice, Poyiadjis, the perpetrator responsible for the dirty money, escaped a custodial sentence by voluntarily returning to the United States, where he pleaded guilty to conspiracy to commit security fraud and reached a settlement with the US Securities and Exchange Commission to pay a record fine of $200 million. Conversely, Trevor and Wendy Baines lost their freedom and everything they owned after having to auction their home and its contents in order to settle their debts.

JEAN-MARIE BALESTRE

Addicted to power

When the *News of the World* made clumsy attempts to suggest that Max Mosley (see Chapter 42), who had served as FIA President, was a Nazi sympathiser, the reality was that, despite his parents' politics and friendship with Adolf Hitler, there was nothing to incriminate him. As for Mosley's predecessor as FIA President, Jean-Marie Balestre most definitely did have Nazi associations, even if he claimed that these resulted from his work as an undercover double agent.

Born in 1921, Jean-Marie Balestre was a successful publisher who, with self-confessed wartime collaborator Robert Hersant, started *Auto Journal* magazine in 1950 and built up a media empire by buying newspaper titles such as *Le Figaro* in 1975. Racing was his passion and he chose to direct his energies to the political side of the sport. He was a founding member of the French national motorsports body, the Fédération Française du Sport Automobile (FFSA), and was elected its President in 1973.

Alongside his role in the governance of French motorsport, he was soon active within the Paris-based Fédération Internationale de l'Automobile (FIA), the organisation responsible for all automotive matters worldwide, and became President of its Commission Sportive Internationale (CSI), the subsidiary body responsible for motorsport, in 1978. That same year he transformed the CSI into the Fédération Internationale du Sport Automobile (FISA) as a stand-alone body to govern international motor racing, particularly Formula 1. By 1986 he was also President of the FIA and continued in both roles until 1991, when Max Mosley defeated him in an election for the FISA Presidency.

Two years later, with an election due for the FIA Presidency, Balestre stood down, knowing that he would lose to Mosley.

Once installed as FISA President in 1978, Balestre became one of the most powerful men in global motorsport. He spent much of his time locked in battle with Bernie Ecclestone over the ownership and control of Formula 1's commercial and television rights. Although he lost that fight, he contributed a great deal to motorsport, particularly in bringing increased attention to safety. Under his leadership, the governing body was transformed from a compliant, docile organisation into an assertive, well-respected, credible institution.

Renowned for his volcanic temper and volatile personality, Jean-Marie Balestre was also known for having been 'economical with the truth' before his career in motorsport governance. He painted a colourful picture of his youth, claiming to have fought in the Spanish Civil War, even though he would have been only 15 years old at the time of its outbreak. Particular interest, however, focused upon his activities during the Second World War.

As journalist and motor racing historian Joe Saward wrote: 'His CV says he was in the French military during the Battle of France, but French police records show he was arrested for *escroquerie* (fraud) in 1940 and was only liberated when the Germans arrived in Paris in June. Two months later he helped Robert Hersant establish the *Jeune Front*, a pro-Nazi organisation, funded by the Germans. After that the two men set up a pro-Vichy training camp named after Marshal Pétain in the Paris suburbs. Then in May 1943, at the age of 22, Balestre joined the Waffen SS. Of this there was no doubt. There are official SS documents, photographs and even articles in the French SS magazine, signed by SS Sergeant Balestre.'

Balestre himself had a different version of events in which he claimed that he became involved in organising an anti-German initiative in Paris when the war began and went on to become active in the French resistance. When, in 1968, he was presented with the *Légion d'Honneur* for his services in the war, it seemed to lend some support to his story although it prompted anger from a great many of those people who had played a proper part and become genuine heroes. However, when photographs circulated in the late 1970s showing Balestre wearing a German uniform, his credibility suffered and he took legal action to suppress their publication. By way of explanation, he maintained that he had joined the SS when working under cover for the resistance as a double agent.

'Balestre claimed he was arrested by the Germans in May 1944 and was sent to Dachau,' stated Saward. 'Others insist he was arrested by the

Although he always denied it, Jean-Marie Balestre — president of FISA, the governing body of motor sport, from 1978 to 1991 — was a member of the Waffen SS during the Second World War, as seen here in uniform.

Americans a few months later and was in Dachau after it had become an Allied detention centre. Resistance people insisted he was SS and not a resistant. When he returned to Paris in May 1945, he was arrested and would spend two years on remand before being sentenced to a 10-year loss of civil rights for collaboration. Hersant suffered a similar fate, but was rehabilitated by an amnesty in 1952. He admitted what he had done and said it was down to youthful errors. Balestre denied everything and sued anyone who suggested otherwise. During the 1950s he collected various official certifications that he had been a resistant. His critics said these had been purchased.'

Once the revelations had come to light, Balestre's involvement with the SS during the war was never in doubt, even if his real intentions couldn't be clarified. Despite his post-war demeanour giving every impression of a staunch patriot, he remained a contradiction in terms. He continued to deny everything and sued anyone who dared question his past.

Of course, as the years passed no one was ever able to prove or disprove Balestre's version of events because all of those who might have been able to shine light on his background were no longer alive. Although he won all of his many legal actions taken to defend his version of events, they were really only Pyrrhic victories and damages were rarely awarded. When he died in 2008, doubts and suspicions still swirled, for he had never managed to convince people that he had been anything other than a willing Nazi collaborator.

CHAPTER 8
TED BALL
Collision course

The final proprietor of Brabham in Formula 1 was a Japanese engineering company that poured money into funding the acquisition of the failing team on loans secured from a fraudulent finance company. This led to the sad demise of the team whose rich heritage included winning four drivers' and two constructors World Championship titles and 35 Grands Prix between 1964 and 1985.

After the arrest and subsequent disappearance of Joachim Lüthi (see Chapter 39) in August 1989 after his brief and malign spell as owner of Brabham, the beleaguered Formula 1 team seemed to lurch out of the frying pan and into the fire. Although it struggled on for another two and a half seasons under the stewardship of Herbie Blash, it had been brought to its knees and Lüthi's short-lived ownership marked the beginning of the end. Unable to source meaningful sponsorship, Brabham remained desperately underfunded and would only achieve three points-scoring finishes in its last three seasons of existence.

Stefano Modena and David Brabham, the youngest of founder Jack Brabham's three racing sons, were the team's drivers in 1990, when Modena managed a best placing of fifth in the United States Grand Prix at Phoenix. A British duo, Martin Brundle and Mark Blundell, joined the team for 1991, but their cars, now equipped with disappointing Yamaha engines, were always also-rans. Lacklustre results in the first half of the season forced the once-great team into the indignity of having to pre-qualify in the second half, but to their great credit the drivers almost always made it through to the starting grid and in fact achieved a couple of decent results, with Blundell sixth in Belgium and Brundle fifth in Japan. In 1992, Eric van de Poele joined Brabham, partnered mainly by Damon Hill, who made his Grand Prix début for the team after Giovanna Amati (see Chapter 3) had been dropped. Hill gave the team its final hurrah at the Hungarian Grand Prix when he crossed the finish line in 11th and last place, four laps behind Ayrton Senna's winning McLaren.

Perversely, the Brabham team's ultimate downfall was brought about by involvement with more dishonesty. After Lüthi's arrest, Middlebridge Group Ltd, a Japanese engineering firm owned by Koji Nakauchi, gained ownership of Brabham for the 1990 season. Middlebridge, which was already running a Formula 3000 team, covered the cost of the acquisition and the subsequent running of the team using loans from a fraudulent finance company called Landhurst Leasing.

Ted Ball established Landhurst Leasing in 1984 as a vehicle finance company that started out by specialising in leasing expensive luxury and classic cars to wealthy customers. Within a year, it was turning over £2 million and by 1991 it had grown to £38 million. As the lucrative business expanded, the company increasingly diversified into other areas that included company car fleets and even plant and office equipment. Passionate about Formula 1, Ball was determined to become a major player in motorsport.

In Oliver Shah's book *Damaged Goods: The Rise and Fall of Philip Green*, Ball is described as: 'The hard-drinking boss who had grown up on a council estate in South London and felt the need to prove himself by throwing money around. When Landhurst secured a £120 million credit line from a syndicate of banks led by Guinness Mahon in 1990, he gifted all his staff Dom Pérignon champagne and Montblanc fountain pens.'

By 1988, Landhurst was supplying lease finance to Middlebridge, starting with a £1 million loan, and had also provided much-needed loans to Lotus, another ailing Formula 1 team with a glorious past. Quite quickly, Middlebridge struggled to meet the lease repayments to Landhurst. When the Brabham team became available for purchase, Ball and his finance director, David Ashworth, put pressure on struggling Middlebridge by lending £8 million for the acquisition. Middlebridge's dependence on Landhurst made its directors vulnerable to improper pressure and in return for the loans they were persuaded to make illegal cash payments to Ball and

Ashworth. At the time of the original £1 million loan, Ball requested and was paid £25,000 in cash, but this was just the first in a web of corrupt payments later uncovered by accountants Arthur Andersen that would ultimately total £420,000.

Middlebridge's difficulty in making repayments put Landhurst in breach of bank covenants. Instead of reporting these, Landhurst hid the problem by falsifying accounts and rolling over leases, often extending further credit on assets of minimal value, including almost worthless piles of parts and equipment. When the original leases expired, instead of terminating the contracts, Landhurst would write new ones on other Middlebridge assets with the money from the new leases being used to pay off the old ones. This was a time of recession and the cycle of concealment and spiralling debt got out of control as the economic climate worsened. Eventually, in early 1992, Ashworth had no choice but to report a breach of covenant to the banks. In August, just after the Hungarian Grand Prix, Landhurst was put into receivership as a result of the investigating accountants' report and Middlebridge's assets were effectively frozen, so it too collapsed shortly afterwards.

The Serious Fraud Office's investigation in conjunction with the City of London Police established that the deceit had resulted in Landhurst owing banks — led by Guinness Mahon but also including the Prudential and several Swiss and Canadian financial institutions — a total of £121 million. Of this, only £70 million was recoverable. Middlebridge owed Landhurst £7.2 million, of which only £1 million was recoverable.

In the subsequent trial at the Old Bailey in London, prosecuting QC Timothy Langdale related that Middlebridge had run out of assets on which leases could be written even though, he said, 'Ted Ball would have written a lease on the tyres changed after a pitstop.'

On 15th September 1997, Ashworth, 45, changed his not-guilty plea to guilty of two counts of corruption. Ball, 50, had already pleaded guilty to eight counts of corruption relating to the net shortfall of £50 million in addition to accepting a raft of illegal bribes and backhander payments that were received from Middlebridge in cash. On 20th October 1997, Mr Justice Pownall sentenced Ball to three years' imprisonment and Ashworth to 18 months.

Ball had seen his dream of being a major player in Grand Prix racing shattered. Of far greater importance to racing enthusiasts was the inauspicious and sad demise of Brabham, one of the most illustrious names in motor racing history.

JOHN BARTLETT

Chequered Justice?

A sports car driver and team owner in the 1980s, his life
was derailed when his childhood dream turned into a
nightmare and he lost everything. Due to the precarious
nature of his profession, he had acquired various Payment
Protection Insurance (PPI) policies and believed that he
was well covered against most eventualities. However, a
battle with one company over its unwillingness to pay out
on a claim evolved into a criminal investigation that
led to a jail sentence for fraud.

When, as a seven-year-old schoolboy, John Bartlett saw newspaper
reports of the accident that almost claimed the life of Stirling Moss
at Goodwood in 1962, he became intrigued by motor racing and the big-
name drivers of the time such as Jack Brabham, John Surtees and Jim Clark
ignited his imagination. When Graham Hill came to stay at his parents'
hotel, The Claremont in Brighton, the excitement was so great that he
decided he had to become a racing driver.

Although he gained limited experience on a go-kart while at school, he
was a late starter, aged 24, when he took the first step towards turning his
dream into reality by enrolling for a trial lesson with Motor Racing Stables
at Brands Hatch. After experiencing the thrill of driving a Formula Ford
Royale RP26, he decided to abandon a promising business career — he was
running his own electronics company specialising in fire alarm and security
systems — and focus his attentions full-time on becoming a professional
racing driver.

He embarked on Formula Ford in 1980 after buying a ten-year-old Lotus

61 with an equally old and tired engine. Although the ancient car was hopelessly outclassed by more modern machinery, it was ideal for him to learn his craft and proved sufficiently robust to withstand the occasional off-track excursion until he was able to upgrade to a more recent Royale RP24, which was only three years old. Away from the circuits, he quickly proved adept at finding commercial sponsorship to help fund his racing and by 1983, with the help and backing of actor Gareth Hunt, he was able to move up to the more senior level of Formula Ford 2000 with a Delta T82. However, another car hit his Delta broadside in his first race and the accident landed him in hospital.

As his results and finishing record improved, he wanted to climb another rung of the ladder. Recognising that age was now against him in making it onto the international stage in single-seaters, he elected to pursue the sports car route and, in his naivety and exuberance, chose to launch himself straight into the top echelons. Despite limited experience that extended no further than a lightweight 160bhp single-seater, he acquired a Group C Lola T610 fitted with a 450bhp Ford Cosworth DFL engine, a car that was much faster than anything he had driven before. In what was only his fourth season of racing, his newly formed team took part not only in the British Thundersports series but also the BRDC Sportscar Championship and selected World Endurance Championship (WEC) rounds, including the Le Mans 24 Hours and even the Sandown Park event in Australia.

Bartlett used his entrepreneurial skills to good effect to land a healthy portfolio of sponsors, most notably Goodmans, a hi-fi manufacturer that would become one of his most loyal long-term supporters. In 1985, Goodmans put up the necessary funding to have the one-off Chevron B62 built to contest the Group C2 class but the car wasn't completed in time for the start of the WEC season and he missed the first three rounds, so the campaign was fruitless. By 1987 he was racing the unique Bardon DB2, which had begun life as the Arundel C200 commissioned and driven by Eddie Arundel, otherwise known as the Earl of Arundel, but he was unable even to finish an event.

The 1988 season, however, proved to be the most successful of Bartlett's career. Partnered by David Mercer in a Harrier, he claimed three wins, two second places and five lap records. These strong performances led to an invitation to race a Group C2 Tiga in two World Sports-Prototype Championship (WS-PC) rounds for British team owner Roy Baker. The second of these was back at Sandown Park in Australia at the end of the year and ended with suspension failure.

John Bartlett took his wife Mary on the trip to Australia and the couple enjoyed a stay in a penthouse suite at the Hilton Hotel in Melbourne provided as part of a sponsorship deal with Hilton International. Before returning home, they extended their stay by stopping off in Malaysia for a few days' holiday. While there, Bartlett rode a frisky ex-racehorse on a beach and got thrown off, landing awkwardly and badly hurting his back. By the time he got home, the pain was so severe that he feared he would be unable to even walk, let alone drive a racing car, so he instructed his insurance broker to make claims against his PPI policies. It took a further six months before he was cleared to race again but this was just the start of the nightmare yet to unfold.

PPI — Payment Protection Insurance — is a form of income security that covers monthly repayments on loans if the policyholder is unable to work through illness, accident or involuntary unemployment. The end of the 1980s was a time of recession with a high rate of unemployment and a huge increase in the weight of claims against insurance companies. This added to the existing problems of many such companies that had also ill-advisedly bought large quantities of now worthless junk bonds and were being sued by their underwriters. Bartlett's initial claim was for a couple of months' worth of payments and thereafter was on a sporadic on/off basis when the back pain was so great that his doctor advised him to rest rather than race.

He raced from time to time between 1989 and 1992, including a brief foray into the American IMSA championship in a Spice and class victory at Snetterton in the 24-hour Esso Willhire event driving a Ford Sierra Cosworth, without knowing the gravity of his injury, which was only established when a specialist eventually diagnosed that he had in fact broken his spine. Meanwhile, he was claiming against both his redundancy and sickness/injury policies but still in ignorance of his true medical predicament. The situation evolved into a criminal investigation after his claim that his insurer had 'hidden' a report confirming that he should never race again because this would have triggered a liability to pay out a much larger lump sum than the total of £6,000 that the company had already paid over an 18-month period.

Bartlett claimed that an unlicensed private detective had erroneously suggested that he couldn't be suffering from his injuries because he had been observed riding horses and mucking out stables at his property when in fact the individual under surveillance had been someone else of similar age who had been renting the stables. This was the catalyst for the Metropolitan Police to raid the family home near Arundel, West Sussex by

John Bartlett took his first steps in racing in 1980 with a 10-year-old Lotus 61, with loyal wife Mary by his side.

making, according to Bartlett, a forced entry at 5.30am with no fewer than 13 officers and removing some documents. When Bartlett returned home from holiday two days later, his immediate reaction was to threaten to sue all parties including the police, his insurer, the private detective and even the bank that had sold him the policy in the first place, to which the response of the police was to arrest him.

Prior to this, Bartlett's bank had bounced cheques even though these had been for trivial sums and had totalled only £16. Incensed about the PPI policies this bank had sold him and by the police raid, he issued proceedings against the bank in the High Court and won his case, leaving the bank not only facing the embarrassing publicity of having to pay him damages of £4,000 but also the ignominy of being sued by means of a legal costs policy that the bank itself had provided. Bartlett had also previously written to BBC TV's *Watchdog* programme about his plight and this prompted an exposé that put PPI policies under national scrutiny for the first time, although no specific details of his claims were cited.

None of this made Bartlett any friends and as a result he felt that he had put himself on the radar of the insurer, which, he believed, had reached the position where it wouldn't pay out again. He felt that his history with the company now conspired against him and influenced its unwillingness to meet its liabilities. After a second police raid on his house, this time during his youngest son's sixth birthday party, according to his account, he was charged with several serious offences, all based on the insurer's conclusion that his claims were fraudulent because they had been variously made on the supposedly contradictory basis of being both injured (therefore unable to work) and redundant (therefore trying to find work).

By the time the case came to court, Bartlett had conclusive proof — including doctors' reports, X-rays and scans — confirming that his spine had not only been broken in two places but had also been knocked forward in the lumbar area by a quarter of an inch. On this basis he was receiving sickness payments while at the same time claiming redundancy payments. His defence was that he was claiming from an accident policy rather than a sickness one and that it obliged the insurer to pay out regardless of whether or not he was employed, sick or looking for work. An additional complication was the suggestion that he had somehow contrived to deliberately bring down his own John Bartlett Racing team as a motive to claim redundancy, when in fact its bankruptcy had been a combination of bad debt and the default of two of his co-driver's sponsors. Lending weight to his conspiracy theory, he stated that all company records that would have confirmed this background had been destroyed or mislaid by the Official Receiver, which would normally retain them for a minimum of seven years.

Further distraction presented itself in the form of prize indemnity insurance that Bartlett had taken out with Tyser Special Risks. Prize indemnity insurance was common at the time in various professional sports and was an entirely legitimate and legal 'bet', whereby payment of a premium could trigger a large pay-out in the event of a certain pre-agreed result being achieved. Specifically, the prize indemnity agreement at issue concerned races in the Interserie championship, a Europe-wide series for sports cars. To compete in the Interserie in 1992, Bartlett had hired a Porsche 966 Spyder owned and run by Gunnar Racing and had been sharing the driving of it with Robin Donovan. After Bartlett finished ninth at Brands Hatch on 26th July, Donovan drove the car at Zolder in Belgium on 9th August and brought it home fifth, a result that triggered the substantial pay-out of £160,000 from Bartlett's prize indemnity policy. With this windfall, Bartlett intended to buy the Porsche, together with equipment and spare parts, and set up a new racing team the following season, although he later changed his mind about the choice of car and instead acquired a pair of much cheaper Lola T89 Indycar chassis that could be converted into sports cars.

Once the Crown Prosecution Service accepted that the riding accident in Malaysia had actually occurred and the insurance company had agreed under cross-examination that Bartlett was eligible to claim for both unemployment and injury, the only avenue left for the insurer was to pursue him about the prize indemnity. Their argument was that if Bartlett knew that he was injured and was already claiming or planning to claim a lump sum, then racing the Porsche had been fraudulent. The insurance company's lawyers therefore focused their attention on charges of obtaining £160,000 by deception.

According to Bartlett, this accusation didn't take into account the timing of his discovery of the true nature of his back injury, as established by an orthopaedic surgeon appointed by the insurance company. Although he had been examined by this specialist on 21st July, five days before he raced at Brands Hatch, he didn't receive the medical report until 10th August and was therefore unaware of the gravity of his injuries when he raced the Porsche. From a medical perspective, it was undoubtedly a foolish decision to have even considered taking part in the race but it was an even bigger mistake to have omitted to tell his insurance broker either that he was going to compete or that he had actually done so. This was especially foolhardy ahead of making a lump sum claim for what seemed likely to be classified as a permanent claim to replace the sporadic payments that had been made up until this point.

When the case came to court in November 1994, the jury returned guilty verdicts on charges of 'obtaining by deception' and of 'furnishing false information'. His Honour Judge MacRae handed down a prison sentence of four years increased to six if Bartlett didn't pay a compensation order of £90,640 to the various insurers he was accused of having defrauded. As a result, the two Lola sports cars that had been stored in his garage at home were confiscated.

This is a convoluted and complex story in which the prosecution claimed that the racing driver had embarked on a web of deception whereby he orchestrated an elaborate fraud involving the collapse of his own racing team, his resulting redundancy and a separate injury claim through which he dishonestly obtained money. At the time of the hearing, the jury wouldn't have been aware of the scandal of mis-selling of PPI policies although it has since been highlighted that millions of people were coerced by unscrupulous insurance agents to buy them as a condition of taking out loans, hire purchase agreements or mortgages.

Since his release from prison, John Bartlett has pursued a crusade to prove his innocence and nowadays seeks to publicise his mission by means of a website on which he states: 'My hope is, by finally publishing the facts behind my case and making public the reality of what can happen within our justice system, it will help raise awareness and understanding by shining a light on the many ways individuals and groups within the police, CPS [Crown Prosecution Service], and courts misuse and abuse power and control. Converging misinformation with fact, creates the predestined and inevitable outcome... an unjust guilty verdict, a verdict based on a set of lies agreed upon.'

CHAPTER 10
DAVID BLAKELY
A fast but tragic life

A tempestuous and violent relationship
culminated in the murder of a debonair and
promising young British racing driver, shot dead
by his vengeful and jealous lover on the pavement
outside a North London pub one Easter Sunday.
The murderer became the last woman to be
hanged in Britain and this had ramifications that
led to reforms and, eventually, the abolition of the
death penalty in Britain 10 years later.

Ruth Hornby was born on 9th October 1926 in the seaside town of Rhyl in North Wales into a dysfunctional and loveless family, one of six children, and spent her formative years in Basingstoke in Hampshire. Her Belgian mother, Bertha, a First World War refugee, was a deeply religious Catholic. Her English father, Arthur, was a former cello player from Manchester who had had to find menial employment when the music halls in which he had played fell out of fashion, leading his family to become increasingly impoverished. An embittered and violent man, he sexually abused his daughters, in Ruth's case from the age of 10. By the time of the Second World War, the family was living in London, eventually settling in Brixton after a spell in Southwark.

After her unhappy childhood, 17-year-old Ruth had a short-lived relationship with a Canadian soldier by whom she had an illegitimate son, Andrei. Despite the soldier professing his commitment to her, when he returned to his home country, on what she was led to believe was a temporary basis, it transpired that he was married with three children, and she never saw him again. Desperate to escape the drudgery of life working with her sister in the Oxo factory in South London, and with her mother looking after her small child, she switched jobs to become a waitress in a fashionable Lyons' café, which represented a step up the ladder and boosted her self-confidence as well as exposing her to a more glamorous life.

The connections the attractive blonde made at the café led her to become involved with The Camera Club, a seedy set-up where members photographed her nude, and where private liaisons led inexorably towards occasional prostitution. She obtained a new job as a hostess at the Court Club in Mayfair, where the manager, Morris Conley, demanded regular sexual favours in return for her employment and accommodation. In a short space of time, her weekly wages had increased dramatically from £2 in the factory to at least £20, although what was even more important to her was the perception that her social standing had improved enormously, something that she so desperately craved.

It was here that the popular Ruth met George Ellis, a 41-year-old divorced dentist whom she married, aged 24, on 8th November 1950, although their time together was brief and unhappy. Ellis was a violent alcoholic and underwent treatment at a clinic at Warlingham Park hospital, where his frequent visits led the insecure Ruth to believe that he was having an affair. She stalked him and created such tempestuous scenes that she had to be prescribed anti-depressants and tranquilisers, which she took for the rest of her life.

Early in the marriage, a connection with Diana Dors, who was on the brink of becoming a big film star, secured a walk-on part as a beauty queen in *Lady Godiva Rides Again*, although neither Ruth nor another glamorous young hopeful, Joan Collins, appeared in the credits. At the time Ruth was four months' pregnant and a daughter, Georgina, was duly born, although her husband denied paternity.

In 1953, Ruth left George Ellis and returned to an independent life working as manager of the Carroll Club, followed by a move, also as manager, to a more respectable establishment, the Little Club in Knightsbridge, whose membership included King Hussein of Jordan, actors Douglas Fairbanks Jr and Burt Lancaster, and Stephen Ward, who became infamous for his part in the John Profumo spy scandal of the early 1960s. The Little Club was located almost directly opposite the Steering Wheel Club, so it was often frequented by well-known British racing drivers of the time, including Stirling Moss and Mike Hawthorn. It was Hawthorn who introduced Ruth to David Blakely.

David Moffett Drummond Blakely was born on 17th June 1929 in Sheffield, Yorkshire, the youngest son of a well-to-do Scottish doctor, John Blakely, and an Irish mother, Annie. The family lived in a large house in the Crookes district of the city from which his father opened his medical practice soon after the end of the First World War, becoming extremely popular with his mainly lower-middle-class patients.

In February 1934, David's adulterous father appeared in court on remand, charged with the murder of Phyllis Staton, a 25-year-old unemployed waitress who, after a two-year affair with him, had become pregnant with his child. The prosecution case alleged that Blakely had illegally administered the drug Pituitrin in order to cause a miscarriage and this had led to her death in hospital from acute septicaemia. The case was discharged by the magistrate, Mr A.J. Slight, on the grounds that although Blakely admitted supplying the drug to the girl, he denied carrying out an operation on her. As the prosecution was unable to prove otherwise, it was decided that, if the case were to proceed, it would be unlikely that a jury would be able to convict. Despite the story being one of national interest that was widely reported in the press and inevitably stained Blakely's character, the family remained highly respected and the episode appeared to have no adverse effect on the doctor's practice, due to the goodwill that he had built up. The strain of the trial, however, added further pressure to an already fragile marriage and divorce followed. In early 1941, only two months after her decree absolute had been granted, Annie, a sophisticated and outgoing character, remarried.

Her new husband was Humphrey Cook, a wealthy man who had inherited his father's thriving wholesale drapery business and fortune at the age of 12. A shy and private character, Cook loved motor racing and had been a competent driver who, despite his girth and portly stature, had regularly competed at a high level in Vauxhalls, Bentleys and Aston Martins at Brooklands and elsewhere, including in the Tourist Trophy and at Le Mans. He had become best known in racing circles for directing £75,000 of his wealth to Raymond Mays and his patriotic venture English Racing Automobiles (ERA), which became active in 1934 and achieved considerable fame and success in the 1,500cc supercharged *voiturette* category during the years leading up to the Second World War. Cook withdrew his patronage of ERA in 1939 after a disagreement with Mays and his direct involvement in the sport ceased with the coming of war.

As Cook's stepson, David Blakely received a good private education at Shrewsbury School, where he was an average pupil, before going on to

Ruth Ellis sometimes accompanied David Blakely to race meetings, this occasion being a Goodwood event in 1954.

compulsory National Service with the Highland Light Infantry, from which he was released within weeks with no official explanation. He tried his hand briefly at a career in hotel management but was ignominiously fired, possibly because of increasing distraction from his all-consuming passion for motor racing. Despite sharing strong mutual interest in this sport with his stepfather, there was no love lost between them. Cook appears to have endured rather than enjoyed his stepson's company whenever the young man visited The Old Park, the grand house in Penn, Buckinghamshire, where the couple lived, but there is evidence that he offered the budding racer some encouragement and support, presumably to please Annie.

The aspiring young driver's appetite was whetted when he entered an amateur race meeting at Silverstone on 28th July 1951 in an HRG and won three minor handicap races. After this encouraging start, he was part of the third-placed HRG team in the 750 Motor Club's six-hour relay event at Silverstone a month later. In 1952, and still very much an amateur, he concentrated on learning his craft in the HRG in more club events at both Goodwood and Silverstone, and also rubbed shoulders with many of the best British drivers of the time in two important internationals, the Jersey Road Race and the Goodwood Nine Hours. Convinced of his talents, he not only raced his HRG into 1953 but also persuaded Lionel Leonard to let him co-drive his modified Leonard MG-engined Tojeiro in the

Nürburgring 1,000Km, a round of that year's inaugural World Sports Car Championship, but he and the car's owner didn't make the finish. Widening his repertoire of racing circuits at home, Blakely's best results that year in the HRG included a win at Castle Combe, a second place at Snetterton and third places at Crystal Palace and Snetterton. A full season with Leonard's car followed in 1954 but results were disappointing, with two third places at Snetterton the best he could manage.

Meanwhile, Blakely had constructed his own open-top sports racer. Known as the Emperor, it was built around a tubular chassis clothed in attractive green full-width aluminium bodywork reminiscent of a Ferrari Monza. Having established a good rapport with HRG from the start of his racing career, he was able to obtain a special experimental version of a twin-cam derivative of the company's Singer-based 1,500cc engine, and it was one of the most promising engines he could have procured at that time. He débuted the Emperor at the Brands Hatch Boxing Day meeting at the end of 1954 and finished second in the 15-lap Kent Cup race.

Self-centred, arrogant and widely disliked, Blakely was exceedingly fortunate in being able to afford to race, thanks to his stepfather's indulgence as well as an inheritance from his father, who had died in 1952. Besides racing, he seems to have spent much of his time and money on womanising, clubbing and hard drinking, revelling in the playboy lifestyle that for some was synonymous with the sport. One of his regular haunts was the Little Club in Knightsbridge and it was here, in 1953, that the good-looking 24-year-old first met Ruth Ellis. Despite the unlikely match of affluent public schoolboy and promiscuous working-class single mother, it wasn't long before the two became lovers and within just a few weeks he moved into her flat above the club, even though he was engaged to another woman, Mary Dawson, and she remained married to George Ellis. She was so desperate to better herself and breach their very different backgrounds and class barriers that she affected a distinctly middle-class accent so that she could fit in better with the smart, fast set and exalted circles in which her new boyfriend moved. This charming young racing driver must have seemed to be the stuff of her dreams.

There were strains on their relationship from the outset. The continual partying fuelled her already heavy drinking habit and her feelings for him were never sufficiently reciprocated, as indicated by his unwillingness to take her home to Penn to meet his mother, despite having proposed to her. Ruth, who by this stage had evolved into a part-time prostitute, openly continued with her daytime liaisons with clients, one of whom got her

In the months leading up to his murder, David Blakely began to compete with his own 'special', the HRG-engined Emperor, seen at the Brands Hatch Boxing Day meeting in 1954.

pregnant, leading to an illegal back-street abortion. The young racer also took up the many opportunities that his lifestyle presented and pursued a string of romantic prospects, often with friends of hers, which added to the friction between the couple. Despite this, their relationship was a passionate one and he referred to her as his fiancée, possibly in the forlorn hope of retaining a degree of exclusivity over the insecure girl.

Unsurprisingly, in such a dysfunctional, destructive and physically abusive relationship, the promiscuity and double standards of both parties led to extreme jealousy that regularly erupted into heated exchanges in public. Their rows often happened in front of club members and guests, who included friends from the racing community such as John Cooper. These spats would invariably lead to Ruth throwing Blakely out, leaving him to seek refuge with his best friend Anthony Findlater, a former Aston Martin engineer who had been heavily involved in building the Emperor, and wife Carole, a one-time girlfriend of Blakely's. The Findlaters were a peculiar and eccentric couple whom Ruth disliked and in her paranoia she became obsessed with the belief that they were scheming to force David apart from her. However, the couple's love/hate relationship continued as she would always forgive him for his numerous indiscretions and violence, and passionate reconciliations would follow.

Another man who became important to Ruth was Desmond Cussen, an ex-RAF pilot who had flown Lancaster bombers in the war and acquired considerable wealth after inheriting his family's chain of tobacconists. Smitten by the vivacious blonde hostess, he became one of her lovers in June 1954. This developed into more than just a casual liaison as she became genuinely fond of Cussen and looked on him differently because he offered the security that she craved and had never had. Four years older than Ruth and significantly more mature than either her or David, he was something of a father figure in whom she could confide, and was the only man in her life who had never abused her or let her down. Indeed, when she lost her job at the club together with the accommodation that went with it, Cussen stepped in to offer not only a roof over her head at his flat in Devonshire Street but also payment of her son Andrei's private boarding school fees, even while the increasingly violent and embittered relationship with Blakely continued.

By the start of the 1955 racing season, Blakely still hadn't won a race of any consequence but held high hopes that the Emperor would make his reputation as a future star. One encouraging prospect was an entry in the Le Mans 24 Hours in June as reserve driver for the three-car works Bristol team. Meanwhile, his first event of the season with the Emperor was the British Empire Trophy at Oulton Park in Cheshire over the first weekend of April but its special HRG engine blew up in practice. The following weekend, which was Easter, he had been due to compete at Aintree, the newly constructed circuit near Liverpool, but the damaged engine meant that he couldn't attend. Instead, he decided to stay in London and promised to spend some time with Ruth after a particularly fierce conflict between them two weeks earlier.

David Blakely detested Desmond Cussen and was furious at having had to become part of a love triangle not of his making. When, on 28th March 1955, Ruth announced to Blakely she was pregnant with his baby, in the forlorn and desperate hope that it would cement their relationship and draw them together, it led to a violent fight during which Blakely punched her in the stomach several times, causing a miscarriage and all the emotional torment and anguish that went with it.

Come the Easter weekend, the unreliable Blakely, true to form, didn't show up to see Ruth as arranged, deciding instead to stay with the Findlaters. She wasn't in a good state, still physically suffering with bleeding from the miscarriage and in mental turmoil, feeling both rejected and betrayed by the man she undeniably loved and desperately wanted to cling to. Furious about his non-appearance, she asked Cussen to help her find him. Sensing an opportunity to break up her relationship with his younger and more glamorous love rival, perhaps just by allowing her to scare him, Cussen provided the impressionable and troubled woman with a .38 Smith & Wesson revolver. Early on Easter Sunday, 10th April, he drove her with her son Andrei to Blakely's parents' house in Buckinghamshire, stopping nearby to teach her how to fire the gun in nearby woodland. On discovering that Blakely wasn't there, they returned to London and correctly surmised that the next most likely place to find him would be at the Findlaters' flat in Tanza Road, near Hampstead Heath.

When they drew up outside that evening, they saw Blakely's car drive away. Guessing that he was heading to a nearby favourite watering hole, The Magdala in South Hill Park, Ruth walked there alone as Cussen didn't want to risk being seen by any witnesses in the vicinity of the pub. She was in a particularly irrational state, having been drinking for much of the afternoon on top of taking her usual sedatives. A topic of conversation in the crowded bar on that balmy spring evening may well have been a recent and well-publicised murder case in the vicinity. A Greek woman, Styllou Christofi, who had lived only a few doors away from The Magdala, had murdered her daughter-in-law, Hella, and had been hanged a few months earlier.

By the time Ruth reached the pub at around 9.30pm, Blakely and a friend, Clive Gunnell, had emerged to enjoy their drinks outside. Having finally tracked him down, she stepped out from the doorway of the newsagent next door and as she approached him said 'Hello David'. Intent on avoiding another scene, he ignored her and immediately turned away to leave, fumbling for his car keys. At this point, his tormented and deeply humiliated lover took the revolver from her handbag and, in a final act of rejection, fired five shots at him. The first shot missed him as he ducked behind his parked car but the second shot felled him. She then fired three more bullets into him at point-blank range as he lay on the pavement. Reports suggest that the gun then jammed briefly before she managed to fire it a sixth time, the bullet ricocheting off the road and hitting a woman pedestrian, Gladys Yule, on her thumb.

In a state of shock, and traumatised by the gravity of the situation and the stark realisation that she had killed her lover, Ruth asked Gunnell to call the police, although an off-duty police officer, Alan Thompson, was able to take the still-smoking weapon from her and immediately arrest her before any other officers arrived. She offered no resistance and in an apparently cold and detached manner immediately told Thompson, 'I am guilty. I am a little confused.' She was taken to Hampstead Police Station and, after making a detailed confession, duly charged with murder.

After appearing in front of magistrates two days later, Ruth was incarcerated in Holloway Prison. The police investigation, by officers who viewed the crime as an open-and-shut case and wanted to wrap things up as quickly as possible, was brief and wholly inadequate. The police never fully investigated the motive or properly questioned the source of the firearm, which Ruth — loyally protecting Cussen and refusing to implicate him — claimed to have received from someone at the club as security for a debt, although she couldn't remember who. Cussen, of course, was involved in the crime but his name wasn't mentioned in court and the jury was never made aware of his existence, even though she had been living at his address. As far as can be ascertained, the police omitted to pursue any line of inquiry with him. The serial number of the Smith & Wesson revolver proved that it was of military issue but there were no records to connect it with Cussen.

Ruth's trial opened on Monday 20th June, a mere eight weeks after the shooting and just one week after the Le Mans 24 Hours in which Blakely had been due to compete. She appeared in front of Mr Justice Havers in the dock of Number One Court at The Old Bailey in London dressed in a two-piece black suit and white blouse with her hair redyed peroxide blonde.

The case of the murderous jilted lover had, of course, attracted a great deal of media attention and Dougie Howell of the *Sunday Mirror* secured the rights to the full story, which was serialised in four parts. At the time it was not uncommon for a tabloid newspaper to pay the costs of legal defence for an accused murderer and, while there's no proof that this occurred in Ruth's case, the choice of solicitor to represent her, John Bickford, was an indication. It transpired that his background included work as a crime journalist for the same newspaper and that he was also friendly with Cussen.

Ruth never tried to deny the killing or excuse her actions in any way. She certainly helped seal her fate and sign her own death warrant when Mr Christmas Humphreys, counsel for the prosecution in court, asked, 'When you fired that revolver at close range into the body of David Blakely, what did you intend to do?' To which her response was, 'It is obvious that when I shot him I intended to kill him.' What the court never knew was that, according to psychiatric evidence, she was mentally ill, had been beaten mercilessly by the lover whom she had shot, and had been sexually abused by her father.

In one of the shortest murder trials in history, the hearing was finished after less than a day and a half. The jury retired for an extraordinarily brief 14 minutes after finding her 'of sound mind' and returned a unanimous verdict of guilty of premeditated murder. The judge, Mr Justice Havers, had no alternative but to hand down the verdict of death by hanging. The diminutive figure standing impassively in the dock simply and sadly replied: 'Thank you.'

Ruth never wanted to implicate anyone else and nor did she seek to appeal against the court's decision. She was reconciled to her fate and felt it was fair, correct and just. A few days before her execution she told her elder sister Muriel on a prison visit that she wanted to die so that she could be reunited with Blakely. This was a sentiment that she reiterated in a moving and apologetic letter she wrote to his mother, whom she had never been allowed to meet, stating, 'I've taken a life and my life is forfeit for that' and adding 'I've always loved your son and will never stop loving him'. She also told her mother that she didn't support the petition that Bickford presented to the Home Secretary to reprieve her and nor did she want to get involved in the campaign that her relatives orchestrated on her behalf.

However, only a few days before being sent to the gallows, she wanted to make her will and requested a visit in prison from Victor Mishcon, a lawyer who had handled her divorce from George Ellis and also a prominent Labour politician. At the eleventh hour, he and his clerk managed to persuade her to tell the full story if only for the sake of her two children whom he felt deserved to know the truth. In a new confession, she admitted that she had spent much of the day drinking Pernod with Desmond Cussen and revealed that he had indeed supplied her with the loaded gun, taught her how to shoot and driven her first to Penn and then to Hampstead. This contradicted her previous formal statement to the police and would have been crucial to her case had it been available for use in her defence because it identified Cussen as her accomplice.

As Britain was beginning to become uncomfortable about capital punishment, particularly for women, Mishcon felt that there was a realistic chance of Ruth's sentence being commuted to life in prison, but he underestimated the personal prejudice of Gwilym Lloyd George, the Home Secretary, in whose gift a review was possible. As a firm believer in the death penalty, his opinion was that 'if a reprieve is granted in this case, then we should seriously have to consider whether capital punishment is retained as a penalty'.

Mishcon campaigned tirelessly on Ruth's behalf for the last 60 hours of her life, feeling strongly that Cussen was not only culpable but could even have been charged as principal and not just accessory. Time, however, ran out. Lloyd George refused an application for a temporary stay of execution and a last-minute search for Cussen was called off after only eight hours.

Ruth's fate, as the only person who could have testified against him, was sealed. Her last visitors, on the day before the execution, were her parents and brother Granville. When they left Holloway Prison at 5.15pm, Granville told reporters that 'she seemed absolutely calm and unafraid of what was going to happen to her'.

On the day of the execution, as was his well-practised routine, Albert Pierrepoint, the country's infamous and most experienced executioner, entered the condemned cell for what would be the penultimate time in his 24-year career. Ruth's arms would have been secured with a soft calf leather strap behind her back before she was led by him and his assistant, Royston Rickard, together with both the prison governor and medical officer, through a door into the adjoining execution chamber. Once she was in position on the trap door, Pierrepoint would have placed a white cotton hood over her head and slipped a leather-covered noose around her neck before securing it to a rope. Ruth apparently didn't utter a word in the last few minutes of her life. In his autobiography, Pierrepoint described her as the bravest and calmest person ever to have stood in front of him when facing the gallows. He stated that he remained haunted by her attempt to smile.

A crowd of over 1,000 people congregated outside Holloway praying for 28-year-old Ruth Ellis, aka prisoner number 9656, when she was hanged at 9.00am on Wednesday 19th July. Despite her portrayal in some publications as a harlot, there was considerable pressure from the public and the press for clemency and a petition was signed by 50,000 people. The case became the catalyst for national debate on capital punishment and ultimately the decision to change the law to 'end legal murder' with the abolition of hanging 10 years later. She was the 50th and last woman to be hanged in Britain. As was customary for executed prisoners, she was buried in an unmarked grave within the walls of Holloway Prison.

There were several sad postscripts to her story. As a young and impressionable 10-year-old at the time, her son Andrei, more usually known as Andy, never got over her death or that of Blakely, who had been the only real father figure he had known. As an adult, he had a troubled life, suffering depression, and after his mother's remains were moved to a plot at St Mary's Church in Amersham, he smashed the headstone in his despair. Not long after, in 1982, he took his own life, aged 37 and living as a recluse in a bedsit in London. Much earlier, in 1969, Ruth's mother had also attempted suicide in her flat in Hemel Hempstead and never properly recovered. Earlier still, the life of Ruth's ex-husband, George Ellis, had spiralled out of control into alcoholism and he had committed suicide in a hotel in 1958.

CHAPTER 11
BOB BOSTON
In the Zloop

Zloop appeared to be a company with a worthy objective — the recycling of out-of-date electronic equipment — but the boss of this start-up venture deceived and defrauded lenders, franchisees and investors of more than $25 million, much of which was spent on furthering his son's NASCAR career.

Born in Sparks, Maryland on 12th September 1989, Justin Boston was exceptionally young when he was first exposed to motorsport after receiving a motocross bike as a present on his fifth birthday. The child practised riding it in the state fairgrounds but was soon competing all over North America and by the age of 13 he had won over 300 motocross events. After a frightening accident in which his bike hit him on the head, his interest transferred to car racing, and at the age of 16 this precocious talent signed up for a course at the Buck Baker Racing School in Charlotte.

He began his career in motor racing by competing in Legend Cars before showing potential in a limited programme of USAR Pro Cup and other events in 2009. His career came to a temporary halt due to a lack of funding but was rescued in 2013 by the arrival of healthy sponsorship from Zloop. This company, which recycled electronic waste such as computers and mobile phones, had been co-founded only a few months earlier by his father, Robert 'Bob' Boston, its Chief Executive Officer, and Robert LaBarge, its Chief Marketing Officer. Zloop backed Justin to compete in the full ARCA racing series for Venturini Motorsports in 2013 driving a Toyota Camry. At the age of 23, he was one of the oldest rookies to take part but continued to show promise and, although he didn't win a race, his consistency was enough for him to end up third in the championship and his performance was sufficiently impressive to bring him the accolade of 'rookie of the year'.

Building on his experience for the 2014 season, Justin scored the first win for his team in 27 years at the Toledo Speedway in a car emblazoned with Zloop's logos and branding, then followed up with another victory at the Madison International Speedway. The Venturini/Boston combination planned to progress into NASCAR's truck series in 2015 but Zloop changed its allegiance and decided to move its driver to Kyle Busch Motorsports, signing a two-year deal as primary sponsor worth $3.2 million per season. As it turned out, Zloop's name appeared on the team's Toyota truck at only two NASCAR events and Boston competed in only nine of the 23 events scheduled for 2015 before he and the team parted company, after a best result of seventh place at Kansas Speedway.

Speculation at the time suggested that Boston's departure had come about because performance clauses hadn't been met and that his requests for changes had been ignored. In an interview he was quoted as saying, 'It just didn't work out.' However, it was established that the driver had been released for monetary reasons because Zloop had defaulted on payments to the team, which later had to resort to suing the company for more than $4 million.

The reason for Zloop failing to meet its obligations to Kyle Busch Motorsports was a financial predicament that led to its filing for bankruptcy before the year was out. At that time NASCAR boasted the largest spectator attendance of any sport in the US and Zloop wanted to use its sponsorship to raise awareness about the unnecessarily high level of 'e-waste'. The company took a mobile recycling unit to all the circuits for racegoers to dispose of unwanted and out-of-date electronic equipment.

From the outset, Bob Boston and Robert LaBarge began selling franchises in Zloop but without disclosing crucial information to their franchise holders. Court records later revealed that Boston's previous company had filed for bankruptcy and that he himself had been personally bankrupt and had had a judgment against him for fraud. In addition, it was recorded that he had been held liable in an action alleging that he had knowingly submitted false financial documentation to a bank to obtain a $2.9 million line of credit.

During Zloop's bankruptcy proceedings, a court-appointed trustee stated that the company had spent 'significant' amounts of money on goods and services unrelated to running the business, even after filing for Chapter 11 under the United States Bankruptcy Code. One example given was a payment of $338 for ammunition. When asked in court to justify the expense, Boston testified, 'I guess if someone came to break in, I would shoot them!' After the bankruptcy proceedings, the company became embroiled in numerous lawsuits, one of which involved a contract that it had won from a manufacturer of infant car seats to destroy and recycle defective seats as necessary, only to discover that Zloop had sold the seats onwards to third parties that in turn had retailed them to the public online.

However, the lawsuits and bankruptcy were only the start of their problems facing the two co-founders of Zloop, for criminal charges were also brought against them. In September 2017, a grand jury at the US District Court of North Carolina indicted both men on charges of securities fraud, money laundering and conspiracy to commit wire fraud. In November, LaBarge pleaded guilty to the charge of conspiracy to commit wire fraud as part of a plea deal with the Attorney's Office.

According to court documents and evidence presented at the trial, Boston and LaBarge defrauded franchisees, investors and lenders involved in their start-up company. Through their dishonesty, they obtained millions of dollars, much of which was spent on expensive personal real estate, a private aircraft — and Justin's racing career. The court also heard that at the end of 2012 Boston and LaBarge had circulated a misleading private placement memo (a legal document provided to prospective investors) that contained material half-truths and made some illegal omissions, such as failing to mention Boston's history of litigation and bankruptcy, or that Zloop was planning to use investors' money to pay off a $4 million debt owed to an earlier lender. Nor did the memo make any reference to the fact that Boston and LaBarge had already spent more than $1.5 million of company funds on personal real estate, and evidence showed that company records had been falsified to conceal this.

When, in 2013, investors demanded the return of their money, Boston managed to satisfy them by securing a loan from another individual. He persuaded this new victim to underwrite a S14 million line of credit from a bank by repeatedly falsifying emails to make Zloop look more attractive than it really was. From this new credit facility, the company drew approximately $3.5 million and spent some of it on a private aircraft and new road cars.

As quoted by ESPN, Boston's lawyer, Kevin Tate, was correct in his assessment that, 'A failed business plan is not a crime.' Indeed, Zloop was

Justin Boston's racing received much of its funding from his father Bob Boston's seemingly worthy but fraudulent electronic recycling business called Zloop, as seen on the son's Toyota Camry at Kentucky Speedway in September 2014.

a legitimate entity that could have been a viable start-up and could have made Boston a significant return on his large equity stake. Instead, the Attorney's Office contended that he defrauded investors and diverted funds from the company so that he could live a lavish lifestyle and his son could be a NASCAR driver. It was stated that Boston's 'greed deprived Zloop of crucial funding it needed to thrive'.

Federal prosecutors argued that Justin's racing was among the motives to commit crimes and that it was inconceivable for any start-up company to justify spending more than $6 million on marketing when it had raised $33 million from investors but less than $4 million from third-party transactions. The federal prosecutor, Taylor Phillips, confirmed in his closing argument that Zloop had 'spent more on their marketing than they did over their entire operational revenue'. The trial in December 2017 lasted five days and the jury took two hours to declare Boston guilty of all charges. The defrauding of investors totalled $25 million of the $33 million brought into the company.

Judge Robert Conrad sentenced 54-year-old Boston to ten years in prison plus two years of supervised release. The judge also ordered him liable for more than $27 million in restitution to victims and ordered him to forfeit his interest in several properties. As a result of his cooperation with the prosecution and his testimony against Boston at the trial, his co-defendant, LaBarge, was given a substantially reduced sentence of two years in prison and two years of supervised release.

Despite his father's cynical attitude — 'My son is a NASCAR driver,

I spend five million a year so he can play race car driver' — there was never any suggestion that Justin Boston was ever aware that his racing was being illegitimately funded. However, as part of the Zloop bankruptcy proceedings, Kyle Busch Motorsports had to return $452,500 to disgruntled investors but in turn the team was awarded a judgment of $442,561 against the unfortunate racing driver whose blossoming career had been brought to a premature halt.

JOHN WES TOWNLEY
Out of control

Justin Boston's last NASCAR truck race was at Iowa Speedway, where he qualified 11th on the grid to start one place ahead of John Wes Townley. Like his rival, Townley was funded by a wealthy father's business, in this case an entirely legitimate one, a chain of restaurants called Zaxby's. Townley started 186 races across various NASCAR series between 2008 and 2016, mainly in the truck series, and during that time his sole national-level victory came in a truck race at Las Vegas Motor Speedway in 2015.

After his retirement from the sport, he married Laura, a professional nurse and public health worker whom he had met through a dating app. However, in August 2019 he was charged with three counts of 'misdemeanor', including family violence battery after, according to court documents, he had thrown his wife to the floor and 'placed her in reasonable fear of the safety of her life, limb and health'. He pleaded guilty to disorderly conduct and was sentenced to 12 months' probation, but prosecutors agreed to drop the battery charges as part of a plea deal. Not surprisingly, the union was short-lived, and their marriage was formally dissolved.

A few days later, on Saturday 2nd October 2021, Townley went to his 30-year-old ex-wife's home and attacked her and her companion Zachary Anderson with a hatchet. In an act of self-defence, as reported by Officer Lt. Shaun Barnett, 'Anderson fired several shots with his firearm.' Townley was 'shot through the chest' and taken to hospital, where he was pronounced dead, aged just 31. Anderson also 'accidentally struck Ms Townley' in the abdomen and she suffered serious but not life-threatening injuries.

CHAPTER 12

CHARLES BROCKET

The Lord and Ferrari fraud

Polo-playing acquaintance of the Royal Family and friend of Prime Minister Margaret Thatcher, Charles Brocket collected rare Ferraris and Maseratis. The Old Etonian peer was first betrayed by a former racer whom he employed and later by his wife, which resulted in him swapping his ancestral home for a prison cell. In an act of desperation to save the inherited family estate from financial ruin, he dismantled four extremely rare sports racing cars and staged their theft in order to make a fraudulent insurance claim.

Charles Nall-Cain's father died when he was nine and he inherited his family seat and peerage aged just 15 when his grandfather, millionaire businessman Sir Arthur Nall-Cain, died in 1967. After finishing his education at Eton, one of England's finest public schools, the now 3rd Baron Brocket started work as a trainee architect before joining the army and spending five years in the 14th/20th King's Hussars, serving in Northern Ireland, Cyprus and Germany at the same time as gaining a growing reputation as a playboy.

When the young Lord Brocket inherited the family's 1,400-acre estate near Welwyn Garden City in Hertfordshire, much of the 25-bedroom Georgian mansion was semi-derelict but thanks to a loan from American Express he converted it into a hotel and conference centre, with more bedrooms in the old stable blocks, and two golf courses in the grounds. By the early 1980s Brocket Hall had been transformed into one of Europe's leading conference venues, business was booming and by the end of the decade it was being hired out for as much as £25,000 per day.

As the enterprise began to make money, initially as a film location, Brocket decided to indulge his passion for fast cars and in 1979 hired Jim Bosisto, a former 500cc racing driver, to assemble a small collection for him. An early purchase was an original Ferrari chassis plate (3565 GT) for £5,500, a crazy amount for a small piece of metal with a number stamped on it, but justified because it belonged to a Ferrari 250 GT SWB (Short Wheelbase) Berlinetta; they believed this gave them the right to rebuild an ordinary, rusty 250 GTE into this different model of much higher value. Bosisto spent the next few years gathering contemporary SWB parts as they came available and this would later come back to haunt his employer.

Old cars are frequently given total restorations in which all the major parts are replaced with brand-new ones. The identity of an historic car is defined by an easily removable chassis plate but the law states that so long as you have the original then the rest of the car could have been made yesterday — which has led to never-ending arguments about originality. This is especially true of historic racing and sports cars, where the more races they have done, the greater the likelihood that at least one major component (engine, body, gearbox or chassis) has been replaced because of wear, tear and/or damage. Over the years several cars have appeared with identical chassis numbers because someone has fabricated a new car from discarded parts and had a new plate made and attached to it despite the 'donor' car still being in existence, having been rebuilt, albeit with replacement components. This unsatisfactory situation continually frustrates and angers historians and owners but has led to grudging acceptance that for some high-value models there are now several more examples in existence than were ever built in period, a situation that provides welcome sustenance for lawyers from time to time.

As Brocket Hall started making even more money through the early and mid-1980s, the peer bought more cars, including three inexpensive Maseratis that needed restoration. Thanks to Bosisto, who was now living on site, the random assortment of cars evolved into a collection that he curated and restored. As well as the now much tidier-looking Ferrari and the Maseratis, there were a couple of Mercedes that Brocket had picked up when in the army, and then Bosisto bought another Ferrari, this time a 365 GTB/4 Boxer. When Victor Gauntlett, then owner of Aston Martin, hired Brocket Hall for a weekend to entertain favoured clients, the guests were able to inspect an array of Astons in front of the house and then asked if they could see the comparatively modest contents of Brocket's garage. This planted the idea that a decent car collection could prove to be an added attraction that might increase the profile of the house and its facilities. Over the next few months Bosisto added three more Ferraris, including a 1956 250 GT Europa that cost £12,000, a figure that Brocket was assured would double within a year but, with the boom in classic car values now in full flow, actually rose considerably more.

Brocket decided to borrow money to buy more cars. His bankers, observing that the four Ferraris in particular were fast-appreciating assets, agreed to lend him £1 million on condition that the collection traded as a limited company with 72-year-old Bosisto as managing director. Brocket and Bosisto were soon in America spending the bank's loan and bought so many cars that there wasn't enough space to store them, so construction began on a vast new showroom. By the end of 1988 the £1 million batch of Ferraris bought in the US was valued at £3 million and the bank was so pleased that in March 1989 it offered an additional loan of £5 million, even though the profits on paper had not actually been realised as only a few of the cars had been sold at that stage. Knowing that The Brocket Collection had money to burn, the more unruly members of the motor trade took advantage.

Brocket lost $300,000 after buying a 1966 Ferrari from an American dealer only to find that it had been resold to someone else for twice the price before the necessary restoration was even finished. Another $120,000 was lost in buying a 'complete' Maserati 450S engine that was in reality just a pile of scrap. Worse still was a Ferrari believed to be an authentic competition 250 GT SWB that was later deemed by a well-known Ferrari expert to be a fake and was sold at a huge loss.

Eventually Brocket's enviable collection was valued at £20 million and numbered over 40 cars. Among them were some historically important sports and racing models, including a 1974 Ferrari 312B3 Formula 1 car driven by Niki Lauda and Clay Regazzoni and a Maserati 300S raced by Juan Manuel Fangio and Stirling Moss. Brocket competed in some of the cars, especially his Ferrari 250 MM, in historic racing events in the US and Europe. His cars were frequently invited to participate at the Goodwood Festival of Speed and he regularly competed in the annual House of Lords vs House of Commons races at Brands Hatch, one of which he recalls winning.

However, the cars had started to become more of a burden than a pleasure to Brocket by 1990. The classic car company had generated £1 million of profits on trading but overall had made big losses thanks to various poor deals, dishonesty within the trade and tax disputes with HM Customs & Excise on cars that had been imported. With interest rates in the UK having doubled to 15 percent in little more than a year, repaying the bank loans, which now totalled £7.5 million, had become cripplingly expensive. Some of Bosisto's deals had been excellent, for example Ferrari Daytonas that had been bought for £80,000 were selling for £250,000, but others had been disastrous. Not only was the collection in debt but in March 1990 Brocket had his first real disagreement with Bosisto after he paid far too much for three Maseratis from the US that turned out to be total wrecks.

Bosisto threatened to leave Brocket's employment if his decisions were questioned, saying that without him the bank would pull the plug on the whole operation. Worse was to come when Bosisto was found dead in his home under what Brocket was convinced were suspicious circumstances. He knew Bosisto, who lived in a mobile home, had always kept a pistol for his personal protection in a bedside drawer but when his body was found the weapon was on top of the drawer, suggesting that he had been expecting trouble. In addition, the keys that he would have used to open his exterior door were nowhere to be seen so it was likely that someone had removed them, and there was £3,000 cash in his jacket pocket. Later that morning an Italian phoned the showroom asking if Bosisto had left for

Part of Charles Brocket's collection as it was in 1988, two years before he came up with the plan to solve his financial difficulties by dismantling four of the most valuable cars, fake their theft and claim on his insurance. Ferraris predominated in the collection.

London, saying that he was expecting payment of £30,000 cash, but no one knew for what and whether the banknotes found were a deposit.

After Bosisto's burial near the Pembrokeshire coast in his native Wales, the executors of his will contacted Brocket to inform him that one of Bosisto's bank accounts contained £120,000, which was an astounding amount for an old man who had always professed to having no savings. When the only surviving relative came to collect the former racing driver's possessions, he unearthed paperwork that explained everything, namely that the prices that Bosisto had actually paid for cars were generally very much lower than what had been charged to the collection, with the discrepancies sometimes being as much as three-fold. It also transpired that he had been siphoning money from the company into his own account, so it seemed likely that the £120,000 was the tip of the iceberg and that other bank accounts probably existed — but the truth had gone with him to the grave.

Meanwhile, Brocket found an American called Rick Furtado to take Bosisto's place as an agent but in due course discovered that his new employee had more than a dozen convictions in his home country, including larceny of controlled substances, breaking and entering, cheque fraud and falsifying number plates. With the classic car market by now showing signs of overheating, Brocket, anxious to clear his debts, accepted an offer from a Japanese consortium of £15 million for ten of the cars sourced by Furtado, but several months passed and the deal didn't materialise. By this time, it was too late as Brocket's car business, and more, was about to crash. As the collection had been used as security, the bank's position was that Brocket Hall and the estate would have to be sold.

In 1990, the British economy was in recession. Many banks were guilty of irresponsible lending of money to people who, like Brocket, could no longer afford to service their debt after interest rates spiralled. The property market was on the verge of crashing and the collector car market was not too far behind it. In August, Saddam Hussein invaded Kuwait and the rise in international tensions impacted the travel industry and led to a decline in corporate bookings at Brocket Hall. By Christmas, with the Gulf War against Iraq soon to begin, there were signs that prices of collector cars had peaked. Sales of even the most historically important cars stopped abruptly and there was suddenly a shortage of buyers at any price.

The value of Brocket Hall, around £9 million, was almost the same amount as Brocket now owed to his bank. One evening when discussing the dire financial problems with his wife Isabel and two shocked mechanics,

Mark Caswell and Steve Gwyther, he told them that the conference business was solid, despite its problems, but that the car collection was where the serious worries lay. He explained that he couldn't simply close the car company and turn the stock over to the bank because he had given a personal guarantee to them using the house as security, which meant that this was at risk of being seized by the bank. The four calculated that £4.5 million was the sum needed to ease the immediate financial pressure by reducing the debt and lowering the interest repayments for long enough for the market to recover.

They all knew that most of the cars were insured for more than their actual values, so the idea was hatched to dispose of four cars, each worth over £1 million, and claim on the insurance. The problem was how best to do it. Caswell, a tough cockney who had worked in his spare time as a nightclub bouncer and a special policeman, proposed that the cars be destroyed in a crusher owned by one of his contacts. Brocket declined this suggestion on the basis that it would be sacrilege to eradicate works of art. Instead, they plotted to dismantle the chosen cars, remove them from the estate, report them as stolen and then claim on the insurance policy. This plan had the advantage that if the claim went ahead, the dismantled cars could be hidden, but if for any reason it was rejected, they could be miraculously discovered after a 'tip-off' and be rebuilt. Gwyther agreed to help for a sum of £25,000, enough to buy his dream car, a second-hand Porsche 911 Targa, but Caswell insisted on £40,000 (later increased to £100,000) as he still favoured the finality of his crusher plan.

The cars they decided to report as missing were a 1960 Maserati 'Birdcage' and three Ferraris, a 1950 195 Berlinetta Sport, a 1952 340 America and a competition 1955 250 GT Europa. Brocket later pointed out that the choices were arrived at not just because of insurance value but because of shortcomings in the cars: 'The Maserati had a replica body, the 195's body had rotted and had to be scrapped, and the 340 and Europa's bodies were made from steel which could be more easily replaced.' He also later recalled that it was with heavy heart that the demolition took place: 'I again promised myself that these cars would, one day, be rebuilt.'

It took the men three nights of hard work to dismantle the four 'stolen' cars and grind the incriminating chassis and engine numbers off various components, because, for once, the fraudsters didn't want them to be identifiable in any way. Larger parts of beautifully sculpted bodywork were burned in the vast furnace used for heating the garage complex.

In May 1991, the 'theft' was reported, and the story made headlines across Britain. At first the police thought that the cars had been taken to order and whisked away on a transporter under cover of darkness, although suspicions did arise because it seemed unlikely that thieves would have been able to disable the sophisticated alarm system without leaving signs. Despite subsequent widespread conjecture in the press, the dismantled cars were neither buried under the park's golf course nor submerged in the lake but were transported to a less glamorous location on the outskirts of London where they were stored in a shipping container. However, as the cars went to pieces, so too did Lady Brocket.

In 1982, Charles had been forbidden from marrying Judy, the previous love of his life, by his family and trustees of the estate because they disapproved after discovering that she had done some nude modelling to make ends meet as an impoverished student at Cambridge. On the rebound, he rushed into a mismatched union with Isabel Lorenzo, an American who had once been one of the world's most successful supermodels. The relationship had been doomed from the outset and became increasingly fractious due to his wife's drug addiction combined with a heavy dependency on prescription painkillers that had a profound and destructive effect. As things deteriorated, she had repeatedly made threats to tell the police about the false insurance claim and had already chosen to tell certain people, including her husband's mother and some of their close friends.

In some respects, things also looked up for Brocket. In an extraordinary turnaround, his bank recognised that the local manager, with whom the loans had been arranged, had been out of his depth and decided to take responsibility for having lent £5 million at the height of the market and then leaving the combined businesses stranded when car prices collapsed. In recognition of this, the bank's board of directors agreed a rescue package in which it offered to lend Brocket £15 million interest-free over ten years. In return it would take a 25 percent stake in the business that could later be bought back at extremely favourable terms and all Brocket would need to do was meet the capital repayments. Fulfilment of this obligation required Brocket Hall to trade at an easily achievable minimum occupancy rate of only 15 percent. By the end of 1993, the attractive interest-free deal was done.

The security of the working capital meant that Brocket himself no longer needed, nor wanted, to pursue his fraudulent insurance claim, which the insurance company, General Accident, continued to contest, refusing to pay out until theft could actually be proven. But there was the matter of how to go about dropping the claim after the various legal actions and

In 1995, after the unravelling of his attempt to defraud an insurance company following the disappearance of four historic racing cars, Charles Brocket was sentenced to five years in prison.

prolonged delay along the way. It was decided that, through his lawyer, Brocket would tell General Accident that he was going to take the company to court, a move that encouraged the insurer to apply to the court asking it to order him to lodge his share of the costs (£700,000) to prove that he could afford the proposed action. However, Brocket didn't have the means to pay this himself and the bank wasn't prepared to allow its loan to be used on a lawsuit that he might lose, so he was forced to drop his case against the insurer and the claim was formally withdrawn. It seemed to be an elegant escape from a hole: General Accident had won the battle, no suspicion could be attached to him as he hadn't received a penny in compensation, and he and his accomplices would be in the clear — or so he thought.

Isabel's drug abuse was now out of control and she was descending into self-destruction, unwilling to seek help or treatment. The couple were living separately and divorce was inevitable. Her irrational behaviour was the result of hallucinations caused by taking vast amounts of painkillers that she obtained by means of duplicate prescriptions from a pharmacy in

PATRICK BARDINON
French connection

One of the world's most notable collections of Ferraris was assembled by Pierre Bardinon. Born in 1931, he was a descendant of the French Chapal family and inherited a fortune that included the sizeable luxury leather goods business of that name. Fascinated by cars from childhood, he became a passionate racing fan and in the late 1960s began buying competition Ferraris, especially Le Mans winners, quite inexpensively in the days before they were sought-after by collectors. Over the years he built up one of the largest private collections of Ferraris in the world, one that was admired and respected by Enzo Ferrari himself.

It has been estimated that Bardinon accumulated as many as 500 cars, of which 300 were Ferraris, including no fewer than four examples of the 250 GTO, one of the most desirable cars in the world with fewer than 40 built. Believing that the cars should be used rather than left standing on display in a museum, he built an impressive two-mile private track in the grounds of his family château at Mas du Clos.

In his later years, Bardinon thinned the collection to a mere 20 cars and after his death in 2012 ownership passed to his wife Yanne. When she died only a year later, the French tax authorities began to take an interest in the value of these remaining cars because the couple's three children were liable for payment of death duties on their mother's estate. A legal battle ensued with the family valuing the cars at $70 million, which was far less than their real worth. In the dispute that followed, the remaining GTO in the collection became the centre of controversy and resulted in the squabbling siblings going to court.

The oldest of the three, Patrick, sold the GTO in 2014 for a reputed €38 million on the premise that it belonged to him alone. He maintained that after a severe racing accident in 1978 his father had gifted him the car, but he was unable to produce any documentation or evidence to support that claim. His younger brother and sister, Jean-François and Anne, disputed his claim and sued him for breach of trust and for their share of the car's value. They initially lost the case but took it all the way to the Cour de Cassation, the highest court in France, where they won on appeal. In August 2021, Patrick was finally ordered to reimburse his brother and sister a total of €58 million to cover the sale proceeds, auction commission and interest.

the nearby town, Welwyn Garden City, and taking them to other chemists to get the extra supplies. In September 1994 she was arrested for forging prescriptions. In retaliation for her mistaken belief that her husband had hidden some of her pills, she finally carried out her threat and told the police about the plot, making detailed criminal allegations. Despite the police having no physical evidence of the cars or their whereabouts, Brocket and his accomplices were arrested in February 1995. Under questioning and fearful of a heavy sentence, Caswell cracked and divulged where the cars were stored.

Almost exactly a year later at Luton Crown Court, 43-year-old Charles Brocket was sentenced to five years imprisonment by Judge Daniel Rodwell, who described his coercion of two men 'previously of good record to take part in a criminal operation as quite disgraceful'. Caswell and Gwyther were each given 21-month sentences suspended for two years. Part of Brocket's more severe sentence was for obtaining money by deception.

This offence involved the aforementioned fake Ferrari 250 GT SWB Berlinetta with the 3565 GT chassis plate. In late 1992 the car had been put up for sale with an asking price of $750,000 and well-known Ferrari collector Jon Shirley, a top Microsoft executive, had bought it through an intermediary, Ron Spangler, after believing that its provenance had been thoroughly checked. The truth only emerged in 1994 when the real 3565 GT was discovered in a garage in France where it had lain unused for many years. Brocket was adamant that he hadn't been involved in the transaction but pleaded guilty in any case to secure a move from Littlehey prison, near Huntingdon, where he had been on the receiving end of vicious knife attacks.

After serving two and a half years of his sentence in seven different prisons, Lord Brocket was released after remission in August 1998. The butchered cars have all been reassembled and returned to their former glory.

IAN BURGESS

A stalled career

This Grand Prix driver was notable more for his colourful character and decidedly shady associations than for his success on the track. His career never reached its full potential and went off the rails due to a lack of funding while it was later found that his business activities included dealing in large quantities of heroin. Unsurprisingly the talented driver was unable to convince the judiciary of his claims that it had been supplied to him by MI5 by way of payment for services rendered and this culminated in a long spell of confinement.

T he subject of this chapter was born as David William Allan in St Pancras, London in July 1930 and was the son of a Scottish journalist from Hampstead. For reasons unknown, he was adopted as a baby by a couple called Burgess, who were also Scottish, and they renamed him Ian John Burgess and brought him up in Bletchingley, Surrey. After growing up through the Second World War and seeing the Battle of Britain waged in the skies above his home, he embarked on studies to qualify in engineering and became involved in motor racing in its early years of post-war revival.

Not far from Burgess's home, Brands Hatch opened as a permanent race circuit in 1950 and the 500 Club — an organising body for low-cost single-seaters powered by 500cc engines — ran lots of events there. Burgess was among the many young enthusiasts drawn to the new track and was soon achieving superb results in a Cooper MkV, starting with second place in June in one of four heats, another of which was won by Stirling Moss, the 500cc world's brightest star. Several wins at Brands followed before the year was out and several offers came his way.

One opportunity came from Jaguar, which already had Moss on board as a works driver and was looking for other promising prospects for its new racing programme with the C-type. With Stirling, Burgess was dispatched in February 1951 to reconnoitre the Mille Miglia route in an XK120. On a long stretch of road near Ferrara, Moss had just taken over the driving from Burgess when an overtaking van appeared in front of their Jaguar and hit it. Fortunately, no one was injured and with the help of a local garage they straightened out the car sufficiently to drive it home. Although Burgess hadn't been behind the wheel at the time, he learned several years later that a third party with a vested interest had put around the false rumour that he had been responsible for the accident, and that was why he never heard anything more from Jaguar.

Sometimes the most ambitious British competitors ventured to 500cc events in mainland Europe and Burgess joined them with his Cooper in June 1951 at the *Eifelrennen* meeting at the Nürburgring, where, in pouring rain, he shocked everyone by winning. Four weeks later, he made another strong impression by finishing second in a heat and eighth in the final at the AVUS track in Berlin, also setting a lap record. As the 1951 season wore on, however, he couldn't afford to do much more racing and only competed intermittently when people offered drives. One good chance came in 1953 with a works Kieft sports car in the Tourist Trophy at Dundrod in Northern Ireland and Burgess, who described this road course as 'the most frightening circuit ever devised', was leading the 2-litre class when a wheel collapsed.

It was only when Burgess got a job at the Cooper Car Company, initially as sales and office manager, that his career was rescued from obscurity and started to look like it might prosper again. His big break came in 1957 when the company launched its new and very popular Cooper Racing School based at Brands Hatch. Ron Searls, one of Cooper's managers, had come up with the idea inspired by the Suez Crisis because the shortage of petrol posed a serious threat to motor racing. There was a staggering response to the idea, with over 2,000 replies in the first week, and Burgess recalled that after every course pupils would write back to argue at length about how they were the next Fangio. As well as overseeing sales of Coopers, Burgess became one of the first instructors at the racing school, teaching pupils on Tuesdays and Thursdays, before being promoted to the role of principal, managing the entire operation.

It didn't take long for Burgess to gain a reputation at the factory as something of a lovable rogue and he was one of very few of the staff brave enough to stand up to the authoritarian Charles Cooper, with whom he was regularly heard arguing but nonetheless remained a favourite, such that he was apparently the only employee able to call the burly boss 'Charlie' to his face and get away with it. He had endless opportunities to cajole both Charlie and son John to give him the chance to race their new works-entered T43 Formula 2 cars in a couple of late-season events in 1957. In the International Gold Cup at Oulton Park, he backed up his winning team leader, Jack Brabham, by finishing fourth, which was enough to earn him the reward of a full 1958 season with the High Efficiency Motors team, which was owned by C.T. 'Tommy' Atkins and ran Coopers.

Atkins was an unusual character. Notoriously short-tempered and an ex-boxer, he raced at Brooklands pre-war and then made a fortune during the war through government contracts for precision engineering, hence the title of both his engineering firm and racing team. Strictly teetotal, he was a control freak who was obsessively jealous of his young wife's movements and would arrange to pre-pay everything for her, from hair appointments to tipping waiters, to avoid allowing her to have any cash in her purse. Burgess related that on one occasion, having heard that she had visited the local swimming baths, he arranged for contractors to come in the next morning to start digging a private pool for her in the grounds of their mansion in Guildford.

Burgess found Atkins a difficult man to race for. A fiercely competitive individual, he seemed to resent the fact that his driver lived nearby and would race him to work in the mornings as his company was near Cooper's premises. Similarly, he would constantly try to outdo Rob Walker: when his fellow entrant acquired a new Mercedes 300SL, Atkins immediately ordered a superior lightweight version to replace the Lancia Aurelia GT he had been using. A bathroom cabinet full of pills hinted at hypochondria, although it finally transpired that he had cancer of the throat and one day in 1965, having eaten breakfast with his young children, he locked the door of his study behind him and tragically shot himself.

A brilliant start to 1958 saw Burgess win at Crystal Palace and Snetterton and he also performed well at overseas events, taking fourth at both Montlhéry and Reims. He made his Formula 1 début in a third works Cooper T45 in the British Grand Prix at Silverstone, retiring with clutch failure, but did finish seventh (and third in the Formula 2 classification) in the German Grand Prix at the Nürburgring driving for Atkins. However, in the Formula 2 Berlin Grand Prix at AVUS, another car tangled with his little Cooper approaching the terrifying brick-laid banking and pitched the car into a concrete post. Serious injuries to his back and legs meant a long and painful recovery that put him out of racing until the following season and ended his chances of securing a permanent works Cooper Formula 1 seat alongside Jack Brabham, Bruce McLaren instead getting that drive.

When Burgess returned to the cockpit in 1959, he returned to Formula 1, via an introduction by Dennis Druitt, BP's racing manager, with the Italian Scuderia Centro Sud team in a 2.5-litre Maserati-engined Cooper T51. His strongest result from four starts was a career-best Grand Prix finish of sixth place back at AVUS, which that year staged the German Grand Prix as a one-off. He continued with the team for 1960 but with poorer results, although a trip to New Zealand at the start of the season at least resulted in a win in the Teretonga Trophy in Atkins's Formula 2 Cooper.

That year, the wealthy ex-PanAm pilot and American entrepreneur Lloyd 'Lucky' Casner took up motor racing as a hobby and established Camoradi (an acronym for Casner Motor Racing Division). This team set the FIA World Sports Car Championship series alight with some startling performances from its Maserati *Tipo* 61 'Birdcage' cars, driven by Casner himself, Dan Gurney, Masten Gregory and, on occasion, even Stirling Moss. For 1961, Gregory persuaded the flamboyant Casner that the team should also try its hand at Formula 1, so Camoradi International was formed with a base in Europe and Burgess was taken on as the number two driver in a Lotus-Climax 18 while Gregory was given a 'lowline' Cooper-Climax T53.

The association got off to an inauspicious start as chief mechanic Bob Wallace was left with so little time to get Burgess's new car ready for the first outing of the 1961 season, the non-championship race around the streets of Pau, that he was still working on it in the back of the transporter as it trundled down to the south of France, so it was no surprise that the car performed unreliably. This debacle was followed by three more non-championship events: Burgess finished eighth on the Heysel circuit in Brussels; he was disqualified from the Aintree 200 for taking on oil during the race, something that was specifically prohibited under the newly introduced regulations for 1½-litre Formula 1; and in Naples, a minor race with a low-quality field, he came home fourth after surviving a lurid spin.

Camoradi was a serious effort but it was becoming increasingly difficult for a private entrant, especially one that seemed to be run perpetually on a shoestring, to compete on even terms with the works teams, even those using supposedly identical engines. Burgess didn't make the grid for his first two World Championship Grands Prix, non-starting in Holland and failing to qualify in Belgium, and thereafter the combination was seldom better than an also-ran but did at least finish the next two races, with Burgess twice posting 14th places, in blistering heat in the French Grand Prix at Reims and in a downpour in the British Grand Prix at Aintree. Masten Gregory wasn't doing much better and decided to jump ship, to the UDT Laystall Racing Team, so Burgess took over his Cooper and used it to finish 12th in the German Grand Prix at the Nürburgring. And with that, Camoradi International's Formula 1 World Championship campaign fizzled out.

Burgess raced in 1962 for another American benefactor, British-domiciled Louise Bryden-Brown, who had been an occasional competitor in US sports car racing in the 1950s. She was a society figure and heiress to the Parke Davis drug company, once the world's largest pharmaceutical company, as well as a major shareholder in Alcoa. Despite her wealth, her Anglo-American Equipe team didn't have the necessary clout to get its hands on the new Coventry Climax V8 engine so had to make do with the increasingly under-powered four-cylinder Climax FPF, used mainly in a novel Cooper-based 'Special' put together by mechanic-cum-designer Hugh Aiden-Jones. Based on a Formula Junior T59 chassis, this car sported side-mounted radiators to reduce frontal area, a configuration that would become normal in later years, but it didn't work well enough without a competitive engine. As a result, the team's main focus was the plethora of non-championship continental races that invariably offered lucrative prize funds and these yielded some decent results, including fourth place at Solitude (Germany) and fifth places at Posillipo (Italy), Karlskoga (Sweden) and Roskilde (Denmark). In three World Championship Grands Prix, Burgess finished twice — 12th at Silverstone and 11th at the Nürburgring — but didn't manage to qualify at Monza. By the end of the year, the team's patron was suffering from the excesses of high living, alcohol and drug problems and she had lost interest in spending any more money, so the enterprise folded.

Burgess raced on for one last season. Together with Aiden-Jones, he joined yet another new team, the ill-fated Scirocco-Powell Formula 1 enterprise, which was intermittently bankrolled by young American socialite Hugh Powell Jr, who had come into huge wealth at a very young age. Rich and bored, and barely out of his teens, Powell travelled to Britain with family friend and guardian Tony Settember, a sports car racer, to buy a Formula Junior car from Emeryson but ended up purchasing the company. This laid the foundations for a Formula 1 project as Settember persuaded his youthful charge to fund the construction of a brand-new car for him to drive, with Burgess also joining the team. In workshops behind a pub in London's Goldhawk Road, the new team and its cars, with BRM V8

Ian Burgess (left) and Bruce McLaren pose with their works Formula 2
Coopers before the Berlin Grand Prix at the AVUS circuit in 1958.
During the race, Burgess crashed and was badly injured.

engines, took shape and prospects looked good. However, it proved to be
a dismal and expensive exercise for the owner and an unhappy experience
for both drivers. In particular, BRM overstretched itself in offering its new
V8 to customers, to the extent that engines were rarely delivered on time
and seemed to need a rebuild after every test session. Burgess's car wasn't
ready until the British Grand Prix at Silverstone, where it retired, and then
he dramatically crashed out of the German Grand Prix at the Nürburgring
when a steering arm broke.

As the team struggled on through 1963, the boy millionaire's interest
dwindled and he became obsessed with a girlfriend with whom he spent
days closeted in a motel near Heathrow airport before disappearing home
to America. Finances became erratic, wages dried up, and the team was
twice stranded abroad with no money. Burgess, who ended up effectively
managing the outfit, discovered that it was all running on an overdraft. He
negotiated a short-term stay of execution from the bank but when further
funding was refused it was left to him and Setterper to clear up the mess,
so the assets were sold to Tim Parnell and they covered what bills they
could. Burgess never raced again and left the sport behind him.

By now he had left formal employment with Cooper and was married to
Swede Solveig Ranberg. For a while he ran his own company, Laminates
Ltd in nearby Weybridge, to manufacture glass-fibre bodies for cars and

boats. Eventually he moved abroad, first to Switzerland, then Greece, where he established two factories to construct prefabricated housing for extreme climates such as the Middle East, where he claimed to have been involved in military intelligence. He also established a yacht charter business in the Mediterranean.

The first inkling that Ian Burgess might not be entirely honest came in the early 1960s when Charles Cooper's holiday home was burgled with the loss of a large quantity of the racing school's cash takings hidden under floorboards. Seemingly the only other person who knew of the existence and whereabouts of this cash was Burgess, but nothing was ever proven because Cooper could hardly report the robbery without potentially inviting awkward and embarrassing questions from the tax authorities.

Nearly two decades later, Burgess re-emerged into the public spotlight when he was arrested in possession of a large quantity of heroin when passing through Customs. He claimed that it had been 'given' to him by MI5, by way of payment for intelligence work he had carried out on its behalf in the Middle East, prior to dispensing with his services. Unsurprisingly, MI5, being a secret organisation, refused to corroborate this unlikely story, and in any case the credibility of Burgess's claim was further undermined by the fact that he seemed to get his security services mixed up: MI5 is responsible for protecting Britain, its citizens and interests, at home and overseas, against threats to national security; MI6 is responsible for gathering intelligence outside Britain in support of the government's security, defence, foreign and economic policies. In any case, an illegal Class A drug wouldn't generally be a currency for remunerating spies.

Needless to say, the judge didn't believe Burgess's claims and there was no evidence to support his convoluted story. The court dismissed his protestations and sent the 51-year-old to prison in August 1981 for 10 years for possession of heroin valued at £1 million and for dealing in drugs. Once he had served sufficient time, Burgess was accorded the status of a low-risk prisoner and transferred to Ford open prison in West Sussex. Even in prison, a connection with Cooper surfaced. John Cooper's daughter Sally, a lawyer, visited a client at Ford and later phoned her father to say, 'Dad, I met a chap today who asked to be remembered to you; his name was something Burgess.'

Before the end of his sentence, Burgess escaped. One day he quietly walked out, met a Czech girlfriend who was waiting outside, and together they absconded to her home country, which at that time was still behind the

GUY JASON-HENRY
A racer to watch

The wealthy heir to the Johnnie Walker whisky business who gave his occupation in his passport as 'Gentleman', Rob Walker was one of the biggest personalities in motor racing. While an undergraduate at Cambridge, he bought a Delahaye 135 *Competition Speciale* previously raced by Prince Bira and began to compete, finishing eighth at Le Mans in 1939, wearing a dark pinstripe suit during daylight and a grey check one at night. However, when he married the following year, he honoured a pledge to his new wife Betty to stop racing and instead became an entrant when racing resumed post-war.

He became friendly with Guy Jason-Henry, who was not only an excellent driver but also a good mechanic. The pair came to an agreement whereby Jason-Henry bought a half share in the Delahaye and raced it, including at the first post-war Le Mans, in 1949, when he and future Le Mans winner Tony Rolt were lying fifth before the main bearings failed, having not been replaced since Walker's outing ten years earlier.

Three months later, Walker received a phone call asking whether he had heard that his partner had been arrested trying to smuggle over 3,000 Swiss watches into the country in a false petrol tank. Walker roared with laughter saying, 'Silly Bugger... Just the sort of stunt he would try to pull.' He was less amused when told that the false tank was fixed to his Delahaye and that the car had been impounded at Newhaven docks.

Jason-Henry had entered the Delahaye for a 1,000km race at Montlhéry near Paris but didn't start the race because the car supposedly broke down in practice. However, the event provided an ideal opportunity to use the car to conceal watches that could be sold at a healthy premium on the black market in the austerity of post-war Britain. Walker had no idea that the Delahaye was even out of the country let alone entered in the race, so although the episode made newspaper headlines there could be no suggestion that he had been involved in any way.

Although the authorities brought Jason-Henry to trial, they recognised that he was small fry. He became a co-operative witness and was acquitted of complicity, although fined for the possession of a revolver that had been found in the car. As the car had been seized for carrying contraband, Walker was left to buy it back from the government.

Iron Curtain. Within hours, he was safely ensconced in Prague, but in later years he flitted around Europe for a while before moving to Spain more permanently. From time to time he would appear in Britain, making brief but necessarily unannounced visits, and always maintaining a low profile. He finally moved back to Britain and settled in Harrow where he lived quietly but, despite increasing frailty and poor health, still tried to keep links with motorsport and his old racing friends. He died there in 2012, aged 81.

It remains a mystery why, despite being a fugitive, he appeared able to travel unchallenged, albeit *incognito*, with such regularity in and out of London, or could it be that the authorities simply turned a blind eye to his movements? Fantastical though his story may have sounded, the complicated world of counter espionage often involves some ambiguity, and it may just be possible that his version of events wasn't entirely fictitious.

DIDIER CALMELS

Getting away with murder

Following the successful Formula 1 exploits of the all-French Ligier and Renault teams, Gérard Larrousse, a highly successful racing driver turned team manager, decided that he also wanted to fly the *Tricolore* in Grand Prix racing and went into partnership with business associate Didier Calmels to set up their eponymous Larrousse-Calmels team, which hit the tracks in 1987. Two years after the team's first race, however, its entire future was turned upside down when one of the co-founders murdered his wife.

Born in 1951, Didier Calmels became mad about motor racing from an early age and competed as an enthusiastic amateur in club events in his native France for nearly ten years, first in a Triumph, then a Porsche. After studying law and economics in Paris at Assas University, the country's most renowned law school, he made a name for himself professionally in a very short time, becoming the youngest Administrateur Judiciaire (trustee in bankruptcy) in France, specialising in the takeover and restructuring of insolvent companies. By 1980, he was running his own successful commercial law practice, Calmels Meille Harpillard & Associés, and soon accumulated an enviable portfolio of clients. As his meteoric career took off, he started to make a great deal of money.

Among Calmels's friends was the racing driver Philippe Alliot, whom he helped into Formula 1 in 1984. After two unsuccessful seasons with the small Skoal Bandit RAM team, Alliot joined Ligier midway through 1986, taking the place of the French team's long-time and very successful driver, Jacques Laffite, who had suffered a career-ending crash at the British

Grand Prix at Brands Hatch. This all-French team, which Guy Ligier had taken into Formula 1 ten years earlier, was a much better proposition and within six races Alliot had scored his first World Championship points, bringing his Ligier-Renault JS27 home in sixth place in Mexico, even if former World Champion turned TV commentator James Hunt never thought much of him, describing him as 'one of the worst Grand Prix drivers ever'.

The team manager at Ligier was Gérard Larrousse, a distinguished name in French motorsport, and through Alliot he got to know Calmels. The two men started to discuss the possibility of a new French racing team.

Larrousse had enjoyed a very successful and versatile career as a driver, starting in rallying. After winning the French Rally Championship in 1967 with an Alpine A110, he achieved his best success with Porsche 911s, winning the Tour de Corse in 1969 and finishing second in the Monte Carlo Rally in 1969, 1970 and 1972. Gradually his focus transferred to racing and he competed in sports cars at the highest level as a works driver variously with Renault, Porsche and Matra. Back-to-back victories in the Le Mans 24 Hours partnered by Henri Pescarolo in Matras in 1973–74 were the highlights of his track success, supplementing a pair of second places in the French classic with Porsches in 1969–70. He also tried his hand at Grand Prix racing in 1974 but it wasn't a happy experience as it involved just two 'rent-a-drive' outings with the short-lived Scuderia Finotto team in a poorly prepared Brabham BT42 with which he just scraped onto the grid at Nivelles in Belgium but failed to qualify for his home race at Dijon-Prenois. After a season of Formula 2 in 1975, he hung up his helmet at the end of the season and moved into team management, initially as competitions manager at Renault. There, he oversaw the development and introduction of turbocharged engines into Formula 1, and steered Renault's own team through a very successful period that brought 15 Grand Prix victories between 1979 and 1983. When Renault disbanded the operation at the end of 1985, Larrousse moved to Ligier.

By now, Larrousse felt that the wealth of experience he had accumulated in so many different facets of the sport should now be channelled into team ownership and quickly discovered that the charismatic Calmels, with his all-important business connections, was the man to help him achieve that. The two men formed a partnership, with Calmels taking on responsibility for finance and commercial operations, and during the autumn of 1986 the Larrousse-Calmels Formula 1 team was established with a view to having a car on the grid for the first race of the 1987 World Championship season. Based in Antony in the southern suburbs of Paris, the new team commissioned a car from Lola, the well-known British manufacturer, with power supplied by the reliable Cosworth DFZ V8 engine. Designed by Eric Broadley and Ralph Bellamy, the car was called the LC87 in recognition of the co-founders' initials, although it was closely related to Lola's existing Formula 3000 contender.

The team began its first season by running just one car, driven by Alliot, although a second entry appeared at the last three races of the season in the hands of débutant Yannick Dalmas. Alliot persevered with the overweight and underpowered car, and in the second half of the season managed to claim three World Championship points with a trio of sixth places, in Germany, Spain and Mexico. In the last race of the year, in Australia, Dalmas went one better by finishing fifth, but he wasn't able to claim the requisite two points because the team had officially entered only one car for the season. It was a respectable start for a new team lacking manufacturer support and using an off-the-shelf engine that was way past its sell-by date.

Unfortunately, the 1988 season with an updated Lola, the LC88, failed to bring the further progress that had been expected. Dalmas did a little better than Alliot by taking two seventh places before being struck down at the end of the season with Legionnaires disease, leading to Aguri Suzuki and Pierre-Henri Raphanel being drafted in for one race apiece. Alliot could manage no better than a pair of ninth places.

Until February 1989, fortune had smiled on the high-flying Didier Calmels in every respect. As well as his myriad professional and business achievements, including co-ownership of a Formula 1 team, he had a strikingly good-looking and intelligent wife, Dominique, whom he had met when they were fellow students at the Assas University. When they had children, she put her own promising legal career to one side to raise their young family.

One evening in June 1988, Dominique met another man, an artist who was the complete opposite to the successful but increasingly distant and distracted lawyer and businessman she had married. Three months later she told her husband about her inappropriate relationship and he, still in love with her, resolved to win her back and rebuild their marriage. As the racing season drew to a close, he planned to spend more time over the autumn and winter months with her and their four young children, who were all under 11 years old.

On the evening of 28th February 1989, Dominique's 70-year-old mother arrived at the couple's chic Paris apartment in Avenue Henri-Martin to visit her young grandchildren. After they had been put to bed, an alcohol-fuelled argument developed between her daughter and son-in-law, and she stayed on for a while to try to act as peacemaker. Sensing that a break-up of the family might not be far away, she pleaded with them to consider the ramifications and the impact on their children, but to no avail. After she left them, the exhausted and unhappy couple continued arguing for several hours over Dominique's infidelity, justified in her state of mind by her belief that her husband had been having a physical relationship with one of his drivers.

In his frenzy, Calmels loaded a shotgun that he used for hunting and threatened to kill himself. In what he later described as a foolish game of emotional blackmail, he related that she repeatedly taunted him that he didn't have it in him to pull the trigger. In the ensuing shouting match, she screamed what were to be her last and fateful words: 'If you want courage, I'll give you some! I saw him again!'

Moments later, just before midnight, Calmels shot his wife in the chest at close range. She died from her injuries in hospital the next day. He later said that he had jumped up from where he had been sitting and lost control of his emotions in a moment of unpremeditated madness. In that instant, six lives were broken. Nearly 24 hours passed before Calmels, grief-stricken and in a state of severe shock, was even physically able to talk to the police.

He was duly charged with murder and just over 12 months later, in the week before the San Marino Grand Prix of 1990, he appeared at the Assize Court in Paris. His mother-in-law Madame Lecrueur, although unforgiving of his actions, made a point of offering moral support and speaking on his behalf. Overcome with emotion, she described him as a loving father and stated: 'I will never destroy the image of dad, he loves his children and they love their father. I had a passion. This passion is dead [but] I still have my grandchildren.' The prosecution had demanded that he be incarcerated for a minimum of seven to ten years but his defence lawyer, Georges Kiejman, successfully pleaded that there were mitigating circumstances and the court ruled that his client's actions were a *crime passionelle* for which he received the more lenient sentence of six years in prison. After only two years and not being deemed to be a danger to the public, he was granted parole and given permission to leave the prison at Melun, south-east of Paris, for work during the daytime before controversially receiving an early release.

After Didier Calmels murdered his wife Dominique on 28th February 1989, his Formula 1 partnership with Gérard Larrousse came to a sudden and dramatic end.

The best result achieved by the Larrousse-Calmels Formula 1 team was Yannick Dalmas's fifth place in the 1987 Australian Grand Prix.

Using his wide network of contacts, many of whom demonstrated their loyalty to him despite his dark past, Calmels was able to rebuild his life and start what soon evolved into a new financial empire by establishing an investment fund specialising in business recovery. However, controversy continued to haunt him and, despite his successful career, he was accused in 1997 of conflicts of interest while advising the Rivaud Bank, leading to his dismissal from the role. The same year he and his second wife, Elisabeth, were indicted in an embezzlement case under suspicion of concealing debts although charges were subsequently dropped.

Many years later Calmels attempted a return to international motorsport with the Schmidt-Peterson Motorsports team by supporting the entry of Frenchman Tristan Gommendy in the 2018 Indianapolis 500. Unfortunately for the driver, the team cancelled the partnership within two months of the announcement after a torrent of bad publicity, although Calmels himself has returned to his roots by racing a classic Porsche.

The Larrousse-Calmels Formula 1 team had been testing on a rain-soaked track at the Paul Ricard circuit near Le Castellet in the South of France when news broke of the events surrounding the arrest of Didier Calmels. Most devastated by the tragedy was Philippe Alliot, who was a close friend of the family and godfather to the couple's son Martin. Amid their feelings of shock and disbelief as more details gradually emerged, everyone in the team became fearful about their futures as Calmels had not only been instrumental in putting the team structures in place but had also been responsible for bringing together the operating budget.

Gérard Larrousse had secured an agreement with Chrysler for the supply of Lamborghini-badged V12 engines and moved quickly to assure the American company and other technical partners that the smooth running of the team wouldn't be affected in any way. He immediately dropped the murderer's name from the team's title, renaming it Équipe Larrousse, and disassociated the team from Calmels in every respect, including making arrangements to take over his shareholding.

Despite the excitement surrounding the team's new Lamborghini-powered Lola LC89, the early-season dramas weren't a good portent for the future and the campaign failed to live up to its potential, partly because of woeful mechanical unreliability. Although Yannick Dalmas returned after his illness, it had clearly affected him and now he fell short of team-mate Alliot. After failing to qualify for four of the first five Grands Prix, Dalmas was dropped, although his career certainly didn't end there because he went on to have a successful career in sports cars, winning the Le Mans 24 Hours no fewer than four times. Éric Bernard replaced him for two races before Michele Alboreto, in the twilight of his career, took over for the rest of the season, but without any success. The only bright spot came near the end of the year, when Alliot qualified fifth for the Japanese Grand Prix at Suzuka and scored a solitary point by finishing sixth.

For the 1990 season, a Japanese company, ESPO Communications, arrived as title sponsor and bought 50 per cent of the team, but a disagreement about the amount of money due led to a contractual dispute and relations were broken off before the end of the year. Nonetheless, the team still recorded its best results yet, despite having to pre-qualify for the first half of the season. While Alliot left to return to Ligier, Aguri Suzuki and Éric Bernard both returned in a full-time capacity and between them scored 11 points in six races, the highlight being Suzuki's third place in Japan. This proved to be the team's only podium placing in its entire history and contributed to what would also turn out to be its most triumphant year, with sixth place in the constructors' championship.

From here, things went downhill, and Gérard Larrousse found himself mixed up with more wrongdoing, first by employing a driver with a criminal record (see Chapter 22), then by entering into a business partnership with an exceedingly unpleasant fraudster who met his end in a shoot-out with police (see Chapter 39).

CHAPTER 15
COLIN CHAPMAN
Winning at any cost

The most innovative racing car designer of his era, Colin Chapman masterminded the super-successful Lotus Formula 1 team but wider business success proved more elusive. Drawn into a toxic relationship with John DeLorean, a smooth-talking American automotive executive, he became embroiled in a huge financial scandal in which the British government and taxpayers were defrauded. Chapman's premature death in 1982 meant that he took his secrets to the grave and avoided the ignominy of legal proceedings and a lengthy jail sentence.

Colin Chapman was one of the most original thinkers in the motor industry. Born in May 1928, he was the son of a hotel manager who grew up in Hornsey and studied structural engineering at University College, London. There he learned to fly with the University of London Air Squadron and subsequently he enrolled for National Service with the Royal Air Force, these experiences instilling a passion for aviation. He started trading in second-hand cars to supplement his income and was introduced to motorsport through his membership of the 750 Motor Club, a fertile training ground for many young men who went on to become top engineers in racing.

Chapman's first competition car, created while still at university, was a modified 1930 Austin Seven trials car in which he achieved enough success to win some prize money. This was immediately reinvested in a developed MkII version built while on leave from the RAF. Always looking for the 'unfair advantage', his creative mind exploited loopholes in the regulations that enabled him to extract more power from his engines and by the time the rules were changed to outlaw his modifications his reputation as a racing driver and engineer had grown sufficiently for other competitors to want copies of his cars. Meeting that demand, he called his cars 'Lotus'.

Helped by a £25 loan from his fiancée, Hazel Williams, he established the Lotus Engineering Company in ramshackle workshops set up in an old stable block behind the Railway Hotel in Hornsey, London run by his father. He initially managed the business in his spare time while working as a salesman for the British Aluminium Company but gradually took on employees. The success of the Lotus MkVI, with over 100 sold in kit form, allowed him to leave his job and concentrate full-time on Lotus, producing both racing and road-going cars. Mike Costin joined from De Havilland and was instrumental in bringing in his brother Frank, who had also worked for the aircraft manufacturer, as a consultant to apply his aerodynamic expertise to Chapman's racing cars.

Fred Bushell, a chartered accountant working in the City of London, often walked past the Railway Hotel on his way home and became curious about the unusual-looking cars being made there. One day he met Chapman by chance when both happened to be using the 'gents' outside the hotel and they got talking. Bushell came on board to look after the finances of Chapman's growing business and soon became an integral and vital part of it. It was Bushell who persuaded Chapman to move into road-car production with the Lotus Seven, followed by the Elite and — after a move to new premises in Cheshunt, Hertfordshire in 1959 — the Elan, all of which proved to be very profitable and helped to fund the all-important racing activities.

As Lotus grew through the mid-1950s, Chapman continued to make a name for himself as a racing driver, so much so that Vanwall entered him for the 1956 French Grand Prix at Reims as Mike Hawthorn's team-mate. Through consultancy work for Vanwall, Chapman had also been responsible for the design of the car's spaceframe chassis and had recommended Frank Costin to create its slippery body. Although Chapman was fifth fastest in practice, impressively beating Hawthorn, an embarrassing collision with his team-mate due to brake failure didn't help his prospects as a Formula 1 driver and prevented him from starting the race. By now married to Hazel and with their first child imminent, he decided to put his own driving aspirations to one side and focus on his business, although he continued to compete at club level in his own cars. Winning at Brands Hatch's Boxing Day meeting in 1958, he beat a talented youngster, Jim Clark, and continued to keep a watching eye on the Scotsman's progress. His offer to bring Clark into Lotus's Formula Junior team in 1960 heralded the start of one of the most celebrated partnerships in the history of motor racing.

Chapman built his first single-seater racing car, the Lotus 12, in 1956 and after it proved its worth in Formula 2 his own team made its Grand Prix début in 1958, fielding cars for Graham Hill and Cliff Allison at Monaco. The breakthrough first Grand Prix victory came at Monaco in 1960 in the hands of Stirling Moss in Rob Walker's privately entered rear-engine Lotus 18. This marked the start of a remarkable two-decade period of Lotus success in which Chapman's ideas and concepts dominated Formula 1.

Until the arrival of the winning Vanwall design, Britain had been an outsider in Grand Prix racing, which had been dominated by Italian, German and French constructors, but Chapman, following in the footsteps of John Cooper, helped to change all that and between them they revolutionised Formula 1. What their small, lightweight, rear-engine designs gave away in terms of horsepower was more than made up by superior handling. Applying the same philosophy that had gone into his first trials cars, Chapman always thought that rules and regulations were to be challenged and circumvented, and that lightness made you faster everywhere, even if that philosophy sometimes compromised safety. Aesthetically, his designs — for road cars as well as racers — were invariably pleasing and adhered to the principles of elegance, refinement and simplicity.

By 1962, Clark had justified his mentor's confidence and had become a proven and regular winner, finishing second in the World Championship in the ground-breaking Lotus 25 with its lightweight monocoque chassis. Chapman and Clark developed a huge rapport built on friendship and mutual respect and their partnership led to great success as Lotus progressed to claim its first world title in 1963 with victories in seven of the year's ten Grands Prix. The normally irascible Chapman never once lost his temper with his shy, introverted driver, who shunned the limelight and preferred to return to his roots and his farm in the Scottish Borders between races whenever possible.

The 1965 season not only saw the Chapman/Clark partnership win the World Championship again, this time with six wins from nine starts, but also brought a famous victory in the Indianapolis 500. Soon after, Chapman's powers of persuasion were used to great effect when Ford agreed to invest £100,000 in a new V8 engine that won on its début in Clark's hands, fitted to the new Lotus 49 at the 1967 Dutch Grand Prix. Designed and manufactured by Cosworth, a company jointly owned by Mike Costin, Chapman's former employee, and Keith Duckworth, the DFV (Double Four

By the time this photo was taken, in 1982 at the Belgian Grand Prix,
Colin Chapman (left) had become deeply involved with John DeLorean;
with him is Bernie Ecclestone (see Chapter 25).

Valve) not only rendered the competition almost obsolete overnight but also developed into one of the most successful and long-lived racing engines ever produced. Quite apart from its neat packaging, a great attraction for Chapman's creative mind was that it had been designed to serve as part of the chassis and double up as a stressed member, so he was able to satisfy his obsession with making his cars lighter and more efficient.

High hopes for the 1968 Formula 1 season were confirmed when Clark won the opening South African Grand Prix only to be dashed three months later with his death when he crashed into trees at 140mph in a Formula 2 race at Hockenheim. Chapman was devastated. He adored his driver, the top talent of his generation, who only ever drove for Lotus in Formula 1, and described him as 'the best friend I ever had'. Such was the superiority of the Cosworth-powered Lotus 49 that the team's other driver, 1962 World Champion Graham Hill, was able to step into the breach, lift shattered morale and take that year's Formula 1 title.

Having resolved never again to allow himself to get so close to one of his drivers, Chapman had an entirely different relationship with his next World Champion and it was decidedly tense from the outset. Jochen Rindt was a highly ambitious and impatient Austrian whose inflated ego was at least equal to that of his boss, guaranteeing that clashes between the two volatile characters were inevitable. Although Rindt needed a great deal of persuasion to drive for Lotus, so desperate was he to become World Champion that he reluctantly put his reservations about the fragility of Chapman's cars to one side and rationalised that driving a Lotus offered him the greatest chance of success.

Rindt's fears were justified in only his second Grand Prix with the team in Spain when he crashed out of the lead. A suspension-mounted rear wing on team-mate Hill's Lotus 49 broke off, causing a violent 150mph accident, and ten laps later Rindt suffered an identical failure on the same part of the Montjuich circuit and his car smashed into the wreckage of Hill's. Either driver could have been killed in these separate accidents but both escaped without serious injury. Rindt was incandescent and publicly outspoken in his criticism of Chapman, laying the blame squarely at his door for sacrificing safety in his relentless quest for speed. In an Austrian TV interview, Rindt stated that the high wings proliferating in Formula 1 at that time were 'an insanity' and that 'they should never be allowed on racing cars but to get any wisdom into Colin Chapman's head is impossible'. When asked if he had lost trust in Lotus after the accident, the impetuous driver was candid in his response: 'I never had any trust in Lotus.'

In 1970, Rindt reluctantly moved on to race the radical wedge-shaped 72 but was always wary of it. At one stage he even told his friend Erich Glavitza that he didn't know how much longer he could drive for Lotus, adding that he couldn't 'stand the sight of Colin'. He didn't survive the year, losing his life in a crash in his 72 during practice for that year's Italian Grand Prix at Monza. His accumulated points from five victories meant that the World Championship crown he had craved for so long eventually became his anyway and after the penultimate race of the season he was declared Formula 1's only posthumous champion. Under the requirements of Italian law, which decreed that someone must be culpable, Chapman was charged with manslaughter. Although the accusations were dismissed years later and his name was cleared, ill feeling about the safety of his racing cars would never go away.

Chapman himself was shattered. So soon after the deaths of Jim Clark and Mike Spence, who had been killed just four weeks after Clark during practice for the Indianapolis 500, Lotus's founder seriously considered whether he should stop racing. 'When I lost Jimmy I thought nothing worse could happen. That it should happen again with Jochen, with whom I had started to be friends, is more than I can bear,' he said.

The 1971 season was fallow due to the team's failure to get the 72 to work properly with the latest tyres as well as the distraction of trying to develop the turbine-powered 56B model. In 1972, however, 23-year-old Emerson Fittipaldi became the sport's youngest World Champion in an updated 72, a car that had been so advanced at its introduction that it remained Lotus's chosen mainstay until 1974, when it still won races in Ronnie Peterson's hands.

Chapman, ever the innovator, became the first man in Formula 1 to fulfil the potential of 'ground effect', working tirelessly with his top engineers to refine this aerodynamic concept that essentially made the underside of a car act as an inverted wing and suck it downwards, providing unprecedented levels of downforce and grip. The team's first attempt at a 'wing' car was the Lotus 78, introduced in 1977. Had it not been for five engine failures that year, Mario Andretti would easily have won the World Championship, but the following season Lotus swept all before it with the 78's exquisitely beautiful successor, the 79, and Andretti, supported by Ronnie Peterson, took the title in a car that was recognised at the time as hugely significant and went on to influence the design of racing machinery for generations to come. Andretti secured the crown at the Italian Grand Prix at Monza but the elation was short-lived because the following morning Peterson unexpectedly died in hospital with severe leg injuries inflicted in a pile-up at the start of the race — and again Chapman found himself on the wrong side of the Italian legal system.

After Peterson's death, it became apparent to those closest to Chapman that he was losing some of his passion for racing, although the desire to win at absolutely any cost, human or financial, in both business and in sport, continued to motivate him. While his innovative thinking would continue to create new ideas like the twin-chassis Lotus 88, which was banned by the authorities, the fortunes of his racing team waned. There would be no more championship titles and Chapman would see his renowned team win only one more race in the remaining four years of his life, courtesy of Elio de Angelis at the 1982 Austrian Grand Prix. Although there was a three-year resurgence in form after Chapman's death thanks to the mercurial talent of Ayrton Senna, who won six Grands Prix in the period 1985–87, the team became a shadow of its former self without its founder and guiding light.

Away from the track, Lotus continued to produce its increasingly popular sports cars throughout the 1960s and 1970s. When Lotus first manufactured its distinctive road-going designs, the British motor industry was the second-largest producer of cars in the world after the United States but in general the products were old-fashioned, overweight and clumsy. In stark contrast, anything that came out of the Lotus factory was modern, light and agile, and these sports cars established a fine reputation in Europe and America. Despite Chapman becoming a millionaire at the age of 40 when 48 percent of his company was floated on the London Stock Exchange, his rushed decision to take the company public was a mistake and arguably the beginning of his downfall. He simply wasn't suited to managing a publicly listed company because he ran Lotus as his personal fiefdom and his cavalier attitude was such that he wasn't prepared to answer to shareholders and didn't give them or anyone else a second thought. He was either incapable of or unwilling to differentiate between the balance sheets and finances of private operations such as the racing team and the publicly listed company, with funds often transferred from one entity to the other.

Ironically for someone who hated smoking, one of Chapman's commercial triumphs had been to attract big-money sponsorship to Formula 1 by persuading Imperial Tobacco to back his team, first by promoting its Gold Leaf cigarettes, then the John Player Special brand. To the outside world, appearances suggested that Team Lotus was in an extremely strong financial position and indeed this partnership coincided with an unprecedented level of success for Chapman and his team. The reality, however, was that an underlying lack of money was a huge problem and Chapman desperately needed additional funding for Group Lotus, its subsidiaries and the constant stream of new ideas that emanated from his restless mind.

Born in 1925, Zachary DeLorean, or 'John Zee' as he liked to be known, was the eldest of four sons. His parents, of Hungarian descent, divorced when he was 17, after which he saw little of his estranged and violent father, who became a drug addict. The boy was raised and educated in and around 'Motor City' — Detroit — so a career in the automotive industry was always likely, especially as his academic talents won him a scholarship at the local Lawrence Institute of Technology, which produced some of the industry's finest engineers. After the US entered the Second World War in 1941, he was drafted into the army and his studies were interrupted, so he didn't finally graduate until 1948.

The first signs of DeLorean's dishonesty came that year when he became involved in a scam in which he masqueraded as *Yellow Pages* — the directory of local businesses — by registering a company with an almost identical name. He cut out advertisements for 2,700 companies and sent each one to the appropriate advertiser with a fake invoice for 'renewal' in the following year's edition. The police were on to him very quickly and he was extremely fortunate that *Yellow Pages* didn't press charges.

When he completed his degree, he initially spurned engineering and embarked on lucrative work as a life-insurance salesman. In his autobiography, he claimed to have sold policies worth a staggering but unlikely $850,000 in commission and said that he pursued this line of work in order to 'improve his communication skills'. It was here that he honed the very effective sales techniques that he used with such success in later years.

After gaining a post-graduate degree in automotive engineering from the Chrysler Institute in 1952, he had brief spells in the engineering teams at Chrysler and Packard before moving to General Motors in 1956. This marked the start of an impressive 16-year ascent as one of GM's most dynamic young executives. He became the group's youngest divisional manager when he took charge of the Pontiac brand and was credited with returning the small and run-down brand to profitability. This was largely due to the hugely popular GTO 'Muscle Car' for which he took responsibility for design, engineering and marketing. However, by the time he moved across to GM's Chevrolet brand, in 1969, it was well known that he was topping up his already considerable salary by wheeling and dealing on the side, in company time.

In what was perhaps the manifestation of a mid-life crisis, he gave his personal image a makeover at this time. After divorcing his first wife, Elizabeth, in 1969, he had a short-lived marriage to actress Kelly Harmon, who was 23 years his junior, then in 1973 he wedded fashion model and actress Cristina Ferrare, who was 25 years younger. Vanity about his personal appearance led him to undergo plastic surgery to modify the profile of his nose and chin and he adopted an increasingly non-conformist appearance that included dyeing his hair, growing sideburns and wearing his shirts unbuttoned. All this began to grate with more conservative peers within GM's senior management and many of them also became increasingly concerned about the Hollywood lifestyle and celebrity status that DeLorean was cultivating, feeling that it was unbecoming and inappropriate for an executive of his standing.

His appointment in 1972 as vice-president of car and truck production for the whole of GM could have paved the way to eventual promotion to the company's presidency but internal politics conspired against him. He left GM a year later, ostensibly by mutual agreement. An arrangement was reached whereby GM gave him not only a handsome leaving package of a Cadillac franchise in Florida but also generously continued to pay him his $200,000 salary while he acted as president of a business charity. He went to great lengths to suggest that he was the only man in history who 'had sacked GM', which might have made a great soundbite but was untrue. He had been forced to resign after upsetting too many people and there were also rumours of grave financial misdemeanours.

At the end of 1975, he founded his own DeLorean Motor Company using loans from the Bank of America and seed capital from some of his celebrity friends and contacts. His plan was to build a competitively priced two-seater sports car to rival Porsche. Unlike most US-manufactured cars with built-in obsolescence, it would be long-lasting because it would be constructed from rust-proof stainless steel and plastics, and it would also be very fuel-efficient. This, he pronounced, would make his product ethical, a laudable if somewhat ironic quality that the silver-tongued marketing genius touted to potential partners across the US and Europe.

His business model was heavily dependent on building manufacturing facilities in an area of high unemployment and specifically where government grants and financial incentives were available to fund the enterprise. Slick though his presentation may have been, most of his many business pitches were turned down because his big plans looked like an expensive gamble. He was on the verge of accepting a proposal in Puerto Rico when he found an eager and willing bidder in the form of the British government. The incumbent Labour Party agreed to provide him with an initial payment of £53 million to build a new factory in Northern Ireland, in strife-torn west Belfast. Government ministers optimistically justified this as an economic solution to sectarian conflict that would create 2,000 new jobs and lead to Catholics and Protestants working in harmony alongside one another. DeLorean claimed that his personal investment in the project was $4 million but the true figure was $750,000 and even that money was his wife's.

A critical part of DeLorean's pitch had been the pledge to turn the prototype DMC-12 — the '12' reflected the intended retail price of $12,000 — into production reality in the unrealistically short timeframe of 18 months. This was just a quarter of the time that industry standards and process would normally have dictated and he desperately needed a design and manufacturing partner to help him deliver his wild promise at the same time as ensuring that the new car would comply with stringent US safety

John DeLorean and his third wife, model Cristina Ferrare, pose for a publicity photograph with the gullwing-doored DeLorean DMC-12.

and emissions regulations. Porsche was his first port of call but the company told him that the task would take seven years and cost £70 million. He tried BMW, which quoted four years and £50 million, and in any case wasn't really interested.

Undeterred, DeLorean embarked on discussions with Colin Chapman, whom he admired immensely. Their dialogue couldn't have been more timely. Despite Lotus's great success in Formula 1, the broader operation, Group Lotus, was struggling and finance director Fred Bushell was constantly having to transfer funds between the public and the private companies to balance the books and maintain the illusion that all the separate divisions were solvent. Added to this, Chapman was furious with the British government because he felt that it had personally snubbed him only days before the DeLorean announcement by rejecting his own much smaller application for a development grant of £400,000. Irrespective of the government's rationale about job creation, he would never accept its willingness to spurn his British company and yet spend vast amounts of British taxpayers' money funding an American start-up venture that could potentially damage Lotus in one of its strongest markets. Perhaps he felt that if he wasn't going to be supported directly, then maybe he should benefit indirectly from the government's flawed decision.

In some respects, DeLorean and Chapman were complementary characters but they were also worryingly alike in far too many ways and the relationship between them was never going to be easy. Both were anti-establishment and at the time of his company's flotation Chapman had railed against the power of the trade unions, over-regulation and government interference. Both men had risen from humble beginnings through hard work to become urbane, egotistical and extremely wealthy. Both were fiercely strong characters and ruthlessly ambitious risk-takers who also wanted more. Both were sometimes prepared to put morals to one side and use their charisma and persuasive skills to get their way, irrespective of the consequences.

With its 'gull-wing' doors, the rear-engine DeLorean DMC-12 had striking styling by Giorgetto Giugiaro, one of Italy's top car designers, but it was based on an exercise that went back to the early 1970s and already looked outdated. Chapman really disliked the 'gull-wing' doors, which he considered not only impractical and expensive to manufacture, but also, somewhat ironically, unsafe because they could lead to the occupants of a car becoming trapped if it were to roll over onto its roof in an accident. Neither did he approve of the insistence that there had to be enough room to stow a set of golf clubs behind the seats because this meant that the car couldn't be built to the ideal mid-engine format.

Chapman declined DeLorean's first offer of $12 million for Lotus to re-engineer and develop the original design. However, when DeLorean raised the fee to $17.65 million, Bushell was quick to persuade his boss to accept the deal, but only on condition that the funds were paid upfront and into a particular offshore bank account.

More than 15 years earlier, Chapman and Bushell had created a company called GPD Services so that Team Lotus — the racing team — could circumvent high British taxes when paying its drivers. The initials originally stood for 'Grand Prix Drivers' but later represented 'General Production Development'. With its roots in Panama, GPD had been set up with an address in Geneva but possessed neither assets nor physical offices and was no more than a PO box. This was the conduit for the funds that were paid by DeLorean as 'consultancy fees' but were never received by or credited to Group Lotus.

November 1978 marked the peak of Chapman's racing career. Only five days after being made a Freeman of the City of Norwich in Norfolk, just up the road from his factory, in recognition and celebration of Mario Andretti winning the Formula 1 World Championship, he signed the deal with DeLorean in which he crossed the line from bending the rules to serious fraud. This coincided with a stage in his life when the relentless pressures of his workload included distractions in the aviation and marine industries. It all took a severe toll on his health and it was known that he was becoming ever more reliant on a cocktail of sleeping tablets and amphetamines. In addition, marital infidelities meant that the distinction between family and private life was becoming increasingly blurred at a time when his business life was just about to get a whole lot more complicated.

In the DeLorean project, Chapman had found much-needed cash flow, as indeed had the architect of the enterprise. Lotus invoiced its client for many millions of pounds, only some of which was spent on re-engineering the flawed design, allowing other Lotus offshoots also to benefit from the largesse of the British government and its unwitting taxpayers. Meanwhile, DeLorean himself concentrated on funding the excesses of his gilded lifestyle from company headquarters in New York where he lived in a 20-room apartment while also owning a country mansion and an avocado farm. Several members of his management team tried to curtail his use of company money on personal expenditure due to their concerns that an impending parliamentary inquiry would uncover unreported and hidden costs, but when anyone dared to get in his way a henchman would threaten them and their families.

When production of the DMC-12 eventually began in early 1981, the project was already massively behind the scheduled start date. Among the elements that conspired against the company were adverse foreign-exchange movements and cost overruns due to dock strikes in Britain that delayed parts deliveries. The 'finished' product was effectively just a diluted version of the Lotus Esprit with a tweaked Renault V6 engine, not the innovative design that had been promised. It was an unmitigated and embarrassing disaster, justifiably slated by critics worldwide. When cars finally landed with US dealers, they were barely fit for purpose let alone worthy of delivery to customers due to their awful quality and poor reliability. The much-heralded stainless-steel body was actually only a coating over a plastic shell and meant that there could be no colour options, added to which the bare-metal bodywork was a nightmare to keep clean because anyone touching it left visible fingerprints. Senior managers at both

Lotus and DeLorean were ignored when they said production had to be paused in order to fix the problems.

John DeLorean had forecast sales of 30,000 units a year and estimated that the company would need to sell between 10,000–12,000 a year just to break even, but it never got close to the first-year production target and was unable to manufacture and sell enough cars to meet costs. Less than 9,000 cars were produced in 21 months and 3,000 of those remained unsold.

Despite the magnitude of the sums involved, the Labour government never did sufficient due diligence on the man and his less-than-immaculate credentials before pledging taxpayers' millions. By the time he went back to ask for yet more funding, there had been a general election and a Conservative government was now in place. Amid reports of DeLorean's personal extravagances and unsavoury tactics, Prime Minister Margaret Thatcher wasn't prepared to give in to his repeated threats to close the company unless he received further bailouts. A total of £80 million in public funds had already been lost on a badly managed company that had underperformed and was essentially worthless and she was reluctant to throw more good money after bad by providing a further £30 million. He claimed that this sum was due as an inflation adjustment and that non-payment would jeopardise guarantees on £24 million that the company had borrowed from banks. By February 1982, the DeLorean Motor Company was in receivership, and in November the government ordered the factory to be closed after considering and rejecting various rescue packages.

To widespread consternation, Mrs Thatcher vetoed a rescue plan by a British consortium to save the DeLorean Motor Company when it was in receivership. This might have secured 1,500 jobs, recouped part of the government's $160 million investment and, critically, restricted direct involvement by DeLorean himself. Weeks earlier she had learned of the millions of dollars that had been siphoned from the company's accounts and that the culprits were almost certainly DeLorean and his associates.

When DeLorean was forced to shelve ambitious plans to take his company public in the US, in desperation to save it from imminent insolvency and with the more pressing need to protect his extravagant standard of living, he came up with several proposals to fund its revival. While the reasons weren't divulged, Mrs Thatcher's government repeatedly gave the DeLorean Motor Company more time and extended deadlines — flexibility that the politicians hadn't been willing to offer the British consortium — and during this period the personal and business phones of key employees were tapped by authorities on both sides of the Atlantic. It has since been the subject of much conjecture as to whether or not Mrs Thatcher was aware of an impending drugs sting on DeLorean when she rejected the British consortium, but it seems likely that she was.

In June 1982, three weeks after Mrs Thatcher met US President Ronald Reagan in London, DeLorean received a phone call from an FBI agent posing as a cocaine dealer and in desperation he took the bait. For Reagan, who was just about to launch his 'War on Drugs' initiative, catching someone like DeLorean trafficking drugs would have been a significant success. Hidden cameras set up by the FBI in a hotel at Los Angeles International Airport duly showed him dealing in 100kg of cocaine with a street value of $24 million that he intended to distribute in southern California.

After his arrest, DeLorean spent time in prison, during which he claimed to have become a born-again Christian. When the trial eventually came to court, in 1984, his lawyers successfully argued that he had been set up and had been a victim of illegal government entrapment, targeted because he was known to be financially vulnerable. Despite his acquittal after a not-guilty plea, his reputation had been irrevocably damaged.

A year later he was back in court, this time indicted on charges of tax evasion, defrauding investors and laundering money from the DeLorean Motor Company. Remarkably, he managed to escape justice once again when the jury cleared him of all charges of misappropriation, but he spent most of the rest of his life fighting legal cases relating to the collapse of his eponymous car company and all this ultimately led to personal bankruptcy in 1999. As for the DeLorean DMC-12, its greatest claim to fame was immortalisation in the aptly titled 1985 comedy sci-fi film *Back to the Future*.

After the DeLorean Motor Company had finally been declared bankrupt, the official receiver was called in and the subsequent investigation by the Serious Fraud Office showed that some design work had in fact been carried out by Lotus but nothing like the amount for which the British government had been billed. It was also clear that the government had effectively been invoiced twice after taking into consideration the funds paid to the mysterious GPD Services.

While DeLorean hid behind his assertion that all payments had been approved by the Bank of England and the Secretary of State for Northern Ireland, Colin Chapman initially denied all knowledge of the $17.5 million payment but later suggested that it had been an introductory fee for 'bringing the parties together'. Whatever the truth, the fact remains that, at the very least, he and Fred Bushell had defrauded Group Lotus by concealing the consultancy fee, which should have been declared in company accounts as an upfront profit but instead remained hidden in Swiss bank accounts. The sum was alleged to have been split as 50 percent for DeLorean, 45 percent for Chapman and 5 percent for Bushell.

Entirely of his own making, the issue of the missing millions would haunt Chapman for the rest of his days. By the end of 1982, it must have seemed that his world was in danger of collapsing around him as the net tightened with the nightmare prospect of imprisonment, financial ruin and disgrace threatening to overwhelm him. On 16th December he flew himself back from an FIA meeting in Paris and died of a massive heart attack later that night in the arms of his wife, aged just 54.

Like so many other Lotus employees, Bushell was completely in awe of Chapman and had worked tirelessly for the man who manipulated him. Not only was he Group Lotus's company accountant but he was also Chapman's right-hand man, close friend and confidant, and it was largely through his efforts that Lotus Cars remained afloat during the tough times of the late 1970s and early 1980s, a period of industrial decline that affected many British car manufacturers. Recalling Bushell's activities, Lotus Formula 1 designer Martin Ogilvie stated: 'Team Lotus's financial year used to be about six months different from Lotus Engineering and Lotus Cars. They used to swap the money around. Fred Bushell got the money in and looked after it and Chapman used to spend it. He would say, "Fred, your job is just to get the money so I can spend it."' Lotus's efforts in Grand Prix racing increasingly became a black hole, especially after lavish funding from David Thieme (see Chapter 54) and his Essex Petroleum company dried up with his arrest early in April 1981, and sponsors suspected that some of their money was being used to pay off debts.

After Chapman's death, Bushell took over as Group Lotus chairman and continued to manage finances and stave off creditors until David Wickens of British Car Auctions arrived as chairman in 1983 with much-needed investment capital. Thereafter, Bushell's role focused on Team Lotus while the British investigation into the whole DeLorean/Lotus scandal rumbled on for years. In July 1989, Bushell was arrested and the case finally went to trial at Belfast Crown Court in 1992, fully ten years after Chapman's death. Bushell pleaded guilty to conspiring to defraud the DeLorean Motor Company and was sentenced to three years in jail, fined £1.5 million and ordered to pay costs of more than £800,000; as he wasn't able to pay the fine, he had to spend an additional year in prison.

As his conviction proved, Bushell was undoubtedly complicit and possibly

'CHUNKY'
Punching above his weight

Although Colin Chapman's untimely death ensured that he escaped a criminal conviction and jail sentence, he did spend two nights behind bars during his lifetime. In an early example of his hot-headed nature and lack of respect for the law, he punched a policeman who was trying to block his way in the paddock at the 1965 Dutch Grand Prix at Zandvoort and after the race, which Jim Clark won for Lotus, he was arrested. It was unfortunate for him that his misdemeanour occurred in the Netherlands because, like the UK, it also has a royal family. It has long been said that this is why he could never have been considered for a knighthood, although in 1970 he did receive the lower accolade of a CBE in recognition of his achievements.

even instrumental in the deception and fraudulent activity. That said, his contribution to Lotus was immense and a large part of his downfall has to be attributed to the misguided but unstinting loyalty to his former boss for whom, instead of trying to save himself, he went to prison. He refused to say anything that might incriminate his friend in order to protect the reputation of the man he revered and thought of as a legend. At the trial, judge Lord Justice Murray made the point that if Chapman and DeLorean had been in the dock, they would have each received a minimum sentence of ten years for 'an outrageous and massive fraud'.

Definitely not a saint and both contradictory and controversial, Chapman was nonetheless a giant of motor racing who ranked alongside Enzo Ferrari in terms of influence and stature, and similarly bestrode the sport while also building superb road cars. Under his direction between 1960 and 1982, Team Lotus achieved 72 wins and 88 pole positions in Grand Prix racing, claimed seven constructors' titles and six drivers' titles, won the Indianapolis 500, and scored numerous successes in other branches of racing. In doing so, he was unique in the history of motor racing and his legacy is of an outstanding mind and unprecedented flair that made Britain dominant in Formula 1 and changed the face of motor racing. He was also a fine talent-spotter when it came to hiring drivers and employees, but he wasn't always quite so astute when it came to judging the character of business associates, as his dealings with John DeLorean attest.

CHAPTER 16
DOMINIC
CHAPPELL
Chicanery

A serial bankrupt and playboy who was even more out of his depth in business than he was when he raced cars, he bought an ailing chain of British department stores for a token £1 in a well-publicised and highly controversial deal but blatantly disregarded the corporate liabilities in order to fund his champagne lifestyle. His shameless spending of company money cost the jobs and livelihoods of 11,000 employees but when he was eventually convicted and sent to prison it was after being found guilty of tax evasion.

Dominic Chappell was born in 1966 and brought up in Sunbury, on the banks of the River Thames in Middlesex. He was privately educated in Somerset at the prestigious Millfield School, which is best known for the outstanding sporting achievements of many of its former pupils rather than their academic prowess, and his competitive instincts developed there. He started motor racing in 1986 and was competing in Formula Ford 2000 by 1988. He graduated to British Formula 3 in 1989 driving for his family-run Long Ridge Racing team (named after the family home) in a VW-powered Ralt RT32. It isn't clear how these early forays in motorsport were financed but in an interview with the BBC he claimed that his family had a long-standing involvement in the oil industry in Libya where he said that he had had personal dealings with the dictator Colonel Gaddafi.

Chappell dabbled in Formula 3 for three seasons. They marked the high point of his racing achievements because he found himself sharing the track with future Formula 1 stars such as Mika Salo, Christian Fittipaldi and — notably — Mika Häkkinen (later to become a double World Champion), although he competed mostly in the Class B division. Very few drivers contested more than a handful of events in this poorly supported subsidiary category, which existed to make up numbers, so the competition was sparse and inconsistent. This meant that in 1990, driving a Ralt for the Racefax team, Chappell benefited from being the only driver to take part in every round and finished runner-up in the class standings. He competed in just two more rounds the following season before progressing in 1993 to more powerful Formula 2 cars in the British championship. Back with his family-operated team, now known as Apache Racing, he campaigned a Ralt RT23 and later a Reynard 92D for two seasons, again without much success.

He also turned his attention to GT cars in 1994 and made his first attempt at the Le Mans 24 Hours in the ADA team's untested De Tomaso Pantera with two British co-drivers, Phil Andrews and amateur Jonathan Baker. After a last-minute change of plan, he was deputed to take the start of the race but beached the car in the gravel at the first chicane on the first lap. Unfortunately for the small team, the marshals damaged the car's gearbox when dragging it from its resting place, so more than 90 minutes were lost while the car was recovered to the pits and then repaired. Although the Pantera did reach the finish, 21st on the road, it was unclassified in the results because it hadn't covered sufficient distance.

Chappell entered Le Mans three more times. In 1995 he drove a Lister Storm GTS with experienced former Grand Prix drivers Geoff Lees and Rupert Keegan but the car didn't make it to the finish after Keegan put the car into gravel and wrecked the clutch extricating it. The Roock Racing Porsche 911 GT2 Chappell drove in 1996 also failed to finish due to engine problems at the halfway mark. As for 1997, the Marcos Mantara 600 in which he was entered didn't even make the start, having failed to qualify.

After a largely undistinguished career as a driver, that should probably have been the last that motorsport ever heard of Chappell. However, the aspiring entrepreneur re-emerged a few years later and left a legacy for which he remains bitterly remembered.

In an abortive and short-lived attempt at being a race promoter, Dominic Chappell launched the ill-fated Interactive Sportscar Championship (ISC) in Britain in 2001. This series, which pledged to revolutionise television coverage and promotion of events, folded after just one badly supported race, leaving almost everybody involved unpaid and promises of payment unfulfilled.

The special feature of the ISC was that dashboard-mounted cameras would provide what was described as 'a truly immersive experience for the television viewer' whereby subscribers would be able to flick between the top eight cars, choosing which one they wanted to watch. The concept behind the series was ahead of its time and these days, of course, the use of on-board cameras by broadcasters is widespread. Launching the race series with great fanfare at a reception in London's Berkeley Square, Chappell was full of his characteristic bonhomie, bluster and optimism. In a convincing sales pitch, he promised the assembled journalists and other interested parties that his concept was going to be a spectacular success, despite the challenging technology. He announced a television deal with the Granada Media Group and told *Autosport* magazine: 'We will have a combination of broadband, internet and terrestrial television with mid-week and weekend slots on terrestrial and a full race package live on digital/satellite television.' He claimed his pipedream would be expanded to include powerboat and motorcycle racing.

It all sounded most exciting and he raised expectations to such an extent that, even if he were only to deliver a fraction of what he promised, the ISC would indeed be a great success. He made wildly optimistic predictions that it would attract a quarter of a million subscribers and the revenue from this would provide a highly attractive prize fund of £500,000 for the inaugural series. The teams were to be offered healthy starting money of £14,000 per car and the top three drivers at each race were to get £15,000, £7,000 and £3,000. It all seemed too good to be true — and, inevitably, it was.

Due to his naivety and inexperience of business, Chappell was blind to all the precautionary advice he had been given. Importantly, he ignored the fact that even Bernie Ecclestone, who had more expertise in this field than anybody else, had already tried to market a more sophisticated version of a similar idea in 1996, and had failed. In a rare mistake, the Formula 1 promoter had reputedly invested $35 million in a digital television offering that at times struggled to attract even 9,000 pay-per-view punters. If the concept couldn't be made to work for Formula 1, with its global reach, then it was unlikely to succeed for Chappell's series of glorified club racing, notwithstanding the internet growth that had occurred during the intervening five years. In what was an ill-conceived and under-financed proposal without a business plan or realistic targets, there was no hope that a new and unproven national championship would ever be able to attract even a tiny fraction of the requisite number of subscribers, and so it proved, to the detriment of all the participants.

Alarm bells quickly rang after the cancellation of the first two rounds due to lack of entries, leading to widespread speculation that the series would never get off the ground. However, the first ISC race did eventually take place at Donington Park on 3rd June 2001, despite considerable scepticism from the teams about the financial health and viability of the series, and their mounting concerns as to what they were letting themselves in for. After several teams encountered various pre-race mechanical setbacks, only nine cars took part. The teams' problems were nothing compared with those of the organisers, who had failed to supply entrants with the requisite interactive electronics in time for the race, which itself had to be shortened because the obligatory mid-race pitstop couldn't involve refuelling due to the absence of refuelling rigs. The winners of the hour-long race were David Warnock and James Pickford in a Lister Storm.

The next race was due to take place at Silverstone the following weekend but it was cancelled immediately after the Donington event because the all-important broadcasting rights weren't in place with Silverstone's owners. That left Rockingham as the next scheduled event amidst recriminations from Chappell, who was quick to issue ultimatums, threatening teams with fines and exclusions from the event if they didn't support the series and run the two-car line-ups that they had agreed to. Within two weeks of the disappointment of the Donington race, the ISC was facing a mass withdrawal by teams if the organisers didn't meet certain financial demands — and, despite further assurances, they didn't.

One of the compromised teams was Brookspeed, whose director, Martin Braybrook, said: 'The team, and I personally, feel very let down by the ISC. Brookspeed has been one of its strongest advocates from day one. With better organisation, communication and commercial skills, the series would have been a major success. Sadly for all concerned, it does not appear to be heading that way.'

It was no surprise to anybody, except perhaps Chappell himself, when the axe finally fell on the ISC after another fortnight of uncertainty. No prize money was ever distributed and numerous bills were left unpaid. Even the caterers for the Donington event were left out of pocket. Chappell insisted that he had done everything possible to make it work and that the teams were, in his words, 'fully aware of what was going on'. He added, 'They knew it was going to be difficult.' Commenting many years later, he was still defiant and unrepentant that everyone involved in the sorry mess had lost large sums of money, insisting that the series didn't collapse but simply 'merged' with other championships, although this is strongly refuted by those who took part.

Much more financial irregularity was to follow Dominic Chappell's disastrous ISC venture, including three personal bankruptcies. Even before the ISC fiasco, he had already experienced his first insolvency, having entered an Individual Voluntary Arrangement (IVA) — a mechanism that enables individual debtors to avoid bankruptcy — after supposedly making a personal guarantee to a failed Formula 1 team.

His first bankruptcy occurred in 2005. Twelve years earlier he had become a director of Eyot, a property company that he ran alongside his father Joe. Following a dispute with Foxton's estate agents over unpaid fees related to the sale of a £1.2 million property in Fulham, south-west London, he declared himself bankrupt. He was discharged a year later but was still a director in 2008 when Eyot fell into administration owing £230,000 to Lloyds Bank.

His second bankruptcy came in 2009 as the result of a failed property venture on a much larger scale, once again in partnership with his father. Their grand plans to develop the Isle of Wight's Island Harbour Marina included building 48 new holiday homes and 26 luxury waterside properties with private moorings on a peaceful offshoot of the River Medina, two miles from Cowes. But after just six months the project went into administration when loans of £24 million were called in by Anglo Irish Bank following its discovery that substantial amounts of the money had been spent on excesses that included boats, cars and a helicopter. The only signs of construction work appeared to be some giant slabs of concrete, forming a giant white 'H' in a muddy field behind the marina's restaurant, and a tattered orange windsock. Apart from this unused helipad, the only thing that remained in the immediate aftermath of the disastrous project was another trail of debt and a string of extremely unhappy creditors, many of which were smaller local businesses.

For the next three years, Chappell listed himself on LinkedIn as chief executive of a Gibraltar-based start-up company called Olivia Petroleum SA in which he held a 40 percent stake. The company had been set up to acquire and develop a 5.5-million-gallon oil-storage facility called Istamelsa in Cadiz, on Spain's south-western coast, but the project was never completed and Istamelsa went into administration when it was unable to settle outstanding tax liabilities. The rest of the shares were owned by private investors who are understood to have ousted Chappell from the business in 2012 by diluting his shareholding following the discovery of missing funds of €400,000 that had been moved personally by Chappell without the knowledge or permission of his fellow shareholders. Allegedly,

After several court appearances, the law finally caught up with one-time amateur racing driver Dominic Chappell in 2020 when he was jailed for six years for tax fraud during his custodianship of British Home Stores.

the money was diverted into other accounts, including one belonging to Chappell's wife, and some of it spent on various luxuries. Chappell was by this time a keen sailor so it was no coincidence that there were also signs of expenditure at a chandlery business that fitted out yachts and supplied parts and equipment for them. The concerns of the shareholders were highlighted in November 2011 by a lawyer acting for Olivia Petroleum in an email that stated: 'There is an awful amount of money spent in travel, restaurants, shopping and UK, which indicates that this could be considered as hidden salaries or payment in species to employees. Big liability here. The company is not trading and this is not in accordance with that.'

When questioned by *The Guardian* newspaper, Chappell said that the idea that he had taken large amounts of money from the company for his personal use was 'totally untrue', before stating that the monies he received from Olivia Petroleum amounted to 'less than €200,000'. He added: 'That was my salary. That's what I drew from the company.' He later changed his story and said he hadn't drawn a salary but had taken 'a directors' loan' amounting to '€212,000, I think'. He also claimed 'I still own a significant amount of it [Olivia Petroleum]' before contradicting that by saying he had sold his stake.

British Home Stores, established in 1928 and known simply as BHS, was one of Britain's best-known and most respected retailers, its department stores a fixture of British high streets. BHS was listed on the London Stock Exchange and was a constituent of the FTSE 100 Index when Monaco-based billionaire Sir Philip Green, a retailing tycoon and brother-in-law of Sir Stirling Moss, bought it in 2000 for £200 million. Green then took BHS into private ownership as part of his Arcadia Group, which he acquired in 2002, to form Britain's second-largest clothing retailer, after Marks & Spencer. Following several loss-making years in difficult trading conditions, BHS began to struggle and reached a point where it was losing £1 million a week and had accumulated a vast shortfall in its pension fund estimated to be in the region of £250 million to £500 million. Green became so desperate to find a buyer, and especially to offload his liabilities to the group's present and future pensioners, that he sold BHS in March 2015 for a nominal £1 plus £10 million equity injection.

The buyer was Dominic Chappell. The purchase was made through Retail Acquisitions Limited, a name presumably chosen to inspire confidence and lend credibility. Green went ahead with the sale despite having been warned that Chappell had no retail experience and had also been bankrupt twice. People in the City of London were mystified about Chappell's background and business credentials because no one in the financial world had ever heard of the 49-year-old public schoolboy with a taste for racing cars, skiing and yachting. Neither was anyone familiar with his newly formed investment company. When Retail Acquisitions Limited took over BHS, *The Sunday Times* quoted Chappell as saying that he had made a 'bonanza' from an oil-storage facility in Cadiz and cited his 'very successful' time at Olivia Petroleum as proof of his suitability to win the takeover bid.

Chappell had also given his professional advisers the name of Olivia Petroleum when asked for examples of his background in turning around struggling companies and this supposed credential was used to counter criticisms that he had no relevant experience. Numerous media outlets reported that Chappell's Retail Acquisitions Limited was a consortium that included the 'oil distribution firm Olivia Petroleum'. He told *The Guardian* that the money he put into BHS had been made through 'Olivia Investments' but under further questioning stated he had made money from a different oil-storage facility in Cadiz that he refused to name, and also from a different 'Olivia Petroleum', this second one supposedly based in Gibraltar. Not surprisingly, this obfuscation led to confusion in the media and incorrect reports that the real Olivia Petroleum SA was involved in the consortium, but he did nothing to set the record straight.

Chappell had previously had business dealings with Paul Sutton, a fraudster who had been convicted of embezzlement in France in 2002 and in 2014, and had put in his own bid for BHS. As soon as Green was notified of Sutton's past, the fraudster was barred from any further involvement in the deal, at which point Chappell stepped in and started negotiating with Green himself. Chappell subsequently denied any past association with Sutton even though he had briefly tried to buy property from him in 2006. At a parliamentary enquiry into the fiasco, Chappell contradicted himself by telling Members of Parliament that he had been hired by Sutton to work on his bid for the department store. Sutton refuted that and said that he had in fact employed Chappell to work as his chauffeur because he had lost £160,000 in the failed property development on the Isle of Wight and giving him a job as a driver was the only way he could recoup some of his money. That all seemed rather less credible once it emerged, soon after completion of the BHS deal, that Sutton and his 'driver' were partners in a Panama-registered company called Clarberry Investments. However, none of this stopped Sutton from claiming, like most observers, astonishment that Chappell's bid had been successful.

Instead of injecting new capital into cash-strapped BHS as agreed with Arcadia, Chappell extracted large sums of money from it. BHS limped on, falling into deeper financial difficulty, while Chappell spent his new-found wealth lavishly on expensive overseas holidays and luxury yachts. Indeed, he behaved more like a child in a sweetshop than as an employer responsible for the livelihoods of 11,000 people.

By his own admission, he took a total of £2.6 million from BHS during his 'stewardship', although the true amount may well have been more. This sum was said to include £650,000 in salary and bonuses together with consultancy fees directed to another of his companies, Swiss Rock Limited, which itself was put into liquidation with unpaid VAT debts of £365,000 and outstanding Corporation Tax of £197,306. Within three months of taking control, he diverted £1.5 million so that he could pay off the mortgage on his parents' home.

The inevitable happened when the beleaguered retail chain went into administration on 25th April 2016 after 88 years of trading and just 13 months after Chappell's arrival. Total collapse gradually followed and by 28th August all stores had been closed for good. More undisclosed financial wrongdoing on Chappell's part came to light during subsequent investigations by Her Majesty's Revenue & Customs (HMRC) and a Parliamentary Inquiry.

The day after the BHS board discussed placing the company into receivership, Chappell diverted £1.5 million to a company owned by a Sweden-based friend who was also a board member of Retail Acquisitions Limited. Unlike so much of Chappell's thieving, this transaction was quickly uncovered and refunded on the insistence of BHS's horrified chief executive Darren Topp. Chappell also transferred to Retail Acquisitions Limited more than £1 million in takings from two specific BHS stores, on London's Oxford Street and in Sunderland.

Hindered by inadequate record-keeping, HMRC investigations failed to establish the circumstances behind other large payments from BHS, totalling £2 million to Retail Acquisitions Limited and over £1 million direct to Chappell. There was also an unexplained £500,000 loan to Retail Acquisitions Limited that Chappell had arranged without the knowledge of his co-directors. It transpired that £275,000 of this loan was used by Retail Acquisitions Limited to buy an American company and a further £221,960 was paid to another company, one where Chappell's father was a director, before being transferred to Chappell. The American company never traded but was later sold for $201,000, with the proceeds paid into Chappell's personal bank account.

The Parliamentary Inquiry was held in July 2016. This concluded in a damning indictment by MPs who branded Chappell out of his depth, incompetent and self-serving, a chancer with his hands in the till. They heard from the company's interim chief financial officer, Michael Hitchcock, that rather than investing much-needed funds, Retail Acquisitions Limited had taken £17 million out of BHS over 13 months and only £10 million had been reinvested. Darren Topp described a personal argument with Chappell about money being taken out of the business during which the embezzler allegedly threatened to murder him, saying: 'If you kick off about it, I'll come down and kill you.' Although Chappell denied making the threat, Topp was aware that he owned guns and took it seriously.

Just before the Parliamentary Inquiry, news emerged that not only did Chappell have several County Court Judgments against him for personal debts but also had been declared bankrupt three times rather than twice as had been originally believed. *The Sunday Times* revealed that he had been made bankrupt when aged just 25 and the bankruptcy order had been handed down in Slough County Court on 3rd June 1992. This was confirmed by a notice in *The London Gazette*, the UK's official public record, stating Chappell's occupation as 'car salesman'. In keeping with his character, he was quick to claim that it was '100 percent' untrue but when shown the notice, he answered: 'It was annulled or dissolved, or whatever they do. It definitely didn't stand. I can't even remember about it, to be honest.' However, the newspaper reported that the Insolvency Service had no record of the bankruptcy being annulled.

By the time of the collapse, the pension shortfall at BHS had ballooned to a staggering £571 million. In 2017, The Pensions Regulator began an investigation. The short-tempered Green was heavily criticised for pushing ahead with the deal and was pressed into providing a £363 million cash settlement towards plugging the gap in order to rescue two schemes representing 19,000 members of staff. As The Pensions Regulator was unsuccessful in its attempts to obtain information from Chappell in relation to the scheme, he was charged with neglecting or refusing to respond to its demands to hand over vital documents and information relating to the acquisition.

At Chappell's ensuing trial brought by The Pensions Regulator, he represented himself at Brighton Magistrates' Court in January 2018 and was found guilty on three charges of failing to provide vital documents. He was ordered to pay a fine of £50,000 plus £37,000 court costs but said he couldn't pay because he had 'no funds' and extensive outgoings of £9,000 per month, which included £3,800 rent for a large period house in Dorset, £2,666 on the lease of a brand-new Range Rover, and £2,500 (plus arrears) on school fees for his two young children. In September 2018, he appealed against the judgment and lost.

The 52-year-old had originally told the court that he hadn't seen the summons from The Pensions Regulator or any of the formal documentation. When asked why by the district judge, he replied: 'Because I was away, I did not have internet access when I was away. I was offshore, on a boat.' Although he didn't elaborate, at the time of the summons he was on his recently acquired yacht, *Maverick 5*, taking part in the Rolex Fastnet, the world's largest offshore yacht race. He also denied that the summons had arrived at his country home but the judge branded Chappell 'evasive' and said that his evidence was 'incomprehensible', 'unreliable' and 'not credible'.

Meanwhile, HMRC was also investigating Chappell's unwillingness to pay tax. Prosecutors said that HMRC had originally been seeking as much as £17 million from him and from Retail Acquisitions Limited and had tried repeatedly to chase down the missing payments. However, Chappell had been obstructive and had continued to ignore HMRC's requests, at one point going on a skiing break in Kitzbühel before asking for more time to pay the money upon his return. On other occasions he gave excuses that he had been ill or abroad during the period in question and that these circumstances had prevented him from assisting investigators, although no evidence of medical attention or travel was ever provided. Retail Acquisitions Limited was wound up by the High Court of Justice in May 2017 on the petition of BHS, which was owed £6.1 million in respect of an unpaid loan.

In October 2019, Chappell was in the dock again, this time at Southwark Crown Court in London accused of tax fraud. There were three charges of tax evasion: failing to register Swiss Rock, his bankrupt finance company, for taxes from the correct date; giving false information to tax authorities and not declaring profits; and failing to submit VAT returns. He had originally faced two additional charges of money laundering but these were dropped. He pleaded not guilty to the three charges and the trial was adjourned for almost a year.

In November 2019, the Government's Insolvency Service, which handles corporate failures, detailed a litany of wrongdoing by Chappell. It concluded that he had carried out 'reckless financial transactions' and 'failed to maintain adequate company records'. It condemned him for spending large sums of money at a time when he should have been trying to save BHS and its employees. He was disqualified from being a company director for a period of ten years.

In January 2020, The Pensions Regulator added to his troubles by ordering him to pay £9.5 million into BHS's retirement schemes. This was never likely to happen as he had already claimed that he was — yet again — facing bankruptcy and wouldn't be able to pay anything, not even the fine and court costs that had been imposed two years earlier.

In October 2020, Chappell was back in Southwark Crown Court to answer charges that he had failed to pay almost £600,000 of VAT, income tax and corporation tax on the £2.2 million he had received after buying BHS.

Portraying himself as a victim of broken promises and the incompetence of others, he tried putting the blame on everyone else, principally Sir Philip Green and his accountants Price Waterhouse Coopers (PwC). He claimed that he had been 'simply too busy' to sort out his business affairs properly, that he had been 'let down by others', and that 'we were given forged and misleading documents by PwC and I was lied to by Sir Philip Green, as were my board'.

The judge, Mr Justice Bryan, was unimpressed: 'You were not overwhelmed by your other pressures, and you were not too busy or under too much pressure to spare the time to buy yourself trappings of luxury with monies that would have been better deployed to pay the taxes due.' The court heard that, instead of paying those taxes, Chappell had shamelessly spent hundreds of thousands of pounds on luxuries, including another yacht and a holiday in the Bahamas. On his return from the holiday, which was a day after £86,000 income tax should have been paid, he had bought a £91,000 Bentley Continental and a pair of Beretta shotguns costing £11,000. A little time later he spent a further £33,000 on a Land Rover. An unedifying email written by Chappell was circulated in the courtroom and said: 'I am having to slum it in the Bahamas for the next three weeks. I know you will all feel my pain.'

After a trial lasting almost four weeks, Chappell did indeed feel some pain. The jury was unsympathetic and found him guilty on all three charges of cheating the public revenue. Sentencing him to six years in prison, Mr Justice Bryan pointed out that not paying VAT or corporation tax, taking receipts out of the company and then putting it into liquidation was 'one of the oldest tricks in the book'. Chappell, he said, had engaged in a 'long and consistent course of conduct designed to cheat the revenue'. He also told him: 'You are not of positive good character. Your offending occurs against a backdrop of successive bankruptcies.'

Whether or not it was the glamour of motorsport that initiated his expensive tastes, Dominic Chappell's profligate lifestyle and excessive spending of other people's money came to an abrupt halt in that courtroom on 5th November 2020. At best, the former racing driver and self-styled entrepreneur will go down as a disgraced businessman but more likely he'll be viewed as no more than a persistent fraudster. His blatant financial engineering, litany of creditors, court judgments, insolvencies and bankruptcies proved him to be nothing more than a compulsive liar.

CHAPTER 17

JACK COTTLE

Boy racer caught on camera

In an irresponsible act of sheer lunacy
at Brands Hatch in 2014, an ignorant
spectator managed to get onto the track
mid-race in an ordinary low-powered VW
Polo and completed a whole lap, laughing
all the way. Like everyone else, the police
didn't find it so funny and arrested him.
Unrepentant, the arrogant prankster
found himself jailed for eight months.

Motor racing can be dangerous and this is highlighted on every admission ticket sold at a race meeting. Drivers and spectators have been killed or injured since the first wheel was turned in competition although thankfully such instances are now rare thanks to advances in all sorts of areas, from car structures to driver protection, from circuit design to marshalling standards. Anyone involved in the sport at any level — competitors, officials, marshals, spectators — is well aware of the inherent dangers. It doesn't require great imagination to understand that every time a car or motorcycle makes contact with another competitor or leaves the circuit, it presents a hazard and potential danger to life. However, no one who enjoys motor racing could possibly have envisaged the incident that occurred at Brands Hatch on 14th June 2014 and could have had unimaginably serious consequences.

Originally conceived by Belgian racing driver Franz Dubois (see Chapter 14) in 1997 and first run in Britain in 2002, the VW Fun Cup is a hugely popular one-make championship for relatively inexpensive Beetle lookalikes built to identical specification. Beneath glass-reinforced plastic

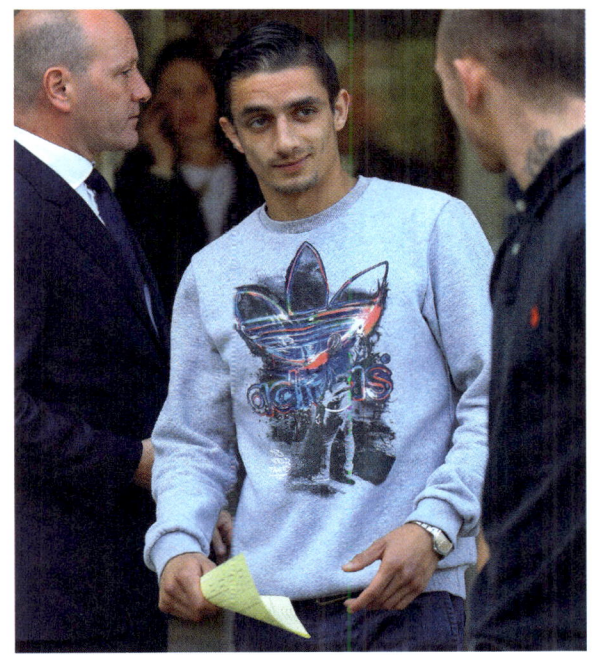

Jack Cottle's idiotic escapade at Brands Hatch didn't seem quite so funny when it landed him with an eight-month prison sentence.

bodywork in the silhouette shape of the iconic VW Beetle, the cars have spaceframe chassis and mid-mounted 130bhp 1,800cc engines as used in production VWs and Audis. Although the Fun Cup racers may look like the much-loved Beetle, they are actually very serious race-engineered machines that offer impressive performance combined with remarkable value for money due to engines and gearboxes being sealed to ensure parity in performance. With strictly controlled regulations, the series attracts a wide variety of professional teams running cars for predominately amateur drivers, and the racing is extremely close. The races are endurance events lasting between three and eight hours, with each car being shared by between two and six drivers.

Among the spectators who had each paid £14 to watch the four-hour Fun Cup race at Brands Hatch in 2014 were 22-year-old Jack Cottle and 20-year-old Zac Copson, who had travelled there with 18-year-old Saskia Fisk in her new white VW Polo. Cottle and Copson were labourers whom Saskia, a pupil in the midst of her A-levels at Sevenoaks Grammar School, had met a few months earlier. Having watched most of the race from the spectator enclosures on the outside of the circuit, Cottle thought they should try to get much closer to the action for its final half hour.

Despite access to the pits and paddock area in the middle of the circuit requiring an entry pass, Cottle somehow managed to drive Saskia's bottom-of-the-range Polo, a 1.2-litre two-door model, through the access tunnel and into the paddock, where he drove along looking for access to the track. Somehow, the pre-race assembly area in the paddock had been left unmanned and the gate leading to the pitlane was open. For reasons known only to him, Cottle steered the Polo through the opening and, ignoring frantic gesticulations from marshals, sped down the pitlane. He drove straight through the traffic lights at the pitlane exit and accelerated onto the circuit and into its notoriously difficult, fast and heavily cambered Paddock Hill Bend. His understandably terrified girlfriend in the passenger seat, fearing both for her safety and her car, screamed hysterically and repeatedly begged him to stop, but he just laughed as several cars bore down on the Polo at speeds of up to 100mph.

The incredulous race commentator immediately saw what was happening and announced, mistakenly, that a 'Volkswagen Golf' was on the track and kept saying that this was 'not quite right' before the race was red-flagged to a halt, by which time Cottle had completed a full lap of the circuit. As the racing drivers flew past the little Polo, some assumed it was a doctor's car or safety vehicle. Fortunately, all of them avoided it. The drama is most graphically seen on a video that can still be viewed on YouTube and was recorded by Copson on his phone from the back seat of the Polo.

Once out of the car, Saskia had to be taken to the onsite medical centre in shock, having suffered a panic attack, while Cottle himself was still laughing when questioned by furious circuit officials. He played down the controversy at the time, saying 'you only live once' and that people had 'blown it out of all proportion', but Kent Police disagreed and arrested him. In subsequent interviews with the police, he admitted that he hadn't driven onto the track 'by accident' and claimed he was dared to do it. Incredibly, although he said he was sorry, he also said he would do it again. After being released from police custody, he defended his actions by posting a foul-mouthed rant on social media insisting that he knew 'how to drive a car', was 'proud to be different' and still thought the whole thing was 'quite funny'.

Copson's video was used in evidence against Cottle in the court case that followed at Maidstone Crown Court a few months later, on 14th November. Judge Martin Joy told the defendant, from Wadhurst in East Sussex, that he had 'endangered many lives' and branded his actions 'premeditated' and 'inexcusable'. Just as the extraordinarily dangerous prank had taken only a few minutes, the judge needed only a few minutes to hand down a sentence of eight months in prison. Other than during his spell of incarceration, Cottle was surprisingly still permitted to drive on public roads, as it wasn't within the power of the police or the judge to disqualify him, because his foolish prank had occurred on private land.

Jonathan Palmer (see Chapter 32), the retired Formula 1 driver and chief executive of MotorSport Vision, which owns Brands Hatch, was pleased with the outcome of the trial: 'His idiotic and selfish behaviour, aggravated by his unrepentant attitude in subsequent media coverage, received much immediate condemnation. His conviction and prison sentence will serve to reinforce the message that this kind of anti-social behaviour is not only stupid but will lead to prosecution.'

NEIL HORAN
The dancing priest

Silverstone witnessed another moment of lunacy by a spectator on lap 12 of the British Grand Prix of 2003. An Irish priest, 56-year-old Father Neil Horan, scaled the trackside barriers and ran onto Hangar Straight, the fastest part of the circuit where cars would have been travelling at speeds of over 170mph. The race was still in its early stages and the cars were quite tightly bunched as he ran along the track towards them, dressed in a green shirt and an orange kilt with a Star of David pinned on the front of it, and brandishing a banner stating 'Read the Bible, the Bible is always right'. Many drivers had to take avoiding action and David Coulthard in his McLaren came particularly close to disaster. Eventually, an extremely brave marshal, Stephen Green, wrestled the man to the ground and out of harm's way. After a spell under the safety car, the race resumed and Rubens Barrichello went on to win it for Ferrari.

Horan was arrested and charged with aggravated trespass, to which he pleaded guilty and received two months in prison. The following summer, after his release, he attempted two more similar stunts. At the Epsom Derby he tried to run out in front of the racehorses but police managed to stop him, while in Athens at the Olympic Games he disrupted the men's marathon and pushed race leader Vanderlei de Lima into the crowds. In 2005, *The Irish Times* reported that he had been defrocked by the Catholic Church.

CHAPTER 18
JERRY DOMINELLI
Crash and burn

An unlikely couple in their Californian social scene, Jerry Dominelli and Nancy Hoover wreaked financial havoc among the high-profile friends they cultivated. Exponents of a Ponzi scheme, they claimed to trade in foreign-currency markets and promised absurdly high rates of return for their clients, but instead funded a celebrity lifestyle. This included sponsorship of a racing team that finished fourth at Le Mans in 1982 and might have been in contention for the World Endurance Championship in 1984 had the law not caught up with them.

Jerry Dominelli's arrival in motor racing in 1981 revolved around John Fitzpatrick, a highly respected and very experienced British racing driver who was fast becoming one of the finest exponents of endurance racing at the time. In 1980, Fitzpatrick had been hired by Californian Dick Barbour as lead driver in a two-car team of Porsche 935 K3s and had proceeded to blitz the American IMSA championship by winning half of the races, including all the blue-riband events. Further successes in Europe that year with Barbour and the German Kremer team ensured that Fitzpatrick won his third Porsche Cup, a coveted trophy awarded annually by the factory to the most successful private Porsche driver.

As the deal with Barbour was a five-year one, it had been the catalyst for Fitzpatrick and his wife Sandra to sell everything they owned in Britain and relocate to San Diego, but Barbour ran into financial difficulties after just one year. Not surprisingly after his impressive 1980 season, Fitzpatrick wasn't short of offers from rival outfits for 1981 but decided that it was a good moment to take the plunge and start his own team. Entering a

Porsche 935 K3 bought from Kremer, he had a difficult IMSA season by his standards, despite winning races at Road Atlanta and Riverside. Towards the end of the season, his prime sponsor, Sachs, a German manufacturer of clutches and shock absorbers, announced a cutback, which meant that his team would struggle to fund the $100,000 needed to compete in the finale at Daytona. Fitzpatrick elected to skip the race secure in the knowledge that, whatever the outcome, he couldn't improve on his third place in the championship.

'Then, out of the blue,' Fitzpatrick told *Motor Sport* magazine, 'I had a call at the workshop. "Mr Fitzpatrick, my name is Jerry Dominelli. I love Porsches, I love racing, I'd like to get involved. Come and see me at my office in La Jolla." I was sure he'd be a time waster, but I went because you should always be courteous. It was Saturday morning; he was sitting in a big suite of offices, a very quiet guy, about 50, expensive suit, silk tie. I told him I wanted to do IMSA the following year but I hadn't got the budget yet. "And Le Mans?" Well, to do IMSA and Le Mans, that's got to be a couple of million dollars. "OK, John, let's do it. When you get back from Daytona, come and see me and we'll get it planned." "Well, I'm not going to Daytona, because I need a new engine." "Of course, you must do Daytona, John" — and there and then he wrote out a cheque for $100,000. I still thought it was all bull, but on Monday morning I went to the bank, and the cheque was good.'

Dominelli didn't attend the race at Daytona but wanted to meet Fitzpatrick again on his return. However, wary of the presence of the prolific amount of drugs money present in the sport at that time, Fitzpatrick first took time to canvass advice and opinion from friends and contacts in San Diego who had been investing with Dominelli. They were all delighted with the money Dominelli's company, J. David, was making for them, so Fitzpatrick, satisfied that his new sponsor was legitimate, visited his saviour once again at his plush offices to plan the forthcoming season.

Now flush with funds, Fitzpatrick bought another 935 derivative, a K4, from Kremer and straight away started winning IMSA races with it. He also added a heavily modified special 935 'Moby Dick' from the Joest team specifically to contest Le Mans, where he and fellow British driver David Hobbs finished a very creditable fourth behind three new works Porsche 956s and won the IMSA class. A few weeks earlier in America, Fitzpatrick had romped to an IMSA victory at Mid-Ohio in the K4, beating the talented John Paul Jr, but at the next championship round, at Lime Rock, John Paul Sr (see Chapter 45), who also raced in IMSA, armed his son with a new Lola T600. Junior put it on pole position while Fitzpatrick qualified alongside him on the front row, with Senior behind in his 935.

'Dominelli only came to a couple of races,' said Fitzpatrick. 'Something always cropped up that kept him in his office, but he did turn up at Lime Rock in a big black stretched limo. I had a good start and was leading Junior in his Lola, when we came up to lap Senior in his 935. He saw me coming and made it difficult for me to pass. Dominelli saw this and began cursing, and the next lap he was on the wall with the mechanics. I'd got past Senior when we came round, and then Dominelli is yelling at him "you son of a bitch" and hurled a wrench at his windscreen! The mechanics had to bundle him off the wall and out of sight, it was hilarious!'

Fitzpatrick's J. David team raced an eye-watering line-up of state-of-the-art Porsches for two seasons, the two 935s joined for 1983 by two 956s. All were painted white with various shades of blue and had 'JDavid' logos emblazoned over them. In return for the funding he put in, Dominelli took 50 per cent ownership of John Fitzpatrick Racing (JFR), investing an estimated $5 million in the team over the two years.

Another rare appearance by the team's patron, this time entertaining important clients, came at the prestigious *Los Angeles Times* Grand Prix at Riverside in April 1983. This six-hour race brought an important win for JFR but it proved to be a very sad occasion. The team entered two 935s, one for Fitzpatrick and Hobbs, the other for Derek Bell and Rolf Stommelen. During his first stint, Stommelen had to avoid a slower car that moved over on him and he spun backwards into a crash barrier and lightly touched an earth bank. After driving a slow lap, he didn't feel that his car was damaged and so got back up to racing speed, only for the rear wing to collapse at the end of a straight at close to 200mph, launching the car out of control. In the ensuing accident, the 39-year-old German driver was fatally injured. Fitzpatrick, meanwhile, had no idea of the tragic outcome, having been told that Stommelen had only suffered a broken leg, and so continued racing with Bell drafted into his car. The three British drivers won the race outright, for the third time in four years in Fitzpatrick's case, but there could be no celebration once they learned of the loss of the man whom Fitzpatrick described as the quickest he had ever worked with.

The chastened team carried on and raced its two 956 Group C cars at Le Mans, where Fitzpatrick finished fifth sharing with Rupert Keegan and Guy Edwards, his car featuring additional sponsorship from Skoal Bandit, an American brand of chewing tobacco. The team had better luck at the British round of the World Endurance Championship (WEC), the Brands

Jerry Dominelli's high life came to a sudden end early in 1984 when the financial trickery behind his J. David 'investment' empire finally came to light.

Hatch 1,000Km, when Fitzpatrick and co-driver Derek Warwick beat the all-conquering works Porsches to win in monsoon-like conditions.

In the weeks leading up to Le Mans, Dominelli had overlooked two reminders to pay the balance of funds due to Porsche for the team's second new 956 for the 24-hour race. With payment having to be made in full before Porsche would release the car, there was a frantic episode in which Fitzpatrick had to track down Dominelli to his office in London and fly there from California to collect a cheque for $200,000 in person and then transfer the money to Porsche in Stuttgart in time for the car to be delivered. Little did Fitzpatrick know that this marked the beginning of financial problems for his team.

J. David 'Jerry' Dominelli was born in Chicago in 1941, graduated from the University of San Diego, and went on to become a stockbroker. He worked at a variety of firms, one of which was Bache Halsey Stuart. There he met Nancy Hoover, who sat at an adjacent desk in the dealing room. At the time they were both married with children but, despite this, romance blossomed for the mismatched couple, who were very different characters both politically and socially. He, a Republican who voted for Ronald Reagan, was a quiet, small and rather nondescript-looking man, distinguished in appearance only by extremely thick horn-rimmed glasses, with twin passions of cars and the arts. She, glamorous and statuesque, a fitness fanatic and party animal, was active in local politics in Del Mar as a Democrat, serving on environmental committees and getting elected to the city council in 1974, two years later taking her turn in the rotating job of mayor.

In 1979, Dominelli founded his own firm, J. David & Company, in the basement of a Mexican restaurant but soon moved into swish offices in La Jolla. J. David was an investment boutique that made the completely unrealistic claim that it could achieve returns of 40–50 percent per annum on international currency markets. Despite widespread scepticism, the illusion of success from the outset led enough hungry investors to plough in their money. Hoover, having left her husband to move in with Dominelli, soon joined her lover's business, becoming an officer of the firm. With her gregarious personality, the vivacious blonde proved to be an invaluable asset and an ideal business partner. She became very effective in charming gullible new investors to open their wallets. As the money poured in, the self-styled 'Captain Money' and his 'Golden Girl' partner used it to make personal investments into areas as diverse as property, gold mining and life insurance. This enabled them to live the high life, which included ownership of an island in the British West Indies that for them was more a legal and accounting mirage than an exotic holiday retreat. For tax and regulatory purposes, they were able to demonstrate that their company's financial activities were based there.

According to Louis Metzger, the court-appointed bankruptcy trustee who would later oversee the liquidation of the Dominelli companies, the pair bought at least five homes, dozens of cars, a Grumman Gulfstream jet aircraft, two Learjets and at least one racehorse. Nancy was reported to have sometimes spent $10,000 a day on clothes and the couple hosted numerous lavish parties. It was in the field of philanthropy, however, where they really excelled, publicly promoting themselves as rich people who cared. Reflecting Dominelli's interest in the arts, they donated large six-figure sums to local causes, including a symphony orchestra to save it from collapse and a university for a new theatre. Closer to Nancy's heart was funding for an Olympic-size swimming pool at that university and the creation of the J. David triathlon team, with selected athletes paid salaries and expenses so they could travel around the country to compete.

Jerry Dominelli's munificence with other people's money included sponsorship of John Fitzpatrick's successful racing team; a high point came in 1983 when Fitzpatrick and co-driver Derek Warwick won the Brands Hatch 1,000Km, a round of the World Endurance Championship, in their Porsche 956.

Dominelli stated that his original intention had been to enable ordinary investors to profit from movements in foreign-currency markets. He promoted a financial model similar in structure to a mutual fund whereby client's money was pooled, enabling him to make dozens of trading positions simultaneously. However, the foreign-exchange markets are extremely volatile and require specialist knowledge. Although he professed to be a well-practised expert, he wasn't. The wildly exaggerated returns that were publicised were a complete fabrication, partly because of incompetence but also because, according to *MoneyWeek* magazine, only a relatively small $28 million of the $200 million raised was ever actually traded. In a classic Ponzi-style scam, the money from new investors was used to pay returns to earlier investors.

Clients were in awe of him and were drawn from the great and good of San Diego. They numbered a large swathe of the city's tight-knit social and political hierarchy, including illustrious surgeons, businessmen and entrepreneurs. Ironically, even bankers, lawyers and judges entrusted hard-earned money to Dominelli, assuming that his conspicuous extravagance was a sure sign that he too was getting good reward. However, as they all received monthly statements showing profits of more than three per cent, which annualised to as much as 40 percent, very few wanted to withdraw funds. Meanwhile, Dominelli took a hefty commission of 20 percent of the fictitious returns, but over a four-year spending spree he and his girlfriend also used most of the investors' money to fund their opulent lifestyle.

Although it had never crossed Fitzpatrick's mind that there was anything untoward about the money Dominelli had been putting into the team, towards the end of 1983 things began to unravel. After crashing heavily in practice for the last WEC race of 1983 at Fuji in Japan, Fitzpatrick decided that it was time for him to retire from driving. Henceforth, he would devote his energies to management of his team, for which his sponsor had grand plans. As well as full-blown sports car campaigns in 1984 in America (IMSA) and Europe (WEC), Dominelli wanted to enter the team for the Indianapolis 500, so Fitzpatrick ordered three Marches and five engines for that venture.

As had often been the case, Fitzpatrick went to see Dominelli at his offices early one morning, at 6am, to discuss these projects. Although the company's proprietor was normally at his desk by dawn, this time there was no sign of him, just his English assistant, Mark Yarry, who was busy clearing his desk and packing his possessions into a cardboard box. When Fitzpatrick asked when he could expect to see Dominelli, Yarry told him that the boss wouldn't be coming in that day. Fitzpatrick related to *Motor Sport* what happened next.

'As he [Yarry] opened his desk drawers, I saw he had a gun. I said, "What's the gun for?" He said a big San Diego investor had come into the office the previous day asking for his money. "He says he'll be back this morning, and if he doesn't get it he's going to shoot everyone in the building." At that moment I realised everything, the whole lot, was a fraud. I went cold, and the hair stood up on the back of my neck. I went home and said to Sandra, "It's all over."'

The shortage of money at J. David became obvious to the wider world when some investors began attempting to withdraw their money and found that the company's cheques bounced. Inevitably, panic set in as word spread, causing a snowball effect as more and more clients desperately tried to liquidate their investments. An angry group of them sued Dominelli and, despite his attempts to reassure investors by falsely claiming that the company was solvent, it was forced to declare bankruptcy in February 1984. As no courtroom in San Diego was big enough to accommodate the enormous number of attendees, the bankruptcy hearing was held in the auditorium of the Veterans War Memorial Building.

When his empire collapsed, Dominelli fled to the Caribbean island of

DANIEL UCKERMANN
On the run

Well known in Germany for his overtly luxurious lifestyle, Daniel Uckermann also accumulated his wealth through a Ponzi scheme and spent some of it on motor racing. After accumulating a big collection of Aston Martin, Lamborghini, Ferrari and Maserati sports cars, he started racing in 2013 and soon achieved success by winning the amateur class of the European GT4 Championship in 2015 driving a KTM X-BOW coupé that had been purpose-built for the series. He won pairs of races at Zandvoort in the Netherlands and the Red Bull Ring in Austria in addition to six other podium finishes, and never finished lower than third place.

After securing the title at the Nürburgring in Germany, with two rounds at Misano in Italy still to go, the delighted driver stated: 'I had never expected that we could go for the championship with a brand-new race car. The ZaWotec team had a great vision and I'm extremely happy that we could secure the title before the final round. We will now be focusing on the final races at Misano. I must be able to race with a clear head and with a lot of fun, although we're still pushing to secure the teams' title.'

However, 32-year-old Uckermann never got to compete at the Italian circuit or to collect his championship trophy at the end-of-season prize-giving ceremony. Living up to his nickname of 'Fast Daniel', he went on the run from creditors together with his Romanian wife and child after his investment company, 'Premium Safe Ltd', was exposed as fraudulent. By promising unrealistically high returns of as much as 42 percent per annum, he was alleged to have cheated investors of €100 million.

Writing in *Road & Track* magazine, Graham Goodwin stated: 'German authorities believed that Uckermann has fled to Africa, possibly to the Democratic Republic of Congo.' While there, it was alleged that he had bought the title of 'Honorary Consul', possibly as a precautionary insurance policy. In November 2016, *Sports Car Racing News* reported that after a year as a fugitive, Uckermann had been arrested in Innsbruck and incarcerated in Stadelheim prison awaiting trial. He was later sentenced to several years in prison by the Munich Regional Court. Meanwhile, 3,200 investors suffered the ignominy of potentially having to return profits that they had withdrawn because some of Uckermann's creditors took them to court demanding repayment.

Montserrat, where the one-time darling of San Diego was eventually arrested and returned to the city to face prosecution on charges of bankruptcy, fraud and conspiracy to commit fraud. By 1985, his spectacular fall from grace was complete, 'Captain Money' now unable even to afford his legal bills. At his trial, under a plea-bargain agreement, he pleaded guilty to four felony charges. The *Los Angeles Times* reported that in his statement, written as part of the plea-bargain process, he admitted that he 'had commingled and misused' investors' funds for his personal use, that he had fashioned a complicated business empire to prevent anyone from tracing his assets, that he had lied about his track record as a successful money trader, that he had fabricated investors' statements to show profits that didn't exist, and that he had needed new investor funds to pay off existing clients. The nature of the scam was such that the trial generated unprecedented interest from San Diego's elite and business community, many of whom had been duped. For all of them, there was some sense of closure and relief when, in July 1985, 44-year-old Dominelli was duly given the maximum sentence of 20 years in prison. He was required by the court to repay $82 million but there was never the remotest possibility that he could do so. US District Judge William Enright described Dominelli's crimes as 'a monumental fraud' and also handed down a sentence of 10 years to his girlfriend Nancy Hoover for her role.

It is unclear how many people invested in J. David but bankruptcy officials estimated the figure at between 1,000 and 1,500. By the time of the company's closure in late 1983, it had received over $200 million from which Dominelli and Hoover had taken $80 million.

John Fitzpatrick Racing may have benefited from Dominelli's largesse, which had brought two seasons of considerable success, but the team's proprietor never personally took a penny out of the team or its sponsorship, instead just retaining prize money. Indeed, he and his wife were amongst the many victims because they had also placed some of their hard-earned money with the so-called financier.

In the aftermath of the financial chaos, John Fitzpatrick Racing found itself the subject of intense scrutiny from the authorities. Between them, the FBI, the IRS and anti-racketeering agencies insisted on inspecting every scrap of paper, invoice and bank statement to see if Dominelli had used the team as a vehicle for money laundering, but it was eventually established that the relationship had been entirely legitimate. However, as Dominelli legally owned half of the team, representatives of the investors understandably felt they were now entitled to that half. With the team having been valued at $5 million, the bankruptcy trustees therefore wanted Fitzpatrick to pay $2.5 million — which he couldn't possibly have done. Fortunately for Fitzpatrick, he was represented by 'a brilliant lawyer', a friend of Dick Barbour, and after a year of argument he was able to settle for $250,000 and buy back the other half of his team. The cars and all equipment were shipped back to England, where he rented new premises at Silverstone and continued to compete in 1984 with funding from Skoal Bandit.

While Nancy Hoover was released from prison after just 30 months, Dominelli served ten and a half years before being paroled to his native Chicago in 1995 after suffering a stroke. He died penniless in 2009, with newspaper headlines proclaiming 'Dead at 68' giving a macabre ring to his passing.

JUAN MANUEL FANGIO

In a tight corner

One of the strangest events in the history of
motor racing occurred away from the track
when, in February 1958, a small band of Cuban
revolutionaries from Fidel Castro's movement
kidnapped Juan Manuel Fangio soon after he
had been crowned Formula 1 World Champion
for the fifth time. Unwittingly, one of the
greatest sportsmen of the 20th century became
embroiled in an audacious political stunt.

Motorsport can have a conveniently blinkered approach when it suits
and especially when money is involved. Hence, its history of travelling
to parts of the world where other sports wouldn't dare go, such as South
Africa in the Apartheid era and Bahrain in recent years. In the late 1950s,
Cuba was another such dubious destination.

Cuba at that time was a repressive right-wing dictatorship under the
detested President Fulgencio Batista. He had come to prominence after a
military coup in 1933 and had been first elected President in 1940 on a
populist platform, after which he led an increasingly corrupt regime that
openly did business with money-laundering mobsters. He was ousted in an
election in 1945 but returned to power in 1952 after orchestrating another
coup. Thereafter, his brutal rule turned Cuba into his personal fiefdom,
beset by unrest with opponents jailed and thousands of citizens killed.
Resistance centred around a guerrilla movement that aimed to depose
Batista and was led by Fidel Castro.

The country was also a playground for America's rich and famous, attracted by plentiful hotels, restaurants, casinos and nightlife, with prostitution rife and open. As part of the government's efforts to keep the dollars coming in and to try to present an illusion of normality to the outside world, Batista decided to stage a high-profile international sports car race on a circuit around the streets of the capital. Havana was a vibrant place, almost a Monaco of the Caribbean, and many of the top drivers of the day were attracted by the remuneration, hospitality and scenic location.

The inaugural Cuban Grand Prix was held on 25th February 1957 and amongst the drivers who took part were Juan Manuel Fangio, Stirling Moss, Peter Collins, Carroll Shelby, Eugenio Castellotti, Alfonso de Portago, Phil Hill and Harry Schell. The Malecón circuit, named after the esplanade along the city's seafront that formed part of the track, measured 3.5 miles and the race was planned to be a long one, with 90 laps equating to 312 miles or exactly 500 kilometres. There was a lucrative prize fund and the leading drivers also received start (or appearance) money, which in Fangio's case amounted to $7,000 ($50,000 today), plus generous expenses. Fangio won in a Maserati 300S from the Ferraris of Shelby and de Portago.

The race was so successful in every respect, including propaganda purposes, that it was repeated in 1958, again over the last weekend of February, a public holiday. By this time, Fangio had secured his fifth World Championship title and was without doubt the sport's most famous figure.

Juan Manuel Fangio was born in Balcarce, a small town 200 miles from Buenos Aires, on 24th June 1911, San Juan's day, after which he was named. His parents were Italian immigrants, his father Loreto a builder and his mother Herminia a seamstress. Fangio said, 'We were a humble family, but we never lacked anything, we never missed anything.' At school he excelled at football and his goal-scoring abilities earned him the nickname *El Chueco* ('Bandy Legs'), which stuck throughout his life.

After doing odd jobs for a local garage while still at school, he qualified as a mechanic at the age of 17. One day a customer asked if he would like to be riding mechanic in a race for Model T Fords, an experience that left him transfixed and wanting more. However, his aspirations were twice delayed, first by a serious bout of pneumonia that almost killed him and then by military service. On his return home, his father gave him a loan and he started a small garage business with his friend José Duffard, another talented footballer. At the end of 1934, six years after his first Model T experience, he took up the offer of a loan for a similar car to go racing. By

1938, he had built his own Ford V8-engined special in which he finished third on his début with it at Necochea.

Recognising his talent, supporters in Balcarce raised sufficient funds to buy him a Chevrolet coupé in 1939. His first big victory came in a 10,000-kilometre marathon, the Gran Premio del Norte, in 1940, and he also became Argentine national champion that year and in 1941. Racing in his country was finally halted in 1942 but after a spell working as a taxi driver he resumed his winning ways in 1947 with Chevrolets, by now aged 36. The Argentine government, led by President Juan Perón, a great racing enthusiast, resolved to send a group of drivers to Europe (via a visit to Indianapolis) in 1948 to assess the level of competition. Once there, Fangio was pleased to be invited by Amédée Gordini to drive his Simca-Gordini in the French Grand Prix at Reims, but the little car was outclassed.

The 1949 season saw the Argentine Automobile Club lend Fangio first an older Maserati 4CL and then a new 4CLT. After he beat all the visiting European drivers in the Mar del Plata Grand Prix, the club paid for him to take part in a limited programme of races in Europe. Although his backers chose lower-profile events, they were delighted that his patriotically presented blue-and-yellow Maserati won at San Remo, Pau, Perpignan and Marseille, but funds ran low. Further assistance led to an outing in a Ferrari 166C at Monza in which he beat the works team, and he also won at Albi in the 4CLT, but by the end of the summer the team had no money left and headed home.

For the inaugural Formula 1 World Championship in 1950, Alfa Romeo signed Fangio to join Luigi Fagioli and Giuseppe Farina. After débuting in the non-championship San Remo Grand Prix, where after a poor start he managed to win in teeming rain, he won in Monaco, Belgium and France, putting him at the top of the points table going into the last race at Monza. After his car broke its gearbox, he took over team-mate Piero Taruffi's Alfa but that failed too, leaving Farina to win both the race and the championship.

Staying with Alfa Romeo for 1951, when he also drove for Mercedes-Benz in an unrewarding sportscar programme, Fangio made up for the disappointment of the previous year to become World Champion after winning the Swiss, French and Spanish Grands Prix.

When Alfa Romeo then pulled out, he signed for Maserati for the World Championship, which was now to be held for Formula 2 cars, and for BRM for some non-championship Formula 1 races. The season started well with six wins in South America in a trusty 2-litre supercharged Ferrari 166C, but

During the evening before the Cuban Grand Prix of 1958, the event's star driver, Juan Manuel Fangio, was kidnapped by members of Fidel Castro's '26th of July Movement'.

once in Europe everything went wrong, with the unreliable BRM letting him down at Albi and Dundrod. After that second event, the Ulster Trophy in Northern Ireland, he was due to take part in a Formula 2 race at Monza the next day, flying from Belfast to Milan via Lyons. Bad weather delayed the first leg of his journey and he missed his connecting flight, so he drove a borrowed car through the night and arrived at Monza just in time for the race. As he hadn't practised, he had to start his Maserati A6GCM from the back of the grid and was clawing his way through the field when he touched a straw bale, lost control and was thrown out of the car in the resulting somersault. The accident, which was put down to fatigue, landed him in hospital for six weeks and ended his season.

Back in a Maserati in January 1953 in time for the first Argentine Grand Prix, he showed that his enforced absence hadn't blunted his ability and soon took the lead in his A6GCM-53 before its fragile gearbox let him down. It wasn't until the season-ending Italian Grand Prix that he was finally able to win a World Championship round.

Mercedes planned to enter Formula 1 in 1954 and signed Fangio. The new team wasn't ready for the first two Grands Prix, in Argentina and Belgium, so he drove Maserati's new 250F in these races and won both. When the Mercedes W196 was ready, in 'streamliner' form for the French Grand Prix at Reims, he won on its début and followed up with victories in Germany, Switzerland and Italy, taking his second title in style.

He carried the momentum into 1955, taking another title after four wins. However, Mercedes withdrew at the end of the season after the innocent involvement of one of its cars in the Le Mans tragedy, when Pierre Levegh's 300 SLR was propelled into the crowd, killing the driver and 83 spectators, and injuring 180 more.

Fangio moved to Ferrari for 1956 and won another title, but he didn't enjoy his season with the team and returned to Maserati for 1957. After another home victory in Argentina, he won in Monaco, France and Germany to claim his fifth championship crown. The German Grand Prix at the fearsome Nürburgring was his last and arguably most famous Formula 1 success after an extraordinary recovery drive. His lead of 28 seconds turned into a deficit of 28 seconds due to a botched pitstop, after which he broke the lap record nine times in his efforts to overhaul the Ferraris of British drivers Peter Collins and Mike Hawthorn to win by 3.6 seconds. Afterwards, he stated: 'I never want to drive like that again.'

Fangio's performance at the Nürburgring undoubtedly influenced his decision to decline offers from other works teams and compete as an independent in 1958. For the first time in four years, he failed to win the Argentine Grand Prix, although he did claim the *Formule Libre* Buenos Aires Grand Prix a fortnight later. After that, he headed off to Cuba for the sportscar race.

Fangio was inevitably the star attraction for the second Cuban Grand Prix, especially as his 47th birthday was approaching and it was likely that he would soon retire. Driving a powerful Maserati 450S loaned by American entrant Temple Buell, he duly qualified on pole position.

In the 12 months since the first race, Cuba had changed dramatically, with Castro's resistance movement having gained momentum against increasing repression. Behind its apparent glitz, Havana wasn't a comfortable, happy or secure place. With the country now teetering on the brink of revolution, the political environment was becoming increasingly unstable and the illusion surrounding the big race was about to be shattered.

In common with many of the other drivers, Fangio was staying in the

This imaginary scene of Fangio during his abduction filled the front page of an Italian newspaper.

luxurious Hotel Lincoln, which ran on American money to such an extent that at one time the entire building was painted as a dollar bill. Just before 9.00pm on the Sunday evening before Monday's race, Fangio was in the hotel's lobby near its busy bar with several friends and competitors. As the most popular sporting icon in the whole of South America, he was inevitably the centre of attention and fans and autograph hunters surrounded him as he headed for dinner with Alejandro de Tomaso, his manager Marcello Giambertone and mechanic Guerino Bertocchi.

Unknown to him, the onlookers included a group of revolutionaries who were waiting for him. As he stepped forward to sign what he assumed would be yet another autograph, he was surprised to be accosted by a bearded and nervous young man shakily brandishing a Colt 45 pistol rather than proffering a pen. As the gun was pressed into his ribs, Fangio's first reaction was that it was a joke, until he was politely told that he was being kidnapped. Three henchmen in the lobby disarmed the personal bodyguard that the government had provided for Fangio's protection and ushered their hostage outside to a group of three waiting cars. More accomplices armed with machine guns pointed at the door of the hotel to keep the astonished crowd at a distance while they made their escape. As some of the other competitors also had armed bodyguards, the World Champion's main concern was that a gun battle could break out, but to his relief there was no gunfire.

Fangio was bundled into a black Plymouth with a machine gun trained on his face until he told the man holding it to put it down because he wouldn't offer any resistance. So as not to attract attention, the Plymouth, with the hostage ordered to crouch down out of sight, was driven with the two accompanying cars slowly through the streets of Havana to a small villa in a quiet suburb. As Fangio described it, 'We went into a room where there was a woman with a small child. The woman asked me to give an autograph to her son. I put down the date and the child's name and signed it. We went by car to a second house, then a third, where I was kept overnight.'

The group of revolutionaries numbered ten people. Their leader was Oscar Lucero, who masterminded covert activities in Havana, and the several women amongst them included Lucero's wife. They explained to Fangio that they were members of Castro's '26th of July Movement' — named after a 1953 attempt to overthrow Batista — and had tried but failed to abduct him at the previous year's race. They provided a dinner of steak, eggs and potatoes, and as they all settled down to eat, they explained their motives. By capturing the biggest name in motorsport, they would draw worldwide attention to their struggle to topple the regime.

Relaxed now that he knew they meant no harm to him, Fangio listened sympathetically to the rebels, many of whom were students. He heard about their experience of horrific repression and violence, which included the murder of friends and relatives, for it had become commonplace for dissenters to be gunned down in the streets or simply to 'disappear'. They told him of the strict censorship imposed on the media and how human rights and freedoms were constantly abused by the authorities. In his own words, Fangio said that he retired to bed 'sleeping like a blessed one', with his only fear now that he might get caught up in a shoot-out between his kidnappers and the police if they succeeded in finding him.

Back at the Hotel Lincoln, security measures had been increased and each competing driver was now assigned his own personal guard. As the next-biggest name after Fangio, Stirling Moss was kept under special surveillance throughout the night, with a watchman disrupting his sleep by regularly knocking on the door of his hotel bedroom to make sure he was still safely in his bed. 'It was a very disturbing night,' Moss recalled. 'Fangio told the rebels, "You mustn't take Stirling because he's on his honeymoon" — which was a lie of course, but nevertheless was very decent of him.'

After capturing Fangio, the rebels had been quick to make sure that the news agencies and radio stations knew about it. The story caused a sensation around the world and the newspaper headlines the next morning proved how successful their strategy had been in moving the spotlight away from Batista's glamorous motor race to the politics of an unaccountable government with a long history of crimes against its own people.

Although the police had initiated a big manhunt to track down the kidnappers and had set up roadblocks all over the city, their efforts failed to provide any clue about the World Champion's location. Batista, refusing to be outdone despite the unfavourable news spreading across the world, was in no doubt that the race had to go ahead as planned, in front of a 150,000-strong crowd. Prompted by unfounded rumours of Fangio's impending release, the organisers delayed the start for 90 minutes but eventually the grid assembled without him, with Maurice Trintignant slipping into the empty seat of his blue Maserati.

The hostage, meanwhile, continued to be treated respectfully in comfortable surroundings. His kidnappers even supplied him with a television so that he could follow the race, although he later said that he would have preferred not to watch it, knowing that he should have been participating — and because of how it unfolded. Before Fangio settled down in front of the television, Faustino Pérez, another of Castro's senior men in Havana, visited to apologise for the kidnap and to assure him that he would be freed once the race was over.

Moss soon took the lead in his Ferrari followed by the American Masten Gregory in another Ferrari, while Trintignant fell way back in Fangio's car. Almost from the start, one of the cars had trailed oil from a split pipe all around the circuit and by the end of the fifth lap there was a liberal coating of it on nearly every corner. Next time around, an inexperienced Cuban driver, 26-year-old Armando Garcia Cifuentes, lost control of his yellow-and-black Ferrari on a bend next to the American Embassy and ploughed into the crowd, tragically killing seven spectators and injuring almost 40 more. As people escaped from the scene of devastation, they swarmed across the track despite the danger from cars still racing at full speed, the police powerless to control them. After just six laps, the race was stopped and Moss declared the winner with Gregory second and Shelby third.

Castro's men, mindful of the need not to come across as the murdering bandits that Batista made them out to be, now had the problem of how best to safely release their hostage. They were concerned that government thugs might kill Fangio in rigged circumstances to make it look as if the kidnappers were responsible. It was Fangio himself who suggested that the safest and most elegant way would be to involve Raul Lynch, Argentina's ambassador in Havana, and later that evening, after 29 hours in captivity, he was duly delivered to the apartment of an Argentinian military attaché for the handover.

The rebels again apologised for inconveniencing him and called him an honorary member of the revolution, while Fangio in return introduced them as his 'new Cuban friends'. Before making their escape, they handed him a letter addressed to the government of Argentina expressing their regret in having to use the great man for political purposes and promising him that, when the revolution was successful, he would be invited back to Cuba by their new government as a guest of honour. Fangio himself was philosophical about the experience saying: 'Well, this is one more adventure. If what the rebels did was in a good cause, then I, as an Argentine, accept it.'

In terms of propaganda, the entire episode was a disaster for Batista. Not only had the worldwide headlines shone a spotlight over his ugly dictatorship, but his failure to track down the captors looked like he was losing his grip. Recriminations began and blame started to be apportioned. Cifuentes was still fighting for his life in hospital when he was charged with manslaughter, although the lack of crowd control didn't result in any action against the event's organising body, which happened to be headed by Batista's brother-in-law.

Within nine months of the kidnap, Batista fled the country into exile and Castro's revolution entered its final stages. Another Cuban Grand Prix had been planned for 1959 but it was abandoned, although a low-key race was reinstated the following year at a new venue using the service roads of a disused military airfield outside Havana. The main event, titled the *Gran Premio Libertad* (Freedom Grand Prix), was again won by Moss, this time in a Maserati 'Birdcage' privately entered by the Camoradi team, with Pedro Rodríguez in a NART Ferrari 250 Testa Rossa a distant second. Sadly, this race was also fated, this time by the death of Ettore Chimeri after he crashed his Ferrari through a barrier and plunged 150 feet into a ravine. Thereafter, racing ceased altogether as Cuba, now in the grip of a different form of extremism under Castro's socialist leadership, became increasingly isolated from the Free World during the Cold War years.

Fangio later told the media that he bore no ill will towards his captors and admitted that he sympathised with what they had done and with their concerns that the huge sums of money spent on the race would have been better used to help the half-million unemployed in Cuba. Castro was true to his word and did invite Fangio to return once he was in power, but that didn't happen until 1981, by which time the great champion was honorary president of Mercedes-Benz Argentina and used the trip to sign a deal to supply trucks to the Cuban government. One of the men he had encountered while in captivity, Faustino Pérez, was now a minister and looked after him during his stay.

Afterwards, Fangio flew on to New York. where he was paid $1,000 to appear on the Ed Sullivan TV show. During his interview with Sullivan, he said: 'I had won the World Championship five times but what made me big in the United States was being kidnapped in Cuba — which I thought was a bit strange!'

ENRIQUE MANSILLA
Dire straights

In the final year of Fangio's career, Enrique Mansilla was born in Buenos Aires and would become another Argentinian racing driver to be kidnapped. On the British racing scene, he was a fierce rival and team-mate of Ayrton Senna in Formula Ford 1600 in 1981, and in Formula 3 with West Surrey Engineering in 1982. That year he almost won the championship despite sponsorship difficulties resulting from the economic ramifications of the Falklands War, but his performances still earned him the coveted prize of a Formula 1 test with McLaren. After an unsuccessful 1983 season in European Formula 2, he went to America to race in Can-Am in 1984 and in CART Indycar in 1985, but then his career petered out.

After retirement from racing, Mansilla became a gold and diamond prospector in Africa. While in Liberia during the country's civil war, he was kidnapped and held captive for five months by President Charles Taylor's henchmen. As a foreign national, he became something of a political pawn, but his high profile probably helped to save his life. After his release, he surprisingly stayed in Liberia and continued in the same line of work before returning to Argentina.

CHAPTER 20
LUIS FONTES
'Manslaughter by Car'

A British racing driver, aviator and powerboat racer of Brazilian parentage, Fontés was a virtual unknown when he won the Le Mans 24 Hours in 1935. Despite his studious appearance, he had a reputation as a daredevil and hell raiser whose drunken antics got him into trouble with the law on numerous occasions and tragically culminated in him killing a young motorcyclist for which he was sent to prison for manslaughter.

The son of an English mother and a Brazilian father, Luis Fontés was born in Hampstead, London on Boxing Day in 1912. His father, Antonio, had prospered during the Brazilian rubber boom and subsequently became a property developer, shipping tycoon and London-based government official. His father, who didn't believe in the formalities of marriage, started several families and after his death, when Luis was just one year old, left generous legacies to the mothers and their respective children. So it was that on his 21st birthday in 1933, Luis inherited a fortune that enabled him to take up motor racing and begin flying lessons, qualifying as a pilot the following year.

Early cars included two MGs, a J2 and a J3, the latter the car in which he started competing. Quickly showing himself to be an incredibly competitive driver, the young novice bought an Invicta S-type with which he had several outings, including the 1934 Tourist Trophy at the Ards circuit in Northern Ireland, where he came up against some of the fastest British drivers of the day. Despite being thwarted by engine maladies, he greatly impressed rival entrant Arthur Fox.

Pictured at Brooklands in 1935 perched on his Alfa Romeo Monza, Luis Fontés may have looked earnest and studious but he was a heavy-drinking tearaway who ended up in prison for manslaughter after crashing into a motorcyclist at high speed.

The wealthy newcomer's racing career took off when, still a relative unknown, he ambitiously hired an ex-Scuderia Ferrari Alfa Romeo 2.3-litre 8C Monza from John Cobb, after the engine in his own MG had failed, and sensationally went on to win the 1935 International Trophy race at Brooklands. He had specifically requested the racing number 13 and then painted the car in the generally accepted 'unlucky' green and reportedly his post-race party was memorable.

Fontés was fast becoming the 1935 season's driving sensation and on the strength of his performances Arthur Fox decided to take a chance by inviting the young ace to drive his ex-works 4.5-litre Lagonda Rapide in the Le Mans 24 Hours. Fontés shared the car with John Hindmarsh, a Hawker Siddeley test pilot and successful Talbot team driver, and despite relentless rain and a delay after incurring damage from debris from another car's accident, the pair took the lead at 10.00am on Sunday, with six hours of the race to go. They survived a late puncture but of far greater concern was very low oil pressure due to a leaking sump that forced Fontés to pit several times. With no time to attempt a repair to the leak and knowing that they would be disqualified if they topped up the oil level, Fox had no alternative but to instruct his drivers to keep going. It was only their skill in using their aviation experience and mechanical sympathy that allowed them to complete the final stages, nursing the car to victory at an average speed of 77.84mph with its gearbox locked in top gear. It's doubtful that the car would have been able to complete another lap of the race as the sump contained only half a litre of oil instead of the normal 12. As this was the 13th running of the race, Fontés had again defied conventional superstitions. He was also the youngest winner of the race, a record that wasn't broken until Alex Wurz won in 1996.

The press reported the impressive performance of the gangly 23-year-old whose bespectacled appearance made him an unlikely looking racing driver. Fellow racer Sammy Davis wrote in *The Autocar* that he 'resembled an earnest student' and added that after a race he became 'the wildest of wild men, and took the art of "making whoopee" to new heights'.

In the meantime, Fontés had bought Cobb's three-year-old Alfa Monza and competed regularly with it that year in high-profile races in Britain and Ireland. Highlights included third place in the Mannin Moar on the Isle of Man, victory in the inaugural Limerick Grand Prix and second place in the Phoenix Park Trophy Handicap in Dublin, his last outing in the car.

A few weeks later he recorded his first success in an air race with his new Miles Hawk Speed Six when he took second place in the Grosvenor Challenge Cup at Leicester. However, a near disaster followed in September in the 14th King's Cup Jubilee Air Race, a 1,000-mile race around Britain, when a broken oil pipe forced him to crash land in County Durham. There was significant damage to the aircraft but the pilot escaped without injury.

The next motor race he entered was the BRDC 500-mile event at Brooklands in a newly acquired Squire single-seater but he was so frustrated with its fragility, which caused him to retire after 54 laps, that he sold it back to the works. To replace it, he ordered a new Alfa Romeo *Tipo* B but sadly he would never have the opportunity to race the car.

A man of contradictions and something of a Jekyll and Hyde character, Luis Fontés's post-race celebrations were memorable and had led to a reputation as a heavy drinker and hell raiser. His antics were infamous and included balancing on a window ledge of a four-storey building with a girl on his shoulders and another when police chased his Invicta round and round Trafalgar Square in London and only caught him when he ran out of petrol. Another led to a conviction under the Railways Act after an incident when passengers on the Torbay Express heard footsteps on the roof of the carriage and pulled the alarm cord. As the train slowed to a halt, Fontés scrambled down and ran off over fields, chased by the driver and fireman and eventually by police.

ANDY SUTCLIFFE
Don't get fuelled again

Andy Sutcliffe was another British racing driver who had a habit of driving while intoxicated and he became embroiled in a drunken car chase with police.

Born in Mildenhall, Suffolk, he began his racing career in 1969 with a Ginetta G12 before going on to compete in Formula 3 with some success in the period 1970–73 winning four races in 1972, the year he also made his Formula 2 début in a works GRD. He raised sponsorship to compete in a one-off race in a works March 732 the following season at Karlskoga in Sweden and made an impression by out-qualifying Lotus Grand Prix star and local hero Ronnie Peterson and finishing third in his heat before retiring from the final. He contested the 1974 European Formula 2 Championship in another March 732, ending up tenth in the standings, his best results a promising fifth in Barcelona and a career-best third in the rain at Pau.

This marked the zenith of his career because his expected entry in that year's British Grand Prix in a private Brabham BT42 never materialised. In 1977 he managed to secure sponsorship to compete in supposedly five Grands Prix in a RAM Racing March 761 but by this time he was race-rusty and his backing was withdrawn after he failed to pre-qualify for the British Grand Prix on his first time out.

Sutcliffe turned to work as a market gardener in Kent and developed a severe drink problem. He was so intoxicated when he left his local pub in Pluckley on 14th April 2006 that he fell over in the car park before getting into his car and driving off. Alerted by an onlooker, police found his car up a grass bank but before they could apprehend the driver he reversed down the bank and sped off, swerving all over the road. At one point Sutcliffe stopped the car and reversed it into the front of the police car before driving off again. The chase only ended when he ploughed through a hedge and into a field. When breathalysed, he was found to be four times over the legal limit. Although he didn't go to prison, Maidstone Crown Court heard that he had previous convictions for alcohol-related offences, including drink driving, and gave him a 12-month sentence suspended for two years and banned him from driving for four years.

His short racing career came to an abrupt end on 6th October 1935. After having too much to drink, he indulged in a race on public roads in Warwickshire against an unidentified rival. Over the course of nine miles there were several reports of reckless driving with Fontés often on the wrong side of the road and tragically this led to a head-on collision with a 19-year-old motorcyclist, Reginald Mordike, who died of his injuries the following day. One report of the accident stated that it had occurred just after a humpback bridge that had launched both speeding cars into the air.

Neither driver stopped at the scene but Fontés was forced to pull in at a nearby garage to have a deflated tyre repaired. When he was arrested, he was found by a doctor to be driving under the influence of alcohol and remanded on bail.

When the case was tried at the Warwickshire Assizes in December, he pleaded guilty but Justice Herbert du Parcq was determined to make an example of the irresponsible young man and on learning of his previous record of four driving offences felt that he had been treated with 'deplorable leniency'. The verdict was manslaughter for which he received a three-year prison sentence and a 10-year driving ban. The case generated extensive coverage, with *The Times* newspaper, under the headline 'Manslaughter by Car', reporting that 'Fontes desired to express his deep regret that his conduct should have resulted as it had done'.

The withdrawal of his driving licence meant that he was no longer eligible for an RAC competition licence, so on his early release from prison in March 1938 he maintained a low profile and ran a speedboat business in Torquay. Unable to race cars, he had the engine from his Alfa Romeo *Tipo B* installed in a Ventnor speedboat that he named *Miss Torbay* and piloted with some success in the British Hydroplane Racing Club Championship.

Having gained a new aviator's certificate, he also resumed air racing and reignited his passion for flying by a fine fourth place in a race from London to the Isle of Man. The outbreak of the Second World War brought an end to this pastime and after his application to join the RAF was turned down he signed up, as did several motor racing contemporaries, with the Air Transport Auxiliary as a civilian pilot ferrying military aircraft between airfields and maintenance units, soon becoming First Officer. On 12th October 1940 he was delivering a Wellington bomber to an RAF storage unit at Llandow in South Wales when the aircraft stalled after an engine failed while circling the airfield and crashed in a field near the neighbouring village of Llysworney. The 1935 Le Mans winner died in the wreckage aged just 27.

CHAPTER 21

JONATHAN FRANCE

Lapping up a life of luxury

This rogue Yorkshire scrap metal dealer turned motor racing entrepreneur and team owner repeatedly broke laws by running companies while barred from being a director. To fund his opulent lifestyle, he fraudulently siphoned more than £6 million from his businesses and diverted company cash and assets into his own pockets, using funds that should have gone to creditors after he was declared bankrupt. He was jailed for multi-million-pound fraud, money laundering and later for receiving stolen goods.

Jonathan France established Mansfield-based Embassy Racing in 2003, initially in conjunction with the Xero Competition team. France headed the EFS Group, which had grown from a family scrap metal and recycling business called Eric France and Son into what was described as a full 'metal solutions' operation with an annual turnover of £100 million. Having first dipped his toes in the sport as a sponsor, France decided to run his own racing team and entered the British GT Championship, the country's premier sports car series.

After a difficult first season with a Chevrolet Corvette punctuated by accidents and mechanical failures, Embassy Racing expanded to become an independent operation and switched to a Porsche 996 GT3 RSR for 2005. With a much more competitive car at their disposal, Neil Cunningham and Ben Collins, who later became notable for his role as 'The Stig' on BBC TV's *Top Gear*, were immediately on the pace and won the third round of the year at Knockhill in Scotland. A succession of podium finishes followed, including another win at Silverstone, and at the end of the year they occupied joint second place in the drivers' standings.

Embassy Racing took a one-year sabbatical in 2006 in order to prepare for an entry into the International Le Mans Series for sports prototypes the following season, when the team raced customer versions of cars built by both Pilbeam and Radical. After unfruitful relationships with both manufacturers, the ambitious outfit decided to make the move from entrant to fully fledged constructor in its own right for 2008. France said he had always 'dreamed of building his own car since he was a child' and 'simply didn't want to be a customer again'.

Despite the team principal's profound lack of experience at this level, his lofty aspirations were clear from the outset when he engaged Peter Elleray — the brains behind the Bentley Speed 8 LMP1 prototype that won Le Mans in 2003 — to design his new carbon-fibre chassis, designated the WF01, the 'WF' representing the initials of William France, his son. He also voiced his intention to create a motorsport engineering operation of excellence along the lines of top-ranking and hugely successful British enterprises like Prodrive and RML (Ray Mallock Ltd). Embassy Racing knew that it had to prove itself at this level before selling its engineering skills and, hopefully, its cars as cost-effective alternatives to the benchmark but very expensive Porsche RS Spyder.

Embassy Racing entered two of its Zytek-powered WF01 cars in the LMP2 class of the five-round 2008 Le Mans Series. Although late delivery of parts from suppliers delayed the new challengers, optimism abounded and lead driver Warren Hughes, in his second season with the team, had high hopes. However, although the team managed to complete two cars just in time, they were virtually untried when they arrived at the opening round at Barcelona's Catalunya circuit. In what was basically a very public test session, the elegant Embassy WF01s made steady progress through the weekend until a steering component failed on one car, leading to the withdrawal of the other on the grounds of safety. This was a typical hurdle in a frustrating season that was blighted by unreliability, although there were flashes of promise, including a first championship point as a manufacturer at Monza and fourth place in class at the Nürburgring. At mid-season, the Le Mans 24 Hours should have been the highlight of the team's year but its single-car entry retired after 15 hours.

At the final round of the Le Mans Series at Silverstone, Hughes missed out on an LMP2 podium finish when a time penalty handed to his team-mate Jonny Kane for ignoring the red light at the end of the pitlane saw them lose third place in the class. All the same, both WF01s finished in the points for the first time and the season ended on a positive note that left the team looking forward to proving the car's undoubted potential the following year.

Only two weeks after the Silverstone race, however, France dropped the bombshell that he was closing Embassy Racing's doors. It was not only an enormous shock to his staff but also to the entire endurance racing community and all those who had listened to his bullish predictions.

As well as becoming a racing car constructor, France had also embarked on a seemingly unnecessary distraction by deciding to enter a pair of Triumph Daytona 675 motorcycles in the junior Supersport category of the British Superbike Championship, complete with factory support. The team operated as a separate division of Embassy Racing for two seasons before its equally sudden and unexpected closure.

At first, Jonathan France suggested that he planned to mothball Embassy Racing only temporarily due to the difficult economic climate, but in March 2009 it was announced that the team's entire assets were to be sold in an online auction. The reasons behind the closure were indeed money-related but the prevailing global financial crisis was a handy excuse to obscure a rather different reality. France had been declared personally bankrupt in November 2008 with accumulated debts of more than £7 million after the collapse not only of Embassy Racing but also of the family scrap metals business, Eric France and Son (Metals) Ltd, four years earlier. In addition, mismanagement behind the insolvency of the scrap metals business had resulted in France receiving a 14-year ban from acting as a company director, effective from 2004, so he had been operating Embassy Racing illegally.

A new racing entity, Team WFR, emerged for the 2009 season and entered a Ginetta G50 in the British GT Championship for two drivers, one of whom was Jody Firth, Embassy Racing's team manager during 2008. France — continuing to ignore the restrictions placed upon him — operated and controlled Team WFR, although it was Firth whom he listed as company director. Towards the end of the year, the team also gave one Embassy WF01 a short-lived comeback at the Silverstone finale of the Le Mans Series, with Firth joining Darren Manning and Warren Hughes behind the wheel. The car's potential was again demonstrated by the trio finishing fourth in class.

Showing further disregard for the law, at this time France also established a new metal-trading firm, JKL (Wakefield) Ltd, with Firth named as the company director. With a certain inevitability, this business was declared insolvent in 2013 with debts totalling tens of millions of pounds, most of which, according to the liquidators, represented unpaid VAT and PAYE/National Insurance contributions. By this time France had also widened his motorsport activities into two businesses, WFR Ltd and WFR Holdings Ltd, with another associate, Graham Myles Schofield, given as their official director, and they duly followed into liquidation.

As well as illegally running these businesses, France was also pillaging money from JKL and diverting it to various business and personal accounts in his name. He falsified company cheques, invoices and other paperwork to make it look as if payments totalling £6 million had been made to bona fide creditors of his companies when in fact they had been spent on luxurious living. He bought a five-bedroom house in a village near Huddersfield and furnished it lavishly. He splashed out on a variety of expensive cars, including three Aston Martins, two Ferraris, a Rolls-Royce and a McLaren. Other high-value purchases included Rolex watches, jewellery, paintings and a collection of fine wines.

Following Embassy Racing's collapse and France's personal bankruptcy, his discredited affairs had been put in the hands of an official receiver and trustee in bankruptcy. With Schofield's help, France repeatedly failed to disclose to them the true extent of his property and possessions, by engineering false and misleading explanations that tricked them into believing that he had no means of raising funds to pay back his debts. A particular example concerned the concealment of a 'bonus payment' of £850,000 in January 2011. It all caught up with him in 2013 with the conclusion of an investigation by the government's Insolvency Service that inevitably led to criminal charges. Although he claimed to be penniless, almost £7 million of assets were subsequently recovered by the trustee in bankruptcy.

In July 2018 at Leeds Crown Court, 46-year-old France pleaded guilty to four counts of fraudulently transferring property, three counts of acting as a director while bankrupt, and one count each of failing to disclose property to the official receiver or trustee. He was also found guilty of perjury, fraudulent trading, false accounting and money laundering. He was jailed for 10 years as well being disqualified, again, from being a company director, this time for 12 years.

Also in court were his two accomplices: Jody Firth admitted money laundering and helping France run a company despite being bankrupt and was jailed for five years four months while Schofield also pleaded guilty to

A catalogue of
legal and financial
misdemeanours lay
behind Jonathan
France's exploits
in motor racing
and earned him ten
years in prison.

Jonathan France's
Embassy Racing even
built its own car, the
Embassy WF01, and
raced it in the Le Mans
24 Hours of 2008,
driven by Warren
Hughes, Jonny Kane
and Joey Foster.

161

money laundering and was jailed for two and a half years. Their association with France's wrongdoing went back to at least 2008, the Insolvency Service having discovered that in the months before France's bankruptcy that year they had received £180,000 between them in cash and assets from his personal estate to hide the money from his creditors.

In a separate case, six men were jailed in December 2020 for a major copper-wire theft conspiracy that had occurred over a period of 17 months. In a well-choreographed and organised crime, the gang stole almost 57 miles of valuable hard-drawn copper wire belonging to the railway network and electricity distribution companies. During 250 separate thefts, they cut down live electric power cables before stripping them and leaving 45,000 homes without power across northern England. Gang members would deliver the wiring to business premises operated by Jonathan France and the appropriately named John Crookes, who arranged the onward sale of the high-value metal.

Since 2013 it has been an offence to buy scrap metal for cash and dealers are obliged to verify identity documentation before they buy from anyone. However, Crookes got round this by using fake identity documents, including driving licences, and software that falsified records despite complying with the necessary legislation. France bought most of the stolen wiring and sent a series of text messages offering to arrange collection of it and promising to pay for it 'in reddies', meaning cash. As he was bankrupt at the time, France hid his illegal earnings from creditors by using an associate's bank account and ultimately deposited over £500,000 by this means. In return for keeping five percent of the money, his associate withdrew cash and handed it over to France. The net closed in when two banks, Barclays and Lloyds, became suspicious and froze the accounts.

In a further appearance at Leeds Crown Court in December 2020, France had two and a half years added to the 10-year prison sentence he was already serving after pleading guilty to handling stolen goods and false accounting. By this time, it appeared that he had only £6,000 of assets left from the proceeds of his crimes, but yet another secret was revealed in February 2021 when it was established that he had a pension fund, so the Judge ordered this to be confiscated upon reaching maturity six years hence in order to raise around £92,000 to go towards repaying his debts.

CHAPTER 22
BERTRAND GACHOT
Road rage

In 1991, Bertrand Gachot, a promising young Formula 1 driver, was involved in a so-called road-rage incident with a London taxi driver. After an altercation involving illegal and dangerous use of tear gas, the impetuous young man was jailed and his moment of madness almost left his career in ruins. It also had far-reaching implications for the world of Grand Prix racing as it set in motion a chain of events that changed the course of its history by opening the door for another driver who would become a record-breaking legend of the sport.

Bertrand Gachot was born in Luxembourg on 23rd December 1962 to a German mother and a French father who was a diplomat who worked for the European Commission. Although a French national, his cosmopolitan background often led to debate as to his nationality, which he did nothing to dispel by incorporating the EU flag in the design of his crash helmet, although throughout his career he raced under a Belgian licence.

A relatively late starter in racing terms, Gachot was 15 when he began karting and a 21-year-old university student by the time he enrolled on a course at the well-respected Winfield Racing School at Paul Ricard in the South of France. Each year Winfield's best driver received a prize, the Volant Elf (sponsored by the French national oil company), which provided a fully paid season in Formula Renault. Although Gachot narrowly missed out on the prize to Éric Bernard, the bug had well and truly bitten. He gave up his studies to concentrate on racing and competed in Formula Ford 1600 with a Reynard 84FF during 1984, concluding a promising season with third place at Brands Hatch in the 1984 Formula Ford Festival, a knock-out competition that attracted the cream of young hopefuls not only on the British scene but from Europe and even beyond.

In 1985, Gachot transferred to a Van Diemen RF85 run by Pacific Racing and won two championships, the ultra-competitive RAC British Formula Ford 1600 Championship — after an acrimonious battle with Mark Blundell — and the EFDA Euroseries. When both drivers graduated to Formula Ford 2000 for 1986, Gachot, still with Pacific Racing but now driving a Reynard 86SF, won the British title while Blundell took the European one. For 1987, with Marlboro backing, Gachot progressed to the prestigious British Formula 3 Championship with Dick Bennetts's crack West Surrey Engineering team and won three races to finish runner-up to champion Johnny Herbert. He was able to step up again in 1988 by competing in the FIA European Formula 3000 Vhampionship with a Spirit Racing Reynard 88D and ended the season fifth in the standings, with a pair of second places his best results.

By this time Gachot was on the radar of the Formula 1 teams and considered to be one of the sport's hottest young prospects. For 1989 he signed to drive alongside Stefan Johansson at newly formed Onyx, having played a key role in attracting the team's Moneytron sponsorship from Belgian businessman Jean-Pierre Van Rossem (see Chapter 58), to whom he had been introduced by Belgian racer Pascal Witmeur. At this time in Formula 1, there were as many as 39 cars fighting for grid positions, which meant that the newer and lesser teams had to 'pre-qualify' for the privilege of being allowed to participate in the official and still oversubscribed qualifying sessions. As a new team, Onyx struggled. Progress was so slow that Gachot was unable to break through the pre-qualifying barrier at the first six rounds, which meant packing up for the weekend by 10.00am on a Friday morning.

It wasn't until the French Grand Prix at Paul Ricard that Gachot made his first Formula 1 start, from an encouraging 11th on the grid, two places ahead of his experienced team-mate. Even more impressive was that in the race he was running in the top six when electrical woes dropped him to an unlucky 13th at the finish. Also making their Grand Prix débuts that day were two young Winfield contemporaries — Éric Bernard at Larrousse and Jean Alesi at Tyrrell — whom he had encountered at the circuit six years earlier. After this breakthrough, and despite heroic efforts in hauling the recalcitrant Onyx ORE-1 into four of the next five races, he was unceremoniously fired by the team's eccentric sponsor. Gachot's privately aired grievances about the lack of much-needed testing time had been

Racing for Jordan in 1991, Bertrand Gachot looked to have an assured
future in Formula 1, especially after setting fastest lap in the
Hungarian Grand Prix, where this photo was taken.

reported in the press and Van Rossem took exception, replacing him with JJ
Lehto (see Chapter 59) for the last four races of the season. For the last two
races, Gachot managed to find a berth at Rial Racing, a tiny and even less
competitive team that was soon to be disbanded, but he failed to qualify.

A move to Coloni for 1990 initially looked more encouraging but turned
out to be a case of 'out of the frying pan and into the fire'. The single-
car team had exclusive use of a Subaru-badged flat-12 engine designed by
renowned engineer Carlo Chiti and built by Motori Moderni but the unit
was underpowered and overweight. At the first race, the gear-selector rod
snapped on Gachot's first flying lap of pre-qualifying and this proved to be
a portent of things to come, with the next seven outings also progressing
no further than Friday's preliminaries. Wanting to limit damage to its
brand, Subaru withdrew after the British Grand Prix, forcing the under-
resourced team to turn to the Cosworth DFR V8 engine. Combined with
the withdrawal of his old team, Onyx, which promoted Gachot to the main
qualifying sessions, this led to a marked improvement in performance but it
still wasn't sufficient for him to make the grid for any of the remaining races
of a thoroughly dispiriting season.

For the previous 18 months, Eddie Jordan, a flamboyant Irish former racing driver turned team owner, had been working on a plan to break into Formula 1. He had achieved great success as an entrant first in Formula 3, where his driver, Johnny Herbert, had beaten Gachot to the 1987 title, and in Formula 3000, where Jean Alesi had delivered the 1989 crown. Jordan prepared his Formula 1 plans with the misplaced confidence that one of his major backers, the Camel cigarette brand, would continue to support his fledgling team, but when that didn't happen he decided to go it alone anyway, at great personal risk. Until this point, Jordan's team had been able to rely on customer chassis from companies such as Ralt and Reynard, but that wasn't an option for Formula 1: Jordan had to become a constructor in his own right. This resulted in the Gary Anderson-designed Jordan-Ford 191's presentation to the media at the team's Silverstone-based factory in plain emerald green in deference to the owner's origins and the fact that there was minimal commercial sponsorship for the two-car team.

For his drivers, Eddie Jordan signed the experienced but erratic Andrea de Cesaris, who was always well-funded, and decided that Gachot would be a good choice for the other car. Despite his miserable first two seasons at the top level, Gachot was as enthusiastic as ever and determined to show what he could do. As a new entrant, the Jordan team initially had to pre-qualify but Gachot always managed not only to do that successfully but also to get through proper qualifying as well. After some early-season reliability problems, the beautifully elegant Jordan cars, now resplendent in a very attractive green-and-blue livery with primary sponsorship from 7Up, proved competitive. At the fifth race, in Canada, Gachot claimed his first World Championship points with fifth place, while De Cesaris completed a great day for the team by finishing fourth.

By this stage of his career, Gachot had also taken part in a few sportscar races, including his first Le Mans 24 Hours, with Mazda in 1990. Pleased with his performance, Mazda invited him back to race its unusual rotary-powered 787B in the 1991 event, which took place three weeks after the Canadian Grand Prix. Partnered by Johnny Herbert and Volker Weidler, and now brimming with confidence, Gachot played his part in achieving an unexpected and famous victory, the first by a Japanese manufacturer.

Back on the Formula 1 trail, Gachot had justifiable expectations of being able to do even better through the second half of the season. Sixth places in Britain and Germany followed on the back of his Le Mans success, and at the next race, in Hungary, he even managed to set the fastest lap. The early promise of his undoubted talent was finally being realised after two exceptionally difficult and character-building seasons. With his star in the ascendency, he had very good reason to be confident for his home race, the Belgian Grand Prix at Spa-Francorchamps, so much so that he even bet designer Gary Anderson that he would put the car on pole position.

Bertrand Gachot never got to the Belgian Grand Prix. Ten days before it, he was sent to jail after being convicted of causing Actual Bodily Harm (ABH) to a taxi driver following a minor collision in London eight months earlier. Having only recently signed for Jordan, he had been on his way to a meeting at the Carlton Towers Hotel in London to help his new team boss pitch to a prospective sponsor, 7Up. He was driving there with his English girlfriend, Kate Palmer, in her Alfa Romeo, and as he picked his way through dense traffic at Hyde Park Corner he had an altercation with a black cab.

'The taxi tried to cut me up and I wasn't having it,' he said. 'Eventually he cut in and started brake-testing me. I thought to myself, if he does it again, I'm not going to brake. He did and I didn't. We touched but very lightly.'

The taxi driver, Eric Court, got out of his vehicle, yanked open the driver's door of the Alfa, grabbed the smartly dressed Gachot by his tie, and threatened him with a clenched fist. During the ensuing argument, and trying to shake off the aggressor, the racing driver sprayed CS gas in Court's face. Although CS gas, more commonly called tear gas, is available in small canisters in other countries and permitted for use in self-defence, its sale, possession and use is, and was, illegal in Britain. Gachot took the precaution of reporting the incident at a local police station and thought little more of it until he was eventually arrested and charged.

In the court case that followed eight months later at Southwark Crown Court, Gachot pleaded not guilty and his lawyers, confident that he would be cleared of assault, predicted a fine or at the very worst a suspended sentence. They were wrong and as shocked as everyone else when the jury returned its verdict, finding Gachot guilty by a 10–2 majority. Justice Gerald Butler handed down sentences of six months in prison for possession and 18 months for assault to run concurrently. He told Gachot: 'The possession of a CS gas canister is in itself a serious offence. When you use it as you did on the streets of London to spray into the face of a man who, I am satisfied, had offered you the most minimal violence, the only possible course I can take is an immediate custodial sentence.' The Judge also rejected an application for bail, ensuring that Gachot, rather than leaving immediately after the hearing for a scheduled tyre test at Monza, would remain in jail at least until his appeal could be heard. This also meant that he would miss not only his home Grand Prix but several more as well.

'I just couldn't believe what was happening,' said Gachot in an interview with *Autosport* magazine. 'For me it was a clear case of [legitimate] self-defence and I think that people who know me know that I would not aggress anybody. The judge considered that I used too much force on someone who came only with his hands. I cannot understand his judgment and I will never accept it. It was an incredible sentence.' Many years later he contended: 'I really didn't think it was an issue. We are talking about something that was really petty and basically I defended myself using tear gas. I never knew it was considered a weapon. I really felt I was within my rights and didn't do anything wrong and had no idea that my freedom was at stake.'

Had he known, he would have had even more reason to be aggrieved by his sentence as, in a similar case at the time, a Master of the Hunt was found guilty of the same offence, ABH, against a fox-hunting demonstrator and given only a two-month suspended sentence. Even the aptly named taxi driver, who received £500 compensation, was amazed at the sentence, telling the *Daily Mirror* that he had only wanted to be reimbursed for his soiled clothes and business lost as a result of the incident.

As news spread that Gachot's application for bail pending an appeal had been rejected, thousands of Belgian sympathisers demonstrated outside the British Embassy in Brussels. Amongst them were fellow Belgian drivers Thierry Boutsen of Ligier and Eric van de Poele of Modena. A non-profit organisation, 'Gachot Why?', was initiated by Kate Palmer, Harald Huysman (a close friend and fellow driver), Rodolphe Gachot (Bertrand's father) and Jean-Marc Goossens (a Belgian lawyer) to publicise and protest against what they considered to be a gross miscarriage of justice. Pascal Witmeur started the 'Free Gachot' initiative over the weekend of the Belgian Grand Prix. His Formula 3000 car carried prominent logos, flags were flown, banners and posters displayed. Campaign T-shirts were worn by thousands of fans and several of the drivers, including Ferrari's Alain Prost. Graffiti messages of support were painted strategically on sections of the circuit in front of grandstands and TV cameras.

Gachot was initially held at one of England's most notorious and severe prisons, Brixton in south-west London, in a cell measuring 10 square metres with visiting allowed for only 30 minutes every 14 days. 'It was like any prison you would imagine but worse because you were locked in 23 hours a day,' he said. 'You didn't have a table on which to eat or anything. There was no toilet in the cell, you couldn't even switch the light

Four days after the Hungarian Grand Prix, Gachot appeared at Southwark Crown Court and was convicted of assaulting a London taxi driver.

on and off. I was trying to look out of the windows to see normal life and people. You wouldn't treat an animal as badly as that.' He considered that the experience strengthened him mentally: 'I had to be philosophical and laugh about it and not get miserable. At the end I was surprised how man can adapt and how [some] other prisoners were not such bad people at all. I discovered things which I never believed were possible.'

He was later transferred to Northeye Prison in Bexhill-on Sea, East Sussex, where he says he read a lot of books and learned how to play chess. 'It was not at all what I imagined a prison to be,' he said. 'We were quite open, quite free. We had to do some gardening but at least I had fresh air and was able to see outside.' Here he was at least able to resume some physical training in preparation for a return to racing, although he had initially blanked racing from his mind: 'I didn't want to know, I didn't want to see F1.'

It was just as well that he didn't have the option of watching the Belgian Grand Prix on television as the performance of his replacement would have added insult to injury. The Jordan team had unlocked even more speed and 'his' car proved to be so competitive that Michael Schumacher qualified it seventh on his Formula 1 début. To rub salt into the wound, in the race De

Cesaris in the sister Jordan closed to within three seconds of Ayrton Senna's leading McLaren before rolling to a halt with an overheating engine.

Gradually Gachot's passion for racing resurfaced: 'I started to watch the Grands Prix and then, when Barcelona was on, I was riveted to the TV. It's something you have inside you. It's difficult to take it out.' With Nigel Mansell at the height of his powers, Formula 1 had reached new levels of popularity in Britain and Gachot found himself perhaps inevitably on the receiving end of quite a lot of ribbing. 'Someone at the prison [a guard] told me that the team had taken a German and they didn't need me anymore,' he said. 'Every time he came in front of my cell he made the noise of a Formula 1 car, telling me that this driver was very good and they didn't need me. However, 99% of the people were really kind and thought it was wrong that I was in jail. They helped me and made life easier. (Obviously you have the 1% who are really bad people and they say: Why does he have it easy? Why should he be treated differently?)'

Gachot valued the support he received from people all over the world: 'I had the most letters from Belgium, France and England but many from America, Japan, Australia. I really enjoyed reading them all and replying to them.' One letter was from De Cesaris, who had become a good friend in their time together, and wrote: 'That new boy — don't worry! I'm gonna get him at the next race!'

'It was just knowing that I was not alone,' added Gachot. 'It kept me calm. When you are in jail you cannot get angry. You have to control yourself at all times and all the support did help me. The other thing which kept me going was that I was convinced that I would get out on appeal because somewhere along the line I still believe in justice. We live in free countries after all and I don't think anyone is interested in putting innocent people in jail. I trained a lot physically and I was really motivated not to eat the wrong things. I prepared for the day of getting out because I still had the contract with Jordan.'

In Gachot's absence, Schumacher had certainly made an impression. He was something of an unknown at that stage — Gachot hadn't even heard of him — and had gone largely unnoticed by Formula 1's talent spotters despite winning the German Formula 3 Championship and the Formula 3 Macau Grand Prix in 1990. However, he had been picked up by Mercedes-Benz, which had signed him to race Group C prototypes in its junior sportscar programme alongside Heinz-Harald Frentzen and Karl Wendlinger. As Schumacher built up experience, he had shown great speed in the World Sports-Prototype Championship, sharing a car with Jochen Mass to win in

Mexico in both 1990 and 1991, and also setting fastest lap at Le Mans in the year of Gachot's triumph.

'I think Eddie must have noticed him winning F3 in Macau,' said former Jordan commercial director Ian Phillips. 'There were various people representing Michael coming to GPs and looking around.' It was rumoured that former World Champion Keke Rosberg was interested in the drive and both Derek Warwick and Stefan Johansson were considered, but they all wanted to be paid and Jordan was on a very tight budget. Such a tight budget, indeed, that bailiffs were knocking at the team's door, so a call from Jochen Neerpasch, competitions chief for Mercedes-Benz as well as an agent for the sports management company that represented Schumacher, couldn't have come at a better moment. While the Jordan team obviously needed a driver, it certainly took a punt on a virtual unknown, even if the reality was that the choice was driven by commercial considerations and the £150,000 raised by Neerpasch with help from sponsors for the one-off drive provided a much-needed lifeline for the team.

Schumacher had a brief session with the team at Silverstone to familiarise himself with the car before heading to Spa-Francorchamps. 'After four laps,' remembered Phillips, 'Trevor Foster came on the radio and said, "I've got to call him in and tell him to slow down. Phone Eddie and tell him we've got a star".' Foster, who had been assigned to be Schumacher's race engineer in Belgium, confirmed the impact made by the youngster: 'We did a very small shakedown after the trucks had already left for Spa, just to let Michael familiarise himself with the controls. Instantly, within three laps, he looked like he'd been in the car all season. He looked totally at home.'

Spa-Francorchamps, then as now the most challenging circuit on the calendar, isn't too far from Schumacher's home town of Kerpen in Germany, so it would have been reasonable to assume that, despite his youth, he would have had experience of the iconic circuit. In fact he had never been there. On the Thursday evening before qualifying, he produced a fold-up bicycle from the boot of his Mercedes coupé and while the team had dinner he cycled four laps to learn the circuit before retiring to bed in a youth hostel, Jordan not having been able to arrange better accommodation. Next day, to all-round disbelief, he posted eighth fastest time before going one better on Saturday, putting his well-established team-mate in the shade. At the start, the overnight sensation momentarily got as high as fifth before clutch failure led to his retirement just after the first corner.

Unusually, the ever-commercial Eddie Jordan had failed to tie his new driver into a binding contract because the deal had been concluded at such

The first Grand Prix after Gachot's imprisonment was in his home country, at Spa-Francorchamps in Belgium, where fans wrote messages of support on the track. The Jordan team's stand-in driver for the race, as pictured, was a little-known newcomer called Michael Schumacher.

short notice, so another team was able to swoop and by the time of the next Grand Prix, at Monza, Schumacher was sitting in a Benetton. And so began his inexorable climb to the top of a record-breaking career in which he would become one of the most successful drivers in the history of the sport, with seven World Championship titles and 91 Grand Prix victories.

After two months of incarceration, Gachot had his appeal heard on Tuesday 15th October, just a few days before the Japanese Grand Prix at Suzuka. The three judges in the Court of Appeal led by Lord Lane agreed that the penalty had been far too severe. The court decided to suspend his six-month sentence for possession of the illegal gas and to reduce his 18-month sentence for assault to nine months, of which six would also be suspended. As an offender is automatically released at the halfway point of a short sentence (one of less than two years), Gachot was immediately freed. Although this was obviously a positive outcome, the court refused to examine the question of whether Gachot was guilty of the crime and merely considered the sentences imposed, so his criminal record stood. He had been calmly confident that he would be released on the day of the appeal but the judgment was nevertheless a massive relief and in his mind represented 'the best proof that they have admitted that they were wrong'. As he left the court, he simply said: 'Common sense has triumphed.'

After the appeal court hearing, Gachot was taken straight to a celebratory party held in his honour that evening at the French Embassy in London, following which he went on to Heathrow Airport (via a Burger King restaurant) and flew to Japan. In a generous touch, one of his personal sponsors, Marlboro, paid for a first-class seat — a dramatic contrast from the prison cell from which he had emerged earlier that day. After a first full night's sleep at his hotel in Japan, he was able, he said, to blank out the experience and feel that his life had immediately returned to normal. It was as if his 'distant nightmare' had never actually happened.

Gachot may have been out of jail but he was also out of a job. He had missed four Grands Prix and Eddie Jordan had by necessity not only replaced him but also legally annulled his contract by invoking a clause about bringing the team into disrepute. After Schumacher's one-off drive at Spa-Francorchamps, Roberto Moreno had occupied Gachot's seat for two races before Alex Zanardi took over for the last three Grands Prix of the season. At Suzuka, therefore, Gachot found himself on the sidelines in the role of unwilling spectator. Fortuitously, he did manage to find a berth for the final race, in Australia, replacing the injured Éric Bernard at struggling

Larrousse. Although he failed to qualify the unfamiliar car, he impressed the team enough to be offered the seat for the following year.

During 1992 with Larrousse, he was sadly unable to replicate the form he had shown at Jordan, scoring just a single point with sixth place at Monaco. He had to sit out the following Formula 1 season but returned as both investor and driver in 1994 with Keith Wiggins's fledgling Pacific team, the same squad with which he had won his Formula Ford 1600 title eight years earlier. He stayed on for a second year and although the new car was a marked improvement, finances were tight and he found himself battling just to get on the back of the grid. At the final race of the year, he equalled the team's best result with eighth place after much of the field had retired. It was Gachot's final Grand Prix. Pacific folded at the end of the 1995 season, by which time Schumacher was already a two-time World

RENE ARNOUX
Wrong turn

Many years before Bertrand Gachot's misdemeanour, Renault Formula 1 driver René Arnoux was involved in a most unusual instance of 'road rage' at the Belgian Grand Prix at Zolder in 1982. After spinning out of the first qualifying session, rain precluded him from improving his time on his final attempt, leaving him second on the grid to team-mate Alain Prost. Not being in the mood to sit in a queue of traffic when leaving the circuit in a Renault 5 road car, the frustrated driver disregarded instructions from marshals and overtook several cars on his way towards the circuit gates. An official tried in vain to block his exit and decided to sit on the bonnet of Arnoux's car. That still didn't stop the furious Frenchman, who simply drove off with the man sprawled over the front of his car and clinging to its windscreen wipers for the duration of the three-mile trip to the team's hotel.

Needless to say, the unfortunate official didn't take kindly to his terrifying and unscheduled journey and immediately summoned the police. Despite Alain Prost making light of it and joking with the police officers that the culprit was actually fellow French driver Jacques Laffite, they went searching for Arnoux. He was eventually found hiding in the kitchens, where he was promptly arrested and put in a cell at the local police station for the next 24 hours.

Champion and about to embark on the next stage of his record-breaking career at Ferrari.

Gachot subsequently drove in occasional sports car and GT races for a variety of manufacturers and privateers but his career never really recovered. When that moment of red mist descended upon him that fateful December evening in congested London traffic, he did irreparable damage to his prospects at the top of the sport — and Michael Schumacher was the immediate beneficiary. Their careers may have taken very different paths, but Gachot insisted that he felt no animosity or bitterness towards Schumacher: 'He deserved the career he had, it was not me that made him, he made himself, he took the opportunity and did the best with it.' To his great credit, Schumacher was one of the first people to come to see Gachot after his release, offering moral support and saying that what had happened hadn't been right. Gachot described him as 'a real gentleman'.

Gachot estimated that legal expenses and lost contracts cost him £1 million. Irrespective of that, he remained remarkably sanguine about the consequences of his indiscretion having been disproportionate to the offence and destroying a career that was on the verge of success, Of the punishment itself, he simply said that he regretted that he wasn't given 'a sentence which was productive, such as helping handicapped children or putting up boards at Customs saying "CS is forbidden in England".'

After his retirement from driving, Gachot focused on business and marketing and is now the owner of Hype, an energy drink. Years later, he eventually returned to Formula 1, this time as a sponsor of Force India, which, via various changes of ownership, had evolved from the original Jordan team.

As well as the ignominy of being the only Grand Prix driver of modern times to have been sent to jail, Bertrand Gachot will forever be remembered as the man who, through a momentary lapse of judgement, inadvertently introduced one of the greatest drivers of all time to Formula 1.

ELMER GEORGE

A sad finish

Hot-headed Elmer George enjoyed little success as a racing driver but did take part in the Indy 500 three times during the period 1957–63 before marrying into the family that owned the Indianapolis Motor Speedway, becoming in effect part of American motor racing royalty. However, in 1976 he became caught up in a love triangle and was shot dead in a confrontation with the family's horse trainer, who had apparently won the heart of his estranged wife and subsequently became her long-time companion.

Born in the now-abandoned mining town of Hockerville, Oklahoma in 1928, Elmer George was one of many inhabitants of similar ghost towns who, as soon as he was old enough, resolved to seek a new life and opportunities in California. After the Second World War, midget racing on the West Coast was an important proving ground for future stars and this is where he started his racing career before progressing to sprint cars with Charlie Curryer's American Racing Association. Elmer then headed to the East Coast in 1954, where he did part of the sprint car season and finished 17th in the final standings, while in midget cars two wins put him 10th in the end-of-season points. He also had his first USAC Champ Car chance that year, in the Hoosier 100 on the dirt track at the Indiana State Fairgrounds, but failed to qualify. In 1955, he failed to qualify for the Indianapolis 500 but did make his Champ Car début towards the end of the season in the Golden State 100 at the California State Fairgrounds in Sacramento, driving a Kurtis-Offenhauser for the HOW racing team.

The co-owner of this team was Mari Hulman. She was the only child of Anton 'Tony' Hulman Jr, who enjoyed inherited wealth from the family business of grocery, alcohol and tobacco wholesaling, and had used some of it to buy the dilapidated Indianapolis Motor Speedway for $750,000 in 1945. At the time, the site was overgrown with weeds, having been idle for four years because of the war, and was in grave danger of being demolished. Indeed, it looked unlikely that the track could ever be viable again but Tony Hulman, through tenacity and dogged persistence, made it work, returning it to its position as the foremost racetrack in the United States. Mari, an 11-year-old at the time of the purchase, had motor racing in her blood and became fascinated by the place. By the age of 21, in 1955, she was a motorsport pioneer in her own right, joining long-time family friend Roger Wolcott to form the HOW team ('H' for Hulman, 'W' for Wolcott), which fielded cars in AAA and USAC sprint and national championship cars for drivers such as Jerry Hoyt, Eddie Sachs, Tony Bettenhausen and Roger McCluskey.

In 1956, Elmer quickly delivered his first USAC sprint car win in his HOW Special at Atlanta's Lakewood Speedway and backed that up a week later with another victory on the steeply banked Winchester Speedway in Indiana. At the season finale at Ohio's New Bremen Speedway, he was one

Mari Hulman, heir to the Indianapolis Motor Speedway, funded her hot-headed husband Elmer George's motor racing in the HOW Special from the mid 1950s to the early 1960s.

of three drivers in contention for the title but lost out and had to settle for third position. He also took part in most of the Champ Car series, scoring a best result of fifth place in Sacramento.

The following year, 1957, was a pivotal one for Elmer. He not only married Mari, becoming Tony Hulman's son-in-law, but also claimed the USAC Midwest sprint car title by 14 points from Andy Linden. After managing to qualify for his first Indy 500, however, he disgraced himself by crashing into the back of Eddie Russo's car on the pace lap, putting them both out of the race before it had even started.

He became known as a particularly aggressive racer whose driving could get wild, dangerous and inaccurate. His 1959 season turned sour at Langhorne Speedway, Pennsylvania, where he was leading the race but driving so raggedly that the USAC stewards decided to disqualify him on the grounds of safety, fearing that a big accident involving Tony Hulman's son-in-law would have serious repercussions. When shown the black flag, Elmer had lapped everyone except second-placed Van Johnson. He ignored the flag for 11 laps and when he finally came into the pitlane he was in a furious mood. He got embroiled in an argument with chief steward Tommy Nicholson and punched him, causing George to be suspended from racing until after the following season's Indy 500.

Following his return to racing, George took his final USAC sprint car win in controversial circumstances at DuQuoin, Illinois in September 1961. He tangled with another driver, Don Branson, and caused the race to be stopped, leaving Parnelli Jones believing himself to be the winner. However, the results were declared as the positions at the end of the previous lap, leaving George as an unpopular victor. At the Arizona State Fairgrounds in Phoenix in November 1962, another accident after contact with a rival propelled his HOW Special through fencing in front of a grandstand where it overturned and injured 22 spectators, and left him with cuts and a damaged shoulder.

His last race was the 1963 Indy 500, where he qualified 28th and dropped out after 21 laps. He made 64 starts in both the AAA and USAC championship series, including three Indy 500 appearances with a single finish of 17th in 1962. Elsewhere, he finished in the top ten 36 times and scored a single victory at Syracuse, New York in 1957.

Following his tumultuous and relatively undistinguished racing career, Elmer George was made a vice-president of the Indianapolis Motor Speedway and given the role of director at the IMS Radio Network, which provided live broadcasting of the event. Mari, who had supported his racing career through all its ups and downs, had four children with him, three of whom were girls — Nancy, Mary and Katherine — and the other a son, Anton, also know as 'Tony'. They lived on a large estate outside Terre Haute, not far from Indianapolis.

After 19 years of marriage, Mari filed for divorce on 3rd May 1976. Twenty-eight days later, on the day of the 60th running of the Indianapolis 500, Elmer had a bitter argument with her. This led to a heated telephone conversation from the family's speedway penthouse with Guy Trollinger, whom he believed to be his wife's lover. Trollinger trained horses for the Hulmans at Terre Haute but George had taken it upon himself to sack him

JACKIE PRETORIUS
Final lap

Jacobus 'Jackie' Pretorius was a Formula 1 driver who also died when attacked in his home. A member of one of South Africa's most famous, affluent and influential families, he was a descendent of one of the earliest Dutch settlers and his first exploits in racing were competing in stock cars before moving on to stunt driving for Buddy Fuller's 'Hell Drivers' demonstration team. After a succession of injuries, he transferred to the relative safety of circuit racing and became one of the stars of the local scene.

Between 1964 and 1973, he competed in the well-supported South African Formula 1 Championship with cars such as a Lotus 21, Lola T140, Brabham BT26 and Surtees TS5. Although he never won the title, his 89 starts produced four wins, nine second places and 15 thirds. Three of these races were the World Championship South African Grand Prix at the Kyalami circuit, the last of them in an ISO-Marlboro FX3B entered by Frank Williams, but he retired on each occasion. He also raced sports cars in the Springbok Trophy Series, most notably Doug Serrurier's Lola T70 during the period 1967–69.

During a burglary at their home in a suburb of Johannesburg in October 2003, his wife Shirley was shot dead and he was viciously assaulted. Six years later, in March 2009, intruders came to the house again and inflicted severe injuries from which he died, aged 74, after three weeks in a coma.

and order him to leave his two-storey home on the estate. Immediately after the race, George left the track and drove to Terre Haute to confront Trollinger, armed with a .22 handgun. Incensed to find that Trollinger was still in the house, he broke in and further argument raged. According to police, gunfire broke out at 1.00am, and investigators estimated that as many as 17 shots were exchanged. Five shots from Trollinger's .22 rifle hit 47-year-old George and killed him. George's gun, which had been fired twice, was found on his body. Trollinger was uninjured.

The 34-year-old Trollinger faced preliminary charges of assault and battery with intent to kill but the hastily convened Vigo County Grand Jury refused to indict him. After interviewing 23 witnesses, including Tony Hulman, charges were dropped and the jury decided that Trollinger had acted in self-defence. Prosecutors dropped the charges with a conclusion of 'justifiable homicide'.

Mari Hulman George became the highly respected matriarch of the Indianapolis Motor Speedway. Chairing its board of directors from 1988 to 2016, she was instrumental in its expansion and continuing success. She became known to millions of fans as the familiar voice that gave drivers the command 'Gentlemen, start your engines' at the start of the Indy 500 and many other races. She died in 2018, aged 83.

Elmer George had raced a variety of sprint cars, midgets and roadsters but is better remembered for the violent nature of his death. His main legacy, however, is that Tony George, the son he had with Mari, eventually took over as the controversial but visionary President and CEO of the Indianapolis Motor Speedway. He founded the Indy Racing League and introduced both the IROC and NASCAR series to the 'Brickyard' as well as inviting the Formula 1 World Championship to compete there.

FERNANDO GONZALEZ LUNA

Speedy González

A fly-by-night 'businessman', he arrived out of the blue with a plan to create a Mexican Formula 1 team in collaboration with Lamborghini but when the car was on the brink of its official launch he disappeared with investors' funds, having taken the Italian supercar manufacturer for a long and very expensive ride.

F erruccio Lamborghini founded his company near Bologna in Italy after the Second World War making tractors and agricultural equipment out of parts from surplus military equipment before diversifying into the manufacturing of air-conditioning units. Riding the wave of the post-war economic boom, his businesses were very successful and by the late 1950s he was able to indulge in his passion for luxury sports cars. He bought several Ferraris produced in nearby Maranello but found them troublesome, particularly with repeated clutch problems. Legend has it that when he took a 250 GT back to the factory to have the problems addressed, he was appalled by how Enzo Ferrari was casually dismissive of any criticism of his cars and seemed unconcerned about his company's poor customer service, reportedly telling Ferruccio that the problem wasn't with the car but with the driver, and following up by suggesting that he should go back to looking after tractors.

Lamborghini was so incensed that he resolved to challenge Ferrari by building his own cars in a new factory in Sant'Agata Bolognese, not far

Shortly before the project came to a shuddering halt in June 1990 with the disappearance of Fernando González Luna and his ill-gotten funding, Mauro Baldi tested the Lamborghini-built GLAS 001 Formula 1 car.

from Maranello. As further retribution, he managed to attract some top Ferrari engineers, including Gianpaolo Dallara, because they had become disaffected with their autocratic employer. Ferruccio's first car, the 350 GTV, a two-seat coupé with a V12 engine, was launched and the company was immediately recognised as being a high-calibre manufacturer of stylish high-performance cars. Highpoints of Ferruccio's involvement in the automotive world were the beautiful Miura (1966), which was the world's first mid-engined supercar with its V12 engine mounted transversely, and the futuristic-looking Countach (1971).

When the oil crisis of 1973–74 threatened the viability of manufacturing high-performance cars, Ferruccio sold his shares in the company. It was a timely decision as the business went bankrupt only a few years later and was bought out of administration by the Swiss Mimran brothers, Patrick and Jean-Claude, who invested heavily in restructuring before selling it on to the Chrysler Corporation in 1987.

As part of chief executive Lee Iacocca's strategy to boost Chrysler's global sales, he wanted Lamborghini to use Formula 1 as a platform to go up against arch-rival Ferrari, although he understood how difficult that would be and initially confined the ambition to building a V12 engine to comply with the new 3.5-litre regulations that would be taking over in 1989. However, this automotive visionary certainly made an ambitious start by hiring two top former Ferrari men in the form of Mauro Forghieri as technical director and Daniele Audetto as manager of a new subsidiary, Lamborghini Engineering, dedicated to the Formula 1 project. The new power unit would be used exclusively by the Larrousse-Calmels team (see Chapter 14) in 1989. Results were dismal, with a best finish that year of just sixth place for Philippe Alliot in the Spanish Grand Prix.

Having failed to get anywhere near its aim of threatening Ferrari during its first year, Lamborghini realised that really it should establish its own works team, but couldn't afford to do so. Instead, an alternative route was to link up with a customer who could fund the construction and development of a Lamborghini chassis to carry the Lamborghini engine. When, towards the end of 1989, an ambitious young Mexican businessman called Fernando González Luna appeared on the scene, he appeared to offer the ideal solution. He was one of many newcomers to pop up in this unprecedented period in the sport when new teams proliferated and there seemed to be a continual queue of genuine entrepreneurs and unrealistic dreamers who wanted to reap the commercial and economic benefits of Formula 1's dramatically increasing popularity.

Apart from providing the flamboyant Rodríguez brothers, Ricardo and Pedro, Mexico hadn't had much to offer in Formula 1 at this point. This shortcoming was recognised by the well-connected González Luna, who announced that he had started a company known as GLAS (González Luna Associates) and was raising money to become the works-affiliated Lamborghini team. The vision he sold to investors and sponsors was to create a team rather like the Brazilian Copersucar-backed operation of Wilson and Emerson Fittipaldi in the late 1970s. Although the venture would benefit from the cachet of involvement with a prestigious Italian sports car manufacturer, it would be entirely Mexican-owned and employ Mexican drivers. Part of the business model was to create a 'staircase of talent' for young drivers and engineers who would be fed into the Formula 1 team by becoming active in a newly formed Formula 3 championship in Mexico.

González Luna was a very good salesman and an extremely persuasive character who was able to attract local backers keen to support his idea of promoting their country. Lamborghini was delighted about being able to compete in Formula 1 in 1991 thanks to the Mexican's promise to provide $20 million that he had raised from various businesses including Pemex, the state-owned oil company, which would be the team's title sponsor. To design the car, the GLAS 001, Forghieri hired Mario Tolentino, who had worked for Alfa Romeo, EuroBrun and Dallara. An extensive testing programme was scheduled, to be divided between Mauro Baldi, an established sports car driver who also had Formula 1 experience with Arrows, Alfa Romeo and Spirit, and little-known Italian-born Mexican Giovanni Aloi, who had raced sporadically in Formula 3.

By June 1990, the car had been completed and was taken to Paris with the intention of being air-freighted onwards to Mexico City. The project was all set to be officially announced to the press during the build-up to the Mexican Grand Prix at the end of that month in the hope of attracting more backing for its début the following year. However, the car never got further than Paris and was then returned to the factory.

Autosport magazine reported: 'GLAS closed its offices when it became known that there were major financial difficulties... The GLAS team is part of a larger corporation, controlled by Fernando González Luna and his brother Alessandro. Neither has been seen since the team collapsed and it appears that something in the region of US$20 million invested in the corporation cannot be accounted for.' Lamborghini Engineering boss Emile Novaro was quoted as saying: 'I am the supplier of the chassis. GLAS is a customer. I'm very upset by this business. Until last week there were no problems, González Luna has been very correct in his dealings. We are not sure if the project is definitely off. There is another contractual obligation to be met on July 10 and we will do nothing until then.'

Sadly, Novaro's good faith and patience were misplaced and it soon became clear that the GLAS project was finished. Left with both an engine and a chassis, and keen that its substantial investment shouldn't be wasted, Lamborghini decided to inject more funds and create its own F1 operation for the 1991 season. As the company was wary about attaching its name to a new team for fear of failure, it registered the venture as Modena Team SpA, reflecting the name of the famous city near its Sant'Agata Bolognese base. Confusingly, the cars were entered as Lambo 291s but they were woefully uncompetitive and only ran for a solitary season in the hands of Eric van de Poele and Nicola Larini.

Meanwhile, the mysterious Fernando González Luna had vanished, his very successful fraud accomplished. After appearing from nowhere, as if by magic, he had disappeared without trace, together with the $20 million that he had raised for the still-born team. No one knows what happened to him and the police and the unfortunate investors are still searching in vain.

CHAPTER 25

GERHARD GRIBKOWSKY

The banker and the used-car dealer

An unknown name in motorsport, this corrupt German investment banker paid a high price for his involvement in it. His dealings with Bernie Ecclestone also had serious repercussions that threatened the power of the Formula 1 supremo over the sport that he had revolutionised and controlled for decades, and that had also made him one of the richest men in Britain.

Bernie Ecclestone should need no introduction to any motorsport enthusiast. The son of a Suffolk trawler captain, he was born in 1930 and as a child used to get up at 5am to deliver newspapers, on two separate rounds, then collect cakes to resell in the school playground. As a young man he progressed from selling motorcycles to owning car dealerships and building up a substantial property portfolio. He also tried his hand as a driver and even made a half-hearted attempt to try to qualify for the 1958 Monaco Grand Prix in a Connaught but didn't succeed. That same year, after his friend Stuart Lewis-Evans suffered fatal burns in a crash in his Vanwall in the Moroccan Grand Prix, he decided to walk away from the sport.

He returned as business partner and manager of Austrian Jochen Rindt, the Lotus driver who died in a crash at Monza in 1970 but still became World Champion posthumously. The following year he bought the celebrated Brabham Formula 1 team from Ron Tauranac and embarked on a 17-year period of ownership that brought much success. Designer

Gordon Murray's technically innovative and invariably pretty cars won a total of 23 races and the team's star driver, Nelson Piquet, became World Champion in 1981 and 1983. Leaner years followed and at the end of 1988 Ecclestone sold the team to Joachim Lüthi (see Chapter 39), allowing him to concentrate on representing the commercial interests of all Formula 1 teams as Chief Executive of FOCA (Formula One Constructors' Association).

It was in this capacity that Ecclestone became best known as the mastermind who transformed Formula 1 into a global phenomenon with vast audiences that rival those for the Olympic Games and World Cup football. As the commercial rights holder of Formula 1, he amassed a vast fortune and his family became one of the richest in Britain. His success as an international and sometimes controversial deal maker made him feared and admired in equal measure but it also made him and his family vulnerable to unwanted attention.

One such threat was a crude attempt at blackmail by Momir Blagojevic, a 48-year-old Croatian who in 1997 naively tried to extort $1 million. *Imperijal*, a Croatian tabloid newspaper, published an interview with Blagojevic about Slavica Ecclestone, Bernie's Croatian second wife, and the four-page spread was accompanied by nude photographs of her. In a series of sensational allegations, the blackmailer claimed to have been her confidant and lover 20 years beforehand and additionally stated that she had worked as a honey-trap spy to lure potentially useful information from the rich and powerful on behalf of the Yugoslavian communist secret police. Blagojevic unwisely threatened to reveal more of Slavica's supposed past in a proposed book that was to be, among other things, 'very dangerous for Formula 1'. Needless to say, this rather clumsy attempt failed and both Blogojevic and the newspaper were forced to make public apologies.

Many years later Bernie found himself on the receiving end of another blackmail attempt.

Gerhard Gribkowsky studied law at the highly respected University of Freiburg and received his doctorate in 1988. He began his career in investment banking at Deutsche Bank before moving on to Bayerische Landesbank in Munich where part of his role required him to sit on the supervisory boards of investee companies. He first made waves, albeit of the wrong kind, after Bayerische Landesbank — more commonly known as BayernLB — misguidedly took a stake in Hypo Alpe Adria, a Croatian company, that resulted in a loss of €3.7 billion. As BayernLB's 'chief risk officer', Gribkowsky was accountable and held partially responsible for losses of such magnitude that the bank had to be rescued by the German state with a cash injection of €10 billion.

BayernLB and two American investment banks, JP Morgan and Lehmans, had collectively made loans totalling $1.55 billion to the Kirch Media Group to buy holdings in Formula 1 from Ecclestone's group of companies and by April 2001 Kirch had a 75 percent stake. However, Deutsche Bank announced in December that the Kirch empire was no longer creditworthy after defaulting on payments of $1.8 billion and the organisation collapsed. The idea of the banks controlling the sport and the business he had built up was unpalatable to Bernie, who also sensed an opportunity to buy back Formula 1 for considerably less than Kirch had paid. However, Gribkowsky thwarted this plan, marking the start of a three-year power struggle between the two men.

The banks were landed with a stake in a business they didn't want. As BayernLB had the biggest exposure, it fell to Gribkowsky to take the leading role of shareholder representative for all three of the institutions. As Tom Bower wrote in his biography of Ecclestone, *No Angel*, Gribkowsky had the task of trying 'to unravel Ecclestone's carefully constructed labyrinthine commercial structure'. Bambino, the Ecclestone family trust in the Channel Islands, owned 25 percent of Formula 1 but controlled the network of 'Formula One' companies. 'The companies can't do a thing without Bambino's permission,' Bower recalled Bernie saying. Unspoken was Ecclestone's unique ability to prevent an outsider's entry and exit from the maze. As Martin Brundle — British former Formula 1 driver, Le Mans winner and top TV commentator — joked, 'Bernie attaches strings to the shares, sells them and then pulls them all back again.'

What also became clear, critically, was that the banks had committed their loans without conducting sufficient due diligence and were unaware of a 'dividend clause' that denied Kirch, or subsequent owners, any income with which to service the interest on their loans, let alone the capital repayments. This not only diluted their control over the business but left Ecclestone's companies taking all the profits from it and meant that Bernie's remaining 25 percent stake was worth a great deal more than the banks' 75 percent, although they recognised that their holding would be worth even less if they didn't retain him as their chief executive.

By early 2005, BayernLB was tiring of Formula 1 and also the man running it. Looking to sell its 47.2 percent stake, the bank tasked Gribkowsky with finding a buyer. As part of the ongoing power struggle between Gribkowsky and Ecclestone, the German had already won a victory the previous

A high-profile court case in Munich in June 2012 surrounding the
ownership of Formula 1 ended with German investment banker
Gerhard Gribkowsky's conviction for corruption.

December when, in London's High Court, Justice Andrew Park had given a
ruling that handed the banks control of Formula One Holdings, one of the
myriad companies created by Ecclestone to manage the sport. Gribkowsky
then turned his attention to the considerably greater prize of Formula One
Administration, which was a much more significant and powerful entity. A
further court case was scheduled to be heard in May 2005 but never took place
because an agreement was reached and the issues settled out of court. By the
end of the year, CVC Capital Partners, a private equity group, had emerged
as a potential buyer and, with Gribkowsky responsible for the negotiations,
Lehmans and JP Morgan took his lead and joined BayernLB in selling their
stakes. By November 2006, CVC had won majority control of Formula 1
after additionally acquiring shares held by Ecclestone's family trusts.

It was during these negotiations that Ecclestone was alleged to have
made a deal with Gribkowsky. At the heart of the legal wrangling that
followed were payments in excess of $44 million made to Gribkowsky
personally, from Bernie himself and his Bambino family trust. Several
years later, German prosecutors brought the case to court in the belief that
this constituted a bribe made to encourage Gribkowsky to sell to CVC on

Formula 1 supremo Bernie Ecclestone gave evidence in court in Munich concerning payments of more than $44 million made to Gribkowsky by him personally and his Bambino family trust.

favourable terms on the condition that the new owner was obliged to retain Bernie's services as chief executive and give him continued autonomy to run and expand their latest investment.

Giving evidence in June 2012 in a court in Munich, 54-year-old Gribkowsky admitted that the claims that he corruptly received $44.4 million were 'essentially true'. The BBC reported that the presiding judge, Peter Noll, said that Gribkowsky had shown 'high criminal energy' as he convicted him on charges of bribery, tax evasion and breach of fiduciary trust, but he also described Ecclestone as the 'driving force' behind the payments. In his testimony, Bernie had admitted paying the money but denied that it was a bribe, saying that he had been worried that if he hadn't paid the money, Gribkowsky would have alerted the UK tax authorities to 'things' that might have led to a tax inquiry.

'The only alternative was that the British tax authorities followed a case that would have been very expensive for me,' stated Ecclestone. 'The tax risk would have exceeded £2 billion. I paid him to keep calm and not to do silly things. I knew he wanted to start a business.'

Gribkowsky's punishment was eight and a half years in prison but the sentence was reduced after he admitted the charges of corruption. He spent 62 months behind bars but escaped serving the rest of his sentence by agreeing to pay his former employer in instalments the funds he had illicitly received. This left him facing financial ruin.

Although Ecclestone had been granted immunity from prosecution for his testimony against the banker, he wasn't yet off the hook. The following year he had to defend another claim in London, this time for $100 million, alleging that he had purposely undervalued Formula 1 in the $2 billion sale to CVC and colluded with Gribkowsky to retain control of the sport. In February the following year he was back in London's High Court. As renowned Formula 1 and business journalist Christian Sylt wrote at the time: 'The alleged bribe was central to the related case last month which was brought by German media rights firm Constantin Medien. It claimed that it lost out through the sale to CVC as it had an agreement entitling it to 10% of the proceeds if the stake sold for more than $1.1 billion. Constantin got nothing as CVC paid $814 million but it argued that higher bidders would have come forward if the sale had not been engineered by Ecclestone, Gribkowsky, Bambino and its former lawyer Stephen Mullens.'

Mr Justice Newey ruled against Constantin, stating that 'it was no part of Mr Ecclestone's purpose (or Mr Mullens') for BayernLB's shares to be sold at an undervalue... no loss to Constantin has been shown to have been caused by the corrupt arrangement with Dr Gribkowsky. That fact is fatal to the claim.' However, he did state that 'the payments were a bribe... Mr Ecclestone's aim was to be rid of the banks. He was strongly averse to their involvement in the Formula One group and was keen that their shares should be transferred to someone more congenial to him.'

Even though Ecclestone's representatives had successfully defended the claim from Constantin, and the Court of Appeal had refused to allow a challenge to that decision, the matter didn't end there. One month later Bernie returned to the same Munich court that he had visited two years earlier to face his own criminal charges that the payment to Gribkowsky had been a bribe, in addition to claims that BayernLB had incurred $66.4 million of damages dating back to a planned stock-market flotation in 1998. Although Bernie was quoted as saying that he had '100 percent confidence in the German judicial system' and that he would be exonerated from any wrongdoing, there was concern that some of Judge Newey's remarks might work against him in the German court.

Had he been sentenced, 83-year-old Ecclestone could have faced up to 10 years in prison. However, German law provides for some criminal cases to be settled with different punishments, such as fines. The country's criminal code allows for trials to be ended under conditions that are 'appropriate for resolving the public interest in a prosecution' as long as the gravity of wrongdoing doesn't outweigh this. The case was abandoned when Ecclestone reached an agreement in 2014 to pay a settlement of $99 million to the German treasury and a further $1 million to a children's hospice. Although the charges were dropped, the magnitude of these payments did raise questions about a system that appears to allow rich defendants to buy their way out of criminal trials.

More litigation followed in 2016, this time when Bernie himself filed a case against BayernLB in the High Court asking it to rule that he had no liability to the bank. BayernLB counter-sued, seeking damages from Ecclestone on the basis that his agreement with Gribkowsky had resulted in the bank's stake being undervalued in the sale to CVC, and the case was settled out of court for an undisclosed sum.

By this time, Ecclestone and his companies had profited to the tune of several billion dollars from no fewer than five changes of ownership since he first considered floating Formula 1 in 1996 and each time one of his most effective tactics had been to sell ownership without actually yielding control. Although the German court proceedings may have appeared to be a close shave, the payment made before the trial concluded meant there was no ruling either way on Ecclestone's guilt or innocence.

Another development occurred in July 2022 with the announcement by the UK's Crown Prosecution Service of its intention to charge Ecclestone, by now aged 91, with tax fraud regarding what authorities stated was a failure to declare over £400 million of overseas assets.

Although Bernie once said of himself 'I'm no Angel', the fact remains that the man who stated that 'my reputation is worth more to me than money' escaped his encounters with Gribkowsky with his reputation intact and was guilty of nothing more than being an exceptionally shrewd businessman.

Before we leave Bernie Ecclestone, let's briefly turn back the years to the Great Train Robbery. Bernie's association with and goodwill towards one of the gang, amateur racer Roy James (see Chapter 29), has led to wild and repeatedly denied speculation that he was in some way connected with the heist. In 2005, Ecclestone announced to *The Independent* newspaper that he hadn't planned the robbery or been involved with it in any way. Known for his dry wit, he added: 'There wasn't enough money on that train; I could have done something better than that.'

CHAPTER 26

ANDRE GUELFI

Speed and adventure

An extremely successful businessman, this one-time Grand Prix driver's remarkable life included early spells as a debt collector and soldier. He made and lost several fortunes, the first of which came from lucrative industrial fishing that led to the unflattering soubriquet '*Dédé la Sardine*'. His impressive network of high-level contacts proved a mixed blessing and ultimately landed him in serious trouble with the law and convictions for embezzlement after he played a pivotal role in corruption scandals involving French and German politicians.

André Guelfi was born in 1919 in Mazagan, Morocco, which was a French protectorate at that time. He was the son of a Spanish mother, a singer and professional pianist, and her husband, a Corsican military officer who had become the local harbour master. The entrepreneurial skills that were to become the hallmark of Guelfi's life were evident from a very early age and when aged only 10 he was not only tri-lingual but already making money by chauffeuring tourists along the local Plage Haouzia, an eight-mile beach, in a car that had been modified so that he was able to reach the pedals. He left school at the age of 16 to work as a messenger boy in a local bank where he discovered a file containing details of unpaid debts and made an agreement with the bank's manager whereby he would collect the money in return for 15 percent of whatever sums he managed to recover. By the time he finished working there, he was earning more than the manager himself and was able to invest his hard-earned cash in a sardine fishing and canning business managed by his uncle.

Although the Second World War broke out when he was still in his teens,

Morocco wasn't actively embroiled in the hostilities until the end of 1942. However, three years earlier the 20-year-old had enlisted in a Moroccan infantry regiment serving in Italy before becoming a driver with General de Gaulle's intelligence operation, the *Bureau Central de Renseignements et d'Action* (BCRA), employed in covert activities in Italy, the combination of which further fuelled his love of speed and excitement. Once the war in Europe was over, he volunteered to go to Indochina and join a select French parachute unit based in Saigon from where he saw service in special missions in Laos. After a brief return to Morocco in 1946, he fled from there to escape a disastrous marriage and settled in Paris, where he bought a bar. When he returned to Morocco once more, he began to build up a sardine fishing and processing business, pioneering a technique to swiftly freeze catches aboard the first refrigerated factory ships. This earned him not only a fortune but also his lifelong and much-disliked nickname of '*Dédé la Sardine*'.

His business success was enhanced by the close relationships that he shrewdly developed with politicians. His wealth enabled him to indulge in two new passions, flying and motor racing, which he first tried in 1950. Confined mainly to North Africa and France, he began competing in a Delahaye before switching to a Jaguar, then came to international prominence in 1953 racing a Gordini in which he scored both class and outright wins at the Grand Prix of Agadir for sports cars. He also shared a factory Gordini with Jean Behra in the Casablanca 12-hour race but they retired with mechanical failure. In 1954 he shared another Gordini with Jacky Pollet to take a class win and finish sixth overall at Le Mans but had less luck racing a single-seater works Gordini at Pescara, retiring when his car caught fire on the first lap.

Guelfi continued to race mainly in Africa, winning the Moroccan championship in 1955, but still made regular forays into Europe, competing again for Gordini in 1956, including at Le Mans with Hermano da Silva Ramos, an outing that ended when their works-entered car retired at half distance with clutch problems. In 1957 he finished seventh in the Pau Grand Prix, although the pale blue Gordinis were now no longer competitive and he was a long way behind the leaders. For the 1958 season, he switched to a new rear-engined Cooper Formula 2 car in which he finished second in the Prix de Paris at Montlhéry, just three seconds behind the winner, Henry Taylor, also in a Cooper. That year he concentrated on racing a Ferrari 250 GT in sports car events but entered Le Mans in a Jaguar D-type that his co-driver, racing under the pseudonym 'Mary', crashed fatally at the Dunlop curve.

In the autumn of 1958, he raced in the first World Championship Grand Prix to be held in Africa and the only one ever staged in Morocco. The organisers were understandably keen to satisfy the new King's wish to have an African driver in the race but there weren't any suitably qualified candidates and instead they settled on two local residents, Guelfi and his compatriot Robert La Caze, who at least raced under the Moroccan flag. Together with Frenchman François Picard and Briton Tommy Bridger, they all made their one and only start in a Formula 1 World Championship event, driving Coopers, albeit underpowered examples in the Formula 2 class that had been added to bolster the field. Guelfi was the last classified finisher, five laps down on the winning Vanwall of Stirling Moss. This marked the end of his top-level racing although he continued to compete sporadically in Morocco throughout the 1960s, most notably when he took second place in a race at Rabat in 1968 in a Porsche 911R.

André Guelfi left Africa in 1971 to return to France, where he settled in Paris and invested in real estate by buying three luxury hotels. Having divorced his wife, he married the niece of the then French president Georges Pompidou and in doing so became the joint owner of 45 percent of a company with a portfolio of 128 buildings in the centre of the city. Within a year he had bought control of the business and used the impressive list of contacts he had acquired to acquire even more property. He was soon well on his way to amassing a second fortune. In 1975 he moved to Lausanne in Switzerland and bought a vast mansion overlooking Lake Geneva where he lived for 25 years. His wealth enabled him to buy a Falcon private jet that he piloted himself and justified the expense of it because he hated wasting time in airport queues.

Encouraged by the French government, he took over ailing sportswear company Le Coq Sportif in 1980. This gave him easy access to sport's largest governing bodies, the *Fédération Internationale de Football Association* (FIFA) and the International Olympics Committee (IOC), and he became a trusted adviser to the latter. He had already played a key role liaising in deals that helped the Soviet Union win the rights to stage the 1980 Olympic Games in Moscow, which won him yet more friends in high places, especially in Eastern Europe.

His impressive network of business and political connections combined with his personal charm and gravitas made him the ideal go-between in deals worth millions of dollars. One valuable connection that he had made during his war years as a BCRA driver was with Pierre Guillaumat, boss

Nearly 40 years after his racing career peaked with an appearance in a Cooper at the 1958 Moroccan Grand Prix, André Guelfi found himself behind bars for embezzlement in a scandal that embroiled the highest levels of French politics.

of Elf Aquitaine, the French national oil company founded by General de Gaulle in 1941. A key part of the company's strategy in the late 1980s and early 1990s was, according to *Malta Today*, 'to secure the oil interests of France in its former African colonies'. Long known in Paris as the 'Ministry of Oil', Elf's riches were used 'to maintain Paris-friendly dictators in African states'. The newspaper reported the allegation that 'African coups were directly sponsored by Elf and that the company routinely served as a cover for secret French governmental operations, which included the bribing of African leaders and money laundering in Latin America. Elf used a system of split commissions as a way of maintaining French influence and later subsidising Gaullist political activities.'

Guelfi maintained that Elf in this period was determined to expand its petroleum and gas production by exploiting production contracts in the Soviet Union but that its efforts were continually defeated by the ruling Communist Party's resistance to foreign business. However, Elf persisted and, after the toppling of the Soviet regime, used Guelfi as intermediary with Russian stakeholders to gain access to their oilfields. In payment for negotiating government-level deals, he earned sizeable commissions but also offered the use and facilities of his Swiss-registered companies and bank accounts to pay kickbacks and commissions to senior Elf executives. In addition, he became a secret conduit for the transfer of millions of dollars from French politicians to German ones, through his Swiss bank accounts and his involvement in the IOC.

The payments were actually commissions funnelled through Elf Aquitaine for the acquisition of the Leuna oil refinery and the Minol network of 2,500 service stations in the former East Germany after German reunification. The payments were based on the artificially inflated prices paid for the assets and were allegedly part of French President Mitterrand's desire to bolster his political partnership with Germany's Chancellor Helmut Kohl at a time of European consolidation. However, the Leuna affair soon led to Kohl's political downfall when the illicit collaboration between the government and Elf unravelled in the biggest-ever corruption trial in French history.

Guelfi was one of 37 defendants who collectively stood accused of accepting the equivalent of nearly €400 million from Elf Aquitaine for personal enrichment and political kickbacks. The others included former Elf boss Loïk le Floch-Prigent and former French foreign minister Roland Dumas and his mistress Christine Deviers-Joncour, who was paid bribes by Elf in order to influence her lover.

In 2001, *The Guardian* reported the convictions and sentencing of the defendants for their part in the shadowy and illegal dealings of the oil company that had first come to light in 1994. The British newspaper described the sleaze affair as 'the biggest financial scandal in a western democracy since the end of the Second World War... Elf became a private bank for executives who spent millions of pounds on political favours, mistresses, jewellery, fine art, villas and apartments.' As the link for approximately €30 million of commissions from Elf's 'black box' of secret funds to German businessmen and lobbyists, Guelfi was not only inextricably linked with the scandal but also at the very centre of it. The newspaper also reported that an estimated €300 million removed from Elf's accounts was under the cover of commissions on big oil deals or property investments. Approximately €25 million of this slush fund, the newspaper added, had been converted into cash. It reported that Elf acted as an undercover arm of government, serving submerged French interests mainly in French-speaking African countries but also in Asia and later in Europe.

Guelfi had already spent 36 days behind bars at La Sante Prison in Montparnasse, Paris in the spring of 1997 on suspicion of pocketing tens of millions of francs while dealing in overseas contracts on Elf's behalf. When it was later established that he was at the heart of the wider scandal in 2005, he was sentenced by the Paris Criminal Court of Appeal to three years in prison with 18 months suspended and fined €1.5 million for the 'abuse of social property'. Despite his central role in the corrupt dealings between business and government, by the time of his sentence he was over 80 years old and was spared from serving any more time in prison.

Guelfi wrote an autobiography, *l'Original*, published in 1999. In this he told of how his Swiss bank accounts had been unfairly frozen as part of the Elf Aquitaine scandal and how he continued to fight (unsuccessfully) in the courts from his new home in Malta. He also detailed a long-standing dispute with Bernard Tapie, the controversial entrepreneur and politician whom he had met in prison in 1997 and was serving a two-year sentence for corruption and witness tampering. Guelfi befriended him and agreed to help him get back on his feet. In the years that followed, Guelfi loaned a total of €14 million to fund Tapie's long legal battle with the state-owned bank Crédit Lyonnais. In return for the financial support, Guelfi claimed that they had agreed to split the proceeds of any settlement, but when Tapie finally won his battle and was awarded €404 million, none of it found its way to Guelfi. This caused extreme bitterness for the disaffected Guelfi for the rest of his days in Malta.

At the time of his death in June 2016, 97-year-old Guelfi had become the oldest living Formula 1 driver, having 'overtaken' his nearest rival, Robert La Caze, in July 2015. Coincidentally, the two had been team-mates when they raced a pair of Cooper-Climax T45s owned by Ken Tyrrell in the one-off Moroccan Grand Prix of 1958.

CHAPTER 27

GENE HAAS

Inside line

Billionaire philanthropist, founder of America's largest computerised machine tool maker and owner of teams in both NASCAR and Formula 1, Gene Haas — no relation to earlier team owner Carl Haas — fell foul of the IRS for orchestrating a tax fraud using 'deceptive and elaborate tax-evasion schemes'. His motive was retribution for his company, Haas Automation, after a previous lawsuit for patent infringement. Haas's deception cost the government almost $34 million and landed him with an 18-month spell in prison.

Born in 1952 in Youngstown, Ohio, Gene Haas had his first exposure to motorsport during high-school holidays while working for LeGrand, the small race car constructor run by Aldin 'Red' LeGrand, learning how to fabricate parts and assemble cars. After enrolling to study engineering at California State University, Haas changed to an accounting course and graduated in 1975. That year, he found some summer work as a mechanic and machinist for Randy Lewis's Wrangler-sponsored Formula 5000 team and attended the Long Beach Grand Prix.

Unable to find employment as an accountant that paid him more than his summer work, he spent three years working as a CNC programmer and machinist before founding a small machine shop of his own, Pro-Turn Engineering, where he and two employees began to produce a self-designed machine-tool indexing head. The reception to this at industry trade shows was so positive that in 1983 he branched out and formed Haas Automation in order to mass-produce indexers. The business quickly evolved from a garage operation into a big American success story, creating innovative, low-cost, user-friendly machine tools and becoming the largest manufacturer of its kind in the US. According to *Business F1* magazine in 2021, the company had annual sales approaching $3 billion with profit margins of close to 30 percent.

Twenty years passed before Haas revived his involvement in motorsport by sponsoring a car run by Rick Hendrick's NASCAR team in 1995. Haas's renewed enthusiasm grew to such an extent that he resolved to start his own team, Haas CNC Racing, which took part in a handful of NASCAR races in 2002 before embarking on a full season the following year. Although Jason Leffler won Haas CNC Racing's first race in the junior Busch Series in 2004, the team's efforts in the main Cup Series saw a high turnover of drivers, none of whom had been very successful in their previous teams, and very little was achieved. Indeed, in 284 starts over seven seasons, Haas CNC Racing never even got close to Victory Lane, managing just one top-five finish in all that time.

Haas readily admitted that he had underestimated the difficulty of succeeding at the sport's highest level: 'When we first came to NASCAR, we had high expectations. We thought we would be able to run with the big dogs, but it was a lot harder than we thought.' His team manager then suggested that the way forward was to be more ambitious and hire a top driver. So it was that two-time Cup Series champion Tony Stewart, who was one of the hottest properties on the market and had been driving for the crack team Joe Gibbs Racing, reached a partnership agreement whereby he would drive for the newly named Stewart-Haas team and own 50 percent of it. The creation of the Stewart-Haas team wasn't an obvious marriage and came as a great surprise to many people in the sport, including, it seems, Haas himself, who according to ESPN admitted that: 'I thought Tony was a little crazy for doing it, but Tony is a little bit smarter than you think sometimes.' Stewart certainly took a big risk in joining a struggling and unproven operation but his commitment paid off. In its first season, 2009, the team saw immediate success, and in 2011 Stewart won his third Cup Series title as a driver and his first as a team owner. Kevin Harvick won another Cup Series title for the team in 2014.

Earlier that year, Haas announced that he had been granted a licence to enter Formula 1 and subsequently bought some of the assets of the defunct Marussia team and settled into its old base in Banbury, Oxfordshire. With a chassis built by Dallara and a powertrain from Ferrari, with whom the parent company already had a close commercial relationship, the new team pioneered a relatively low-cost model of racing at the highest level and made its début in 2016. This was no vanity project, as Haas explained to *Business*

Before Gene Haas (left) entered Formula 1 with his own team, he co-ran
a NASCAR operation with two-time champion Tony Stewart (right).

F1 magazine: 'It's part of our business plan to expand our sales across the
world. We have a good domestic market and we use NASCAR for that and
Formula 1 is basically an expansion of that for the rest of the world.' To
date, the team's best result in seven seasons has been only a single fourth
place, in the 2018 Austrian Grand Prix, but Haas's continuing commitment
to his endeavour has seen him form an even closer attachment to Ferrari by
establishing a satellite factory close to Maranello.

In certain respects, Haas's approach reflects the way British industrialist
Tony Vandervell went racing with his Vanwall team in the 1950s, using the
sport to showcase his company's technology.

Having built his company, Haas Automation, from nothing, Gene
Haas became one of the largest employers in California's Ventura
County, where he was also known as an extremely generous benefactor
and philanthropist. As he was such a popular figure, his arrest by IRS
agents in June 2006 came as a huge shock to all those who knew him. The
charges were conspiracy, filing false tax returns and witness intimidation.
A 52-page indictment accused him of running a bogus invoicing scheme to
produce sham tax deductions and the Justice Department claimed that his
actions had cost the federal government millions of dollars in lost revenue.

According to Stephanie Hoops, writing in the *Ventura County Star* in
2001, John Phillips, the company's former chief financial officer, was the
whistleblower who went to federal authorities with information about Haas's

JEREMY MAYFIELD
Not so fast

Before Gene Haas's NASCAR team joined forces with Tony Stewart, one of Haas's drivers had been Jeremy Mayfield, who developed an uncomfortable and controversial relationship with NASCAR's authorities. Mayfield started racing for Haas in late 2007 and competed in seven more races in 2008 before Stewart became involved and dispensed with him.

Mayfield's difficulties worsened in 2009 when NASCAR suspended him from racing after he failed a drugs test for methamphetamines. He maintained that the result was due to his use of prescribed Adderall (for ADHD) and over-the-counter Claritin (for allergy relief), as disclosed to the series doctor. He took the governing body to court and won but this proved to be only a temporary reprieve because he was soon suspended again for another alleged failed drug test. The situation, which many observers felt was a personal vendetta against the embattled driver, wasn't helped when ESPN reported his comments about the chairman of NASCAR, implying that he had a drug problem: 'Brian France out there talking about effective drug policy, it's kind of like Al Capone talking about effective law enforcement. That's the way I feel about it. The pot shouldn't be calling the kettle black, you know what I'm saying?' Mayfield could have returned to NASCAR had he been prepared to complete its 'Road to Recovery' treatment programme but he refused because he felt that would be an admission of guilt.

In 2011, police searched Mayfield's home following reports from an informant that he and accomplices had carried out a series of burglaries. After the discovery of over $100,000 worth of stolen goods and 1.5 grams of methamphetamine locked in a gun safe, he was taken into custody. By the time the case was eventually heard in January 2014, almost all the charges had either been dropped or thrown out, with Mayfield pleading guilty to one count of possession of stolen property and one count of possession of drug paraphernalia. He was placed on unsupervised probation for 18 months and ordered to pay $88,000 in restitution plus $1,100 in fines and other costs.

As for Mayfield's comments about Brian France, NASCAR's chief was arrested in 2018 on charges of aggravated driving under the influence and criminal possession of a controlled substance, oxycodone, although the latter charge was subsequently dropped.

creation of tax-fraud schemes, triggering a federal investigation. Phillips told investigators that both Haas and general manager Denis Dupuis had asked him to depart from standard accounting practices in order to avoid federal taxes after Haas Automation lost a patent-infringement lawsuit to industry rival Hurco Companies Inc in the last quarter of 2000, resulting in a furious Haas having to pay an $8.9 million settlement to Hurco. The newspaper reported that Haas's anger was so intense that he vowed to recoup the millions of dollars he lost and blamed the government. As the newspaper put it, quoting federal investigation records, 'Haas told Phillips that he was going to get back his $8.9 million... with an additional $8.9 million ... as punishment by writing off his tax debt.'

Prosecutors claimed that Haas and Dupuis designed a budget to write off $50–$60 million for tax years 2000 and 2001, by orchestrating bogus expenditure that could be deemed business costs. Phillips stated that he was told to create fake invoices for Weldman, a brand of equipment frequently bought by Haas Automation. Invoices, related paperwork and payment cheques were to be sent to the owners of two companies, Bob Cable of Enmark & Associates Inc. in Valencia and Chuck Todd of Supermill Inc. in Reno, Nevada. According to court records, Phillips stated that these two men would keep 2 percent of the proceeds and kick back 98 percent to Haas through one of several subsidiaries set up by Phillips. Cable, Todd and Dupuis all pleaded guilty in connection with the tax-fraud scheme, as did Phillips's successor, Kenneth Greene, who was charged with continuing the deception.

Just before Haas's case was due to go to trial after a six-year investigation, with the prospect of a prison sentence of as long as ten years, a plea agreement was reached whereby the 54-year-old would plead guilty to one charge of conspiracy to commit tax evasion, *The New York Times* reporting that he had defrauded the federal government of $34 million in taxes. As part of his plea agreement, Haas was ordered to pay a $5 million fine and more than $70 million in restitution for back taxes and interest. In a statement, US Attorney Thomas P. O'Brien said: 'Mr. Haas has now paid the government more than twice the amount of taxes he attempted to avoid paying.'

Haas was sentenced to two years in prison and the judge agreed to his lawyer's request that he be placed in a low-security facility in Lompoc, California, near Vandenberg Air Force Base. His imprisonment began in January 2008 and he was released on probation after 18 months. However, it was during this period of incarceration that he made good use of some of his time by successfully persuading Tony Stewart to join forces with him as driver and co-owner of his NASCAR team.

CHAPTER 28
ANGELA HARKNESS
Stripper who ripped off NASCAR

This *femme fatale* created a NASCAR team that was entirely funded with fraudulent bank loans. She paid for nothing, scammed the sport and fled the country, leaving behind a dead husband as well as a business partner and lover languishing in prison. In a story of supreme deception, she bankrupted companies and left in her wake a trail of broken promises, bounced cheques and unpaid employees.

Angela Harkness's life was unstable from the start. She was born Fatemeh Karimkhani in Iran in 1976 into a large family who fled to West Germany when she was three years old during the Iranian Revolution, in which the government was overthrown by extremists. The refugees settled in Osnabruck and, according to subsequent press releases, she allegedly gained a degree in psychology by the age of 19 before moving to Texas with four of her sisters in 1995.

Three years later she moved to California and, going by the name of Angela, found a job working as a stripper in a night club called the Candy Cat. In the first of several attempts to secure US citizenship, she married Rayford Taylor Jr, but the marriage quickly fell apart. At her workplace she then met a 40-year-old judge, Dion Harkness, who was employed by the Californian State Compensation Board. They married but this was also a doomed relationship that soon became violent.

A fellow lawyer, Charles Bentley, told *Car and Driver* magazine that they were a bad combination: 'Angela drank a lot of beer and was using coke.

Dion hit the hard liquor. She had an emotional temperament and would yell and scream when she got tight and started to fight with him.'

After his new wife's repeated accusations of domestic abuse, Dion Harkness was placed on three years' probation by the bar association and his once-flourishing legal career came to an abrupt halt. The birth of a daughter in November 2000 strained the volatile relationship even further and he became severely depressed. In February 2001, he drove to a motel in Thousand Palms, California, where he stayed for several days before shooting himself dead. He left a suicide note in which he stated that it was his wife who had frequently attacked him and that he had never hit her. This was consistent with reports from people who knew the couple and said she was a pathological liar.

In the aftermath of her husband's death, Angela Harkness moved back to Texas and found another job, this time dancing topless at the Yellow Rose night club in Austin. Here she met the married man who would become the next victim of her affections. Gary Jones was a vice-president of a local branch of the Wells Fargo bank whose role there was to arrange and authorise loans. Captivated by the dancer's charms, he left his wife and moved in with his new lover. As with his predecessors, his life quickly became derailed. From the autumn of 2001, she persuaded him to use his position at the bank to make bogus applications for loans in the names of unknowing relatives and associates.

It's unclear when or how Angela Harkness became interested in motor racing, although her various unsubstantiated claims concerning her occupations over the years included being a motocross champion, which, bearing in mind her history of untruths, seems unlikely. She and her latest lover identified NASCAR, which was at the height of its popularity, as an easy way to make some money.

She convinced Jones that a relatively small investment in a team would be returned many times over by attracting multi-million-dollar sponsorship deals from which they could line their own pockets. As a result, he was persuaded to take out further fraudulent loans and in 2002 a new racing team, Angela's Motorsports, was created to run in NASCAR's second-tier Busch Series. The announcement of the new team in October was extremely well received by the media and warmly welcomed by the NASCAR community and motorsport in general for the diversity it brought. The party line was that the arrival of a 26-year-old woman of Middle East origin with a 34-year-old African-American partner would 'open doors for women and

The funding behind Angela's Motorsports, the short-lived NASCAR team set up by Angela Harkness in 2002, was entirely fraudulent.

minorities in stock car racing'. With so many people going out of their way to help them succeed, the couple fully intended to capitalise from the goodwill they had created.

A long-established NASCAR team, Robert Yates Racing, struck a deal for Angela's Motorsports to buy two Ford cars, engines and equipment for $900,000. The new team attracted top personnel, including crew chief Harold Holly. When it was announced that popular driver Mike McLaughlin was available for 2003, having been dropped by Joe Gibbs Racing, the newcomers wasted no time in recruiting him too. McLaughlin was running in the top five in the championship at the time and his reputation was such that he would have been of interest to many of the established teams, but the couple convinced him that their outfit was already fully funded for the coming season and that they would be strong contenders. 'It all happened so fast, I couldn't believe it,' said McLaughlin.

The team owners lied to their star driver by telling him that it had a $5 million sponsorship contract with WiredFlyer, an early example of an internet travel agency. There was indeed an arrangement with wiredflyer.com, whose owner, Rick Barton, was one of Jones's clients at the bank, but it extended no further than help with travel expenses in return for a logo on the car. However, when the car was unveiled at the team's media launch, its green-and-white bodywork carried very prominent WiredFlyer branding and showed no allegiance to any other companies. Jones told a surprised Barton that this was only temporary until the signing of a larger sponsor.

Ahead of the 2003 season with McLaughlin, the team decided to dip its toes in the water and take part in the last two rounds of 2002 with another driver, Jay Sauter. Despite his best efforts, the hastily assembled team failed to qualify first time out, at Phoenix, Arizona, on 9th November. However, a week later at Homestead, Florida, Sauter did get into the race along with Kevin Lepage in a second car, the entry of which was a complete surprise to Barton at WiredFlyer. Although Lepage dropped out at the halfway stage with brake trouble, Sauter did at least finish the race, albeit two laps down on the winner in 25th place. This would turn out to be not only the first race for Angela's Motorsports but also the last.

Many teams start racing with incomplete budgets in the hope of attracting a major sponsorship deal to keep them in business and cover accumulated debts, but it wasn't like this with Angela's Motorsports. As FBI agent Matt Gravelle told *Car and Driver*, the difference in this case was 'that their seed money was stolen'. A few days after the Homestead race, Jones took out a further loan from Wells Fargo for $250,000, this time in the name of Angela's mother, and immediately made two payments. He transferred $150,000 to Robert Yates as part settlement for the equipment that had been delivered and $100,000 to star driver McLaughlin. During the off season, the fraudsters went on a recruitment drive to fill key positions by hiring a respected team manager and a new crew chief. Another loan, for $70,000, was granted in December but by then cheques to suppliers and employees had already started to bounce, with the fraudulent loans being the only source of income for the overspending team. By this time, Jones's employer had become suspicious about the number of loans being authorised and, after an internal investigation, fired him in January 2003.

In the last days of the team's existence, it took part in pre-season testing at Daytona and McLaughlin showed great potential by setting 10th fastest time. However, realising that the team was a sham, Yates was quick to react and sent trucks to the Angela's Motorsports race shop to repossess engines and equipment that hadn't been paid for. The embryonic team closed its doors at the end of January, with employees and dozens of others owed money. Not knowing the truth, fans wrongly assumed that WiredFlyer was to blame for the mess by defaulting on payments, and the bad publicity brought down the small company. Rick Barton, the innocent and entirely honourable president of WiredFlyer, lost $80,000 by charitably taking over some of the fly-by-night team's debts and repaying people who were owed money. Very sadly, Barton died the following July at the early age of 48, his widow believing that the cause was the accumulated stress of the episode added to a pre-existing heart condition. Equally conscientious was the team's disillusioned and now unemployed driver, who raised money to pay off creditors and employees whom he also helped to find new jobs.

After the collapse of the team, Jones initially found work managing a sports bar and Harkness secured her old job at the strip club. It took a year for the FBI to complete its investigations before the truth became public knowledge and the case came to court. Jones pleaded guilty to charges of embezzlement of over $1 million, bank fraud and theft, and was sentenced to three years and ten months in prison. Harkness pleaded guilty to one count of conspiracy to commit bank fraud and was released on bail after promising to testify against her partner. However, she left her job after just one week and moved, with her four-year-old daughter, across the border from Texas into Mexico before fleeing to Dubai, where she found work as a beautician. The FBI eventually tracked her down by rummaging through her sister's garbage and finding a discarded letter that revealed her address. However, as the US doesn't have an extradition agreement with the UAE, it took until 2007 before she could be returned to America to serve a custodial sentence of 40 months. She remained in Texas after her release from prison but has subsequently been arrested again, on charges of theft and violence.

ROY
JAMES

Drive it like you stole it

In a classic case of what might have been, Roy James was an extremely promising young racing driver competing in Formula Junior, the established single-seater training ground for the Formula 1 driver that he yearned to be. However, he led a double life and achieved considerably more fame and notoriety for his criminal activities in his 'day job' — above all for his part in the Great Train Robbery — than for his achievements on the track.

Roy James was born into a dysfunctional and broken family in Fulham, south-west London, in 1935 and spent his formative years in the harsh environment of a post-war London riddled with bomb damage from the blitz. When he was old enough, he trained to be a silversmith, becoming so highly skilled that he was able to sell some of his work at Harrods, the prestigious department store in Knightsbridge that was close to his digs in Nell Gwynn House on Sloane Avenue.

However, his real interests lay in sport, where he showed great talent and versatility. Of small, nimble build, he had a trial for Queens Park Rangers football club and excelled in water skiing, where he was a top British contender in the late 1950s. By the turn of that decade, however, the relatively new sport of go-karting, which had been introduced to Britain by US servicemen stationed at airbases, ignited a passion for speed. In 1962 he graduated to represent Britain at European Championship level and won four out of his five races at a meeting in France. With racing having quickly become his all-consuming interest, he decided to move up the ladder into Formula Junior.

At Brands Hatch's traditional Boxing Day meeting in 1962, he watched New Zealander Denny Hulme score an impressive win first time out in a brand-new Brabham BT6. Now aged 28, the budding racer decided that a Brabham was just what he needed and, despite the not inconsiderable cost, managed to buy Hulme's very car. At his first event, at Oulton Park, he was immediately on the pace, qualifying third but spinning off in the race and badly damaging the car after battling for second place. After pleading with the Brabham factory, he managed to procure a replacement chassis in time for his second event, at Goodwood, where he once again crashed out of second place. Another non-finish followed at Brands Hatch but this time he was leading the race when he spun off on the penultimate lap. His first win came next time out, at Snetterton, where he showed he was a fast learner by beating the *Formule Libre* allcomers.

With that, he became a regular winner in lower-level Formula Junior and *Formule Libre* races, his tally for the year across the two categories numbering 12 wins and 11 fastest laps, including plenty that set new records. One of his winning races, at Brands Hatch, is best remembered for the car-racing début of the celebrated multiple motorcycling champion, Mike Hailwood, who drove a Brabham that day to fifth place. By the summer, major oil companies such as Esso and Shell, which were significant backers of the sport at that time, were sufficiently impressed to be talking in terms of offering contracts for the following season, and the works Brabham set-up also seemed to be interested. His career was certainly moving in the right direction and his prospects of reaching his goal of Grand Prix racing were looking promising.

Unless they have independent means, most aspiring racers face the perennial problem of how to fund their participation in an exorbitantly expensive sport. Before Roy James moved into motor racing, he already had a lucrative sideline that gave him the wherewithal to buy and race his Formula Junior Brabham. He was adept and experienced in crimes such as stealing cars and he also put his athleticism and diminutive build to good use as a cat burglar capable of scaling buildings to break into apartments and steal valuables.

Being a gifted silversmith meant that he didn't need to risk passing on stolen goods as he just melted down precious metals to create new products that he could then sell with impunity. By the time he was 25, he had already served time in prison for a variety of relatively low-level robberies and car thefts. At one point he had even had the audacity to steal Mike Hawthorn's road-going Jaguar to use in a robbery before having the good grace to leave it near the Steering Wheel Club in London so that it would be easily found and returned to its enraged owner, although he only returned the BRDC badge from the car to the family after the World Champion's death in early 1959.

While he was go-karting, he widened his horizons to include a couple of lucrative jewellery thefts from hotels in Monte Carlo with his accomplice Micky Ball. On their return to Britain, the small-time thieves fell into the company of a 'firm' of much more serious criminals and began an association that would lead to his involvement in the big robbery that would define his life. In November 1962, the South-West Gang was responsible for stealing the BOAC airline's payroll in dramatic fashion from London's Heathrow Airport in a violent attack on an armoured truck that left its security guards unconscious after being coshed. James and Ball were employed for their skills as getaway drivers in their stolen Jaguar Mark 2s, with the cash being bundled into Ball's car while James used his to ease their passage. At one junction he was able to ensure unimpeded progress through red traffic lights by holding back oncoming vehicles with the Jaguar, and at one point he barged into a Wolseley to knock it out of the way. Although both drivers were later arrested and James was already well known to the police, he got away without punishment because he hadn't been picked out in an identity parade, but Ball received a five-year prison sentence.

James used part of his share of the BOAC heist to pay for the Brabham that got him started in Formula Junior. Denny Hulme later recalled the surprise with which the newcomer was received at the Brabham factory in Surbiton when he opened a briefcase crammed full of used banknotes to pay designer Ron Tauranac and sales manager Alan Fenn for his car.

As the car of choice for criminals in the 1960s, Jaguar Mark 2s were widely used as getaway cars in countless robberies throughout the decade. They were not only powerful and fast, easily capable of 125mph, but also roomy enough to seat five adults with plenty of space for stolen goods. Although the later 3.8-litre version (with 220bhp) was the faster model by a small margin, James preferred the 3.4-litre (with 210bhp) because he felt it was better balanced. These Jaguars could easily outpace anything in the armoury of the police force, which relied mainly on Ford Zephyrs at this time. James was very particular about his personal Mark 2 and had it improved with lowered suspension, better brakes and an upgraded cylinder head. In addition to making his go-faster modifications, he used his mechanical skills to add hand operation of the brake lights to confuse any pursuers.

At the time of the Great Train Robbery, Roy James was racing his ex-works Brabham BT6 in Formula Junior. He's pictured at Brands Hatch in May 1963.

By 1963, James had become an integral part of the South-West Gang as well as its youngest member. Jockey-sized with crew-cut hair and a mild cockney accent, he was a distinctive figure whom his associates unflatteringly nicknamed 'The Weasel', a source of intense irritation to him. The gang leader was Bruce Reynolds, a prominent member of the criminal underworld who had successfully cultivated an air of respectability by claiming to be an antique dealer. He was a regular spectator at Goodwood where he mixed socially with people involved in the sport and certainly didn't look out of place as the enthusiastic owner of an Aston Martin.

Buoyed by the financial return and success of the airport job, Reynolds set his sights higher and enlisted James to take part in a major plot to rob the overnight Glasgow-to-London Royal Mail train. His plan was to hijack it *en route* to London in a remote part of Buckinghamshire when it would be carrying a substantial quantity of largely untraceable used £1 and £5 banknotes due to be taken out of circulation before being destroyed by the Bank of England. The attraction to James was understandable and he wouldn't have needed much persuasion to take part in his most ambitious theft to date due to the constant need to find money for his motor racing. This job could bring riches beyond his wildest dreams and his share could potentially be enough for him to reach Formula 1, a target that he felt his talents deserved and that he craved to attain.

Legend has it that the plan was hatched in an 18th century pub in Brill, Buckinghamshire called The Pointer, but it's more likely that the real planning was done elsewhere and that any meetings at the pub would have been during last-minute preparations because of its proximity to Leatherslade Farm. This was a run-down property that Reynolds had bought two months earlier because its rural location, 27 miles from the scene of the robbery, would make it an ideal hideaway where the gang could lie low with the contraband in the immediate aftermath of the robbery. The scheme was devised around inside information and planned with military precision and in considerable detail. The thieves all had designated roles and knew exactly what they had to do after plenty of practice beforehand. Other men were recruited from a Brighton-based gang, the South Coast Raiders, because they could provide invaluable experience of robbing trains and rigging railway signals.

Leatherslade Farm was large enough to accommodate all the men and its outbuildings could be used to keep the collection of vehicles needed for the operation under cover and out of sight. The fleet included an army-surplus Austin Loadstar truck, two Land Rovers and a horsebox to be used afterwards to transport the banknotes. Other than one of the Land Rovers, the vehicles had been bought rather than stolen. The Land Rovers were painted the same shade of green and fitted with identical number plates (BMG 757A). The considerable financial investment required for the operation was covered by some of the proceeds from the Heathrow theft. Besides purchase of the vehicles and rental of the farm, other expenses were payment for the necessary inside information from a source, said to be a senior Royal Mail official, and stocking up with provisions for an anticipated two-week stay at the farm.

For his part in the preparations, James marked out different escape routes along country lanes that several small groups of the gang could take separately. He then made repeated trial runs in a Mini Cooper with Bruce Reynolds following in a Lotus Cortina, practising the various options for getting to the farm from the point of ambush. On the night of the robbery, James's tasks, apart from driving one of the Land Rovers, would be to cut telephone wires to all properties near the bridge and help to decouple the train to separate the mail and sorting staff from the carriage carrying the cash.

Just three days after racing his Brabham on Bank Holiday Monday at Aintree, where he finished fifth and set a new lap record, James was one of the gang of 15 men who forced the night train to a halt just south of Leighton Buzzard in the early hours of Thursday 8th August. Having tampered with the signalling system, they unhitched ten carriages at the rear to allow just the front two, the second of which was the 'High Value' carriage containing the money, to travel half a mile further until stopped by a false signal on an isolated stretch of line at Bridego railway bridge, where their vehicles were waiting. This location was chosen because the bridge crossed over a lane near the hamlet of Ledburn that would permit a swift getaway. To take the truncated train that short distance, the gang had recruited an experienced train driver, but he proved to be unfamiliar with the locomotive, an English Electric Type 4. Having stormed the cab and overpowered the young assistant to the driver, David Whitby, some of the men then resorted to extreme force to persuade the unfortunate driver, 57-year-old Jack Mills, to take the train onwards, almost bludgeoning him to death with metal bars in the process. The masked men then smashed their way into the High Value carriage and in a human chain loaded dozens of sacks full of money into the two waiting Land Rovers and Loadstar truck.

Within half an hour, the gang had pulled off one of the most daring and famous thefts in British history. The total haul was £2.6 million, which is worth about £51 million at today's values. Once the loot had been loaded and with James sedately driving one of the Land Rovers, the vehicles took their pre-planned separate routes back to the farmhouse.

One of the thieves had made the mistake of telling postal workers on the train not to move or try to raise the alarm for half an hour. When the police learned this, it suggested to them that gang was likely to be hiding out within that sort of reach in terms of driving time, and therefore no more than about 30 miles away. Having been unable to find any forensic evidence at the crime scene, the police search fanned outwards from there and a £10,000 reward was offered for information. Helped by a tip-off from a neighbour who had observed unusual goings-on at the deserted farmhouse, police raided it five days after the robbery.

As soon as the men heard radio reports that the police were scouring their area, they panicked and made an early and chaotic exit from the farmhouse. In their haste, they didn't clean up properly and left a generous trail of evidence. There were fingerprints galore, including on a Monopoly board with which some of them had whiled away time, reportedly using real money from the robbery. They were careless about other evidence, even managing to leave a few mailbags lying around. As the Loadstar had been seen by one of the railwaymen, some of them had decided to repaint it but they managed to spill incriminating drops in various places, including on the soles of their shoes.

The original plan, much to James's distaste, had been to move the vast quantity of banknotes in a horsebox, but with the need for a swift exit this idea was abandoned and the proceeds of the robbery were hastily distributed. On Saturday 10th August, James fetched his personal Jaguar and used it for three high-speed return trips shuttling money between the farmhouse and the East End of London, where he and Charlie Wilson hid their shares in a lock-up garage. On one of his journeys, James found time to deliver £12,500 from his share to the wife of the imprisoned Micky Ball, his fellow driver in the Heathrow job, as a reward for keeping his silence. James was then able to return, albeit briefly, to his new life in motor racing. At Cadwell Park on 18th August, just ten days after the robbery, he won the Formula Junior and *Formule Libre* events.

By the following Thursday, 22nd August, the investigating officer, Detective Sergeant Jack Slipper, known as 'Slipper of the Yard', was closing in. Photographs of James had been circulated to the press under the heading 'wanted for questioning' and Slipper was keen to apprehend him before he or his contacts saw any coverage. On the very day that James featured in the newspapers, his name was also listed in the specialist weekly motorsport journals as an entrant in the Formula Junior support race at that weekend's big Tourist Trophy meeting at Goodwood. This was finally the budding racing driver's opportunity to prove himself against the very best up-and-coming talents, including future Grand Prix stars such as Peter Arundell, Richard Attwood, David Hobbs, Denny Hulme, Peter Revson and Mike Spence.

After discovering that James would be competing at Goodwood, Slipper, having confirmed with the circuit that his quarry was indeed in attendance, arranged for officers from the Sussex force to go to the track on the Friday practice day. Partly thanks to Slipper's heavy-handed and less-than-subtle inquiries, James received a tip-off and left Goodwood as quickly as he could, apparently passing bell-ringing Wolseley squad cars coming down the road towards him as he departed in a white Jaguar E-type. The following week's edition of *Motoring News* stated in its report of the Formula Junior race: 'A notable non-starter was Roy James, who did not appear on Saturday. Scotland Yard, it seems, wished to interview him and James was not to be found.'

The police already knew that James had a garage in Battersea where he kept the Brabham so two local officers were dispatched in the hope that he could be ambushed there. It wasn't until the following day that his mechanic, Robert Pelham, arrived at the garage with the Brabham on a trailer, so all the waiting officers could do was arrest Pelham and take possession of the racing car. The police had already been to James's flat in

The scene of the Great Train Robbery of 8th August 1963. As an experienced burglar and highly skilled driver, Roy James had a suitable combination of skills to make him a key part of the team behind the heist.

Chelsea where it was clear from its state that he had left in a hurry. In fact he had gone to ground in a flat in Ryders Terrace, St John's Wood.

James hid there for nearly four months until a female informer told the police where he was. In the early hours of 10th December, officers from the Flying Squad forced their way in. James, using his experience as a cat burglar, attempted to flee across rooftops in the freezing temperature wearing only his underwear and carrying a hold-all crammed with more than £12,000 in banknotes. After a dramatic chase, he was arrested in the back garden of a nearby house.

The police had initially linked him to the train robbery because of his known association with some of the other key gang members, but ultimately there was plenty of evidence to connect him to the crime in any case. The serial numbers on some of the banknotes in his hold-all tallied with records of the stolen cash and his fingerprints matched those found on a few items at Leatherslade Farm, including a page from a magazine, a first-aid kit and a Pyrex plate that he had used to give milk to the farm cat.

James was one of 11 defendants when the trial began at Aylesbury Crown

Court on 20th January 1964. At its conclusion, 51 days later, he received prison sentences of 25 years for conspiracy to rob and 30 years for armed robbery, to be served concurrently. When jailing the robbers, all but one of whom received sentences of the same or similar duration, Mr Justice Edmund Davies told the court that 'to deal with this case leniently would be a positively evil thing'. The sentences did seem somewhat disproportionate and excessive for the time but took into account the injuries inflicted on the train driver, although the judge still wasn't consistent with a previous sentence he had imposed where a victim had been shot dead.

James served the first eight months in solitary confinement at Wormwood Scrubs as a deterrent to trying to escape, something that his accomplice Charlie Wilson had succeeded in doing after only four months, and that Ronald Biggs managed within 15 months, before going on to serve a total of 11 years before being freed for good behaviour on parole in 1975. The elation of his early release was dampened by the discovery that the friend whom he had entrusted to 'look after' his share of the stolen money, which he had originally intended to use to finance a Formula 1 drive, had spent it all while he had been behind bars.

His obsession with motor racing continued through his years of confinement, nurtured by the specialist publications he was allowed to receive. After his release, the 40-year-old did the rounds of various teams, including some in Formula 1, looking for drives, but they all told him, unsurprisingly, that he was now too old for a serious racing career. His visits included Max Mosley and Bernie Ecclestone, respective proprietors of March and Brabham, and he also approached Graham Hill, with whom he had been friendly in earlier times and who was now running his own team.

However, there were people in the racing community who did rally around him to help, some feeling that his sentence had been disproportionate to his part in the crime, and mindful that he had been a popular figure on the scene. Amongst those who befriended him whilst he was incarcerated were Val Pirie (Stirling Moss's former secretary) and David Brodie (the successful saloon car racer). Others who tried to help by using their connections were Rod Banting (an old Formula Junior sparring partner) and Nick Syrett (former director of the BRSCC).

Not long after his release, an offer came from David Mills, who in later years became five-time Le Mans winner Derek Bell's manager. Mills agreed to give James a trial at Silverstone in a Formula Atlantic Lola T360, a very much quicker car than anything he'd ever driven before.

'I was asked to help him by all sorts of people in the business,' said Mills. 'I think the racing fraternity felt that it had been a terribly long sentence: 30 years — that's life, after all. He was a nice enough chap, outgoing, many people liked him and felt he had served more than enough time. I had a Lola which Ted Wentz had been driving in Atlantic and then Formula 2, and at the end of the season we put the Ford BDA Atlantic engine back in it for James to test, and I issued a press release saying, "Roy James returns to racing!".'

At only 5ft 4in in height compared with Wentz's 6ft, James had problems in fitting the car properly. In addition, a Formula Atlantic single-seater wasn't the ideal choice after such a long break because its power output, aerodynamic downforce and high levels of grip on slick tyres made it a totally different experience from his Formula Junior exploits 12 years earlier. He soon found himself in trouble: he put a wheel on the grass at Abbey curve while changing up to fifth gear, lost control and slammed into the crash barrier, destroying the car and breaking a leg. Quoted in *Autosport* magazine, he said, 'My times were coming down nicely and I'd have had a decent position on the grid. After 12 years it felt good and I was elated. I can't wait to have a go again. Time is not on my side. I can't afford to miss a day.'

Mills went on to say: 'I think motor racing was his lifeline; he just kept it in his sights that one day he'd come out and be a racing driver again. He was so keen: I can't describe how excited he was to drive a racing car round a circuit again. And he was getting down to some good times when he went off.'

Despite this inauspicious incident, it didn't quite end his dream. As *Autosport*'s man reported a year later from Mallory Park over the Easter weekend, 'the dapper former train robber... made a quiet competition début in a little 85mph Renault 5 Turbo'. However, the words that followed were rather more scathing: 'Entries for Renault 5 racing are so thin that importers have to swell their ranks by making cars available for various "guest" drivers, none of whom looked capable on this occasion of challenging the proper competitors. Of the "guests", Roy James gave the popular press the story that they and Renault presumably wanted by rolling his car (on the fourth lap) at Gerard's while lying ninth but it's a sick sport which has to rely on crime and Renault 5s for publicity.'

It was harsh but probably fair comment, for James had needed just a handful of laps to write off two cars. Mills, who was still trying to help him find a way back into the sport, pointed out that raising sponsorship for him wasn't as easy as it might have looked: 'People with big money to spend are the big companies with boards of directors and it's difficult to argue with them when they say they don't want to upset their shareholders by giving money to a man with a criminal record.'

However, James did find some support for the season and his saviour came in the form of John Webb, managing director of Motor Circuit Developments (MCD), which owned a portfolio of four circuits including the flagship Brands Hatch. Webb always had a keen eye for any promotional opportunity and was quick to seize on the initiative and publicity value of helping the return to racing of a notorious thief whom he argued had served his debt to society. Through his company, Motor Racing Stables, Webb arranged for his new protégé to do a limited programme of racing in Formula Ford 1600 with a Royale RP21.

James débuted the Royale on 1st August 1976 at Mallory Park, where he crashed yet again, knocking all four corners off the car at the Esses. At Brands Hatch four weeks later, he did at least finish a race, managing to take second place in one of the heats. In another incident at Mallory Park, he made himself very unpopular with an angry young Nigel Mansell by taking him off after losing control of the Royale. Back at Brands Hatch in November, he started from pole position and was running second to Don MacLeod before it all went wrong when he attempted to take the lead. He rode over a rear wheel of his opponent's car and was launched into the barriers in a terrifying series of cartwheels from which he was lucky to escape with just a bruised ankle although a photographer was badly injured.

Although he had shown flashes of speed, James never regained his old form, which was no great surprise given his age and time away from the track. In going in for Formula Ford 1600, he was trying to compete with men half his age with ambitions of becoming the stars of tomorrow. Although he made a few one-off appearances the following year, his comeback had proved to be both naive and unrealistic.

With his forlorn hopes of a return to the big time now over, James fell back on his legitimate trade of silversmith, selling items from a market stall and occasionally getting commissions from former racing connections. He made silver trophies for the BRSCC and Bernie Ecclestone commissioned him to create other trophies, including the FOCA Award presented to the promoter of the best-organised Grand Prix of the year at the annual FIA Prizegiving Gala. That's as close to Formula 1 as he ever got.

Regrettably, James, who had moved for a while to Spain, returned to crime and was arrested in 1983 for his involvement in a massive VAT

Less than six months after the Great Train Robbery, Roy James was one of 11 members of the gang who went on trial at Aylesbury Crown Court, following which he spent 11 years behind bars for his part in the crime.

fraud, having allegedly imported melted-down gold without paying excise duty. Along with his old ally Charlie Wilson, he was lucky to be acquitted. However, he was soon once again in even more serious trouble.

At around this time he married 18-year-old Anthea Wadlow, who, rather ironically, was the daughter of a bank manager. Over time, and perhaps unsurprisingly given the 30-year age gap between them, the marriage broke down. Although he won custody of their two young children due to her alcoholism (he neither drank nor smoked), he defaulted on payment of a £150,000 settlement to her. This became a major point of contention and culminated in an acrimonious altercation with her and her father, David Wadlow, that ended in him pulling out a handgun. He shot Wadlow several times, leaving him permanently scarred and partially disabled, as well as beating Anthea with the gun. This time there was no attempt to run and he himself called the police to give himself up.

After 17 years of freedom, he was sent back to jail in 1994. His sentence for attempted murder was a lenient six years, the judge having taken account of his fragile and depressed mental state, which his defence lawyers attributed to the legacy of his involvement in the train robbery. Inside, his continual complaints about feeling physically unwell were initially treated with scepticism by prison officers, but eventually he was allowed to go to a hospital for tests. Heart problems were diagnosed and he had surgery for a triple bypass operation, which led to his early release from prison in 1997. That August, aged 61, he died of a heart attack in Brompton Hospital, West London, not far from his birthplace.

The Great Train Robbery has been chronicled so extensively that there has almost been an industry in the countless books and articles that have been written and the films and TV productions that have been made. As one of the most enduring heists in British history, it captured the nation's imagination and created a mythology that has often been overly romanticised, with the real-life thugs portrayed as glamorous heroes in a *Boys' Own* caper. It may have been a meticulously planned operation of unprecedented proportions but the reality is that it was shambolic in its execution and involved the violent beating of a defenceless train driver who was simply going about his job and suffered serious injuries and trauma from which he never fully recovered. In his summing up at the end of the trial, the judge accurately described the robbery as 'a crime of sordid violence inspired by vast greed'. Although Roy James was neither the mastermind behind the operation nor directly involved in the physical assault, he was quite capable of turning to violence on a whim, as he proved so conclusively when he shot his father-in-law.

Although James only raced cars for little more than half a season before the Great Train Robbery, he was certainly one of the brightest young prospects amongst Formula Junior racers of that time and his raw talent and commitment behind the wheel might well have taken him onto a professional career. Contemporary Formula 1 team owner John Cooper, who had encountered him as a pupil at his racing school and was partly responsible for teaching him, was one of many who thought him an exceptionally good driver who could have been a champion. However, while several of James's erstwhile peers had progressed to Formula 1 and established glittering legacies while he was behind bars, they had already retired from the sport by the time he was released. Meanwhile, he had had plenty of time to ponder and reflect on what might have been, rather than the reality of his infamous place in history as Britain's best-known getaway driver.

CHAPTER 30
MICHAEL JONES
Driving ambition

Many fathers have put considerable sacrifice, dedication and money into furthering the motor racing ambitions of their offspring, often to little avail, but this individual's fraudulent approach — without his innocent son's knowledge — was to get British taxpayers to foot the six-figure bill.

Like so many aspiring young racing drivers these days, Wales-born Nick Jones's interest in motor racing was ignited at a very early age when his father Michael took him karting as a three-year-old. The youngster went on to race karts more seriously as soon as he was able to, before progressing to cars, first a Mini, then a bright yellow Renault Clio entered by Cardiff Advent Motorsport. By 2009 and aged 19, the club-level driver had already tasted some success that culminated in him winning the Welsh Sports and Saloon Car Championship. Mostly he raced in Wales at the Pembrey and Anglesey circuits but occasionally he and his father made forays to venues further afield such as Brands Hatch. So serious was the teenager about making a name for himself on the professional stage that he enrolled at The Silverstone Motorsport Academy in his quest to learn as much as he could about all the different facets of the sport from which he intended to make a living.

Many 'karting parents' live their lives vicariously through the exploits of their children but most such youngsters aren't born into significant wealth.

Seen in his Formula Renault car at Donington Park in 2004, Nick Jones
went racing with his father Michael's support, never knowing that
all the funding came from a tax scam.

In a scenario all too familiar to those parents who desperately want to believe that their offspring is the next Ayrton Senna or Lewis Hamilton, many are from very ordinary backgrounds who will often spend far more money than they can justifiably afford on a sport in which the odds of their child making it into the big time are stacked heavily against them.

Michael Jones was no exception and as a devoted father he wanted to help his only child, Nick, fulfil his dreams. When his son began to show more and more potential, Jones spent a fortune that he didn't have paying for Nick's racing. Soon he was helping the teenager to compete more widely across Britain and even in Belgium to take part in rounds of the Renault Sport Clio Cup. In doing so, Jones racked up enormous debts and his financial difficulties forced him to remortgage the family home for £400,000.

The desperation didn't end there. Michael Jones was a financial adviser who had previously been a tax inspector and when his son was aged just 16 he had established an ostensibly bona fide Cardiff-based company called Nick Jones Racing Ltd (NJR) with his son as the director and himself as the company secretary. This entity formed the basis of an elaborate tax fraud to bankroll Nick's racing career whereby Jones used his knowledge to operate a scheme through which he encouraged clients of his accountancy practice, J&R Business Services, to advertise with NJR. He persuaded 12 companies, mostly locally based, to 'pay' for sponsorship packages on NJR's racing cars and website. In truth the deals didn't actually exist and no real advertising ever occurred but the participating companies falsely reclaimed the VAT on their 'payments'. The directors and sole traders of these companies were personally reimbursed with gifts of 'tax-free' money while Jones falsified the company accounts, failing to show NJR's true income. It was subsequently discovered that when any real sponsors made payments to NJR, the money was quickly transferred to his personal bank accounts within 24 hours, so he was pocketing money that should have been declared to the British tax authorities.

Following an investigation by HM Revenue & Customs, the tax loss was calculated to be in excess of £140,000 in a scam involving a total of £600,000. When Jones appeared at Cardiff Crown Court in 2013, the 60-year-old pleaded guilty to five offences that included cheating the Inland Revenue, VAT fraud and transferring criminal property. Sentencing him to 32 months in prison, the judge described the fraud as 'carefully considered and constructed' using Jones's 'expertise as an accountant'.

Young Nick also appeared in court charged with being part of the swindle but the jury returned unanimous verdicts clearing him of two counts of possessing a total of £400,000 in criminal property. Completely oblivious to what had been going on, he told the court that he had no inkling of what his father was up to nor that he had been fiddling cash from the taxman. He said that he had never had any reason to suspect that anything untoward was going on financially. Nick was clear that had he known that there were any problems with funding, he would have stopped racing. In sentencing his father, the judge said: 'Your son was in ignorance of the criminal nature of your scheme and he was duped by his own father.'

CHAPTER 31

ACHILLEAS KALLAKIS

The gift-bearing Greek poker player

At the end of 2008, Honda shocked Formula 1 and the wider
world of motor racing by announcing that it was pulling out of
the sport with immediate effect. The Japanese manufacturer's
decision set in motion a chain of events that would lead to
a management buy-out and the fairy-tale story of World
Championship success for the hastily created Brawn F1 team.
Before this, however, one of the suitors who attempted to
buy the team emerged as a crook, dubbed by the media as
'Britain's most successful serial confidence trickster'.

Honda enjoyed a long and illustrious history as a Formula 1 engine
manufacturer in the period 1984–92 and won 69 Grands Prix, mainly
with Williams and McLaren, enabling those teams to claim six consecutive
constructors' titles between them. Craving even greater success as a
constructor in its own right, Honda bought British American Racing (BAR)
at the end of 2005. This outfit had been established and funded by British
American Tobacco six years earlier and had risen from the ashes of the
once-great Tyrrell team. Despite vast expenditure and the efforts of former
World Champion driver Jacques Villeneuve, BAR had performed woefully,
only once achieving a podium result with third place at the Spanish Grand
Prix in 2001.

Under Honda's ownership, however, prospects quickly improved and
Jenson Button scored a morale-boosting first victory for himself and for
the team at the 2006 Hungarian Grand Prix. Another big step forward
came at the end of 2007 when, fresh from a one-year sabbatical from the
sport, Ross Brawn joined Honda as team principal. One of the architects

of Michael Schumacher's record-breaking successes at Ferrari, he brought huge expertise and experience to the Northamptonshire-based operation although he arrived too late to influence the design of its 2008 car. For 2009, though, Brawn was hugely influential in the design and concept of the team's new contender and confidence was high.

By this time, the world was in recession. In a period that the International Monetary Fund described as the most severe economic downturn since the Great Depression of the 1930s, the financial services group Lehman Brothers, an institution always considered too big to fail, was allowed to collapse and it filed for bankruptcy in September 2008. The financial meltdown that followed precipitated global fear and panic and led Honda's board of directors in Tokyo to make the snap decision to withdraw from Formula 1 — a devastating blow to the sport as a whole. The people at the top at Honda were under the misapprehension that the Formula 1 team, despite the resources that had been lavished on it over many years, had no market value in the prevailing economic crisis and therefore didn't consider it worth trying to find a buyer. The board's view was that the team should be closed as quickly as possible but Brawn and Nick Fry, the team's chief executive, asked for a stay of execution while they attempted to identify interested parties. Surprised at this development, the Japanese directors agreed to this suggestion and continued to fund operations for a limited period with a necessarily much-reduced workforce.

When it was announced in early December 2008 that the Honda Formula 1 team was up for sale, Fry and Brawn found themselves deluged with expressions of interest, but they were desperately short of time if they were to succeed in putting a deal together in time for the 2009 season. Among the suitors was the well-respected Prodrive operation, run by David Richards, who had been previously involved with the team in its BAR guise and had helped to steer it during its most hopeful season of 2004. Virgin's Richard Branson looked into purchasing the team before deciding instead to confine his company's involvement to prominent sponsorship. Vijay Mallya, owner of the Force India Formula 1 team, was another to express interest.

There was also another potential buyer who turned out to be not at all what he seemed.

As Nick Fry describes it in his book *Survive, Drive, Win*, Achilleas Kallakis introduced himself as a billionaire shipping owner and rather bizarrely referred to himself as 'Ambassador of the Republic of San Marino to the Sultanate of Brunei'. After contacting the team through its sponsorship department, Kallakis invited Fry and Brawn to sumptuously appointed offices in London's Mayfair. Notable was the fact that the coffee table in the reception room was ostentatiously sprinkled with official-looking letters from various charities, art galleries and other esteemed bodies, all of which appeared either to congratulate him on his appointment to senior roles in their organisations or to thank him for his sizeable donations.

Kallakis made it clear from the outset that he wanted to buy the Honda Formula 1 team. He asked to visit its factory in Brackley, Northamptonshire as soon as possible and this was arranged within a matter of days. As the factory's helipad wasn't big enough to accommodate the massive helicopter in which Kallakis would be travelling, the company car park had to be cleared to make way for the VIP's arrival.

A bizarre couple of days in London followed for Fry and Brawn. An invitation to dinner in a private room at the Ritz gave them the first hint that their host might not be all that he appeared when he expressed disbelief that both of them were 'stupid enough' to pay taxes in the UK. This would prove to be a portent of things to come. The following evening saw the two men treated to another dinner, this time at Kallakis's house in Knightsbridge where he gave them a tour of an art collection that he claimed was worth tens of millions of pounds. As Fry pointed out, 'Some paintings were familiar and well-known pieces of artwork but neither Ross nor I was in a position to tell a fraud from the real thing. So we stood around, making suitably enthusiastic comments about how wonderful they were and he was.'

With the team's desperate need for an investor and the severe time constraints, Kallakis was at the top of the list of potential buyers, even though Fry and Brawn nonetheless had reservations about this man who had emerged out of the blue. Naturally, they embarked on a process of due diligence and went to great lengths to establish their potential saviour's credentials. At their own expense, they employed Kroll, an international corporate investigations agency, to dig into Kallakis's background. In addition, they knew that three-time World Champion Sir Jackie Stewart was friendly with the former King of Greece and asked him to check whether he had ever heard of their suitor. Meanwhile, they received two letters of reference on the official-looking letterheads of a junior member of the Royal Family and a Member of Parliament. Suspicions were aroused when it was noticed that the wording of both letters was remarkably similar to another letter that purported to be from a Swiss banker and had been given to them by Kallakis himself.

In the run-up to Christmas, Stewart reported back that the King of Greece

Achilleas Kallakis masqueraded as a billionaire shipping owner when negotiating to buy the Honda Formula 1 operation in 2008 but fortunately the team's senior representatives, Ross Brawn and Nick Fry, smelled a rat, unlike the banks that Kallakis had defrauded on his way to accumulating his riches.

had never heard of their quarry but couldn't rule him out as bona fide. By 23rd December, though, Kroll had come up with some interesting information. The investigators had discovered an American newspaper report describing how a certain 'Stephan Kollakis' had been convicted in 1995 of selling 'bogus British feudal titles to hapless Americans and Australians' while working as a travel agent in the unglamorous South London suburb of Croydon. One of these unsuspecting people was a US congressman who, like the other wealthy victims, believed the ludicrous assurances of a route into the upper echelons of British society that would allow them to call themselves 'Lord' and their wives 'Lady' and that their children could be known as 'The Honourable'. Among the promised perks were priority invitations to royal functions, the right to wear 'heraldic robes of nobility' and an opportunity to ride in the Queen Mother's birthday procession.

With their worst suspicions now confirmed, Fry and Brawn phoned Kallakis to tell him that details about his past had been uncovered and that, due to Honda's very strong ethics and strict compliance requirements, they wouldn't be able to continue their discussions. When the furious

Greek recovered his composure, he tried to play down their concerns by justifying his past mistakes as the result of youthful exuberance. Once he had established that Kroll's report hadn't yet been forwarded to Honda, because of the Christmas holiday, he suggested that if they simply provided a more flattering 'report' from a different agency, the Japanese would never need to find out about it. Not surprisingly, the incredulous men took their cue and ended the call.

Stefan Michalis Kollakis was a renowned poker player who was nicknamed 'The Don' after winning as much as $1 million on the international circuit. He was born in West London in 1968 and brought up in Ealing before going to study at the University of Buckingham, where he met his future partner in crime, Martin Lewis, who was an extremely talented forger. The scam that Kroll had highlighted involved buying titles from the Manorial Society of Great Britain, sub-dividing them into districts and then offering them for sale by advertising in newspapers. They claimed to be taking advantage of an ancient practice known as 'subinfeudation' — the sub-dividing of feudal lands — in order to increase the number of titles, even though this procedure had been banned in 1290. After their convictions for selling fake titles with a price tag of £85,000, both men changed their names: Kollakis became Achilleas Kallakis (with an 'a' instead of an 'o') and Lewis became Alexander Martin Williams. Eight years later, they embarked on their next joint venture, a rather more audacious and elaborate one.

The Guardian newspaper discovered that Kallakis had paid for an entry in *Who's Who in America*, the biographical reference book of notable living people in the US. Among other things, he listed himself as a 'patron of the English National Ballet, member of the development board for the National Portrait Gallery and recipient of the Churchill Award for Excellence from the Churchill Enterprise Foundation', but these were all either exaggerations or fabricated claims. Using his newly established identity, he reinvented himself as a shipping owner and property tycoon, and persuaded banks to lend him hundreds of millions of pounds between 2003 and 2008, using the loans to build one of London's most impressive and enviable property empires.

In keeping with their newly acquired wealth, Kallakis, his wife Pamela and four young children moved into a townhouse on Brompton Square in Knightsbridge where they enjoyed a lavish lifestyle with all the trappings of seemingly huge business success. These embraced a £27 million private jet, a £5.2 million helicopter, a fleet of cars including chauffeur-driven Bentleys, a superyacht moored in Monaco and the collection of high-value artworks that had been flaunted to the executives of the Honda Formula 1 team. He also owned a villa in Mykonos and property in Monaco, where he is said to have been a member of Prince Albert's charitable foundation. Bidding on high-priced commercial properties, Kallakis operated from a sumptuous office suite in Mayfair, doing his deals under the name of the Pacific Group, which was supposedly controlled by a family trust. The 'trophy' properties that were bought in and around London included Orion House in Covent Garden (£80 million in 2003), Astral Towers in Crawley (£21 million in 2005), two Home Office tower blocks in Croydon (£100 million in 2006), the Department of Health's offices in Vauxhall (£75 million in 2006), the Telegraph Media Group's headquarters in Victoria (£225 million in 2007) and a block in St James's Square (£120 million in 2007) that he intended to convert into some of the most exclusive and expensive private apartments in the world.

His spending spree wouldn't have been out of place in a game of Monopoly but this was for real. And it was all based on fraud and forgery using other people's money, secretive offshore trusts and fictional backing from an overseas shipping empire. Among the fraudster's methods was the use of forged references from supposed associates such as Lord Harris of High Cross, the former director of the Institute of Economic Affairs. Harris's reference appeared to confirm Kallakis's credentials, although his widow insisted at the eventual trial that she knew nothing of the purported family friendship that Kallakis claimed.

Too late, several lenders became increasingly suspicious of Kallakis's activities and credibility, chief among them the Allied Irish Bank. AIB had lent Kallakis a total of £740 million on the basis that Hong Kong property giant Sun Hung Kai Properties (SHKP) had supposedly guaranteed to pay prevailing or future rents if any tenants defaulted, thus removing the risk of occupiers not renewing their leases. Astonishingly, by wining and dining the gullible bankers, Kallakis somehow managed to convince them that these guarantees would fall apart if they contacted SHKP directly rather than through him. When it was proposed that AIB representatives should fly to Hong Kong to meet SHKP, Kallakis instead arranged for two executives from the bank's property team to meet a 'Jonathan Lee' at his Mayfair offices. Lee was supposedly a director in the treasury department at SHKP who had agreed to stop off, *en route* to Hong Kong from New York, especially to meet the AIB men. Although they thought it a little odd that he didn't have any business cards with him, he appeared to have good knowledge and understanding of Kallakis's loans and this gave them the confidence they needed, allaying the doubts about the financial guarantees supporting Kallakis's property empire.

Following the credit crunch of 2007, the scam began to unravel in August 2008, just as London's commercial property market was collapsing. To spread its risk, AIB attempted to sell on some of its loans to other banks, one of which was Helaba of Germany. Helaba was aware of Kallakis's previous conviction under his real name and, of course, told AIB about it. In due course AIB discovered that Kallakis had invented his connections with Hong Kong: SHKP had never employed a 'Jonathan Lee', didn't have a treasury department and had never been involved in rental guarantees. It also transpired that Kallakis had defrauded the Bank of Scotland of £22 million.

As prosecutors investigated the allegations that Kallakis's complex and mushrooming empire was founded on fraudulent leases used to secure loans on properties with inflated values from banks, the Serious Fraud Office (SFO) carried out a series of coordinated raids on his operations. While Kallakis was the 'front man', it was the creative skills of Alexander Williams, the prolific forger, that were responsible for the production of the false documents and fake guarantees used to support the loan applications.

At the subsequent trial, Walter Kwok of SHKP appeared by video link from Hong Kong and told the jury that he had never met with the defendants and his signature on multiple documents had been forged. A statement from the SFO said: 'The transactions were structured in a way that the bank loans exceeded the purchase price of the properties. This was achieved by providing the bank with a guarantee from a Hong Kong company, Sun Hung Kai Properties Limited, of long-term payment of rents at top market rates, to the landlord of the commercial properties. SHKP are a large, well established Hong Kong property company with a high credit rating and the guarantees therefore had the effect of increasing the value of the properties substantially. The rationale provided to the banks for SHKP's involvement was that a subsidiary company of SHKP would receive large cash payments called a reverse premium, which was factored into the value of the loans, and a share of the profits on the sale of the properties. However, the reality was that SHKP had not entered into any guarantees and had no knowledge of the transactions or the purported subsidiary companies that had entered into them. The SHKP documents provided by Kallakis and Williams to AIB were forgeries and the reverse premiums were channelled into the pockets of the fraudsters.'

The original trial of 2011 collapsed after three months when Williams attempted suicide but was resumed a year later, in September 2012. When it ended the following January, both of the 44-year-old men were found guilty of numerous charges including conspiracy to defraud, forgery and money laundering. Kallakis was stripped of his assets, which were returned to the banks, and was sentenced to seven years in prison while Williams was given five years. In a rare instance of the government's law officers seeking longer sentences, Solicitor General Oliver Heald took the highly unusual step of taking the case to the Appeal Court, which duly increased Kallakis's sentence by four years and Williams's by two years. Heald said: 'We welcome the Court's finding that the culpability of the offenders was at the highest level because they set out and persisted over a significant period with planning, determination and audacious dishonesty to commit a commercial fraud with international proportion.'

Jailing the men at Southwark Crown Court, Judge Andrew Goymer censured both the Allied Irish Bank and the Bank of Scotland for 'acting carelessly and imprudently by failing to make full enquiries before advancing the money. It almost beggars belief senior management chose to disregard warnings and rushed to complete the deal at all costs. Both the defendants took full advantage of the prevailing banking culture in which corners are cut, and checks on them superficial and cursory.'

Kallakis may have been a renowned and top-ranked poker player but despite his audacity he ultimately lost out in the property game. Like his imaginary title, most of the claims about his connections to establishment figures were fabricated, although there was a genuine one. His uncle was a wealthy Greek shipping tycoon called Pantelis 'Lou' Kollakis. However, when Uncle Lou eventually attended a meeting with concerned AIB bankers in 2008, he told them he had no knowledge of the fictional business that his nephew had conned them into funding.

Of his dealings with Kallakis, Nick Fry concluded: 'In retrospect it seems surprising that we did not share our concerns with the police but at the time we had no grounds to suspect that he was engaged in wholesale criminal activity. It also seems extraordinary, looking back, that we were fairly quickly able to rumble Kallakis and rule him out of doing business with Honda, whereas several major European banks, who lent him hundreds of millions of pounds, failed to adequately investigate him, to their considerable cost.'

The Formula 1 team, which evolved into Brawn GP and won the 2009 World Championship with Jenson Button, had avoided a poisoned chalice.

JONATHAN KERN

Masquerading as a racing driver

A playboy confidence trickster, he enjoyed a jet-set life by travelling the world posing as famous people, in particular a well-known British Formula 1 driver. His deceptions finally caught up with him when he was tracked down by Interpol and arrested at gunpoint on the French Riviera.

Jonathan Palmer is a former British Formula 1 driver who over the course of seven seasons made 83 Grand Prix starts. His early racing exploits in a Marcos sports car ran in tandem with his studies as he qualified in medicine and had a brief career as a doctor until motor racing took over. His performances in a Formula Ford Van Diemen led to a drive in British Formula 3 with the new West Surrey Engineering team for 1981. In a fantastic début season driving a year-old Ralt RT3, he took six pole positions, seven wins and nine fastest laps to claim the championship by a large margin. After a more difficult first season in Formula 2 with the mighty works Ralt-Honda team in 1982, the following year saw more Palmer dominance and he was crowned European Formula 2 Champion after winning six races.

As reward for all the testing work he had been conducting for the Williams Formula 1 team, he made his Grand Prix début with Williams in the 1983 European Grand Prix at Brands Hatch. However, despite his outstanding résumé, he never managed to find the competitive Formula 1 seat that his talent deserved and he spent six largely fruitless seasons racing for RAM, Zakspeed and Tyrrell, with the highlights being occasional finishes in the points and victory in the one-off Jim Clark Trophy, awarded in 1987 to the top-placed driver of a non-turbo car. Palmer also raced Group C sports cars, most notably with Richard Lloyd's team in Porsche 956s, winning the 1984 Brands Hatch 1,000Km and finishing second in the following year's Le Mans 24 Hours. He mixed a season of driving a Porsche 962 for the works-backed Joest Porsche Racing team with Formula 1 testing duties for McLaren in 1990 before his driving career culminated with a British Touring Car Championship campaign for BMW the following year.

After his retirement from racing, Palmer developed an extremely successful business career as a motorsport entrepreneur. He ran driver experience events and track days through his Palmersport company before creating the Formula Palmer Audi championship as a cheaper alternative to Formula 3. He co-founded MotorSport Vision Ltd, which owns the commercial rights to operate several racing series and is best known as owner and operator of an impressive portfolio of racing circuits comprising Brands Hatch, Oulton Park, Snetterton, Cadwell Park and Donington Park.

Jonathan Kern is an international conman who, other than his Christian name and British nationality, shares absolutely no similarities whatsoever with Jonathan Palmer but repeatedly impersonated the racing driver for financial gain. Claiming to be Palmer, Kern racked up unpaid bills for designer clothes, jewellery and top-ranked hotel accommodation all over Europe, before taking his scam to America. There he used his persuasive charms to con his way into the lives of dozens of women, from whom, having won them over, he would borrow thousands of dollars that were never repaid.

One of the many to have been deceived by him during a whirlwind romance was Elizabeth Ballard of Milford, Connecticut. After lending him her bank card, she found that her account had been drained as he used her money to wine and dine other gullible victims at top restaurants, with the result that she was forced into bankruptcy in 1994. It wasn't just unsuspecting women who were duped, for luxury hotel owner David Colby recalled how a car dealer provided Kern with a $78,000 Jaguar: 'They dropped the keys at the desk and said this is for Mr Palmer for his use while he's in America and please make sure that he gets it. We always believed him and that just made us more convinced that everything was OK.'

The first thing Palmer himself heard about the man was when three-time Formula 1 World Champion Jackie Stewart told him that, in Palmer's words, 'someone was going around France driving a BMW cabriolet and saying he was me'. Lisa Davis, Palmer's personal assistant at the time, said: 'We've had Kern claiming to be Jonathan Palmer all over the world, borrowing cars, and we have had numerous invoices for clothes, jewellery and outstanding hotel bills all in Palmer's name. Fortunately, he doesn't resemble Jonathan Palmer in the slightest.'

In 1996, an arrest warrant for Kern was issued in the US on charges of felony, criminal impersonation, second-degree forgery and second-degree larceny but, according to police in Milford, it wasn't extraditable on the grounds of cost. By this time, however, the imposter had returned to Europe and eventually his continued predilection for performance cars led to his downfall. According to *The Guardian* newspaper, Kern contacted Lotus Cars in August 1998 claiming to be the publisher of *Now*, a celebrity magazine, asking to borrow a road-test car to use as the subject of an article. This was an entirely plausible prospect because car manufacturers regularly loan cars to journalists for review.

Having satisfied itself about Kern's credentials, Lotus delivered a 170mph twin-turbo Esprit V8 GT to the home of his mother, sculptor Doreen Kern. That same day, the conman set off across the Channel *en route* to the Belgian Grand Prix, from where he called Lotus a few days later to inform the company that the car had been stolen. He said that he was about to fly to the US and would call again two days later but in fact he drove the £70,000 supercar all the way to Puerto Banús in Spain to see a long-term lover. In the meantime, Lotus had become suspicious, having rechecked Kern's driving licence and identified irregularities.

Lotus assumed that it would never see Kern or the Esprit again. However, as *The Guardian* reported, 'By an extraordinary stroke of luck, Lotus employee Katie Dann was also on holiday in Puerto Banús, where she took a photograph of herself with the silver Lotus as a souvenir. It was only when she got home that colleagues recognised the licence plate as that of the missing car.' After quarrelling with the girlfriend in Spain, Kern continued his travels and headed for France and Italy, spending a while at Lake Como before arriving in Antibes on the French Riviera, where Interpol tracked him down.

Early one morning, a five-man team of French police ambushed him at gunpoint in his hotel. *The Independent* newspaper reported that he was found 'in bed with a prostitute and in possession of a fistful of fraudulent credit cards'. The 44-year-old was detained in prison in Marseille for eight months before being extradited to Britain, where he received a three-year jail sentence. Rather ironically, he was sent to Norwich prison, just a few miles up the road from Lotus's headquarters in Hethel. Although he pleaded guilty at his trial, he claimed that he borrowed the car fully intending to return it. He was quoted as saying: 'I think Lotus have done well out of this. I've given them lots of publicity. I think they should pay me.' Lotus eventually got its car back, albeit with 6,000 more miles on the clock.

Kern, it turned out, had previously pulled off similar stunts. According to journalist Julia Hartley Brewer, writing in *The Guardian*, he committed his first offence of impersonating a policeman at the age of 18, and dishonestly obtained an array of fast cars over the years. Posing as a music producer, he started by 'borrowing' a £44,000 BMW from the company's Park Lane showroom in London. He progressed to 'obtaining' a BMW M3 cabriolet in Italy and a Mercedes 600SL in Florida. As well as the Jaguar in Connecticut, he got hold of at least one Ferrari and also another Lotus Esprit. At the time of his sentencing, several American states were understood to have outstanding arrest warrants for him.

Hartley Brewer visited him in Norwich jail and wrote that not only did he stay in some of the world's most expensive and exclusive hotels, running up huge bills, but he also bought entire wardrobes of designer clothes, jewellery, watches, briefcases and numerous other accessories, sometimes posing as Rolling Stones guitarist Mick Taylor, but more often than not in the name of Jonathan Palmer.

Palmer, a man who is respected throughout the motor racing community for his success as a driver and in business, had to endure many frustrations, including the serving of a county court summons for non-payment of two escort girls booked in his name. When his office received an invoice from Versace in Milan for £12,000, Palmer decided to telephone Kern and berated him for damaging his reputation. Kern apologised, promising never to impersonate him again.

RUSSELL KING

Lord Voldemort of motorsport

The larger-than-life Russell King is a British globetrotting serial fraudster and conman who spread his largesse and largeness across several sports, from football to Formula 1. Those he duped along the way have included a former manager of the England football team and one of the biggest and most prestigious car manufacturers involved in Grand Prix racing.

In the 1980s, Russell King was chairman of a tiny magazine publishing company called Celebrity Group that owned *Basketball Monthly* among other titles and at the same time he was also a director of a local basketball club. In the early 1990s, he was sentenced to two years in prison for an insurance scam after attempting to claim £600,000 for an Aston Martin Zagato that he claimed had been stolen but was later found hidden in his garage. While he was inside, his ailing business went into liquidation after being sued for almost £700,000 by Creditcorp, which alleged fraudulent behaviour by the company's directors. At this time King was also associated with the controversial and disgraced publicist Max Clifford, who was subsequently jailed for sexual offences.

By the early 2000s, King was operating in the world of high finance in Jersey, where he was involved in the so-called Belgravia Financial Services Group, which was registered at his home address although he claimed never to have been a shareholder or officer of the company. Of his several scams in this period, one involved conning the family of his gardener and housekeeper out of their life savings. Demands by Close Finance for repayment of a £2 million loan were unsuccessful, precipitating a police raid on his house, following which he fled to Dubai leaving a trail of financial destruction behind him. From this new base, he convinced the investment bank First London that he was managing billions of dollars for the Bahraini royal family that the bank would be able to access for funding and investment purposes, and earn fees accordingly, provided it rewarded him with a 49 percent shareholding. In an extraordinary lapse of judgement, the bankers omitted to clear the exchange with the financial regulators and agreed to the transaction even though in reality King had no financial connection at all with the Bahraini royal family. Now with ownership of a large slice of an investment bank for which he had paid nothing, he exuded wealth and all the trappings of apparent success.

Aware that Manchester City had been sold in 2008 to Sheikh Mansour, a member of the Abu Dhabi ruling family, King now decided to buy a football club. His target was struggling Notts County, which needed serious investment. In 2009, the fraudster arranged to buy the club from the supporters' trust for a nominal £1 (and take over its debt) after the trust's representatives met one of his supposedly wealthy benefactors in Bahrain. Abid Hyat Khan was introduced as a Middle Eastern prince, but reporters from the BBC later discovered that this man was also a crook and was on the run from the police. The previous year, Khan had absconded before he was due to stand trial for allegedly stealing almost £1 million.

Although King claimed, as was his trademark, to have no legal involvement in the deal and simply acted as negotiator, he negotiated the onward sale of Notts County to Munto Finance, a subsidiary of Qadbak Investments, which was another company trading on non-existent connections with ultra-wealthy Middle Eastern families. One of King's coups was to recruit a distinguished former England team manager, Sven-Goran Eriksson, to lead the ailing football team out of the lower divisions. The fraudster additionally tempted Eriksson with the promise of lucrative rewards from an entity called Swiss Commodity Holdings, a mining and resources company, by giving him what purported to be a substantial shareholding that would yield vast rewards from a flotation on the stock market that was said to be only weeks away. King claimed that the Swiss-based company had assets worth almost $2 trillion because it owned the rights to North Korea's gold, coal and iron ore. Telling Eriksson that the guaranteed funding for Notts County supplied by First London would come from this mining deal, King persuaded him to join a delegation visiting Pyongyang.

'I was in the palace and they were handing over to the North Korean government so-called shares,' Eriksson told the BBC. 'I asked them how much that was and what they told me was not millions, it was billions of dollars. They used my name. Of course they did. At the end it became a big, big mistake. For me as a football man it was fantastic, building a club from the bottom of League Two and having the funding to do it, to be a Premier League club. It's like a dream, so I signed. Big mistake.'

Needless to say, the promised investment never arrived and the club was left £7 million in debt. Eriksson said there were early signs that all wasn't as it seemed: 'I started to have doubts when they came and told me the milk bill has not been paid.' He was in good company as two of First London's advisers, Tim Yeo (a Conservative MP) and Air Marshal Sir John Walker (a former head of Britain's defence intelligence), were also taken in, with their names used to add credibility to King's lies. First London went into administration in 2010 with debts of £8.7 million.

Russell King first appeared on the fringes of motorsport in 2002 when he was linked to a sports agency called Essentially Sport through John Byfield, a respectable lawyer who represented the interests of Formula 1 driver Jenson Button. By 2004, Byfield and King were involved with another company, Grand Prix Investments, which was said to be buying the Jordan Grand Prix team with the blessing of Dubai's Sheikh Ahmed bin Saeed Al Maktoum. All he had actually done was to give his approval for their unrealistic suggestion that the team be based in Dubai, but they didn't have his financial support and the deal never reached fruition.

King reappeared on the scene in 2009 when BMW was looking for a new owner for the Formula 1 team that it had bought from Sauber Motorsport four years earlier. During that time, the team, called BMW Sauber, had performed with impressive reliability but won only one Grand Prix, in Canada in 2008 with Robert Kubica. Now BMW, having decided to leave Formula 1, resolved to find a suitable investor to take over the team. However, the team's very existence was thrown into jeopardy when it transpired that the potential buyer might not be the saviour it purported to be.

In late 2009, it became public knowledge that the offer accepted by BMW was from the mysterious investment consortium Qadbak Investments, the group that was being investigated by the English Football Association about its involvement with Notts County. The insistence on anonymity by the new buyers had already raised suspicions that all was not what it seemed

After conning his way into buying Notts Country football club and leaving it with huge debts, Russell King turned his malign attentions to Formula 1 in 2009, as a potential purchaser of BMW's Formula 1 team.

and discomfort grew further after more research established unfortunate connections with King, whose assets in Jersey had recently been frozen because of unpaid debts and the failure of his Belgravia Financial Services Group. Worrying rumours about the identity of the buyer gained momentum when it was alleged by a Swiss newspaper, *Sonntagszeitung*, that Qadbak was merely a front for a convicted fraudster that it named as Russell King, who, it claimed, intended to fund the team off the back of the commercial income that the BMW-owned outfit had earned from finishing sixth in the 2009 constructors' championship. However, this revenue was conditional on the team being granted an entry for the 2010 season, which was looking increasingly unlikely.

The FIA, already suspicious about King's credentials and the existence of the financial backing, was unwilling to allocate the grid slot to Sauber until the team's management was certain that real money was in place to guarantee the future of the operation and its hundreds of employees. BMW itself was also becoming ever more concerned at the lack of evidence of solid funding behind the deal, which Qadbak consistently claimed was underwritten by Bahrain Capital International. With further doubts about the identity and credibility of Qadbak, the team failed to win the unanimous support that was necessary for it to be granted an automatic slot on the grid for the forthcoming season. As a result, the deal collapsed, primarily because of King's involvement, and BMW was left unable to find an alternative buyer at such short notice.

With that, King left motorsport behind but not his life of fraud. He returned to his old stamping ground of magazines and set up publications using various aliases and making false claims about their circulation figures so that he could rake in millions of dollars in advertising revenue and barter deals. One magazine was called *FT Business Arabia*, which presented itself as an authorised spin-off from the internationally renowned *Financial Times* but was entirely bogus. This deception was pulled off with such meticulous planning and attention to detail that everyone from luxury retail brands to top hospitality groups fell for it.

King was able to evade justice on many occasions by denying and concealing his true connections with fraudulent enterprises and often referred to himself as 'Lord Voldemort', the character from the Harry Potter books who can never be named. However, the law did finally, once again, catch up with the swindler whom the BBC described as the 'Trillion Dollar Conman' when he was extradited from Bahrain to Jersey. There in 2019, 28 years after his first sentence, a court found him guilty on separate counts of laundering funds from the now-defunct Belgravia Financial Services Group and sentenced him to six years in prison. He was released in 2021.

RANDY LANIER

International Marijuana Smuggling Association

It's ironic that Randy Lanier's success in America's premier sports car championship sowed the seeds for his downfall. The authorities, who were already investigating some of his competitors, became suspicious of this brash privateer's ability to beat well-funded and works-supported teams, despite few visible signs of sponsorship. He claimed that a water-sports rental company was behind his huge wealth but the true source was very different. The inevitable happened when his secret life collided with his meteoric racing career.

Although he had always been interested in cars and liked to listen to the Indianapolis 500 on the radio, Randy Lanier was a relative latecomer to racing. He became involved almost by accident after looking around the SCCA's stand at a car show in Miami Beach, picking up a brochure about race-driving tuition and paying on the spot for lessons: 'I thought it would be kind of neat to sign up and maybe do a little amateur racing some time. It was just going to be a hobby, you know, something to do around home.'

In 1979, aged 25 and armed with his newly acquired racing licence, he decided that he was ready to compete and paid $7,500 for a dilapidated Porsche 356 Speedster that he stripped out and equipped with new brakes and a roll cage. He won his first race, an amateur event in West Palm Beach, and was instantly hooked. The following year he managed to win his class in the SCCA Southeast Regional Championship.

Lanier's remarkable ascent in the sport gathered momentum in 1981. At the end of the season he made his début in the IMSA Camel GT series, America's top sportscar competition, by paying to co-drive with Dale

Whittington in a Porsche 935 at the Daytona finale. A few months later, early in 1982, his big break came in the 24-hour race at Daytona when he was called up as a last-minute substitute for an unwell Janet Guthrie in a NART-entered Ferrari 512 BB LM with Bob Wollek as lead driver. Although Lanier damaged the gearbox and managed to crash the car out of third place during his first stint, 18 hours into the race, his raw speed made a strong impression. Again paying for the privilege, he rejoined Whittington for the Sebring 12 Hours, this time driving Preston Henn's Porsche 935 K3.

NART invited Lanier to drive the Ferrari again in that year's Le Mans 24 Hours. He and his wife Pam flew there by private jet and stayed in a 56-room château. 'That's when it hit me,' he said. 'The lifestyle, the racing, the whole package. I told my wife then that this was what I wanted to do the rest of my life. This is something I need to be a part of.' Sharing with Henn and Frenchman Denis Moran, he got very little time behind the wheel as the car ran out of fuel after four hours.

His first strong IMSA result came on a return to Daytona with fourth place in Henn's Porsche in the Paul Revere race two weeks after Le Mans. After that, Lanier took the plunge and bought his own car, a March 83G, and asked Marty Hinze to partner him. Their first three races brought two remarkable third places, at Mosport and Michigan. In a very short time, Lanier had built a fine reputation not just as a quick driver but also one with the all-important financial means to support his racing. Although his 1983 season began impressively with second place in the Daytona 24 Hours in another March, a new 83G, it was otherwise a disappointing year, with sporadic races with Hinze in his older March bringing a succession of retirements.

Keen to make up for it in 1984, Lanier teamed up with Dale Whittington and his brother Bill to form Blue Thunder Racing. At great expense, this new 'money-no-object' team acquired two Chevrolet-powered March 84Gs and recruited a top crew chief, Keith Leyton, who was told to hire the best mechanics in the business irrespective of cost. The new outfit was dismissed by the big manufacturer teams — Jaguar, Porsche and Ford — and other established teams as yet another group of amateurs with more money than sense, let alone talent. However, the team was a spectacular success right from the start, finishing second in its début event, close to home in the Sebring 12 Hours.

Next time out, in the six-hour Grand Prix of Endurance at Riverside, Lanier claimed a dramatic victory. Towards the end he took the lead from Al

Randy Lanier took the IMSA scene by storm in 1984 when he racked up six victories and became champion in his first full season.

Holbert, the reigning IMSA champion, but then a tyre blew. By the time he made it back to his pit for a new wheel, the car was running on a bare rim and had dropped well back, but he charged through the field, caught and repassed Holbert, and won by five seconds. 'Two weeks after,' Lanier recalled, 'I went to Laguna Seca and won. Then I went to Charlotte and won.' And he kept on winning. At Portland, he won in a dramatic finish after the race leader ran out of fuel on the last lap. He followed that up with victories at Michigan and Watkins Glen.

His more experienced co-driver, Bill, whom Lanier described as 'like one of my brothers', helped him improve his driving skills and develop knowledge of car set-up. It was all to good effect as, to the disbelief of his competitors and the press, the little-known Lanier became IMSA champion in his first full-time season.

'These were fabulous racing days,' remembered Lanier. 'It felt awesome. Every day I woke up knowing that I was going to a race track, going to a race shop, or climbing in a race car. I was at the peak of my life, I thought.

I felt so blessed… And I knew then I was capable of competing at any level.'

Brimming with confidence, he set his sights even higher. Despite having no experience in single-seater racing, let alone in immensely powerful Indycars, he focused on a new goal of winning the Indianapolis 500. Frank Arciero, a well-known talent spotter, signed Lanier to drive for his team part-time in 1985 with the intention of doing a full season the following year. At his first Indy 500, which was only his second event in the team's Lola T900, he was not surprisingly out of his depth and failed to make the grid, while his eight other Indycar appearances that season were lacklustre by his standards, although he made steady progress.

Lanier didn't leave sportscar racing behind entirely, but his 1985 outings with Blue Thunder Racing came nowhere near the previous year's achievements, with a best result of fifth place in the end-of-season Daytona Finale. Joest Racing, winners of Le Mans for the past two years, offered him a Porsche 962 seat in the Daytona 24 Hours and Sebring 12 Hours early in 1986, but the car retired so early from both events that he never got to drive.

The Arciero team, meanwhile, acquired a new March 86C for Lanier's 1986 Indycar season and it proved to be much more competitive. This time he not only qualified for the Indy 500 but did so at an average speed of 209.964mph, obliterating the previous record for a rookie set by Michael Andretti two years earlier. His reputation rocketed ahead of the biggest race of his career. Rainstorms of biblical proportions forced postponement of the race by a week but eventually Lanier was able to place his bright red car on the fifth row of the grid just behind double Formula 1 World Champion Emerson Fittipaldi and amongst other Indycar legends, including previous winners such as the great A.J. Foyt, who had the same chassis and engine package, and Mario Andretti. He put in a stunning performance, running near the front at one stage, and finished a very respectable 10th, the only rookie to complete the distance. At the awards banquet, he received the prestigious 'Rookie of the Year' accolade.

Still riding on the crest of a wave and with his performances improving as he gained experience at this level, he went to the Michigan 500 in August for his ninth Indycar race of the season. A tyre exploded at high speed and he smashed into the retaining wall with such force that his right femur was shattered, leaving the bone protruding through his fireproof driving suit. Doctors had to insert a metal rod to rebuild the leg. The highest point in his racing career had quickly been followed by the lowest. And much worse was to follow.

One of Randy Lanier's 1984 wins in his Blue Thunder Racing March 84G
came here at Michigan International Speedway in a 500km race
partnered by Bill Whittington (see Chapter 63).

Randy Lanier's father was an impecunious but hard-working carpenter who moved his wife and four children from a tobacco farm with no running water in Virginia to Melbourne in south Florida at the end of the 1960s when Randy was 13. At a time when TV's *Miami Vice* glamorised the local drug culture and party scene, the lure of a fast-paced lifestyle had a profound impact on the teenager. For Lanier, fiction became reality. His life, he said, 'was so open, so free. There were parks where we'd have pot festivals, and love-ins. I was right in that mix.'

He was enrolled at Miramar High School but had to drop out at the age of 15 after being caught selling marijuana to classmates. 'Honestly, I didn't even think about it as drug dealing,' he said. 'It was just a way for me to smoke without having to pay for it.' The pony-tailed youngster took a job on a construction site and soon he was selling to his fellow workers too, making far more money from this than he could ever earn through back-breaking manual labour at $1.65 an hour. 'Let's just say, I was definitely making more money than I made nailing boards all day,' he said. By the age of 19, in 1973, he had enough money to buy a sleek 27-foot Magnum Sport speedboat for $18,000 for fun at weekends, but within only a few months he used it for another purpose.

'A buddy asked me if I was interested in going to the Bahamas and putting some grass on my boat. It seemed like an adventure, so I did it.' This brought even more easy money and he made further trips. From there, it was all too tempting to move on to ferrying larger quantities of marijuana from offshore ships to drop-off areas on beaches. This marked his transition from a small-time dealer to a trafficker. His first major contract, solicited by south Florida drug barons, was another excursion to the Bahamas to pick up what he estimated to be a ton of marijuana from a 'mother ship' waiting offshore.

The pot-smoking habit exploded in America during the late '70s and early '80s. Florida was a smuggler's paradise with thousands of miles of coastline and labyrinthine inland waterways all in convenient proximity to various Caribbean islands as well as Colombia, where 75 percent of America's marijuana supply was cultivated. Florida's ideally placed marinas and ports became hives of activity and a burgeoning illegal industry grew up, often involving creative logistics to bring in the marijuana away from the inquisitive eyes of Federal agents and the US coastguard and then distribute it.

At the time 'Colombian Gold', an exotic new strain of marijuana grown on the country's wild Guajira Peninsula, was flooding America and fuelling a bonanza on the black market. The peninsula proliferated with loading facilities for 'mother ships' in the form of trawlers or fishing boats capable of transporting bales of marijuana by the ton to islands within easy reach of Florida. Lanier built up a network of strong local connections and formed a close partnership with one individual. This was Ben Kramer, an offshore powerboat racer and owner of Apache Power Boats, a name that adorned Lanier's March 84G during his super-successful 1984 racing season. Kramer was related by marriage to notorious mobster Meyer Lansky and already had a criminal record, having been recently released from prison for drug trafficking. He connected Lanier to his contacts in Colombia and together they moved up a gear. No longer middleman distributors, they were now able to buy premium marijuana direct from source and in doing so dramatically improve their profit margins.

Lanier realised that he needed a bigger boat and bought a 65-foot Norwegian-made wooden fishing trawler, *Ursa Major*, which enabled him to sail to Colombia and return with a vast cargo of marijuana. On the first trip, be brought back 15,000 pounds — seven and a half tons — of Colombian Gold that he sold for nearly $4.5 million the next day. 'That was the beginning, it just evolved,' he said. Over time, his boats became bigger and faster, and eventually the trawler became part of a fleet that included more speedboats as well as barges with tugboats to pull them. A simple but audacious method was to conceal watertight bales of marijuana in secret compartments in the ballast of the barges and dock quite openly. 'We welded compartments into the ballast so the weed was underneath the salt water,' explained Lanier. So successful were they in evading Customs officials that shipments grew even bigger and routinely exceeded 100,000 pounds in weight. Very few traffickers were sufficiently confident or daring to smuggle loads of that magnitude into America.

The first time Lanier and Kramer did it, early in 1983, their barge sailed up New York's East River and docked at the derelict Brooklyn Navy Yard with 130,000 pounds of Colombian Gold on board. That night the partners celebrated their success by renting a private room in a Manhattan restaurant. To further mark the occasion, Lanier bought personalised hats for the entire crew emblazoned with the logo 'The 100 Club' in recognition of their new-found status as smugglers of a 100,000-pound shipment.

Despite meticulous planning, however, the shipments weren't always so successful. During one long voyage with a 22,000-pound load, water leaked into one of the barge's compartments and some of the valuable bales became sodden without anyone realising. As the marijuana decomposed, it emitted methane and some of this detonated when some welding was done. Two of the unfortunate welders died through asphyxiation from methane and there was a danger that the entire barge would explode, so the entire shipment had to be abandoned. The stricken barge, carrying the two dead men wrapped in tarpaulin sheets, was scuttled and sunk out at sea.

When Lanier was 22, he had married his high-school sweetheart, Pam, who knew all about his illicit activities. To create an illusion of legitimacy, he started a business renting out boats and jetskis near Fort Lauderdale and in the sports pages of newspapers and the motorsport press he was routinely described as a regular businessman with a wife and a young daughter. However, racing sportscars at the highest level was, and remains, exorbitantly expensive, and people in the racing world wondered where Blue Thunder Racing was getting the sort of money it needed to embarrass the deep-pocketed factory teams and their highly rated professional drivers during that super-successful 1984 season. 'To compete against the Porsches, the Jaguars… I figured out I had to spend as much as them,' said Lanier. And so he did. At one awards banquet, a competitor approached one of Lanier's crew and remarked, 'I don't know where the hell these Blue Thunder guys came from, but they're the only race team where everyone on the pit crew wears a Rolex!' It just so happened that between races,

Lanier and his partners had just smuggled in a particularly big barge-load of Colombian Gold.

While still in his 20s, Lanier was living a life of unimaginable riches, especially for a country boy from Virginia. He and Pam moved into a sprawling five-bedroom ranch house that was equipped with platinum sinks and patrolled by a pair of Rottweiler dogs in the grounds. They also owned three holiday homes in the Rockies. He bought a fleet of exotic cars, including a new Porsche for himself and a Mercedes for Pam. They flew to races in private jets and hosted lavish parties at their homes, filling the hot tubs with Dom Pérignon champagne. 'Crazy, wild times: Learjets, bales of weed, drawers full of money,' recalled Pam.

The torrent of drug money was so great that Lanier and Kramer had to launder much of it. Using a series of offshore accounts, they routed millions to a front company that built a 100,000-square-foot casino in California called the Bell Gardens Bicycle Club. One of the numerous fictitious companies Lanier created for laundering purposes was reportedly called G. Reedy Holding Co — 'greedy'.

On 11th March 1986, Lanier's former IMSA team-mate, Bill Whittington, was arrested and charged with tax evasion, fraud and smuggling 'multi-ton quantities of marijuana' valued at $73 million. According to press coverage in which Lanier's name was mentioned, but only by association, this put him in an awkward position. When the usually publicity-shy driver was interviewed by the *Sun Sentinel* newspaper, he denied all knowledge of Whittington's activities. 'I didn't even know Bill was in trouble... we heard rumors for years,' said Lanier. 'It's unfortunate, but I don't think less of him as a person. I hope people will take me on my driving skills, not whom I associate with.' Lanier said he knew of no drug money being invested in Blue Thunder Racing's operation when they won the title: 'If it was, I didn't see it.'

This was a period in which Ronald Reagan's administration was relentlessly pursuing all drug crime through its 'War on Drugs' initiative. As Lanier's 1986 Indycar season got underway, he became increasingly nervous that he and his wife were being shadowed by federal agents. He hid in a condominium rented under a false identity and began using untraceable pay phones. His paranoia intensified a week before the Indy 500 when he was visited by the brother of his Louisiana distributor, who had been arrested with a few pounds of cannabis in his broken-down truck and was cooperating with the FBI. This dealer had been a long way down the supply chain but the usual method for investigators was to work up the chain with one dealer after another providing the names of suppliers, like a domino effect. Eventually they were led to Lanier.

At the time the company's barge, carrying the largest load yet, was 10 days off the coast of New Orleans sailing south towards the Panama Canal with the intention of smuggling its cargo into the US through a harbour in California. Despite the risk, the partners decided to continue as there was so much money at stake and so many people involved, although Lanier had resolved that this would be his final shipment. Continuing with it, however, proved to be a mistake because it provided more leads and yet more incriminating evidence. In October 1986, Lanier was one of 11 people to whom the Drug Enforcement Agency (DEA) handed down a series of charges in the federal court in Miami predicated on 'a major drug and money laundering organisation'. As he had still not fully recovered from the injuries sustained two months earlier in his Indycar accident, Lanier immediately surrendered to the authorities and was released on bail.

At about the same time, an unrelated case in England added further weight to the unravelling of his operation. The largest armed robbery in British history had taken place in 1983 when six armed men had stolen three tons of gold bullion, cash and diamonds worth $40 million from a Brink's-Mat warehouse near London's Heathrow Airport (see Chapter 62). The case had remained unsolved until detectives from Scotland Yard identified an accountant in the British Virgin Islands whom they suspected of laundering money for the thieves. In a deal made with the police, this accountant confessed that he had also handled money for some significant US-based drugs operations, one of which included Lanier's laundering of large sums via the Bell Gardens Bicycle Club.

In January 1987, Lanier's predicament became even more serious. The FBI's investigation of the racing team's source of funding and his fabulous wealth provided them with the basis for a watertight case and he was indicted for importing marijuana from Colombia. Prosecutors estimated that he had made $68 million in profits between 1982 and 1986. He had just stopped off at a deli to pick up some breakfast after visiting Pam and their new-born son in hospital when he caught a glimpse of a news report on the television screen behind the counter. To his horror, the scene showed the tall gates in front of his home near Fort Lauderdale, with news crews reporting live and DEA and FBI agents hovering in the background wearing body armour, accompanied by the headline 'Indy race car driver Randy Lanier has been indicted on federal drug-trafficking charges'. As Lanier put it, 'I paid for my bagel, packed my shit and got the fuck out of town.' He later called Pam on a pay phone to tell her he was leaving and wouldn't be able to return to fetch her or his two children, Brandie and Glen.

He was able to slip out of Florida unnoticed in the sleeper cab of an articulated truck and hid in rural Pennsylvania before flying to London on a false passport. There he met up with an old girlfriend, Maria de la Luz Maggi, whom he had known in Florida. With millions of dollars still secreted in offshore bank accounts, he believed it would be possible for him to build an entirely new life and even considered resuming his racing career under a new identity in New Zealand. After staying for a while in Europe, where he spent lavishly on luxury hotels and gambling trips to Monaco, the pair flew to Antigua in the Caribbean. Awaiting them was a 60-foot Hatteras motorboat on which they planned to relax for a few weeks before sailing to Spain.

One late October morning as they steered the Hatteras into a small harbour, a grey ship pulled in behind them, blocking their exit. They watched as the Antiguan vessel dispatched a small boat filled with armed men. As it sped towards them, Lanier quickly launched his own Zodiac tender. Reaching the dock before his pursuers, Lanier sprinted away, barefoot and wearing only swimming shorts. As he climbed a steep hill, spiky vegetation lacerated his feet and they began to bleed badly. Cornered by a convoy of jeeps full of more armed soldiers who threatened to shoot, he had no choice but to limp back down the hillside into the hands of the Antiguan Police, who put the 'undesired alien' on a plane to Puerto Rico. Once on US soil, Lanier was arrested. He had spent eight months as a fugitive.

When Lanier was indicted in the Southern District of Illinois for drug smuggling under the new 'Continuing Criminal Enterprise Law', this superseded the Miami indictment and centred around him, Ben Kramer and Kramer's father, Jack. Lanier claimed that he was offered a deal whereby if he turned informant and testified against key people in his network, he would receive a lesser prison sentence of 22 years, but he told his lawyers that he was only prepared to serve 10 years and insisted they reach agreement with the Justice Department to this effect. His bargaining position was too weak, however, and given the sheer quantities of drugs involved, Lanier was classified as the 'kingpin'. His lawyers warned him that if he were to be convicted of the highest drugs charge possible, it meant life imprisonment with no chance of parole. The authorities decided that Lanier, as well as being a high-profile racing driver, was also the mastermind of one of the largest drug-trafficking operations in American history.

The trial took place over three months during the summer of 1988 with

10,500 pages of court transcripts accumulated from 65 witnesses. These included two dozen associates who testified against him, several of them long-time friends — one was Charles Podesta for whom Lanier had been best man — seeking more lenient sentences for themselves. According to the prosecution, Lanier and his colleagues had trafficked more than 300 tons of marijuana into the US and had overseen a drug-smuggling empire that encompassed a dozen states and employed more than 150 people. The jury found the 34-year-old guilty on three counts that all came with hefty sentences: running a continual criminal enterprise; conspiring to distribute marijuana; and defrauding the IRS. Despite the absence of any violence in the charges, Judge James Foreman chose to stick with the sentencing guidelines and, under what was known as the 'Super Drug Kingpin Law', sentenced Lanier and Kramer to life without parole, colloquially known as the 'natural death sentence'. He also ordered the government to seize the record amount of $180 million from the defendants' collective assets, which included the Bell Gardens Bicycle Club.

With Lanier now in prison, federal agents seized his house in Florida and descended upon his wife, his father and other family members and close friends. They dug up $2 million hidden in PVC pipes buried under his father's lawn (for which he would receive a prison sentence) and discovered $500,000 in a relative's basement. His brother's home was confiscated in 1991 and auctioned because it had been used for illegal activities, although the brother was never charged with any crimes. Although they had already established Lanier's ownership of the casino, they went on to discover a web of overseas bank accounts and more money, houses and cars. In the meantime, Pam took a job on the fruit counter of a grocery store to support the couple's two children. There was also the girlfriend, Maria, whom he married while behind bars before she was sentenced, in 1992, to nine years in prison for money laundering, then deported upon release.

Lanier was held in several medium-security prisons before being transferred to Leavenworth federal penitentiary in Kansas. He made unsuccessful attempts to appeal and his various elaborate escape plans were thwarted. After spending 26 years inside, he was unexpectedly released in October 2014 without explanation from the government. With the motion sealed by a federal judge, neither prosecution nor defence lawyers will ever be permitted to discuss the reasons why the sentence was commuted. However, changing social views about the increasing acceptance of marijuana, which is now legal or decriminalised in several cities and states, is likely to have played a part. Clemency has subsequently been granted to thousands of nonviolent prisoners who would have received lesser sentences had they been tried today. Indeed, the irony isn't lost on Lanier that his daughter Brandie now lives in Colorado, where recreational marijuana has been legal since 2014, and makes her living providing medical marijuana to dispensaries.

Since being freed at the age of 60, Lanier has put his skills and experience to good use working as a health technician at a treatment centre for substance abuse as well as an Uber driver and a performance driving coach in Florida. He has even competed in occasional amateur sportscar races of the kind that got him hooked on the sport back in the 1970s. He talks candidly about how he paid for his racing career: 'I did have some money from sponsors. The [team] wasn't totally from running the grass. But it mostly was.' While he has accepted much of what happened to him, he still thinks that his sentence was ludicrous: 'A person should not have to spend the rest of his life in prison for marijuana.' After his release, he reconnected with Pam, his first wife, and they now live together again.

Regardless of how his racing was funded, there's no doubt that Randy Lanier had great driving talent. For a driver who had raced at Le Mans, won the top sportscar racing title in America and looked to have a bright future in Indycar racing, his conviction as one of America's most prolific marijuana smugglers was a shocking revelation.

DONALD ARONOW
Blue Thunder

Randy Lanier's brazen self-assurance was evident in the naming of his racing team. 'Blue Thunder' was borrowed from the brand name of a 39-foot twin-hulled speedboat designed and built by Donald Aronow, who was a champion powerboat racer. Aronow sold 14 of these high-speed craft to the US Customs Service on the understanding that they could outrun the single-hull boats being used by smugglers, but in fact they didn't prove to be any faster.

Aronow was shot to death in broad daylight in Miami on 3rd February 1987. For many years Lanier's co-defendant, Ben Kramer, was the prime suspect but never charged. Almost ten years later, however, he and a career criminal named Bobby Young pleaded 'no contest' (whereby a charge is neither admitted nor disputed) to the killing, which was reportedly in retaliation for a business deal that had gone wrong.

CHAPTER 35

VIC
LEE
Motorvation

By the early 1990s, Vic Lee Motorsport had developed into one of the most successful teams in the British Touring Car Championship. However, suspicions were raised about the UK-based outfit's frequent trips to 'test' its BMWs at Zandvoort in the Netherlands. All became clear when the team owner and several associates were caught smuggling cocaine valued at £6 million in their transporter. After his release from prison, Lee returned not only to his life in motor racing but also to his old ways, for which he was again put behind bars.

Vic Lee, the son of a milkman, has a long and impressive history in touring car racing as a driver, engineer and team owner. After initial forays building and racing Minis in the Special Saloons category in 1975, he progressed to a Sunbeam Stiletto built by fellow driver Rob Mason, who would play an important role in his life in later years. Lee was involved in a big accident in the Sunbeam at Oulton Park, breaking a leg in three places and fracturing a kneecap, injuries that put him on crutches and out of racing for 14 months. Once fit again, he did a few more races before taking a break from the sport in 1979.

He concentrated on building up two garage businesses, one of which was a Volkswagen Audi specialist that he later had to sell as part of a divorce settlement. Lee continued to work for the purchaser, the Whitehouse Group, a chain of Kent-based car dealerships, and persuaded his new employer to allow him to build a racing VW Golf Mk2 and compete with it under the company's name, a partnership that proved sufficiently successful to lead to a factory deal to run a more potent 16-valve Golf GTi. Competing in the up-to-2,000cc class of the Monroe British Production Saloon Car Championship, Lee became class champion in 1985 and overall champion in 1987. In that latter season another competitor was Jerry Mahony, who we shall encounter again.

Lee's accomplishments led to an approach from building contractors Mulcahy & Hirst offering a paid drive in a brand-new Porsche 944 Club Sport in the Porsche Cars Great Britain (PCGB) Championship. The venture ended prematurely with a crash, again at Oulton Park, but Lee managed to persuade his undeterred sponsor to back his move into the British Touring Car Championship (BTCC), which by this time had become a prestigious and very popular series, thanks in part to television coverage. Lee secured a drive with MIL Motorsport in one of its under-developed but powerful Toyota Supra Turbos but the car proved just as unsuccessful in his hands as it did for part-time team-mates Mark Hales, Ian Flux and Chris Hodgetts. A disastrous campaign saw both Hodgetts and Lee leave before the end of the season but at least the experience provided the catalyst for Lee to fulfil a long-held ambition and establish his own team, believing he could do a better job than most. To be successful, he realised that he would need to concentrate fully on the team's management, so he hung up his helmet.

In his first year of running a team, 1989, he joined forces with Richard Asquith to form Lee Asquith Motorsport and they contested the one-make Honda Civic CRX Championship, which they won. In a parallel programme they also ran a Duckhams-backed Ford Sierra for Karl Jones in the BTCC but funding was tight and they were unable to do the extensive development and testing required to keep up with the bigger teams. After an amicable split with Asquith, the team evolved into Vic Lee Motorsport (VLM) with the aim of focusing its proprietor's energy and resources on running a successful BTCC campaign in 1990. Having decided that a BMW M3 was the weapon of choice, Lee took on the financial risk by mortgaging his house to buy a year-old example that the Italian Bigazzi team had been campaigning in the German championship. He converted it from Group A specification to make it eligible for the forthcoming 2-litre BTCC formula, scraped together a moderate budget and hired Jeff Allam, a long-time BTCC driver. A pleasing season ended with third place in the class standings.

The small team's progress with limited resources impressed businessman Ray Bellm, who signed to drive for 1991. Bellm brought with him Listerine (mouthwash) backing to add to the sponsorship that Lee had already secured from Securicor (security services), allowing the team to become a two-car

Team-mates in their Vic Lee-run BMW 318is, Steve Soper (leading) and
Tim Harvey battle it out during the 1992 British Touring Car Championship.
Unknown to them, Lee was using one of the team's transporters for
drug smuggling and was arrested in September of that year.

effort with Will Hoy as lead driver. A separate deal was done to run two
more cars as a satellite operation for Laurence Bristow and Tim Harvey
with backing from Labatt's (beer). The foundations for the great things to
come lay in the team being able to go down its own route with choice of
tyres (Yokohama), engine builder (Eurotech) and gearbox (Hollinger). This
gave VLM an advantage over the BMWs of the works-supported Prodrive
team, especially when it came to tyres, because Prodrive was contracted to
run on less durable Pirelli rubber.

Bolstered by ever better TV coverage, the BTCC had become the most
popular race series in Britain, and a move to Super Touring regulations
for 1991 meant that for the first time in its history the championship
ran with just a single class. This rulebook change brought interest from
several manufacturers, prompting Vauxhall, Nissan and Toyota to field
works entries, often with high-profile former Formula 1 drivers. By cleverly
spotting a loophole in the regulations, Lee was able, in his words, 'to fit
the fuel cell in the place where it was most logical to put a lot of weight —
very low and just in front of the rear wheels rather than in the spare-wheel
well in the boot behind the rear axle.' The spare-wheel well was where the

previous Group A rules had required fuel to be located. This initiative gave the team's BMW M3s, which this time had been built from scratch, a great advantage with their optimised weight distribution.

Success came quickly to the new team. The BMWs were competitive throughout the season and so reliable that there were only four occasions on which fewer than three of the four VLM-prepared cars finished in the top ten. After a season-long duel with John Cleland's Vauxhall Cavalier, Hoy duly became champion.

With Hoy departing to Toyota for 1992, a rejigged operation saw VLM run three new-shape BMW 318is, with Bellm and Harvey now joined by Steve Soper. Harvey contested the whole season, Bellm stepped down after two-thirds of it, and Soper missed three rounds due to works BMW commitments in Germany. While BMW GB continued to provide engineering and technical support to Prodrive-run Team Mobil, which remained the official works team, the manufacturer also stepped in to assist VLM's operation, which now went under the snappy name 'M Team Shell Racing with Listerine'. BMW's decision proved to be a good one because the team's self-developed cars were more successful, especially after a mid-season redesign of the rear suspension. After a slow start, Harvey enjoyed a fine run of success with five consecutive wins in the second half of the season. In one of the most dramatic finales ever seen in the championship, the top three drivers arrived at the final race at Silverstone separated by only four points. Harvey claimed the title for VLM when his rivals struck trouble, Cleland's Vauxhall retiring after a series of fraught and controversial clashes with VLM team-mate Soper, and Hoy's Toyota going out with engine failure.

By now, the BTCC was becoming dominated by manufacturer-backed teams with multi-million-pound budgets, so what VLM managed to achieve in such a short time, with significantly less means at its disposal, was impressive. Soper related at the time that part of the recipe for the team's success was that the boss was such a highly motivating, uncompromising, energetic character, and such a perfectionist that the only people allowed to wear shoes in his racing cars were the drivers. Soper also stated: 'Cost does not seem to matter to VLM: if there is an advantage to be gained, then money is not a consideration.' Those words would turn out to be unwittingly prescient.

The much-praised team proprietor, however, wasn't around to savour his team's second consecutive BTCC title. Just before the penultimate round, at Donington, Vic Lee had been arrested.

Trackside marshals are the understated and often-unappreciated heroes and lifeblood of all forms of motor racing, without whom no events could take place. They are volunteers and racing enthusiasts who willingly give up their free time for scant reward, other than the dubious privilege of standing unprotected in all weathers in front of the barriers and therefore getting closer to the action than the paying spectators. Vigilance is a vital aspect of the skills they bring to their task. It was unfortunate for Vic Lee that the day job of one vigilant marshal was as a customs officer. Based at Sheerness in Kent, he became suspicious about the regularity of the cross-channel ferry crossings made to Vlissingen in the Netherlands by a large and conspicuous racing transporter belonging to the reigning British Touring Car Champions.

As a knowledgeable enthusiast, the customs officer wondered why a team competing in an exclusively British championship should ever need to travel abroad. Aware that the transporter's destination was Zandvoort, he thought it even stranger that the team should regularly visit a circuit that wasn't even on its race calendar, especially when there were so many suitable and more relevant British circuits available for testing. A far more obvious choice, for example, would have been Brands Hatch, which was almost literally on the team's doorstep in Kent and hosted two BTCC rounds. Zandvoort may have been a challenging circuit in pleasant seaside surroundings, but its attraction for Vic Lee Motorsport lay solely in the fact that it was in the Netherlands, the most 'drug-friendly' country in Europe.

Upon reaching Zandvoort after the three-hour drive from Vlissingen, the big VLM transporter would disgorge its contents — a single BMW and all the equipment needed to run it — and the team would go through the motions of sporadically sending the car out onto the circuit to give the impression that it was running through a bona fide test session, evaluating components, settings and performance data. There was more than met the eye to this transporter: it was a special 'mule' that looked like one of the team's regular trucks but contained secret compartments in the roof of its trailer in which bundles of cocaine could be stowed. In addition, pressurised cylinders of nitrogen — as used for inflating tyres and powering tools — were also emptied, cut open, filled with illicit cargo and welded up again, all under cover of track activity. Just how many illicit operations succeeded before police closed in and impounded the transporter remains a mystery, but it's reasonable to assume that there were a good few.

The mastermind behind the plot was Rob Mason, the man who had built Lee's Sunbeam Stiletto the best part of 15 years earlier. Mason

After five years in prison, Vic Lee returned to motorsport in 1999 — but he hadn't left his criminal past behind and was caught drug trafficking again six years later. He is pictured in 2002 when he ran Halfords-sponsored Peugeot 406 Coupés in the British Touring Car Championship.

constructed and operated the facsimile 'mule' transporter and was kept under investigation for 18 months before being caught. A tip-off from a Spanish truck driver to Dutch police, who were independently monitoring Mason's movements, added to the suspicions of Her Majesty's Customs & Excise and led to the deployment of a surveillance team. The activities of 'Operation Bounce', as it was code-named, included observation of the team's movements from the control tower at Zandvoort. This operation culminated in the interception of the rogue transporter at Sheerness on 10th September 1992 after yet another cross-channel foray. Over a period of several hours, the contraband was removed from the gas cylinders and the secret compartments, fake drugs put in its place, and the truck allowed to continue to the team's base in Northfleet.

No arrests were made at the ferry terminal but more than 50 officers subsequently swooped on the VLM workshops in Northfleet and other addresses in Kent. The words 'Assume Nothing' painted in large capital letters on the walls of the workshop unit in Northfleet, Kent, may have been some sort of motto but they were also prophetic. Vic Lee was in the middle of a meeting with two senior managers from BMW in Munich with whom he was in the process of negotiating a deal to build cars on BMW's behalf for the German and Australian touring car championships. He had to excuse himself from the meeting but his German colleagues were very understanding when he gave them the bogus explanation that he was being visited about a VAT issue.

Together with the other co-conspirators, Mason and Lee were found guilty of smuggling 40kg of pure and unmixed Colombian cocaine with an estimated street value of £6 million. Early in 1993, Mason was sentenced to 18 years in prison and Lee to 12 years, and sent initially to the Category A high-security Belmarsh prison in south-east London.

Lee's arrest led to his team being rapidly wound up and its assets sold by liquidators. Ray Bellm, having withdrawn from the team only a few weeks before the scandal broke, re-emerged in a management capacity to help guide it through to the end of a very successful season, after which he and Steve Neal bought some of the assets. Using these as a basis, Neal formed West Bromwich-based Team Dynamics, which eventually became a major player in the BTCC with Neal's son Matt as lead driver. Matt became one of the most successful drivers in the history of the BTCC, winning more than 60 races and taking three championship titles, in 2005, 2006 and 2011.

After serving five years, Lee was released on parole for good behaviour in 1998 and immediately found temporary employment with Team Dynamics. It wasn't long before he gathered the wherewithal to acquire Bowman Motorsport and use this to resurrect his own operation. Initially he ran a race programme for Peugeot in the National Saloon Cup (NSC) from premises at the manufacturer's Stoke Aldermoor factory complex near Coventry but then returned to the BTCC, with his team now called Vic Lee Racing (VLR). In 2000, Lee ran Peugeot 306 GTis for Alan Morrison in the BTCC and Toni Ruokonen in the NSC, both ending the season as class champions.

On the back of these strong results, Peugeot contracted VLR to run its works entry in the new-look BTCC for 2001. The team signed Dan Eaves, Matt Neal and — in a touch of *déjà vu* — Steve Soper to drive the 406 coupés, but sponsorship difficulties led to Neal being released from his contract after just two rounds. Against a resurgent Vauxhall team, VLR's campaign was nowhere near as successful as Peugeot had envisaged and the company withdrew its backing at the end of the year. VLR persisted with the 406s for the 2002 season but was now rebranded as Team Halfords after Eaves was able to attract significant sponsorship from the car accessory retailer. As Soper had retired after a crash at the end of the previous year, Eaves was joined by another 'blast from the past' in the form of Tim Harvey. Now without manufacturer support, VLR competed in the 'Independents' championship, which Eaves duly won with Harvey third. Midway through the season, Carl Breeze joined as an extra driver and stayed for part of 2003, when the team switched to Peugeot 307s. The new model was uncompetitive and results were poor, leading Eaves to depart — with the Halfords sponsorship — to join Matt Neal at Team Dynamics for 2004, driving Honda Civic Type Rs.

Lee changed direction for 2004, running a two-car team in the Porsche Carrera Cup Great Britain, a 911 GT3 championship run as part of the support programme at BTCC rounds. Lead driver Jason Templeman scored two victories at Brands Hatch on his way to third place in the final standings. VLR also competed in the first round of the British GT Championship at Donington with a four-year-old 996 GT3-R in which Peter Kox and Ian Khan finished second and third in the weekend's two races, but there were no further outings.

During Lee's 'second-time-around' involvement in the BTCC, he reconnected with Jerry Mahony, a racing rival from way back. Mahony's motorsport initiation had come in 1987 with a Formula Ford 2000 test at Goodwood but he was physically too bulky to be able to drive a single-seater comfortably (he didn't have enough space to even operate the gear lever) and instead elected to compete with a Ford Sierra RS Cosworth in the Monroe British Production Saloon Car Championship, where he found himself sharing the track with Lee in his Golf GTi. Mahony was quick from the outset, taking second place on his début and his first win while still racing with a novice cross on his car. After an unusually short baptism, he was able to follow Lee straight into the BTCC for 1988. At the first round, at Silverstone, he managed to score a fairy-tale maiden victory in his Arquati-backed Sierra RS500 thanks to a large helping of beginner's luck and plenty of attrition amongst the frontrunners. As it turned out, he never won again and bowed out of the series in 1990 after a couple of lacklustre seasons with a BMW. After retiring from racing for good the following year, he concentrated on building up a corporate hospitality business that specialised in motorsport events and he found several clients in BTCC circles, where his presence even extended to driving the safety car

GIUSEPPE SPERLINGA
Crack team

Another team boss to have been caught using one of his racing team's vehicles for drug-smuggling is Giuseppe Sperlinga. His Belgium-based team, GPR Racing, was a regular entrant of customer-run Aston Martin GTs all over Europe in both the Belcar and the Blancpain Endurance series. When his team's Fiat Iveco flatbed truck was searched in Dover after driving off a cross-channel ferry, 48lb of cocaine and 2lb of heroin with a street value of £4.1 million was found stashed under its front seats. After admitting two counts of drug smuggling at Canterbury Crown Court in July 2014, the 62-year-old was sentenced to 15 years in prison.

on occasion. He developed an especially close relationship with Lee, whose cars sported branding for Mahony's 'V.I.P. Club'. Their association also had a darker side.

On 20th February 2005, Lee and Mahony were arrested in the car park of the Holiday Inn at High Wycombe in Buckinghamshire. They had been tailed across the home counties by HM Revenue & Customs officers and caught red-handed delivering 19kg of cocaine with a street value of £1.7 million along with three other men, one of whom got away. Lee, the assumed ringleader because of his previous crimes, was allegedly found to have £19,000 in cash in the boot of his BMW M3, which would have been additionally incriminating if true, but he always maintained that its presence in his car was 'fabricated'. Incredibly, and perhaps most shockingly, Lee's return to crime took place very quickly after termination of the jail licence from his original 12-year sentence. However, having held his hands up at the earliest opportunity when apprehended in 1992, Lee this time vehemently maintained his innocence and claimed that he had only become involved unwittingly and indirectly through simply trying to help an old friend who had got himself mixed up with the wrong people. He argued that his presence was an unfortunate case of being in the wrong place at the wrong time.

The BTCC circus was setting up in the paddock at Mondello Park in Ireland when, on 22nd July 2005, Lee and Mahony appeared in the dock at Southwark Crown Court in London alongside two other defendants who had acted as couriers. All four pleaded guilty to drug-trafficking offences and between them were handed prison sentences totalling 38 and a half years. Lee pleaded guilty to dealing in 1.43kg (3lb) of a Class A drug and to offences contrary to the Proceeds of Crime Act 2002. Despite this being a rather lesser misdemeanour that his previous exploits, his prison sentence was the same as before, at 12 years. Mahony, who admitted two counts of supplying drugs, was jailed for 11 years, appropriately serving the last part of his sentence in an open prison almost within earshot of Silverstone.

'It is clear they were deliberately engaged in the supply of cocaine in high-level organised crime,' said Andrew Marshall for the prosecution. Judge Neil Stewart stated in his summing up: 'This was clearly an organised drugs transaction. It was for commercial reasons and it was on a large scale.' Lee's assets were frozen and he was subject to a Confiscation Order issued after further investigation by HMRC. Under the Proceeds of Crime Act, he was ordered to pay £73,230 within six months or face a further two years in prison. Robert Adler, HMRC's assistant director for criminal investigation, was delighted with the result that his team of investigators had achieved: 'This has been a significant success story for us in terms of seizing such a large quantity of cocaine, the dismantling of a major criminal organisation and returning the profits from this crime back to the nation.'

Lee was released in 2010 after serving five years of his 12-year sentence. He again managed to find a way back into the world of motorsport, this time in a peripheral capacity, when he landed a job with Corbeau, a long-time manufacturer of seats and safety harnesses for motorsport use. The company had employed him when he was on day release from Ford open prison and he soon became managing director, a post he still holds at the time of writing. Under his leadership, the company not only managed to sell products into Halfords, formerly a lead sponsor of VLR, but also won a tender in 2020 to manufacture 2,200 'safety' seat modules for prison transport vans. The appointment of a twice-convicted serial drug trafficker into a senior management role inevitably raised controversy at the time but Lee, having worked hard to reinvent himself, staunchly defends his position and answers his critics by saying that he has paid for his crimes and is a 'glittering example' of how the prison system can work properly.

'This is something that I can never get away from,' he said in 2012, 'but it is something for which I have been punished and which I would like to put behind me once and for all.'

CHAPTER 36

COLIN LEES

Road to destruction

A larger-than-life character and successful stalwart of Formula Ford, Colin Lees enjoyed entrepreneurial success in Northern Ireland and became a much-respected multi-millionaire until his businesses ran into severe difficulties and brought a spectacular fall from grace. As his complicated life unravelled, bankruptcy revealed a much darker side and a tangled web of deceit, corruption and criminal activity involving fraud, drug smuggling and money laundering.

ormula Ford was established in Britain in 1967 as an entry-level class of single-seater racing and has traditionally been regarded as the first major stepping stone into open-wheel racing after karting. The relative affordability of the category, thanks to use of the ubiquitous 1,600cc Ford 'Kent' engine, ensured its success and its popularity was so great that some seasons in the 1970s and 1980s saw as many as eight separate championships run in the British Isles. Formula Ford has bred an almost endless list of some of the most famous names who have gone on to become highly successful professionals.

Colin Lees from County Derry, Northern Ireland was 24 years old when he began racing in Formula Ford after some exploratory outings in an Alfa Romeo saloon. He joined the ranks of myriad hopefuls in 1976, competing in an ancient and well-used Lotus 69 before progressing to a newer Van Diemen RF75 in 1977. Driving an up-to-date Crosslé 32F in 1978, he took 12 wins and 18 other podium finishes in races in both mainland Britain and throughout Ireland, winning the Northern Ireland championship. The

Crosslé marque was almost unbeatable at this time as Lees and Irishman Arnie Black were arch-rivals and prolific winners in their epic battles together. Although Lees won over 20 races in 1979, Black prevailed and took both Irish championships, north and south of the border. However, Black was sporting enough to admit that Lees gifted him the Northern Ireland title. Not only had his rival had a problem with his engine at the last race but Black only won after Lees tangled with another driver with whom he was racing unnecessarily because the culprit had jumped the start and would have been penalised anyway. Black is on record as saying that although they had had various incidents with each other over the years, this was only because they always tried so hard: 'There were never any hysterics or recriminations. He was a very good driver and I got on very well with him.'

As Alan Tyndall says in his book *Hidden Glory, The Story of the Crosslé Car Company*: 'Colin Lees had outstanding ability in a racing car and a quiet personality in the paddock, keeping very much to himself. But when he squeezed his considerable frame into his racer, he seemed to grow horns. As his future business partner Dennis McGall remarked, when you were racing against Colin you didn't expect any favours!'

McGall also recounted: 'Colin had a Van Diemen when I met him and I had the (Crosslé) 25F. He was the first person I ever had an accident with. I remember seeing him get out of the car and thinking how big can you be and get into a Formula Ford!'

Further development in 1980 saw the birth of the Crosslé 40F, which was much narrower than its predecessor and therefore an even tighter fit for Lees. This also gave the car nervous handling and made it too difficult for the average club racer to drive, although Lees was talented enough to be able to master it and gave the car one of its first wins at Mondello Park in July. A return to the same circuit the following month saw him win the Irish Formula Ford Festival Trophy and he also dominated the Northern Ireland championship with six wins from seven rounds.

By now it was time for Lees to try to move up the ladder. Formula Ford 2000, which used 2-litre Ford engines, was the logical next step and Black recommended him to team owner Ivor Goodwin. After excelling in his first race in Goodwin Racing's Delta T80, he was offered a contract to race the team's Argo JM9 in the British Formula Atlantic Championship in 1981 but the car wasn't a match for its driver's talents and the season was a disappointment. For 1982, he returned to Formula Ford 2000 in Ireland, back in a Crosslé, and also did some Formula Atlantic with a Ralt RT4.

A change of tack came when Lees, together with erstwhile racing rival Dennis McGall, invested in part-ownership of the new Mondiale Car Company, which Leslie Drysdale, Crosslé's designer, founded in direct competition to his former employer. Helped by some government funding, Mondiale established itself in a new factory in Bangor, County Down and became operational in a remarkably short time, starting in 1984. Its first model, the M84S, was on the pace from the outset and by 1986 Mondiales were being sold all over the world, with multiple orders from the Skip Barber racing schools in America. The factory even received a visit from the Duke of York to present the Northern Ireland Exporter of the Year Award.

Now driving cars built by his own company, Lees continued to achieve racing success, although by this time the competition, especially on the mainland, had become more intense and he was up against drivers who were 10–15 years younger, including future Grand Prix stars Mark Bluncell, Martin Donnelly and Eddie Irvine. As the youngsters moved on in their careers, Lees competed in Mondiales at club level for several more years. In 1992, however, racing had to take a back seat because he found himself in deep trouble.

Colin Lees had worked for his father William's Magherafelt-based family construction business since the age of 17 and eventually took it over midway through his racing career. Under his stewardship, it evolved into the Lees Group of companies and included businesses as diverse as fisheries and forestry. The flamboyant entrepreneur presented himself as an extremely successful businessman who was everybody's friend and was a winner who had charm and good connections in all the right places. A major provider of local employment, at his peak he had as many as 450 people working for him and was known as a significant benefactor whose grand gestures included using his helicopter to deliver Christmas presents to a special-needs school while dressed as Santa Claus.

Lees proved himself to be extremely plausible in his dealings with financiers, businessmen and government ministers. Government funds started to pour into his company's coffers and between 1985 and 1992 he benefited from financial aid of £2.3 million from the Industrial Development Board. In January 1991, he appeared at a news conference alongside local MP John Hume, leader of Northern Ireland's SDLP (Social Democratic and Labour Party), who grandly proclaimed Lees's plan to set up a pulp mill in Derry producing wood chip to sell to Scandinavia and described it as 'one of the most important announcements of the century'. Later that year, Lees was standing beside Richard Needham, the British Government's Industry Minister, when Needham cut the tape at the opening of a shopping centre that Lees had built. However, it all went wrong in 1992 when the empire collapsed under a mountain of debt totalling £35 million, caused by over-ambitious expansion.

Dennis McGall, Lees's co-investor in Mondiale cars, knew him as a tough racing rival and, like most others in the Northern Irish business community, thought him to be solid and successful. He said: 'I suspected that his construction business wasn't working but thought that his extensive forestry interests were sound. The forestry people knew that their side of things was rocky but thought the construction business was sound. Both were in trouble.' As Lees's businesses faltered, he got involved in increasingly desperate attempts to stay afloat.

During Ulster's long-running sectarian violence, the IRA (Irish Republican Army) had murdered several construction workers who were involved in contracts for the security services. These contracts were extremely lucrative and Lees wanted to monetise his close links with the security forces by building pre-fabricated police stations but in such a way that that his connection could be hidden and any threat to his own safety reduced. The British Government needed friends like Lees. An MI6 secret agent alerted him to the availability of a former seaweed factory on the island of North Uist in Scotland's remote Outer Hebrides and this provided the ideal site for his purposes of manufacturing reinforced concrete panels in secrecy. The agent also introduced him to Malcolm Baillie, who was hired as a front man to disguise Lees's interests, and the two of them set up Marine Structures Ltd, registered in Inverness, Scotland.

The clandestine operation didn't last long because the IRA found out about it after only two contracts had been completed. But the company continued, on paper at least. Although the ruse to foil the IRA hadn't worked, Lees and Baillie had an incentive to keep working together because, under the cover of their lucrative government contract, they had started a double leasing scam. Together with Baillie's son Stuart, a former professional footballer, the three men set up Lees Group Scotland, which, financed by fraud, saw rapid expansion between May 1988 and October 1991 to become a major force in forestry and fish farming. Lees also created a company called Plant Corporation of Ireland whose only purpose was to produce false invoices. He would ask banks and leasing companies from all over the UK for big loans, sometimes as much as several hundreds of thousands of pounds, for

With his Ulster-built Formula Ford Mondiale bearing allegiance to his Lees Group of companies, Colin Lees gets stuck in trackside gravel in 1990, nearly 25 years after he began racing in Formula Ford. His criminal activities, which earned him six years in prison, had become extensive by this time.

heavy industrial plant and equipment, then Plant Corporation of Ireland would provide the necessary paperwork to dupe the leasing companies to transfer the funds. In most cases the vehicles and equipment to back up the bogus leases simply didn't exist and in others second-hand equipment was passed off as new and often the same items were the subject of more than one deal.

This scam was replicated in Scotland with a similar operation called The Nationwide Plant Corporation, which was registered at a small terraced house in Inverness with two local labourers listed as the directors. Over the course of four years this entity expanded into more than 20 subsidiary companies and, as the scale of the fraud increased, so did the tension between Lees and the two Baillies. It was later claimed by the prosecution in court that Stuart Baillie had become fed up with the lion's share of the profits going to Lees when he and his father were doing most of the work and eventually they tried to seize control of the Scottish operation.

A mammoth six-month trial at the High Court in Edinburgh in 1999 took place without Malcolm Baillie, who was deemed too ill to take the stand, and ended with Stuart Baillie receiving five years in prison for his part in frauds. These were originally estimated to have netted almost £13 million but after the jury deleted parts of the indictment the figure was reduced by £5 million. In this instance, Lees had escaped prosecution, which made the Baillies understandably very bitter, but in the meantime he was awaiting sentence in a Belfast court after being convicted of separate frauds amounting to £20 million.

Returning to 1992, Lees Group Scotland collapsed in March that year and afterwards the receivers uncovered one of Scotland's biggest frauds. One example concerned leases for 400 salmon cages when only 100 existed while the value of the salmon stock was less than half the £7 million stated in the books. At the same time, Lees's timber and construction company in Northern Ireland also collapsed with debts of £35 million and once again the receiver was unable to find significant amounts of equipment that the business was supposed to own.

An Ulster TV programme later documented how Lees had got involved with a chain-smoking American called Derek Jones, who was notorious for driving around Ballymena in a vintage Rolls-Royce. It told of how Jones was wanted by the FBI for the laundering of money for two of New York's leading Mafia families with funds being transferred from banks in New York to Canada to Dublin to Ballymena and back again to New York. Jones was central to much of Lees's corrupt activities and lived in a house paid for by him. He acted as the front man in running several companies, but the real owner and sleeping partner, who was bankrupt and therefore disqualified from being a director, was, of course, Colin Lees. In Dallas in 1993, the two of them met Richard Worthy, a businessman and former district attorney who, having specialised in prosecuting white-collar crime, should have been the first to spot anything underhand but was taken in by the men and subsequently fleeced of $1 million.

A report in *The Sunday Times* outlined other misdemeanours. There was a trade loan that was never repaid, made by Bass, the brewer, to another Lees company, Leisure Trading, to buy the Loughside Inn in Belfast in 1996. This establishment was used to launder cash from a string of fraudulent operations before it was burned down by loyalists in 1997. Also in 1996, customs officers made a routine search of a boat named *Plongeur Whisky* that had limped into a harbour in County Clare with engine problems and discovered 1.7 tonnes of cannabis resin with a street value of £17 million. The boat had been bought by Derek Jones, whose financial transactions were now under investigation by the Royal Ulster Constabulary.

Lees was arrested in October 1997 once his multiple connections with these crimes had been confirmed. On his first court appearance in April 1999, he admitted 47 charges of theft and fraud totalling £20 million from his own group of companies. In September that year he was in court again to plead guilty to his involvement in a £2 million drinks-smuggling scam, in which he evaded paying duty and VAT by falsifying documents relating to the export of alcohol from Britain to Ireland. At the end of the same month he pleaded guilty to the drug-smuggling operation. Over a year later, at the end of 2000, he was finally sentenced to 12 years for the drug offences and lesser sentences to run concurrently for the other charges.

He was released at the end of 2003 after serving six years behind bars (including time spent on remand) mostly in Maghaberry Prison in County Antrim. Old habits die hard, however, and he had been free for less than two years when a plot was uncovered in which the now 53-year-old had plotted to smuggle quantities of amphetamines worth £32 million and ecstasy worth £1.7 million from the Netherlands to the UK. Concealed inside seven pallets of denim jeans, the drugs were intercepted by police in a Greater Manchester industrial unit used by a legitimate storage and courier company, and were intended for onward distribution in London and north-west England.

After a five-week trial at Liverpool Crown Court, Lees and his associates were found guilty in August 2005 of conspiracy to supply class A and B drugs. Judge John Roberts acknowledged that while Lees might not have been at the very top of the hierarchy, he told him: 'I view you as a major player in both conspiracies.' He was sentenced to 25 years in prison for plotting to supply ecstasy and 13 years for plotting to supply amphetamine with the sentences running concurrently.

In one of Lees's many court cases, a judge referred to his undoubted talents and business acumen and credited him as being 'a man of some intelligence who unfortunately chose to redirect it into crime'. He was also a gifted racing driver but former rival Arnie Black's view that he could have made it as a top international was probably optimistic. Not only was he still racing in the junior categories against very much younger talent when he was in his late 30s but also his disparate off-track activities were taking up far too much of his time and attention.

CHAPTER 37
GREG LOLES
Highway to Hell

For almost a decade, this amateur racing driver turned team owner and self-proclaimed financial genius shamelessly abused the trust of numerous friends, clients and fellow churchgoers by stealing millions of dollars from them. He engaged in what the FBI described as 'a carefully calculated fraud' using sham companies in order to pay for both his racing exploits as well as an extravagant lifestyle that was funded by lies and other people's stolen pensions and life savings.

In the 1980s in West Germany, brothers Hermann and Horst Farnbacher began racing at national level from an early age. Horst, the younger of the two, was more successful, winning two championships in a VW Polo in 1988 before progressing to the German Touring Car Trophy and winning five races in 1990. Two years later, the brothers established Farnbacher Motorsport to field Porsches in several manufacturer-backed series and soon they were competing strongly in the Porsche Carrera Trophy and the Le Mans Series. After much success and many race wins over the next ten years, often with Horst as one of the drivers, their aspirations grew further and they resolved to put their experience to good use and try their luck in the thriving North American sports car scene, although they needed to find the budget to do so.

After a timely introduction, Greg Loles, an amateur driver who had started competing at club level in Porsches in the US, convinced the brothers that he was an extremely wealthy man and duly became the investor they needed. In 2004, in deference to their new majority shareholder, the team, based in

Pictured in 2008 with the Porsche 997 GT3 Cup run by Farnbacher Loles Racing, Greg Loles is flanked by team drivers Bryce Miller (left) and Dirk Werner.

Danbury, Connecticut, was renamed Farnbacher Loles Motorsports and immediately demonstrated great pace, initially campaigning a Porsche 911 in some rounds of the Grand-Am Road Racing Championship. In 2005, with Horst's son Dominik as one of the drivers, the team won the GT class of the Rolex 24 at Daytona. In 2007, running a full season in Grand-Am for the first time, the driver pairing of Dirk Werner and Bryce Miller scored 10 podium finishes in the GT class to secure the teams' championship for Farnbacher Loles Motorsports and the drivers' title and 'rookie of the year' accolade for Werner. The 2008 season was the team's first in the American Le Mans Series and brought official support from Porsche, including occasional participation from its works driver Wolf Henzler, with a best result of a GT2 class win at Road America for Werner and Miller with Richard Westbrook.

With his racing team on a roll, Loles decided to try to capitalise on its success by building a new business servicing high-performance road and race cars, predominantly Porsches. The vast high-specification facility that he opened in Danbury was so beautifully equipped that a senior employee, Spencer Cox, likened it to the Taj Mahal, a comparison not usually associated with car workshops. The relationship with Porsche in racing became stronger and this was confirmed at the start of the 2009 season when Loles announced: 'Everyone at Farnbacher Loles is proud to announce our partnership with Porsche for the 2009 American Le Mans Series season. Many people have worked very hard to gain this recognition from our manufacturer.' The momentum seemed to continue, now with Leh Keen joining Werner on driving duty.

However, the diversification of Farnbacher Loles into other areas outside motorsport had been ill-conceived and its massive cost, with a large staff and big overheads, contributed to the failure of the associated businesses. Whilst the racing team continued to be reasonably successful, it consumed much more capital than could be covered in prize money and sponsorship revenue, and towards the end of the 2009 season it was also in financial difficulties.

To the great surprise of the shocked Farnbacher family, Loles was arrested in December 2009 on charges of embezzling millions of dollars from a church. All the brothers had known about his finances from their original introduction to him was that he had claimed to be involved in hedge funds and his spending certainly suggested that he had very deep pockets. He did — but unfortunately it became clear that those pockets weren't his.

Born in 1959, Greg Loles graduated from Purdue University in Indiana with an engineering degree but later in life, starting in 2001, he portrayed himself as an investment adviser, telling people that he operated Apeiron Capital Management Inc. This entity was registered with the US Securities and Exchange Commission from 1995 to 1998, at which point the registrations were cancelled. However, Loles continued to operate the business and falsely represented it as a legally registered investment management firm and continued to solicit clients. In the mid-1990s he used his Greek parentage to inveigle himself into St Barbara's Greek Orthodox Church in Orange, Connecticut. Not only did the church entrust him and his company with its various investments but he also worked hard to cultivate individual business relationships with churchgoers.

He was elected to serve on the board of the church's endowment fund, which held a significant amount of money that was used for funding scholarships and making charitable contributions. Because he was regarded as an expert stockbroker, he was given, in the words of court documentation, 'authority to trade on behalf of the endowment fund'. Loles told the other

HENRI ZOGAIB
Wrong side of the track

By strange coincidence, Greg Loles and former sports car racer Henri Zogaib were both sentenced within a day of each other in 2014 for scamming people out of millions of dollars in unrelated Ponzi schemes. While Loles had targeted his victims outside the sport, the Lebanese-born Zogaib, who raced in the Rolex Sports Car Series, focused his attention on fellow competitors.

Zogaib burst onto the racing scene as a graduate of the Skip Barber Racing School and claimed to have strong financial connections emanating from his time at an exclusive Swiss school, although in reality he had attended the far more ordinary Sea Breeze High School in Daytona Beach. His scheme, which had promised investors returns of as much as 40 percent, was uncovered in 2009. Many well-known figures in the sport were among more than 30 investors who between them lost $5.4 million. His boss at the SAMAX Motorsport team, Peter Baron, was scammed for approximately $400,000 and his Scottish team-mate, ex-Champ Car driver Ryan Dalziel with whom he had won the Grand-Am race at Laguna Seca in 2008, was taken for $550,000 together with his father.

Autoweek magazine dubbed Zogaib the 'Madoff of Motorsport' after Bernie Madoff, the American financier who orchestrated the largest Ponzi scheme in history, amounting to $65 billion, even though the label would have been even more appropriate for Loles. Zogaib's prison sentence of 15 years compared with the 150 years received by 71-year-old Madoff in 2009.

board members that he was making money for the church and word spread throughout the community about Loles's purported success. He told other members of the church that he could guarantee significant returns from imaginary and fictitious high-yielding bonds without risking the initial sums invested. After the FBI's investigations, it was discovered that Loles had operated a non-existent fund, Knightsbridge Holdings, that had attracted a flood of new clients with the promise of an annual return in the range of 7.0–7.75%.

Three specific cases cited in court documents concerned individuals who had invested $100,000, $1 million and $2 million. Loles had told all three that the money they had invested with Knightsbridge Holdings had been used to buy what he described as 'arbitrage bonds', which he claimed were issued by blue-chip companies like General Electric, Travelers Insurance and Applied Materials. Although there were no such bonds, he created false statements that provided the unfortunate investors with detailed monthly records, interest statements and tax forms, but these were all just figments of his devious imagination.

This was a textbook example of a Ponzi scheme. He simply used incoming capital from fresh investors to make small 'interest payments' to earlier investors when pressed to do so and by this means created the illusion that the promised financial returns were real. For many years, he was able to get away with his deception by moving money around and winning enough new investors to ensure that no one caught up with him. Many of those who were duped were elderly and vulnerable people, including some who were terminally ill, all hoping to leave money for their children or grandchildren. One of those on whom he preyed was a woman whose husband had recently died: Loles not only got his hands on the proceeds of the deceased man's insurance policy but also convinced the widow to take out a second mortgage and transfer that money to him as well. His dishonesty first came to light in 2009 after a parishioner who had loaned $500,000 to the church, via Loles, failed to recoup the money and went directly to the church, which denied ever having received it.

None of the money obtained by Loles was ever actually invested. Instead, it was spent on providing him with an extravagant lifestyle and funding his failed business ventures and loss-making racing team. Among his ill-gotten luxuries was a large mansion equipped with a multi-car garage for his collection of sports cars. Despite not filing a tax return for years, and with the most income he reported in any year between 2000 and 2009 being a mere $32,215, Loles had managed to extract around $27 million from more than 50 victims. As well as the churchgoers and the church itself, these included clients of Farnbacher Loles. Loles's deception tore apart a close-knit Greek community, many of whom stopped going to their church because they were too embarrassed and humiliated.

The greatest loss was suffered by the Misailidis family. Over the week of Christmas in 2008, Loles spent $19,000 wining and dining them in New York City. Afterwards they sent him almost $14 million to invest that he later claimed, falsely, was his profit on Greek share deals he had made with the late John Misailidis. In court during 2011, US District Judge Alvin

Thompson determined not only that the investigation of this specific crime had been obstructed by Loles after his arrest, due to his false statements to the FBI, but he had also wilfully tried to mislead the court during multiple hearings and committed perjury while testifying. In the end, Loles pleaded guilty to charges of mail, wire and securities fraud in addition to money laundering. Judge Thompson told him: 'You are the most sinister defendant I have ever sentenced for this category of crime.'

Loles addressed some of the victims who attended his trial. Looking directly at them, referring to some of them by name, he professed love for them before begging for their forgiveness while repeatedly pausing to fight back tears. He even asked two of them to come and visit him at the Donald W. Wyatt Detention Facility in Rhode Island.

'I know a lot of you have love for me,' he said. 'I hope one day you can forgive me... There are no words to explain what happened.' He said he hoped his acts 'going forward will show it doesn't end today. I will do everything in my power to try to pay you back.' He talked about the importance of having been given the opportunity to confess his sins to a Greek Orthodox priest, saying 'It was wonderful... I feel I'm OK with God. I confessed and repented.'

The judge wasn't impressed and, in 2014, finally handed down a custodial sentence of 25 years, presumably to allow Loles sufficient time to repent at his leisure.

CHAPTER 38

RICARDO LONDONO

Racing cartel

**Officially listed as the first Colombian Formula 1
driver, Ricardo Londoño-Bridge — his unlikely
sounding but entirely genuine full name —
was denied the racing licence that would have
enabled him to compete, ending his dream
before it had even started. Londoño had a more
dangerous pastime than motor racing, however,
for his business involvement with drugs cartels
ultimately led to his murder.**

Most racing fans on both sides of the Atlantic will have heard of the immensely talented and versatile Colombian driver Juan Pablo Montoya. His hugely successful career crossed backwards and forwards between America and Europe, starting with championship titles in International Formula 3000 in 1998 and CART Indycar in his rookie season a year later. In 2000, he entered the Indianapolis 500 for the first time and won it, then between 2001 and 2006 he won seven Formula 1 Grands Prix with Williams and McLaren. He switched to the NASCAR stock cars, where he was also reasonably successful, before moving on to race sportscars. He won the Daytona 24 Hours three times (in 2007, 2008 and 2013) and in recent years he has still been winning in IMSA.

An earlier talent from Colombia was Roberto Guerrero, who was much less successful but still a leading driver who won two Indycar races in 1987 and twice came agonisingly close to victory in the Indianapolis 500. Prior to that, he had become the first Colombian driver to start a Formula 1 Grand Prix and, despite not recording any points finishes in two seasons, with uncompetitive Ensign and Theodore cars in 1982 and 1983, he proved himself more than capable. Technically, however, the accolade of being the country's first Formula 1 driver goes to Ricardo Londoño-Bridge.

Born in Medellín, Colombia's second-largest city, in 1949, Ricardo Londoño was an extraordinary daredevil as a teenager who raced bikes, cars and even boats. His skill and bravery earned him the nickname '*Cuchilla*', which roughly translates as 'Razor'. He competed in local stock-car races in the 1970s, building a great reputation as one of the most promising racing drivers in the country through his performances at circuits such as El Volador and Tocancipá. From 1979, having concentrated his efforts on competing in Colombia, he went further afield and focused his efforts on North America.

His first big race was the Sebring 12 Hours in March 1979 with John Gunn and George Garces in a Porsche 935 Turbo but they didn't finish. At the end of the year he returned to Florida for the 250-mile Daytona Finale and finished 18th in the same car. Back at Daytona for the following year's 24 Hours, he and Albert Naon shared fellow Colombian Mauricio de Narváez's Porsche 911 Carrera to score a fine seventh place and second in the GTO class, while he and the car's owner followed up at Sebring with a less impressive 26th and 10th in class. However, his main focus that year was the Can-Am Challenge in which, competing as the Londoño-Bridge Racing Team with a Lola T530, ostensibly sponsored by Roldan Autos, he achieved some respectable and consistent results, including fifth place at Mosport and sixth places at Sonoma, Road America and Riverside, putting him 12th in the final standings.

As his friend, journalist Mike Doodson, wrote: 'The mistake that Ricardo made in his career was to stay at home, where his ability garnered him increasingly meaningless successes, not to mention enhancing his celebrity. It was only when his fellow countryman Roberto Guerrero, eight years his junior, started to have success in British F3 racing, that he decided to head for England at last.'

When, aged 31, Londoño finally felt ready to try his luck across the Atlantic, he settled on the Aurora AFX Formula 1 Championship, a thinly supported series for pensioned-off Formula 1 machinery and assorted Formula 2 cars, held mainly at British circuits. He bought a one-off drive in Colin Bennett's ex-Mario Andretti Lotus 78 and took part in the 1980 season's final round at Silverstone. Pre-race testing at the circuit saw him turn in some competitive laps in the unfamiliar car but on his sixth lap of official practice he crashed the car before he had been able to post a meaningful time. Hard work by the locally based Hesketh team, which fabricated new components overnight, and by his mechanics enabled him to start the race from the back of the grid. He brought the elderly car home in seventh place.

His 1981 season started with a return to Daytona for the 24 Hours driving the Red Lobster Racing BMW M1 with Dave Cowart and Kenper Miller in the GTO class but that ended in retirement. Meanwhile, having proved his worth against international competition in Can-Am, and full of enthusiasm after his single-seater outing at Silverstone, he now aspired to greater things. An introduction by Bennett to Mo Nunn's Ensign Formula 1 team came at an opportune moment. This cash-strapped little team had endured a torrid season the previous year after its star driver, Clay Regazzoni, suffered a career-ending crash at Long Beach that left him paralysed for the rest of his life. With the team's prime sponsor, Unipart, also having departed, Nunn found himself in urgent need of a cash injection. Bennett had become part-owner of the team and campaigned for his protégé Londoño to be signed up.

Not only did Londoño appear to be capable of making the transition to Formula 1 at World Championship level but he also presented a new market from which to attract sponsorship. In early 1981, desperate for funding, Nunn led a contingent to Colombia to look for backing. Amongst those to pledge their support were Café Colombia and Pasta Doria as well as some other more colourful sponsors. At that point the team realised that it faced a conundrum because its new driver didn't have the requisite FISA-issued 'superlicence', given his limited international experience. This meant that for the first race of the season, the United States Grand Prix West at Long Beach, Swiss driver Marc Surer instead filled the sole Ensign seat.

Things looked up for Londoño prior to the next race, the Brazilian Grand Prix at Jacarepaguá, where there was a handy opportunity for the eager Colombian to impress FISA observers and obtain his superlicence. Rio de Janeiro's new Jacarepaguá track had been the Brazilian Grand Prix's venue for the first time in 1978 but financial problems had forced the event to return to its former home, Interlagos, for the next two years. Because of this, a pre-event acclimatisation session was organised at Jacarepaguá on the Wednesday before the race weekend, something that was normally only accorded to tracks being used for the first time. Londoño was allowed to participate in this test and prove his credentials.

After Surer completed a handful of installation laps, he handed the Ensign N180B over to Londoño for his first experience of the car. Within

The nearest Ricardo Londoño came to achieving his dream to race in Formula 1
came with a one-off drive in this ex-Mario Andretti Lotus 78 in a round of
Britain's Aurora AFX Championship at Silverstone in 1980.

about ten laps, the novice posted a respectable time of 1m 41.7s. Although
this was four seconds adrift of the day's best time, set by Carlos Reutemann
in his Williams FW07C, it was quicker than plenty of established drivers,
including luminaries like Nelson Piquet and René Arnoux, and only a
second or so slower than other big names such as Gilles Villeneuve and
reigning World Champion Alan Jones. However, Londoño's aggressive
style of driving upset some of the other drivers and Keke Rosberg, who
was especially unimpressed, took the opportunity to try a 'brake test'. The
Colombian newcomer couldn't avoid the Finn's Fittipaldi and slammed into
the back of it. Even though Londoño had otherwise acquitted himself well,
the collision led to his application for a superlicence being turned down the
following evening. The team had to replace him with Surer, who managed
to finish a fine fourth in the wet race conditions in one of his and the team's
best-ever performances.

Even though Londoño hadn't been allowed to participate in official
qualifying or the race itself, he had had an entry accepted in his name and
that left him at least able to lay claim to being Colombia's first Formula 1
driver.

The official and valid explanation for his exclusion from the Brazilian Grand Prix was that the authorities didn't feel he had sufficient experience. However, Bernie Ecclestone had also added weight to that decision due to his concerns about the provenance of Londoño's sponsorship. He had discovered that the driver's funding was strongly linked to the notorious Medellín Cartel drugs operation and very understandably he didn't want this association, or the possible laundering of proceeds from those crimes, anywhere near Formula 1. Londoño's habit of wearing a solid-silver razor blade as a pendant around his neck wouldn't have helped to dispel that notion.

Entrenched in Colombia's political, financial and social fabric at the time was the constant war of successive governments against the huge cocaine-trafficking trade, which was bigger financially than the country's GDP and cost thousands of lives. The founder and leader of the Medellín Cartel was Pablo Escobar, who remains infamous as the wealthiest criminal in history having reportedly accumulated $30 billion at the time of his death in a shoot-out with a rival cartel in 1993. The drugs lord, who used terrorism, kidnapping and exceptional violence in the course of amassing his fortune, was a car enthusiast and also a keen racing driver who had funded the construction of some local race circuits.

As with VW Beetles in Germany and Fiat 500s in Italy, one of the most common sights on the roads of Colombia in the 1970s was the box-shaped Renault 4, which remains a cult car there nowadays. It was in one of these underpowered Renaults that Escobar started competing against other wealthy associates from within the cartel before progressing to an ex-Emerson Fittipaldi Porsche 911 RSR that he soon upgraded to a 935 facsimile. Whilst no one dared ask what Escobar did for a living, suspicions were raised at these small-time events by the presence of four race cars (one each for him and his cousin plus two spares), support vehicles, a helicopter and lavish hospitality.

Londoño and Escobar were only a few months apart in age and their paths first crossed at a hillclimb in Medellín. Their association led to financial support for Londoño's racing that benefited his international ambitions in the short term but ultimately led to his downfall.

After his failure to break into Formula 1 in 1981, Londoño returned to Europe to spend some of his illicit budget. He bought some Formula 2 drives with Docking Spitzley alongside Stefan Johansson in the team's Toleman TG280 and Lola T850 before quietly disappearing for a while. He didn't compete at all in 1982 after the arrest of most of his 'sponsors' and

BILL BLACKLEDGE
Running on empty

Ricardo Londoño's continued venture into single-seater racing, taking in a handful of European Formula 2 events, meant that he wasn't able to compete in the 1981 Can-Am Challenge, but the presence there of an expatriate Scottish driver ensured that drugs money still found its way into the championship. Amateur racing driver Bill Blackledge was also a skilled pilot who allegedly flew huge batches of cocaine and marijuana from Colombia to North America for the powerful Cali Cartel in the 1980s and managed to evade capture for decades by using a variety of fake identities. While Londoño's illicit business dealings meant that he didn't survive into old age, the Scottish fugitive was 84 when, in 2021, he was named by Interpol as the oldest individual on its list of most wanted British criminals, having helped smuggle drugs worth billions of pounds across continents. Blackledge has been specifically accused of involvement in a conspiracy to import 1,000kg of marijuana and 5kg of cocaine into the US.

thereafter made sporadic IMSA appearances with a Porsche 911 Carrera, a Chevrolet Corvette and a Pontiac Firebird before hanging up his helmet in 1985.

By this time, through his friendship with Escobar, Londoño was well connected in the burgeoning Colombian drugs racket and he started a business in which he used his extensive network to sell boats, planes and helicopters to recognised drug traffickers. This brought him even closer to the heart of the illicit trade and eventually, in November 1998, 1,200kg of cocaine was discovered at one of his properties. Two years later, the Colombian courts issued a confiscation order whereby classic cars and property valued at $10 million were seized, although he managed to avoid imprisonment.

By this time Londoño had accumulated some very unpleasant enemies. One of the few assets that the authorities allowed him to keep was a hotel in Cispatá Bay, a seaside resort near San Bernardo del Viento. He was staying there on Saturday 18th July 2009 when, surrounded by family and friends and preparing to leave the beachside restaurant where they had enjoyed lunch, six hitmen suddenly appeared on motorcycles and shot him dead.

The horrific assault lasted five minutes and left 12 bullets in his body, including three in his head. Two other men, believed to be his bodyguards, were also killed and police said they believed that the assassinations were part of the settling of accounts in the drugs trade.

Aged 59 at the time of his death, Ricardo Londoño may have had an unremarkable international career in motor racing but, despite the unsavoury backing that ensured that he will forever be known as the racer who was sponsored by the Medellín Cartel, he was a national hero at local level and a much better driver than is generally credited.

CHAPTER 39
JOACHIM LUTHI
Off the straight and narrow

The Swiss financier was
the custodian of a famous
World Championship-winning
Formula 1 team for less than
a season before going on the
run from the authorities, who
eventually caught up with him
in the US where they found him
living under a false name.

J ack Brabham founded his eponymous team in 1960, by which time he was on his way to winning his second Formula 1 World Championship for Cooper. He won his third title in 1966, this time in his own car, thus becoming the first and only man to win the World Championship in a car bearing his own name. When he decided to return to his native Australia in 1970 for family reasons, his partner Ron Tauranac bought his share in Motor Racing Developments, which owned the Brabham name and the production rights for its successful Formula 2 and Formula 3 customer cars. Tauranac was an excellent engineer but soon realised that he didn't have either the commercial skills or interest in managing a team at that level and after a year he sold out to Bernie Ecclestone for £100,000 before leaving the company.

Ecclestone provided much-needed capital to modernise the team and his faith in young South African designer Gordon Murray was rewarded with multiple race wins for several drivers in the years that he owned Brabham, culminating in World Championship titles for Nelson Piquet in 1981 and

1983. After that, things went gradually downhill. The team's final victory came in the 1985 French Grand Prix and at the end of that season, Piquet, dissatisfied with his salary, moved on, with Murray departing a year later. Following engine partner BMW's withdrawal at the end of 1987, Brabham had to take an enforced sabbatical and didn't compete at all in 1988. The heyday for the team with such an illustrious history was well and truly over and by now Ecclestone had lost interest in owning a team as all his time and energy was devoted to managing the commercial interests of the Formula One Constructors' Association (FOCA). Ecclestone sold Motor Racing Developments, including the Brabham name, to Alfa Romeo, who planned to use the team's facilities and expertise to build a contender for a new production car racing series, but when this didn't materialise the Italian manufacturer also lost interest and, under pressure from Fiat, its new parent company, decided to dispose of the team.

Peter Windsor, the award-winning motorsport journalist, was commercial manager of the Williams Formula 1 team at this time. He had long-held aspirations to run his own team and, when it became apparent that there was an opportunity to buy Brabham, he approached a Swiss millionaire to fund a deal. This was Walter Brun, a one-time post office clerk who had made his fortune from slot machines and indulged his passion for motor racing by becoming a notable team owner in world championship sports car racing, running Porsche 956s and 962s. Perhaps letting his ambition run away with itself, Brun arrived in Formula 1 in 1988 with his own EuroBrun team, but it achieved very little, often failing to qualify or even pre-qualify.

In a deal worth £5.5 million handled by Ecclestone, Motor Racing Developments passed into new ownership. Windsor became managing director of Brabham and announced the return of the iconic name for the 1989 season, supported by Brun and an 'anonymous' Swiss banker.

The new investor was 39-year-old Joachim Lüthi, a financier of questionable repute who owned Zürich-based Adiuva Finance, an investment company, and also had a 50 percent interest in a Liechtenstein-based company called Kingside Establishment.

Although Lüthi initially appeared to be the team's saviour, the manner in which he came to acquire it was opaque and untidy. Part of Windsor's deal was that he would receive a 20 percent shareholding in the company but by the end of 1988 Brun had quickly decided that he would sell his shares to Lüthi, who didn't want Windsor involved. Understandably aggrieved that he had been squeezed out, Windsor took legal advice to clarify how his agreement with Brun had been changed now that Lüthi had a controlling interest and he successfully applied for a High Court injunction that froze his 20 percent interest in the company.

As Terry Lovell explained in his book *Bernie's Game*, Lüthi had beaten Windsor to it by effectively moving ownership of the shares and the company out of the UK. Retaining one ordinary share, he transferred the remaining 999 shares to a Liechtenstein-based entity in a move that laid the ground for his real interest in Motor Racing Developments — to use it as cover for a major fraud.

Within two weeks of Lüthi buying the company, Lovell stated: 'He arranged a loan of £2 million to be made by MRD to Kingside Establishment, which then went into liquidation but not before transferring its funds to a newly opened branch office in Zürich from where it was transferred to Lüthi's Adiuva Finance AG before that too went into liquidation. Accountants Robson Rhodes subsequently reported that "no details have been found... to confirm the purpose, terms or recipients" of the £2 million transfer. MRD also paid £250,000 to an unnamed director for loss of office and the company chairman, namely Lüthi, received a payment of £291,000. To cover the transfer to Kingside Establishment, Lüthi arranged for MRD to receive loans totalling £2.285 million from Adiuva.'

Unsurprisingly, Lüthi was keen to maintain a low profile. One of Brabham's drivers that season was Martin Brundle, who was making a return to Formula 1 after winning the World Sports-Prototype Championship for Jaguar. He told *Motor Sport* magazine of a meeting in 1989 when he went to see Ecclestone about driving for Brabham: 'He was sitting in his office with a man in a suit. Bernie said, "Brundle, this is Mr Lüthi. He's just bought Brabham, and he wants you to drive for him. He's in the top end of the finance world and he just wants to keep a low profile, so don't talk about him to anyone." Joachim Lüthi turned up for the first race at Rio with a knotted handkerchief on his bald head and a hooker on each arm. I said to myself, "So this is the man we mustn't talk about. Low profile, right."'

While the new owner amused everyone on the pit wall with his antics, the reborn team posted mixed results during the 1989 season. Driving Brabham BT58 cars with underpowered Judd V8 engines, Brundle and team-mate Stefano Modena often qualified well, helped by effective Pirelli qualifying tyres, but the cars weren't reliable and good results were infrequent. The Monaco Grand Prix marked a fine high, with Modena third and Brundle sixth, while the Englishman added another sixth and a fifth towards the end of the season, in Italy and Japan respectively.

On the Wednesday before the Belgian Grand Prix at the end of August, Lüthi was arrested in Zürich in connection with the suspected embezzlement of $100 million that had been invested by clients of Adiuva Finance who found that they had been unable to withdraw their funds. The investigation that led to Lüthi's arrest had been initiated by the Swiss Banking Commission in conjunction with the investigating magistrate of the Canton of Aargau, where a separate criminal investigation was also underway involving Kingside Establishment. Only two days later at the Court of Appeal in London, Peter Windsor succeeded in obtaining the latest in a series of injunctions preventing any part of Brabham's assets being disposed of, the news of which was obviously cause for great concern for the members of the team whose immediate future looked bleak as a result.

All of this further soiled the already tarnished image of Formula 1 as it came hard on the heels of the arrests of Didier Calmels (see Chapter 14) of the Larrousse-Calmels team on murder charges and of Fred Bushell on

While Martin Brundle talks to an out-of-shot interviewer during his 1989 Formula 1 season with Brabham, the team's sinister new owner, Joachim Lüthi, observes in the background.

PETER WINDSOR
Lights out

Peter Windsor's legal action dragged on and in 1991 he was awarded substantial damages. By this time he was back at Williams, now as team manager, after an interlude with Ferrari. As described in Terry Lovell's book, he had been through an exceedingly unpleasant experience before the conclusion of his court case: 'Six months earlier he had been bundled into a van by two men as he left the Williams team headquarters in Didcot, Oxfordshire. Employees who went to his aid were threatened by what appeared to be a gun. Handcuffed and blindfolded, he was driven out to the countryside, beaten up and later dumped by the roadside. He was taken to hospital for treatment to cuts and bruising.' Whether or not this frightening incident was connected to the dispute over his shares in the Brabham team is conjecture but fortunately he overcame this setback and continued his illustrious career in the sport.

fraud charges and his subsequent resignation from Team Lotus (see Chapter 15).

Lüthi was finally charged with embezzling $133 million from 1,700 investors but before his case could come to court he fled to America, where he adopted the alias Terry Sexton and claimed to be a German national who owned a gold mine. With the help of the Swiss authorities, the fugitive financier was finally tracked down to Marina del Ray, California in 1995 and arrested. After an unsuccessful appeal against an extradition order, he was eventually returned to Switzerland in May 1996 to be convicted of criminal charges that resulted in him serving a prison sentence of seven and a half years.

MALIK ADO IBRAHIM

The 'prince' who left the paddock

Ahead of the 1999 season, a mysterious and self-proclaimed Nigerian 'prince' scammed his way into becoming the co-owner of the Arrows Formula 1 team by promising huge investment. Before that year's campaign was over, he had disappeared along with his unfulfilled promises, leaving behind considerable confusion about his motives and a weakened Arrows team facing severe financial difficulties from which it never recovered.

The engaging but curious Prince Adulmalik Ado Ibrahim, known as Malik, had been privately educated in England, together with his brothers Nazir and Khadril, at Langley School in Norfolk. He claimed that he belonged to one of the 75 royal families of Nigeria, where monarchs have no formal political power, and that he was one of King Attah's 150 grandchildren from 14 wives. This may have entitled him to style himself a 'prince' but it was quite a tenuous connection. He also suggested that he had made his fortune in oil, telecommunications and real estate. He gave the impression of having access to great wealth by living in a suite at the exclusive Lanesborough Hotel on London's Hyde Park Corner and flaunting a collection of expensive road cars.

He first appeared in Formula 1 circles when he promised funding for the proposed Japanese team Dome, which had designed and built a prototype car around the architecture of a Mugen Honda engine. As *Business F1* stated: 'Malik Ado Ibrahim found it frighteningly easy to convince [the team's management] that he was a man of substance and agreed to meet

Prince Malik Ado Ibrahim appeared briefly in Formula 1 in 1999,
joining Tom Walkinshaw in co-ownership of the Arrows team,
but never came up with the money and soon vanished.

them at the Hilton Hotel adjacent to London's Heathrow airport where coincidently there was a meeting of Formula One's team principals happening on the same day. But it was no coincidence. Malik had chosen the same hotel on the same day to help convince the Sasaki brothers (the owners) that he was a Formula One insider. It worked beautifully.'

When they met, Malik told them that he was in negotiation with the sport's supremo, Bernie Ecclestone, to enter his own team, so this appeared to be a marriage made in heaven. The Sasakis were so impressed by the number of team principals present that they agreed to introduce the 'prince' to Hiroshi Honda, president of Mugen, the racing engine subsidiary of Honda, to discuss a supply of engines that Malik would pay for. However, Mr Honda saw through Malik and closed down the negotiations.

Undeterred, Malik continued to pursue his fantasy of owning a Formula 1 team and approached Eddie Jordan with a proposal to buy a share in his company. Jordan was initially interested but became sceptical and soon ceased all dialogue. All the same, Malik enjoyed being in this spotlight and to raise his profile engaged the expensive Freud communications company with the brief to make him as famous as the Irish entrepreneur.

His next target was Tom Walkinshaw, who had bought the Arrows team in 1996 from its previous owner, Footwork, a Japanese logistics company, but after just one season had become desperate for funds despite having come tantalisingly close to winning a race courtesy of Damon Hill at the Hungarian Grand Prix, where he led for most of the distance until hydraulic failure allowed his former team-mate, Jacques Villeneuve, to pass on the final lap and take the win away.

Failing to realise how many royal families there are in Nigeria, Walkinshaw was completely taken in by Malik's overtures and implied connections and was also impressed by the claim that he had competed at the Le Mans 24 Hours under a pseudonym driving a Lamborghini, although there is no evidence of this. As Malik had convinced investment bank Morgan Grenfell to help him in the deal, Walkinshaw, without carrying out sufficient due diligence, accepted the offer of $125 million as a combination of equity and sponsorship for the 1999 season. It looked like an arrangement that would transform the team's fortunes.

Malik had dreamt up a concept whereby he marketed a universal brand name, 't-minus', with the aim of raising funds by licensing it to companies wanting to promote their products using the Arrows Grand Prix team as a platform. However, 't-minus' didn't actually exist and under questioning from sceptical journalists Malik struggled to explain whether it was manufacturer of an energy drink or a brand through which he would launch luxury goods. Indeed, he told Matt Bishop that he would 'publicise the brand, then decide what products it should make'.

By the middle of 1999, it was no surprise that the ludicrous scheme hadn't generated any revenue nor that Malik had made no payment to the team for the purchase of his shareholding. By the end of the season, both the mysterious 't-minus' logos on the side of the cars and the flamboyant 'prince' had vanished from Formula 1.

Arrows lurched through the final phase of its existence before running out of money midway through 2002 and finally collapsing at the end of the season, taking with it Walkinshaw's main business, the highly successful Tom Walkinshaw Racing (TWR). After Arrows's liquidation, Walkinshaw was handed a personal bill estimated to be in excess of £13 million. Mr Justice Lindsay ruled that the Scotsman was liable for an indemnity that he had given in respect of an overdraft with the private-equity division of Morgan Grenfell, which had a legitimate claim as a secured creditor and refused to show any latitude on its terms, a situation that finally brought the team to its knees. The catalyst for this debt was the hole that had been left in the company accounts three years earlier by Malik's non-payment.

A few years later Malik was at it again when he popped up in 2008 and was arrested for the theft of $750,000 provided to him by Robert Richardson Sr to develop his son's career as a young NASCAR driver. The Collin County District Council Special Crimes Unit (SCU) alleged that Malik had stolen the funds by promising they would be deposited in a Bank of America trust account that didn't exist. Although he was cleared of this by the courts, the 44-year-old wasn't allowed to leave the Texas jail where he was being held because he was required to post bail of $35,000 in connection with several other charges concerning perjury and false statements that he had allegedly made during the lead-up to his trial.

More wrongdoing came to light in January 2010 when he was working for a renewable energy company that he had co-founded. After a Texan district attorney received claims that Malik had stolen over $200,000 from it, a warrant was issued for his arrest to face 11 counts of indictment for fraud.

Malik later moved back to his home country and married a wealthy heiress. At the time of writing, he had recently announced his intention to run for the presidency of Nigeria.

CHAPTER 41
SID MILLER
Facing the music

This is the improbable story of two eccentric bachelors who were Anglican lay preachers and became prolific benefactors to numerous young racing drivers. Their sponsorship arrangements were largely funded through a scam in which Sid Miller, aided and abetted by John Bellord, sold electronic organs to churches. When it all ended abruptly, the two men evaded the authorities by clumsily faking suicide and escaping to live as fugitives in a roofless bothy on a remote and uninhabited Scottish island for 262 days before ending up in jail.

During the 1974 and 1975 British racing seasons, it would have been almost impossible to attend a national club race meeting without being aware of the high-profile presence of Southern Organs. Such was the extent of the company's largesse that its name — and those of subsidiaries National Organs and Miller Organs — seemed to be everywhere, with sponsorship deals widely promoting its products. The corporate logos were emblazoned on the flanks of numerous cars and through title support of leading series and championships, all reinforced with additional advertising in race programmes and on trackside banners and hoardings.

Even to the uninitiated, motor racing was an unlikely and incongruous choice of platform through which to promote a company that ostensibly sold electronic organs to churches. However, Southern Organs was an extremely unusual business operated by two extremely unusual characters, Sidney 'Jim' Miller and his associate John Bellord, both of whom were already indulging their taste for fast, expensive cars with a stable that included models from Aston Martin, Facel Vega, Jensen and Rolls-Royce.

Miller and Bellord's growing interest in the world of motor racing came after an introduction to John and Angela Webb, the husband-and-wife team who ran Motor Circuit Developments (MCD), which owned Brands Hatch, Oulton Park, Mallory Park and Snetterton. Over the course of two seasons of involvement, the Southern Organs name became attached to various racing championships, with the British Saloon Car Championship of 1975 perhaps the most prominent, but there were also series for Formula Ford and Formula Atlantic single-seaters and Clubmans sports cars. The portfolio of British drivers who sported allegiance to the mysterious group of companies was as extensive as it was impressive and included many established and rising stars, including ex-Olympic ski champion Divina Galica, Tony Lanfranchi, David Purley, Tony Shaw, Damien Magee, Wil Arif, Barry Andrews, Rod Birley, Clive Baker, Geoff Friswell, and brothers Dave and Richard Morgan. Additionally, Southern Organs supported entire race meetings with generous prize funds, celebrity races and even a racing series for light aircraft.

Among the drivers, Geoff Friswell was one who particularly came to regret his association with Miller and Bellord. Known as 'Frizz the Whizz', he was best known for his success in racing a Mallock in the British Clubmans championship. Having already become champion in 1972, he was looking likely to repeat the feat in 1974 until he ran out of money mid-season and missed some races. Rescue appeared in the form of Southern Organs with Miller offering him enough backing to finish the series, although unfortunately it came too late to be able to take the title. For 1975, Friswell wanted to move on from Clubmans but agreed to Miller's suggestion that he continue for one more year with the promise that, if he won the title, Southern Organs would support him in Formula 2 for 1976. This was a massive incentive and an offer that the driver couldn't refuse. In his Mallock U2 Mk16, Friswell duly obliterated the opposition and won the championship, which his sponsor was also supporting. It was a momentous season in which he won 22 races, scored four more podium finishes, set one outright lap record and another 12 class records, with seven other fastest laps. But despite his unprecedented success, his dream of progressing to Formula 2 was shattered.

Dave Morgan was another driver for whom substantial promises never materialised. His eye-catching rise included a televised punch from James Hunt after a Formula 3 shunt at Crystal Palace in 1970 and an impressive Formula 2 victory at Mallory Park in 1972 against a stellar cast that included Niki Lauda, Jody Scheckter and Ronnie Peterson. After becoming embraced by Southern Organs, he achieved his ambition to reach Formula 1 by getting a seat in a Surtees TS16 for the British Grand Prix of 1975. Miller and Bellord had recently met John Surtees and arranged to place Morgan in the struggling team's second entry alongside John Watson. With sponsorship ascribed to National Organs, the plan was to take in the remaining four European Grands Prix, starting at Silverstone, and possibly the end-of-season United States Grand Prix as well. As things transpired, the Silverstone race proved to be Morgan's first and last Formula 1 outing and effectively killed off his career. It was an inauspicious race that ended for him, as for many other drivers, when he aquaplaned off the track into the catch fencing at Club Corner in the deluge of rain that prematurely halted the race. He later judged that it had been the least competitive performance of his entire career but that he had made the best of an average car and was confidently looking forward to a better run next time out at the Nürburgring in Germany. That never happened because his new sponsor defaulted on payments despite grandiose assurances.

The Southern Organs presence at that Silverstone meeting also extended to the support race for saloon cars as well as the championship in which they competed. The company reached a new level in its hunger for attention by managing to persuade publicity-shy 'glam-rock' star Alvin Stardust to present the trophies to the winning drivers of its race. Stardust, whose real name was Bernard Jewry, admitted to having a long-held ambition to attend a Formula 1 race and accepted the offer, so he was helicoptered to the circuit and lunched with the company's guests. Although commonplace these days, this was an early example of a corporate interest bringing a celebrity to a Grand Prix to exploit their fame by association and Stardust was certainly a 'name' at the peak of his fame and popularity. Another initiative at Silverstone was the distribution of tens of thousands of free copies of a 'Southern Organs Grand Prix' newspaper.

Three months later, in October, the highly competitive Southern Organs British Saloon Car Championship reached its finale at Brands Hatch with the title poised between three drivers. Andy Rouse, who drove a semi-works Broadspeed Triumph Dolomite Sprint, held the advantage because he had scored more class wins than the other two, but there was every chance that class rival Brian Muir in his similar Shellsport-backed car could derail his championship ambitions after pipping him to the class victory in the previous round at Oulton Park. Although a plan had been hatched for Brands Hatch whereby Rouse, if he weren't already in front, would pass Muir at the last moment, an accident late in the race put the final stretch of track leading

The names of Sid Miller's electronic organ businesses — Southern Organs, National Organs and Miller Organs — appeared on numerous racing cars, including Dave Morgan's Surtees TS16 in the 1975 British Grand Prix.

up to the finish line under yellow flags, meaning no overtaking. Ignoring this, Rouse darted past Muir only a few metres from the line, but he was allowed to keep the points and became champion. However, this thrilling climax was completely overshadowed by the fact that the series sponsors, Sid Miller and John Bellord, had long since vanished and there were no cheques available for the prizewinners.

The short-lived but extensive Southern Organs racing programme was managed by Geoff Green, who had been appointed Motor Racing Promotions Manager despite having no interest in cars or motor racing, let alone any relevant experience. He had first met Sid Miller and John Bellord many years previously in 1962, when, aged 21 and newly employed as a builder's labourer, one of his first jobs was to paint the wrought-iron gates of the stable block at the imposing Honeywood House near Horsham in Sussex. Miller and Bellord had turned this rented country mansion into a luxury convalescent and retirement home with charitable status from where Miller, a self-taught psychologist, also ran an unorthodox alternative therapy and healing practice, which although unregulated was entirely legal at the time.

Miller and Bellord were lay preachers with a keen interest in theology and had friendships high up in the Anglican church. Fancying themselves as intellectuals, they had co-authored a book called *A Course of Instruction on Cause and Effect*, published in 1952. Miller was eight years older than his associate and his personality was warm and charismatic, while Bellord, who looked after the accounts, was quieter and more reflective. Bellord had eschewed a career in his family's engineering business and had gone into partnership with Miller in 1950, when they first took on Honeywood House as the base for their endeavours. Always immaculately dressed, the pair became local benefactors as middle-aged men, helping the poor and giving significant sums to charity over a 15-year period. Through their philanthropy, they ingratiated themselves into the local community where they appeared to be genuinely liked and respected. Despite their taste in expensive cars, they weren't otherwise materialistic and lived modestly away from the main house in a small and well-kept studio flat.

Green, who was newly married, became one of many people whom Miller took under his wing to benefit from his 'guidance' and theories on the meaning of life. After setting up his own building and shopfitting business, Green earned most of his income at Honeywood House, which by now was owned by Miller and Bellord rather than rented. He took on increasingly large alteration and refurbishment jobs, one of which included completing the conversion of a stable into a chapel. Having been befriended by the two men, he grew ever closer to them, bonding over regular discussions about life, psychology and philosophy. The enigmatic Miller was very charming and able to attract people from diverse backgrounds. It wasn't long before Green and his wife, together with nurses, gardeners and cleaners on the payroll, were surprised to receive invitations to the many lavish parties and functions held at the house. It was as if the hosts had some sort of hold over their guests, all of whom were treated as part of the 'flock'. Despite initial discomfort, the Greens found themselves mixing with celebrities from the worlds of television and radio as well as bishops, detective inspectors and bankers. And racing drivers.

By 1967, Miller and Bellord felt the need to expand to supplement their existing income. Due to their strong religious leanings and affinity to the church, their solution was to start a business trading in electronic church organs. This idea had been inspired by a visiting clergyman who

Pictured with John Webb, boss of Brands Hatch, Sid Miller (right) became an unlikely but significant sponsor in British motor racing in 1974–75, providing funding for lots of young hopefuls as well as racing championships.

had been so impressed by the sound quality of an organ that his hosts had installed in the recently converted chapel that he wanted one too. Having identified potential demand for electronic organs as replacements for the elderly and costly-to-maintain pipe organs found in the great majority of churches, a new business was born. Within two years they had established their first shop in West Sussex, opened by the Bishop of Guildford, and over the next few years the empire grew to include ten shops in south-east England and the acquisition of another business, coincidentally named Miller Organs. By 1973, the pair had built up a huge empire on borrowed money and established seven companies under the umbrella of the Southern Organs group. Part of their vision was to create a new market in which organs and electronic synthesisers became more widely used in the world of entertainment and so broaden their appeal to a wider demographic. In anticipation of this, they also installed teaching studios in some of the shops and hired musicians to give lessons to customers.

The success of the two bachelors lay largely in their ability to persuade banks and finance companies to hand over money with little or no formal due diligence and based entirely on an illusion of wealth that had very little substance. The sales pitch they gave time and again to anyone in their extensive network of contacts, be they friends, business colleagues or even employees, was that they were selling organs to churches but as clergy were unable to sign hire-purchase agreements, and they therefore needed others to step in and act as 'sponsors' by signing the necessary forms in the capacity of nominees. The unsuspecting individuals felt secure in the knowledge that there was no risk involved because the articulate, convincing Miller and the credible, aristocratic-sounding Bellord would protect them by standing behind the deals and acting as guarantors. The nominees were also assured that the churches involved, all of which were completely unaware of the scheme, would individually repay the capital borrowed through the legacies and donations they received. Innocent and respectable nominees were not only duped but made to feel that they were being charitable and led to believe that they were part of a small group of trusted people who were helping by providing their names to assist the church. Their cooperation also earned a fee as an added incentive. Many impoverished racing drivers were happy to sign up as guarantors of multiple hire-purchase agreements in return for a form of 'sponsorship', much of which was delivered in cash at race circuits.

Through another company owned by the group, Eastbourne Finance, the guarantor scam extended to other money-making projects that encompassed a range of financial products such as mortgages, loans and investments, although the organ transactions continued to provide the most lucrative business. Any sponsored organ could be proven to be legitimate stock, with a traceable serial number, a delivery note and an invoice from the manufacturer. However, it transpired that several finance companies and banks unwittingly financed each individual organ, their decision-makers only too happy to put their faith in the two men who had nurtured such good personal relationships with them. In the 1970s the cost of an organ started at £5,000 (£66,000 at today's values) and in some cases it was later

With partner-in-crime and fellow lay preacher John Bellord, Sid Miller ran
a luxury convalescent and retirement home in Sussex called Honeywood
House, where a room was given over to demonstrating electronic organs.

proved that an individual organ was being financed as many as eight times
over. Oblivious to this, the various banks and finance houses appeared to
queue up to provide favourable terms of credit that the scammers used to
service the accrued liabilities from their previous hire-purchase agreements.
This vicious cycle became a money-raising scheme that initially created
huge wealth before spiralling out of control and turning the two men away
from philanthropy and into the criminal world of fraud from which there
would be no turning back.

As the Southern Organs group grew, so did Geoff Green's building
business. He was well placed to win all the shopfitting contracts as well as
work kitting out a factory and offices in Storrington. He had been making
a good living from this and had also received commissions for innocently
introducing friends and family as sponsors of organs, each time earning the
equivalent of a week's wages. He was now aware that his paymasters wanted
increased sales of church organs, preferably expensive top-of-the-range
models. He also knew that Miller and Bellord had identified motor racing
as a world containing a lot of wealthy people and associated opportunities.
When, out of the blue, he was offered the role of Motor Racing Promotions

Manager, he was caught completely off guard, especially as he had never even been to a motor race. He was flattered that, after more than ten years of friendship, he had finally earned sufficient respect to be brought into his benefactors' small and trusted inner circle. Against his wife's advice and his own better judgement, however, it was with some trepidation that he accepted the offer. As he readily admitted in later years, he was an impressionable young man lured by the promise of good pay and a fast car (a canary yellow Jensen-Healey), and more time to study philosophy and what the fraudsters described as 'our work'. Their justification for his appointment was that he could be trusted not to cheat the group. The job specification included writing press releases, organising track advertising and arranging hospitality suites at race days, but, crucially, didn't involve him in dealing with drivers and their sponsorship contracts until after they had been sealed. Despite his reservations about moving out of his comfort zone in the building trade, he he saw an opportunity to change his life. It certainly did that, but unfortunately not in the way that he had envisaged.

The downfall of Southern Organs came about in the wake of the Labour Government's introduction in July 1974 of a higher 12.5% rate of VAT on various 'luxury' goods, including petrol, and then the doubling of it three months later to 25%. This applied to all the products sold by Southern Organs and prompted the previously negligent finance companies to gradually become more diligent. They started sending letters to organ sponsors demanding to view organs named in hire-purchase agreements. When these letters were initially brought to his attention, Miller dismissed them as administrative errors, but the mounting level of requests couldn't be ignored forever.

Geoff Green, unaware of the full extent of his employers' dishonesty and reassured by the fact that he had delivered organs to churches, became involved in subsequent discussion about the options and what might be done. Bellord, who by now was mentally worn out and fully realised the impossibility of the financial predicament, wanted to face up to the crisis and let the law take its course. Miller, however, couldn't bear to think of the social stigma of people turning against him and wanted to escape for a while, preferably, he joked, to a remote desert island, so that he could have time to meditate, think things through and return refreshed and able to resolve their problems. After yet more debate, both men confessed to Green that they were in trouble and in danger of letting people down, and had decided that the best option really was to disappear.

Green had just read Frank Fraser Darling's book *Island Years*, which told how its author, a Scottish naturalist, had lived for years with his family in the remote Summer Isles, a group of small islands a few miles out to sea from the fishing village of Ullapool. Miller and Bellord knew that area of north-west Scotland as a holiday haunt and Green suggested that they could hide for a while on one of the islands. Although the Summer Isles had become a popular tourist destination, the appropriately named Priest Island wasn't part of the usual tour schedule because of its greater distance from the mainland and unpredictable tidal swell. The tiny island, on which Darling had briefly lived, also contained several freshwater lochans and a little stone bothy that could provide basic shelter. This barren, windswept, rocky tract, no more than half a mile across, wasn't quite what the two men had envisaged as a hideaway and initially they were unimpressed with the plan, but with no viable alternatives and time running out, they reluctantly agreed that Priest Island would be their destination.

Miller and Bellord were now in the hands of their loyal friend Geoff Green, who, by default, became their accomplice because he took on the role of both mastermind and quartermaster. He bought an inflatable rib boat large enough to carry the three of them together with sufficient food, equipment and stores for the two fugitives to survive for up to three months, plus a second smaller dinghy to enable them to fish on calmer days. One essential and non-negotiable item required by the two runaways was a chemical toilet, even though it would take up a lot of space in the boat. All the detailed planning took several weeks during which increasingly persistent creditors had to be fended off.

The two men told their staff that they were going on a two-week holiday to France and, as it would be their first break for years, they would celebrate with a party at Honeywood House. On 10th September 1975, watched by their guests, they took off from the lawns to fly to Calais in the same Bell Jet Ranger helicopter that they had previously chartered for business use. Their innocent pilot acted as the perfect witness to confirm their arrival in Calais and, once landed, they made their presence as conspicuous as possible in local cafés and shops, and sent postcards back to friends and associates in England. Then they returned by ferry to Dover, where Green met them with a Ford Cortina Estate towing a closed trailer crammed with the two boats and all their provisions. Green drove them through the night to north-west Scotland, where they lost an entire day searching for a suitably isolated launch site. They ended up much further from Priest Island than the originally planned departure point and faced a sea trip of 12 miles rather than the expected four. In a fully laden rib with only a

20-horsepower Chrysler outboard motor, that would be quite a challenge in extremely unpredictable seas.

After an incredibly treacherous ten-hour crossing to the island, rocked by huge waves in the unforgiving waters, the three exhausted men unloaded the waterlogged boats. They scaled the cliffs, a difficult task for Miller because he was mildly disabled from childhood polio, and found a temporary pitch for tents. After a night camping on the island, Green left his friends to fend for themselves and find the dilapidated bothy that could provide them with a little more shelter. Alone, he endured an equally unnerving return journey to the mainland, where he dismantled the rib and loaded it back into the trailer before returning to Sussex.

While the fugitives languished on Priest Island, getting used to their transition in attire from sharp business suits to waterproof oilskins, Green returned to work at Honeywood House. He remained the only person who knew the true whereabouts of the men while their trickle of postcards appeared to corroborate the story that they were indeed relaxing in France. By now Southern Organs was facing a deluge of correspondence and visits from nervous bankers and skulking financiers, all of which created considerable unease among the staff.

Of course, suspicions were aroused when the meticulously punctual pair didn't arrive home as expected. Green, the only person in the know, played innocent. As the racing season drew to a close, many thousands of pounds of prize money and sponsorship could not be paid, and Green, who had little idea of the extent of the wrongdoing, was the man who had to face those who wanted their money. His lack of knowledge was consistent with the fact that he was merely a puppet and not privy to any of the financial arrangements that had been made by his employers. His first public commitment after their disappearance was the final Formula One Air Race at Sywell aerodrome in Northamptonshire where he had the embarrassment of making excuses for turning up with only a small silver trophy and none of the contracted prize money. Another task was to deliver a series of letters written by Miller, although Green wasn't privy to the contents. They were in fact clumsily worded and unconvincing fake suicide notes written in the naive belief that they would persuade the finance companies to stop their pursuit and write off the debts.

The lack of due diligence by the financiers was quickly brought into sharp focus. There were reams of contracts guaranteed only by Miller and Bellord. Some of the nominees had previously been refused credit for the smallest of items before suddenly becoming deemed to be creditworthy for thousands of pounds purely on Miller's sanction. With no sign of the fraudsters, it wasn't long before police officers and reporters descended on Honeywood House, while writs poured in from the credit companies that put the blame squarely on the shoulders of the unfortunate nominees, including many of the racing drivers who had been 'sponsored' by the Southern Organs group.

A month after Miller and Bellord's disappearance, the enormity of the fraud was revealed. The *Daily Express* ran a front-page scoop with the headline 'Three Million Pound Help the Church Organ Fraud' with the figure updated the next day to £5 million. The article stated that more than 400 people and 20 finance companies were involved in the scandal and that two briefcases filled with cash had disappeared with the two men. It became clear that Miller's wealth had been an illusion, based on using other people's names to borrow large sums that he then paid back to create healthy credit ratings. In similar style to a Ponzi scheme, both men had been 'robbing Peter to pay Paul', which only worked until the bubble inevitably burst.

By now, the fraud squad was on the case. With reported 'sightings' of the fugitives across Europe and even in Australia and Africa, Interpol also became involved. Some of the more speculative sections of the media even suggested criminal links with the Great Train Robbery and Lord Lucan, whose disappearance the previous November after the alleged murder of his children's nanny appeared to share certain similarities.

Having discovered that the Ullapool area had been a favourite holiday destination for the conmen, the police deployed huge numbers of officers to the area in an unprecedented manhunt and even resorted to employing a psychic to assist them. Despite the pair being on an island only four miles away, no clues were uncovered. Miller and Bellord were presumed dead, which was consistent with the letters that their accomplice had been tricked into delivering.

In his excellent book *Paying for the Past*, Geoff Green described in detail the growing dilemma he faced at this time. On the one hand, through a strong sense of loyalty, he had tried to help the men who had played a major part in his life for many years, befriending him and employing him. On the other hand, he was now complicit in their crimes and guilty of betraying the trust that some of the nominees had placed in him, including his own friends and family members, some of whom had formed a 'fighting group' to share resources and attempt to clear their names and lessen the risk of losing everything through personal bankruptcy.

Green had been assured by Miller that the two men would return to sort things out after coming up with a plausible explanation to point the finger of blame squarely at the complacent and greedy financiers. He knew that barren Priest Island was a harsh habitat, particularly in sub-zero temperatures during winter, and that his benefactors only had enough provisions for a couple of months. Even allowing for catching fish and foraging, they would still have had to make sporadic trips in the tiny dinghy to get supplies from the mainland and that would have been particularly difficult in view of Miller's disability and the fact that neither of them could swim. Like so many others, Green had been taken in by their spell and had also been incredibly gullible in trusting them to eventually do the right thing and confess. He felt increasingly let down that they hadn't kept their word and reappeared.

Early in July 1976, he was shocked to receive a phone call from Miller asking for money to be sent to an address in Ullapool. After eight months in hiding on Priest Island, the fugitives had crossed to the mainland several weeks earlier and moved into a caravan in the garden of a guest house. They had exhausted the £1,000 cash that they'd taken with them and were now desperate. Now that he knew their whereabouts, Green realised that the deception and his misguided loyalty had lasted long enough. After nearly ten months of living a lie to protect the pair, he decided that he had to give them up. After consulting a solicitor, he went to the police. Knowing that without him Miller and Bellord might never be brought to justice, the police were prepared to offer leniency. On 30th July 1976, uniformed officers surrounded the secret hideaway in Ullapool, much to the consternation of the landlady, and arrested the fraudsters. They offered no resistance and assumed that they had been found through the tenacity of the police and the media rather than betrayal by their friend whose loyalty they had abused. They were returned to Sussex and held in prison in Lewes while criminal bankruptcy charges were filed against them.

The men each disclosed debts of £1.5 million with assets of only £2,500, which didn't come remotely close to covering the total sums borrowed — at least £5 million — to pay for church organs that had never been delivered. In unearthing the complexities of the scam, the fraud squad found nearly 3,000 fictitious hire-purchase agreements that required payments of over £50,000 a month to service them. The value of all transactions totalled £7 million.

The case was heard at Lewes Crown Court on 5th January 1977 and character references were provided by the Bishop of Woolwich. Miller, 56, and Bellord, 48, pleaded guilty on 17 counts of theft, conspiracy to defraud, forgery and obtaining pecuniary advantage by deception. They were each sentenced to six years in prison. Part of their defence was the claim that their catalogue of crimes had begun with paying a prostitute's escalating blackmail threats to a friend who was a church leader. The police kept their part of the bargain with Green and he was exonerated, despite his role in assisting the lawbreakers by helping them to abscond and being an accessory to their crimes. He considered himself extremely fortunate to have been spared prosecution and to have escaped jail.

Some of the Southern Organs sponsorship commitments were actually fulfilled. Formula Ford driver Wil Arif was one of the first aspiring drivers to have been summoned to Honeywood House and the first to be signed up on a two-year contract, lured by a weekly salary of £150 and the prospect of being taken into Formula 1. However, having been brought up by his parents to avoid anything to do with hire purchase, the street-wise and deeply suspicious youngster declined to sign a second document that accompanied the agreement and mentioned... electronic organs. After a graphologist was able to prove that left-handed Arif's signatures were forged, because they had been done by a right-handed person, he was lucky to avoid any financial loss. Geoff Friswell was less fortunate as one of many in the racing community who suffered heavily from the fiasco, having to sell his prized Mallock Clubmans sports car to repay debts incurred through his association.

Despite its high profile, grandiose plans and magnanimous promises, Southern Organs was only involved in motor racing for two seasons. But like their products, Sid Miller and John Bellord had certainly made a racket, in more ways than one.

CHAPTER 42
MAX MOSLEY
Head of the sport, in court

A central figure in Formula 1 for nearly 40 years, Max Mosley was an intellectually gifted man from a wealthy but controversial family background. As a racing driver, he rose as far as Formula 2 before establishing a major manufacturer of racing cars. As President of the FIA, the governing body of motorsport, he worked tirelessly to transform the sport and improve road safety. Despite all this, many remember him more for the details of his complicated and colourful private life exposed by a tabloid newspaper and the court battles that followed.

Max Mosley was the second son of Sir Oswald Mosley, leader of the British Union of Fascists during the 1930s, and society aristocrat Lady Diana Mitford, who was admired by both Winston Churchill and Adolf Hitler. They were prominent Nazi sympathisers and their secret marriage in Germany in 1936 took place at the home of Josef Goebbels with Hitler in attendance as guest of honour. During the war, the British government interned the couple from the spring of 1940, one month after Max was born, until the end of 1943.

Educated in Ireland, France and Germany before being sent to Millfield in England, Max read physics at Oxford and then went on to Grays Inn in London to qualify as a barrister. His ambitions to enter politics, for which he would have been well suited, were thwarted by his father's reputation and he was told that his name would be 'electoral poison'. A fascination with motor racing, which began with a trip to Silverstone while at university, grew into a passion that was to become his life.

He started by racing sports cars, competing mainly in club events. His family wealth enabled him to buy a Formula 2 car, a Brabham BT23C, in 1968 and he embarked on a European Championship campaign, starting at the Hockenheim race in which the great Jim Clark was killed. Despite poor results, he persevered into 1969, now with a Lotus 59, but crashed the car during practice for his first race with it, at the Nürburgring. Realising that he was never going to be quick enough to make it into Formula 1, he decided to hang up his helmet.

Very soon afterwards, he joined forces with fellow racer Alan Rees, accountant Graham Coaker and designer Robin Herd to create March Engineering as a new manufacturer of racing cars, its name formed from the initials of the co-founders' surnames. His training as a barrister proved very useful in dealing with the legal and commercial aspects of the fledgling company, where he became *de facto* team manager of works-entered Formula 1 and Formula 2 teams.

After selling his shares in the company at the end of 1977, Mosley used his experience and skills to navigate the politics of Formula 1 alongside Bernie Ecclestone, with whom he had formed a strong but unlikely bond. Together they made a formidable pairing who took on the Fédération Internationale du Sport Automobile (FISA), the sport's authoritarian governing body at that time, and in due course he became legal adviser to the Ecclestone-run Formula One Constructors' Association (FOCA) as it battled with FISA over the commercial interests of the sport.

After a break from the sport during which he unsuccessfully sought a way into British politics with the Conservative Party, Mosley became President of FISA's Manufacturers' Commission in 1986. Then, in the election for the overall FISA Presidency in 1991, he ousted his old adversary, Jean-Marie Balestre (see Chapter 7), by 43 votes to 29. He was responsible for amalgamating FISA into the Fédération Internationale de l'Automobile (FIA) and in 1993 succeeded Balestre as the organisation's President, a position that he kept until 2009 after being re-elected three times.

When he merged the FIA with the International Touring Association (ITA), he established an extremely powerful pressure group for car manufacturers. This gave them the strength to take on governments all over the world and went some way towards satisfying his political aspirations. He also had a major influence in the introduction of the European New Car Assessment Programme (Euro NCAP), the independent crash-test organisation whose work has significantly improved the performance of European cars in road accidents and has been described by the European Commission as the most cost-effective road-safety initiative for 20 years. His swift reaction to the fatal accidents that befell Roland Ratzenberger and Ayrton Senna at the San Marino Grand Prix in 1994 brought immediate and long-lasting benefits through the significant safety changes that he forced Formula 1 to adopt. His efforts to persuade Formula 1 to dramatically reduce operating costs, in part by standardising components and restricting electronic driver aids, established him as a visionary. Although he was named a Chevalier of the Legion d'Honneur in France in 2006 for his contribution to road safety and motorsport, his significant achievements were never officially recognised in Britain.

None of the measures he introduced to Formula 1 were universally popular and one that was particularly controversial was the deal negotiated in 2000 whereby the FIA leased Formula 1's commercial rights to Ecclestone for 100 years for $315 million. While this helped the already very rich Bernie to become even richer, the FIA used the proceeds to create a charitable foundation focused on promoting safety on the road and in motorsport worldwide. Mosley was also at the heart of another controversy when the McLaren team was accused of cheating (see Chapter 49). Although he always denied it, his dictatorial stance, which resulted in an unprecedented fine of $100 million, appeared to be a personal vendetta against team principal Ron Dennis and was inconsistent with the treatment of other teams that got away with similar transgressions almost unpunished.

The strongest public outrage surrounding Max Mosley occurred away from the track. On 30th March 2008, the *News of the World*, a British tabloid newspaper, published salacious revelations of his activities with a group of prostitutes in a London flat, filling its front page with the headline 'F1 Boss Has Sick Nazi Orgy With 5 Hookers'. Mosley described that as 'an outright and deliberate lie', as was the even more offensive fabrication that the group had been re-enacting a scene from a concentration camp. This was part of the newspaper's attempt to discredit the leader of a world-wide organisation, one that included members from a wide variety of ethnic backgrounds, by alluding to his parents' wartime connections and political affiliations in order to lend its story an element of credibility and public interest.

The newspaper denied inventing any elements of the depravity it reported and announced that it would be sending video evidence to the FIA's senate members and general assembly. This move was clearly designed to force Mosley's resignation as FIA President because the organisation states that 'words, deeds or writings that have caused moral injury or loss' breach

Max Mosley as team manager, seen with ear defenders around his neck
at the 1975 Austrian Grand Prix, tending Vittorio Brambilla's March on
the day the Italian driver scored an unexpected victory for the team.

its International Sporting Code and bring the possibility of expulsion. A
few days before an FIA summit meeting in Paris in early June, Ecclestone
said that Mosley should resign, a change of mind after earlier declarations
of support that was seen as an act of betrayal to his friend of 40 years'
standing. At the meeting, a stormy one, BMW and Mercedes lent their
support to Ecclestone's comments although neither company appeared to
reflect on their own respective wartime histories.

Despite the considerable pressure to step down, Mosley refused to do so.
His bedroom activities may have been unconventional but they involved
consenting adults and no crime had been committed.

He embarked on legal action against the *News of the World* on grounds
of 'breach of confidence', claiming that his activities had been inherently
private in nature and that their portrayal in the newspaper was an invasion
of his privacy. A crucial aspect of his case was the contention that there
had been a Nazi theme. In court it transpired that he had been the victim
of a set-up by the newspaper, which had paid one of the women and her

husband, who was employed by MI5, for video footage taken with a hidden camera and published frames from this. He was also able to prove that there had been no elements of the alleged Nazi theme. The judge, Sir David Eady, ruled decisively in his favour and awarded £60,000 in damages and £450,000 in costs. However, it was a pyrrhic victory, for the scandal had already caused irreparable damage to his reputation.

He continued to champion the right to privacy. In 2011 he persuaded Britain's Prime Minister, David Cameron, to establish the Leveson Inquiry into media practices and ethics. He even covered the costs of some of the claimants against the *News of the World* in a phone-hacking scandal that resulted in the newspaper's closure, which must have given him a degree of satisfaction.

Mosley was a classic case of poacher turned gamekeeper and unsurprisingly there was no shortage of people in the Formula 1 paddock, including many of the sport's leading figures, who delighted in the tabloid's revelations and Mosley's discomfort. His authoritarian and often ruthless style over the years ensured that he had enemies and there would have been several of them who might have sought revenge. After the court's judgment, there was still the question of who had initiated the set-up. Whatever the truth, Mosley, who took his life in May 2021 knowing that terminal cancer was about to kill him anyway, had been lured into a trap. As he wrote in his autobiography, 'The conventional wisdom in Formula One has always been that someone [in F1] was behind it.' There are several suspects.

JAMES MUNROE

The not-so-gentlemanly 'gentleman racer'

A serial conman and deluded 'Walter Mitty' fantasist,
James Munroe — born James Cox —appeared to typify
dull, unremarkable respectability but led a very public and
extravagant double life. During the week he was the bespectacled
manager of an accounts department but at weekends he became
an attention-seeking, self-styled 'millionaire businessman'
and 'gentleman racer' of a McLaren F1 GTR. Through his
extraordinary duplicity, the ultimate vanity project was
unwittingly financed by funds embezzled from his employer.

L ike so many schoolboys, James Cox was passionate to the point of obsession about cars as a teenager and dreamt of racing them as soon as he was old enough. Typically for his age, his bedroom walls at home were adorned with large posters of the contemporary Lamborghini Countach and Ferrari Testa Rossa models. Inevitably, like most youngsters with similar aspirations, there was neither the money nor the opportunity to fulfil his ambitions. By the time he had reached his 20s, the nearest he had come to owning any kind of 'performance car' was very much more modest.

'I hocked myself to the hilt just to, albeit briefly, own a MkII Golf GTi 16v,' he said, 'sadly ending its days stolen, ransacked and unlovingly abandoned on bricks on Wentworth golf course. The debts mounted and the bailiffs circled so that I could have that car on the driveway. Then the usual banal examples of company cars came and went; the A-Z of small executive saloons. I dreamt of that day when I could put something special in my garage. But it never materialised. Each day, it seemed ever more remote.'

The reality of his life was such that by the time he was in his early

30s he was married with a young family living in suburban Wokingham, Berkshire, and working in middle management in an accounts department. As disenchantment grew with what he felt was a meaningless existence, it simply fuelled his dreams more strongly. He started to make frequent trips to the nearby showrooms of Maranello Concessionaires, the famous Ferrari importer and main dealer. Although his job prospects and personal life didn't change materially over the next couple of years, he ended up being able to acquire a Ferrari 348tb in the classic and desirable colour combination of Rosso Corsa with cream hide interior.

By 1997, aged 33 and intoxicated by the 348tb's performance, he wanted more. Now going by the name James Munroe, he fooled himself that he was ready to live the second part of his childhood dream: he was going to become a racing driver. He chose the Goodyear-supported Ferrari Challenge, a club-level British championship that catered for drivers competing in a wide variety of Ferrari models divided into two categories, one for older and often standard road models, the other for much quicker 'modified' cars.

He bought a Ferrari F355 Challenge, which was a special race-bred version of the F355, the 348tb's successor. However, the woefully inexperienced driver's performance was underwhelming to say the least and he found himself consistently and hopelessly outclassed, trailing behind not only all the modified cars in his class but also most of the slower standard cars. His fellow competitors found him a very ordinary, quiet and unassuming man who made no attempt to mix with them.

Yet he was a man of contradictions whose ego seemed to grow each time he made one of his sporadic appearances on the starting grid. He so wanted attention and approval that his singular lack of success proved hard for him to bear. Indeed, the only recognition he ever seemed to receive over the course of two seasons with the F355 came at Croft, North Yorkshire, when the race commentator lavished inordinate attention on his car just because its red-and-white harlequin livery looked similar to nearby Sunderland football club's team strip.

Undeterred by his embarrassing lack of results and craving the limelight more than ever before, he resolved to step up into the much higher-profile British GT Championship for the 1999 season. His ambitions knew no boundaries and he acquired from the Parabolica Motorsport team a McLaren F1 GTR, a spectacular racing car that had won the Le Mans 24 Hours in 1995. Introduced in 1993 at a price of more than £500,000, the McLaren F1 in road-going guise had a top speed of 230mph and was capable of 0–60mph in three seconds. Powered by a 6.1-litre BMW V12 engine, it

Accountant and fantasist James Munroe (left) raced this McLaren F1 GTR in 1999 on funds embezzled from his employer; he so enjoyed the limelight that he hired supermodel Caprice to join him for a media launch at a Soho restaurant along with Calum Lockie, his original choice of co-driver.

had a central driving position and dramatic lift-up 'scissor' doors. For more than a decade it was hailed as the world's fastest production road car and immediately became a modern classic with its ground-breaking design. As only 106 examples were ever built, its rarity combined with its eye-watering cost ensured that ownership was confined to a very exclusive club. The elite who recognised it as the ultimate supercar of the time included celebrities such as Elton John, George Harrison and Rowan Atkinson. Very few owned more than one of these incredible machines apart from Ralph Lauren, who had two, the Sultan of Brunei, who had no fewer than five... and James Munroe. He not only acquired an example of the even rarer GTR racing version, of which 28 were made, but also became the proud — and very dishonest — owner of a road-going model as well.

The aspiring racing driver's new venture was announced with great fanfare at a lavish press launch held at the exclusive Mezzo restaurant in London's Soho on 15th January 1999. Glamour was added by the presence of Caprice, the world-famous supermodel who, in return for a hefty appearance fee, was hired to unveil the car, which was finished in McLaren's famous Papaya Orange. She posed next to the car dressed in white racing overalls, together with Munroe and Calum Lockie, the team's professional driver, who was to share driving duties and had been introduced to Munroe by driver coach Les Goble. As the champagne flowed at the Veuve Clicquot-supported event, the slightly chubby accounts manager from Wokingham revelled in all the attention he received from the numerous photographers and journalists, but in reality he looked almost as out of place in those surroundings as he did on a race circuit.

To prepare and run the McLaren, Munroe had engaged the well-respected team AM Racing, owned and managed by Aston Martin dealer Paul Spires, an accomplished racing driver himself who was also scheduled to race the car. Although AM Racing's previous experience had been mainly in the preparation and running of historic Le Mans cars, Spires had put together a very strong group of engineers and the operation proved to be well up to the required standard. Munroe announced to the media: 'We have no pretensions to winning races. We could have put a high-profile professional in the car but we wanted to keep it as a purely privateer team. We will rotate the driving between the three of us and see how it works out. Most importantly, we want to show that we are doing this properly.'

The British GT Championship, which featured cars from the GT1 and GT2 categories, was in its seventh season and in 1999 was sponsored by Privilege Insurance. This was destined to be the final season in which GT1 cars — including the McLaren F1 GTR — could compete, so the series provided a last opportunity for British fans to see top-line grids of these spectacular machines. The season comprised 11 races, one of which was a continental excursion to the daunting Spa-Francorchamps in Belgium. One of the attractions of the championship for entrants was that cars were shared between two drivers and the regulations pandered to the egos of wealthy amateurs by allowing so called 'gentleman' drivers to pair with quicker professionals. Despite this, most of the amateurs at this level were capable drivers, as they needed to be to handle such powerful race-bred machinery. This was not the right arena for someone with as little talent and experience as James Munroe.

Taking advantage of clement winter weather in Spain, AM Racing conducted initial pre-season testing at the Albacete circuit with Calum Lockie. Less than a month after the well-publicised press launch, the McLaren was in action again at Silverstone for more testing on the national circuit. The car was devoid of any signs of external sponsorship except for a strip across the top of the windscreen sporting allegiance to Veuve Clicquot, presumably in deference to the copious quantities that had been quaffed at the launch party. Behind the wheel at Silverstone, however, was not Lockie but Chris Goodwin, who coincidentally had raced the very same chassis for its previous owners in the 1997 FIA GT Championship and had been drafted in for this session. Within a couple of weeks Goodwin was formally signed up as lead driver, replacing Lockie for reasons that were never made clear. Lockie's contract was annulled and paid off in full by the team patron, after which he took up offers of drives in both a Marcos and Porsche in the GT2 class later in the season.

When Goodwin flew in from America, where he had been racing at Sebring, and topped the official pre-season testing sessions at Silverstone, spirits were high and Spires said: 'It couldn't have gone better. We now have a true pro-am [professional-amateur] line-up but I think we can win races.' As Goodwin's international career was in the ascendency, this wasn't a drive he needed or even particularly wanted, but he accepted it on the basis that it would do him no harm, keep him race-sharp and reward him with, in his words, 'a crazy amount of money'.

Come the first round of the championship, at Silverstone on 28th March, the pre-season optimism continued when the team's lead driver put the McLaren on pole position with a lap over eight seconds quicker than the car's custodian could manage. Goodwin leapt in front at the start of the race and led convincingly, building a six-second margin over his nearest rival and setting the fastest lap. Leaving the obligatory driver change until the last moment permissible under the regulations, he then had to watch in frustration as his hard work was undone and Munroe slipped down the field to an eventual fifth place.

For the second round, at picturesque Oulton Park in Cheshire on 3rd May, there was special dispensation for Goodwin to drive solo because the 'self-made multi-millionaire', as Munroe had started to describe himself, was reported by *Autosport* magazine to be 'away on business'. Goodwin again put the car on pole position and recorded the fastest lap of the race on his way to third place, complete with the obligatory pitstop.

Munroe was back in the cockpit for the next race, at Snetterton on 31st May. After an enthralling battle in qualifying, Goodwin just missed out on pole position, beaten by Tim Sugden's EMKA-run McLaren. This time Munroe took the start, with the team's strategy resting on the hope that he would hold up most of the field before handing over to Goodwin after a short but steady stint. That was how it turned out, the pair finishing second just over half a minute behind the winning Lister Storm, with Goodwin diplomatically praising Munroe's flash of promise. This result would be the best of the team's campaign.

For the next round, at Brands Hatch on 20th June, Munroe again took the start for a short stint before handing over to his 'pro' co-driver with the car two laps down. Goodwin managed to reduce the deficit by one lap and bring the car home fourth, his efforts once again rewarded with fastest lap.

In the meantime, Munroe's off-track exploits had started to attract attention. People in the British GT paddock were intrigued about where this previously unknown driver had come from, especially one who not only owned a McLaren for road use but could also afford to own and race another one. By now, Munroe also possessed other high-performance sportscars, all with personalised registration numbers, and turned up at race meetings in a variety of them. He cultivated a growing reputation for big spending and his 'generosity' extended to providing top-of-the-range Ducati motorcycles for his pit crew and mechanics as well as buying a Mercedes C180 for his co-driver.

Immediately after the Brands Hatch race, Munroe funded an extravagant trip to the third round of the American Le Mans Series (ALMS) at Mosport in Canada for Goodwin and several AM Racing personnel. This was supposedly a fact-finding mission to investigate the possibility of running the McLaren in the last three rounds of the ALMS season. Afterwards, Spires enthused to the media about the prospect and added that the team was also considering buying an open-top sports racer for the following ALMS season alongside another British GT campaign. The cost of the round trip, which included flights on Concorde and hotel bills at the Marriott in Toronto, were said to have been over £50,000.

To feed his apparently insatiable appetite for fame and attention, Munroe had hired a public relations specialist, Panic Publicity, at the start of the season, and this company probably organised the original Soho launch. Panic Publicity certainly did an extremely good job, one that in retrospect could be deemed to have been too effective. At the first round, for example, superstar singer Paul Young was present in the team's hospitality unit and everyone assumed he was there because he was a friend of Munroe's, although he was actually just another hired hand who was being paid for his appearance in order to feed the illusion the team benefactor was creating around himself.

Over the next few months, Munroe was highlighted in several magazine articles, including an interview in *Boys Toys*, a so-called 'lad's magazine' whose erroneous headline proclaimed: 'James Munroe: he's filthy rich and owns a racing team'. In the story, Munroe was quoted as saying: 'I've been into fast cars and racing since I was a teenager, but it's a difficult game to get into. I've never had the chance until now. Yes, this is a dream come true, definitely.' Panic Publicity continued to prove its worth by ensuring that its client made a series of television appearances, the most notable of which was on BBC2's *The Car's The Star* in an episode featuring the McLaren F1. After trying unsuccessfully to entice various high-profile owners to take part, the programme's producers had to look elsewhere. In his quest for fame, Munroe needed no persuasion and gleefully accepted the invitation to participate. During his short appearance, he ill-advisedly boasted to presenter Quentin Willson that he had once driven his McLaren F1 at 170mph on the M40 motorway.

The next outing for the AM Racing McLaren F1 GTR was back at Silverstone, this time for the biggest British GT Championship event of the season, as one of the support races for the British Grand Prix on 11th July. In front of a huge crowd, Goodwin sprinted into the lead from the front row of the grid as the pack flooded down into Copse Corner on the first lap. He stayed in front for five laps until encountering a backmarker, a Marcos Mantis, that crossed his path just as he was about to lap it, forcing him to spin in avoidance. He made up the lost time before handing over to Munroe, who brought the car home a disappointing sixth, nearly two laps down on the winner. Goodwin admitted that by now, despite being handsomely paid, he was finding it difficult to maintain his motivation when co-driving with someone who was completely out of his depth.

Goodwin never saw Munroe again. Indeed, his abiding memory of the team patron was watching him leave the Silverstone paddock as pillion passenger on the back of a motorcycle and disappear into the sunset.

Alarm bells started ringing at AM Racing just a few days after the British Grand Prix when team manager Paul Spires called Chris Goodwin to say that there was 'a problem with the money'. Spires didn't know it at the time but Munroe's assets had been frozen by lawyers. By the time of the next round of the British GT Championship, at Donington Park on 7th August, the AM Racing McLaren F1 GTR had vanished from the entry list. The following month, news broke that James Munroe was under investigation.

In 'real life', away from the race circuits, Munroe — real name James Cox — was still a very ordinary accountant, albeit with a little more seniority than in earlier years. McGraw Hill, a highly respected American company that had become one of the world's biggest educational publishers, employed him as head of its accounts department in its European offices in Maidenhead, Berkshire. In 1995, soon after joining the company, he had established ghost companies — Execom Management Services Ltd, Thinexcel Management Services Ltd and Business Visions Ltd — and registered them at his home address of Almond Close, Wokingham, with he and his wife listed as directors. He used these companies to submit bogus invoices to his employer and was perfectly placed to ensure that payments were authorised and made to the respective bank accounts, of which he was the sole beneficiary.

Questions had already been raised about the honesty of this ostensibly very ordinary man who took excessive amounts of sick leave so that he could devote time to his extracurricular activities. His long and creative list of excuses included the claim that he suffered from chronic kidney problems. Even worse, on one occasion he cruelly lied that his young son Adrian was seriously ill and receiving treatment at Great Ormond Street Hospital. This prompted sympathetic colleagues to arrange for flowers to be delivered to the hospital only for their kindness to be repaid with the discovery that no child of that name was at the hospital.

Serious suspicions escalated when a senior McGraw Hill executive watched television coverage of a British GT Championship race on Channel 4. He was astonished to spot one of the company's employees being interviewed about racing what the commentator had described as 'a million-dollar car' in a sport that he correctly assumed was beyond the means of an accountant on an annual salary of £51,000. After internal investigations soon revealed two unauthorised payments, a more extensive audit was instigated with Ernst & Young, the accountancy firm, and this uncovered 15 more illegal transactions made by Munroe, ranging from £46,400 to £549,300.

It was while Munroe was away on a two-week family holiday in Spain that his life of subterfuge began to unravel. In subsequent interviews with Thames Valley Police, he admitted all the charges of fraud, saying that he did it because he was 'disillusioned with his job' and wanted to 'step up'. He said that he fully recognised that his job had put him in a position where it was easy to take advantage. Initially, he said, he had simply intended to use the stolen money to fund a lavish personal lifestyle, which included buying an expensive Rolex watch, before his greed escalated and he progressed to buying expensive sportscars. With it all seeming so easy, the regularity with which he sent phoney invoices to his employers spiralled out of control.

When Munroe appeared at Reading Crown Court in September 2000, the prosecution stated that he had used the stolen money to buy lots of cars as well as to fund the racing team. Besides the cars already mentioned — the two Ferraris and the two McLarens — his fleet of road cars included three Aston Martins, three Mercedes and a Ferrari 550 Maranello. He had also acquired two important historic racing cars, an ex-Gerhard Berger Benetton Formula 1 car and a Silk Cut-liveried Jaguar XJR Le Mans car. He certainly had good automotive taste.

'The whole of this enterprise was funded by unauthorised payments by McGraw Hill,' said Sally Howells for the prosecution. 'As the director of accounting he was responsible for the management of the payment system and had detailed knowledge of the payment process.' Munroe was jailed for five years after he admitted 17 charges of transfer by deception and three of procuring the execution of a valuable security. During a four-year period he stole £2,885,722, of which it was calculated that no more than £830,000 would be recoverable for his employer. In defence of his 36-year-old client, Peter Warne told the court: 'Munroe describes himself, or his creation, as "a monster which he could not stop". He appears to have gained an immense adrenalin rush from what was, in effect, a double life. He became wracked with guilt, wretched.' Judge Josh Lait was not sympathetic and said when summing up: 'This was a serious and continued breach of trust carried out over a substantial period, executed by false documentation.'

The fall from grace of the car-mad fantasist should have ended there. But it didn't.

Even after his early release from prison in 2003, Munroe evidently still felt that the world owed him a living and that crime paid. Within nine months, he had been recruited by Automotive Skills, a charity funded by the Department of Transport to promote training skills in the retail motor industry. He falsified his CV and provided his own references because communications to the email addresses and phone numbers he supplied for two named referees were in fact directed to him. In his senior post as financial manager with a salary of £63,000, he was given free rein over where funds were distributed and forged dozens of cheques to pay for the rental of a £5,000-a-month house, buy a £70,000 Porsche, lease a BMW, a Saab and a Mercedes, and purchase Chelsea football club season tickets costing £12,000. His fraudulent activities over a two-year period were only uncovered after staff stumbled upon a website detailing his earlier crimes. He was suspended the next day and then sacked when he failed to show up for a disciplinary hearing.

After his arrest, he claimed that the executive cars were for use by company directors and that the season tickets were a legitimate business expense for entertaining clients. Although he estimated that he had 'only' forged cheques worth £100,000, Middlesex Guildhall Crown Court heard that in total he had stolen nearly £500,000. Now aged 42, he was convicted on one charge of obtaining pecuniary advantage by deception, three charges of obtaining services by deception and two of theft, but there were 16 other charges that he denied and weren't dealt with. His defence lawyer, Ronald Jaffa, said: 'He owed some money and decided to pay off his credit card. Once it started, he went on to commit these offences. In handing down a four-year prison sentence, Judge Roger Chapple told him, 'Your naked greed is breathtaking.'

Unfortunately, for the victims whose livelihoods were affected by his deceit, the story still didn't end there. Remarkably, he found responsible employment yet again, in March 2015, by which time he was 51 and once again using his real name, James Cox.

This time he managed to con his way into becoming the £65,000-a-year finance director of Britain's Energy Coast (BEC), an organisation set up to assist economic development in Cumbria. In his first month, Cox defrauded his employer out of more than £40,000 that he used to buy a Jaguar XK, which he then part-exchanged for a BMW, and later two Mercedes. When an audit highlighted concerns about him, he left the firm after only five months in the job. After his departure, chief executive Michael Pemberton called in the police. Cox was tracked down and found to be living in a Premier Inn hotel in Weston-super-Mare, Somerset, at the time of his arrest.

In the court hearing that followed, magistrates in Carlisle heard how Cox had been responsible for negotiating a £100,000 loan to a local company. Part of the arrangement had included an option of access to a further £40,000 if required. The Prosecutor, Pamela Fee, told the court that when BEC checked its accounts, it discovered that the full £140,000 had been withdrawn rather than the initial £100,000 that had been agreed, and that on inspection the signature used to authorise the additional amount — £40,490 to be precise — had been forged. Fee said that this sum had been transferred to a Jaguar dealership and that the paperwork was in the name of James Cox.

On 21st April 2016, Cox appeared in front of magistrates and admitted that he had forged a loan agreement and used company funds to buy a Jaguar. Other offences included committing fraud to get the job, obtaining money through fraud and four counts of transferring criminal property.

He was remanded in custody until his sentencing and one month later was jailed for a third time, on this occasion for six years. At Carlisle Crown Court, Recorder Mark Ainsworth described Cox's action as a 'planned and determined deception'. He said: 'Any funds that are siphoned off [from BEC] dishonestly means a reduction of funds that are available for the community and for the regeneration of this area.' This was reiterated by Detective Inspector Dan St Quintin, of Cumbria police, who said: 'James Cox has stolen over £40,000 from a fund set up to help communities in Cumbria that need it most, he has put jobs and community projects at risk. He has used this money to fund a lifestyle he could not afford.' In a rather charitable defence, Paul Tweddle told the court that his client was an 'educated' single man with a degree in accounting and finance from Bristol University, but that is open to question as the university has no record of him. Tweddle continued: 'He has no assets whatsoever. He has no accommodation and as of his release from custody will be of no fixed abode.'

Following his sentencing, Cox was ordered to hand over to BEC all property found in his possession, which included a Mercedes C180, three mobile phones, a laptop and a wireless mouse, and also a pair of silver Aspinal cuff links that he had been given by colleagues upon his departure from the company. These various items were to be sold in an attempt to claw back part of the loss but it was estimated that they were only likely to raise about £15,000.

Cox was back in the news again as recently as December 2018 when, now aged 54, he absconded from an open prison in Norwich, having been allowed out for a pre-arranged medical appointment that he failed to attend. Members of the public were told to be vigilant and warned not to approach him, and anyone sighting him or knowing of his whereabouts was asked to call the police immediately. Having done a full circle, he had returned to his roots and was found a week later 170 miles away in the Reading area, from where he was returned to jail.

We may never fully understand the true reasons why a middle manager living in a mock-Tudor house in Wokingham turned to a life of crime and massive fraud. His own attempt to justify his actions was that he resented his life and felt that he 'deserved' so much more than he had achieved through any efforts of his own. Clearly a troubled individual, his curious mixture of insecurities, ego and stupidity had combined to form a dangerous cocktail. Added to this was his brazen arrogance in publicly bragging to anyone who asked about the source of his wealth at the time he was racing the McLaren

F1 GTR. He claimed that he had started a multi-media company and sold it for £50 million to McGraw Hill, who, he would explain, required him to carry on working there for several years.

As anyone involved in a sport such as motor racing knows, adrenalin is a very powerful hormone that can produce extreme emotions and excitement. In the case of James Cox (aka James Munroe), his craving for attention suggested that he received his highs not so much from racing one of the fastest and most desirable sportscars ever made but more from the publicity and kudos that went with it. His behaviour guaranteed that he would draw attention to himself to such an extent that it was almost as if he wanted to get caught.

For all his many failings, which included a lack of talent behind the wheel of a racing car, what is undeniable is that this figure of intrigue and amusement amongst the paddock crowd was not only passionate about fast cars but also had great taste in them.

CHAPTER 44

DON NICHOLS

Under the Shadow of espionage

Imitation may be viewed as the greatest form of flattery but in the intensely competitive world of Formula 1, where secrets are closely guarded, it is extremely unwelcome. However, in an incestuous sport where morality has never been a high priority, technical skulduggery, plagiarism, copying and improving on ideas from other teams is endemic, part of the DNA and as old as the sport itself. Industrial espionage, though, is a very grey area of ambiguity and controversy that is notoriously difficult to prove when it comes to ideas and concepts.

The most blatant example of copyright infringement in Formula 1 involved the fledgling Arrows team when it burst onto the scene in 1978. Arrows was an acronym made up of the surname initials of the key founders, all of them emigrés from Don Nichols's Shadow team. 'A' stood for financial backer Franco Ambrosio, 'R' for Alan Rees, 'O' for team principal Jackie Oliver, 'W' for engineer Dave Wass and 'S' for designer Tony Southgate. Riccardo Patrese also transferred from Shadow to become one of the team's drivers.

Out of fiscal necessity, the new Arrows team was desperate to be admitted into the Formula One Constructors' Association (FOCA) for its 1978 campaign because this offered huge financial advantages, including subsidised travel, but FOCA's stipulations dictated that to receive the benefits of membership Arrows would only be allowed to miss one non-European race. That meant the team's new car had to be on the grid for the second round of the 1978 World Championship, the Brazilian Grand Prix on 29th January. The first Arrows was built from scratch in the remarkably short timeframe of five weeks and shipped to Brazil straight after a press launch one snowy day at Silverstone.

Partly due to the lack of time, Southgate relied heavily on his recent experience and knowledge by applying many of the same concepts and theories that he had followed when conceiving the Shadow DN9. He had designed much of the DN9 in his home studio and as a self-employed freelance designer it was very easy for him to start working on the new Arrows the day after he left Shadow. This couldn't happen nowadays because teams go to great lengths to protect themselves from the transfer of information or inside knowledge by imposing legally binding 'gardening leave' clauses in their contracts during which time a departing employee isn't permitted to have any contact with a new employer.

When the Arrows FA1 was revealed, it looked very similar to the Shadow DN9, although there were more than 100 features that differentiated the two cars. Southgate explained the similarity in his book *From Drawing Board to Chequered Flag*: 'An area that did present me with difficulties was the suspension and in particular the uprights and assemblies. The lead time of design and manufacture was too long to make the South American date, so something had to be done to circumnavigate the problem. I spoke to a solicitor friend of mine back in Bourne [where Southgate had previously worked when at BRM] and queried the copyright law when applied to race cars. He told me that if the components were to the same design and I had designed them both and they were not going to be offered for sale for profit, then there was no problem in using them. He also gave his opinion that, as a freelance designer of the Shadow cars, the copyright stood with me. This was all going to prove totally incorrect in court.'

Don Nichols was an enigmatic character of whom journalist Pete Lyons said: 'He knew everyone but few people knew him.' He often wore a rather theatrical, large black hat to echo his Shadow team's emblem of a cloaked man with a broad hat hiding his face. He had chosen this spy motif for good reason as he had been a spy with America's Central Intelligence Agency in Japan in the aftermath of the Second World War, using Tokyo as a base for activities in Korea and Vietnam. However, it didn't require any of his skills in espionage to convince him that the new Arrows car was almost identical in design to his Shadow and he instigated legal proceedings.

His action began with his legal team obtaining the type of search warrant used in the fashion business to combat the copying of ideas. When one of the lawyers arrived at the Arrows factory in Milton Keynes, he issued legal

When launched at a snowy Silverstone in January 1978, the Arrows FA1
bore an uncanny resemblance to the Shadow DN9. Don Nichols,
Shadow's owner, took the matter to court and won.

documents to Tony Southgate and proceeded to search for anything that
related to Shadow. Needless to say, he was delighted to discover engineering
drawings in Southgate's possession showing the DN9's upright assemblies
and components.

A summons to court was soon issued. The result of the bitter feud was
that, at the High Court on 31 July 1978, Justice Templeman duly found
the Arrows FA1 to be in breach of copyright. He ruled that 40 percent
of the car's components had been copied from the Shadow DN9, so the
Arrows car was banned with immediate effect and the team ordered to
hand over an array of parts to Nichols and the Shadow team. As Arrows
had correctly anticipated that the court was likely rule against it, the team
had already built a replacement design, this time in less than 60 days, but
was still required to pay damages of £15,000 together with legal expenses
of more than twice that amount.

The court case wasn't the only setback to blight the fledgling team's
inaugural season. Even before the first race, Franco Ambrosio (see
Chapter 4) had run into trouble with the Italian authorities over financial

irregularities, leaving Arrows having to seek new sponsorship in a hurry. The team's original choice of second driver, Gunnar Nilsson, was diagnosed with cancer in December 1977, shortly after signing for Arrows, and the rapid decline in his health meant that he was never able to take up his seat prior to his death ten months later. Helpfully, Rolf Stommelen's recruitment in Nilsson's place also solved the sponsorship dilemma because he brought backing from the German Warsteiner brewery. Much later in the season, Patrese became the target of a witchhunt after being falsely accused of causing Ronnie Peterson's fatal accident at the start of the Italian Grand Prix at Monza, which led to his exclusion from the next race. Finally, the team found itself denied all-important FOCA membership for 1979, leaving it with an additional and unbudgeted £35,000 added to its travelling costs.

Copying the ideas of others has long been part of the cut-and-thrust of Formula 1, just as it is in many fields of endeavour. As far back as 1963, the British Racing Partnership (BRP) introduced a car that was so heavily modelled on the previous year's successful Lotus 25 that Colin Chapman took legal action for copyright infringement, although the case was settled out of court. In 1976, the Penske PC3 outwardly looked almost identical to the team's customer March 751 that had preceded it. In 1979, most of the grid attempted to copy the previous season's all-conquering Lotus 79, the car that ushered in the aerodynamic concept of ground effect.

Back in that era, teams didn't guard their secrets quite as obsessively as they do now, and indeed one rival designer was discovered in the Lotus pit garage during 1978 with a notebook and a tape measure. When the 1979 season began, Ligier was first out of the blocks with its facsimile of the Lotus 79, the JS11, winning the first two races of the season, although the French team's designers soon lost their way by unwittingly altering the all-important under-surface venturi in a way that made them less effective. Conversely, Tyrrell's unscientific copycat design, the 009 model, didn't work at all, despite being designed by an ex-Lotus employee and bearing an extremely close resemblance to the type 79. Héctor Rebaque's private team, having bought and raced a Lotus 78 the previous year, built its own version of the type 79 simply by using the same chassis jigs that it found had been retained by the original sub-contracted fabricator. Rather than take action against this blatant plagiarism, Chapman was so full of misplaced confidence that his follow-up design, the Lotus 80, would render the copies obsolete that he just ignored it all.

RICHARD TOMLINSON
What goes around, comes around

Another member of the Formula 1 community who had been a spy was New Zealander Richard Tomlinson, who worked for six months in the marketing department of the fledgling Stewart Grand Prix team, owned by three-time World Champion Jackie Stewart and his eldest son Paul. Prior to this, he had spent four years working for Britain's Secret Intelligence Service (MI6) until his sudden dismissal in 1995. Embittered by the experience, he embarked on a book detailing his treatment by MI6 and his experiences as a secret agent even though the conditions of Britain's Official Secrets Act prevented him from doing this. After his arrest in 1997, he pleaded guilty and was convicted and imprisoned for 12 months, becoming the first former MI6 officer to be jailed for breaking the Official Secrets Act since George Blake, the KGB traitor, 36 years earlier.

Of all the rivals that adopted ground effect, it was Patrick Head of Williams who best got to grips with the science of the concept, to the extent that eventually he gained a better and more educated understanding of how and why it worked than Lotus's design team ever did. The Williams FW07, which was introduced at the fifth Grand Prix of 1979, in Spain, and became the team's first-ever winning car, was not a direct copy of the Lotus 79 but rather a much better designed and engineered alternative. The FW07B version took Alan Jones to the World Championship title the following year and set the team on the path to long-term success.

Since then, we have had 'Spygate' (see Chapter 49), one of the most publicised episodes of copyright infringement in Formula 1. More recently, the 2020 version of the Racing Point car, the RP20, was dubbed the 'Pink Mercedes' in reference not only to its livery but also to its marked similarity to the previous year's championship-winning Mercedes W10. Essentially, Racing Point had studied enormous numbers of photographs of the Mercedes and, following generally accepted practice, 'reverse engineered' its own interpretation of the Mercedes concept. A furore erupted as several rivals, led by Renault, lodged protests with the governing body suggesting collusion between the two teams, which would have contravened the prevailing rules that required entrants to design and manufacture everything other than the engine, transmission and some suspension parts. Attention focused on the front brake ducts, which were listed as components that couldn't be created by another team. While accusations of sharing or trading data were vehemently denied by both parties, Racing Point was fined $400,000 per car and docked championship points, although the team, somewhat illogically, was allowed to retain the offending items for the rest of the season.

Speaking in the wake of the protest in 2020, Formula 1 technical supremo Ross Brawn told the official F1 website: 'Copying in Formula 1 is standard. Every team has, in normal times, digital photographers in the pitlane out there taking thousands of photos of every car for analysis, with a view of copying the best ideas. We used to give our photographers a shopping list. Racing Point have just taken it to the next stage and done a more thorough job. There is not a single team in this paddock which has not copied something from another. I'd ask every technical director in the paddock to raise their hand if they haven't copied someone else. You won't see any hands. I have certainly copied others. Last year, Racing Point had access to, and could use, 2019-spec Mercedes brake ducts because they were not a listed part. This year, brake ducts are listed parts, so you have to design your own. However, Racing Point cannot forget the knowledge they acquired using the 2019 Mercedes brake ducts. I think it is illogical to think they can wipe their memory banks. It is a tricky problem and one for the FIA experts to resolve.'

Brawn, who won titles when working for Benetton and Ferrari before going on to yet more success with his own eponymous team and the mighty Mercedes operation that evolved from it, had a reputation himself for 'pushing the envelope'. Referring to regulations on fuel capacity, Bernie Ecclestone once suggested that Brawn's Jaguar XJR-14, which won the 1991 World Sports-Prototype Championship, had 'more tanks than the Germans in the Battle of the Bulge'.

JOHN PAUL
SR & JR
Speed and weed

John Paul Sr was a very unpleasant, volatile and abusive bully. He professed to hate both guns and Porsches because of what he had seen the Nazis do in his homeland as a child, so it was ironic that his life should become inextricably linked with both. A competent racing driver, he launched his supremely gifted son, John Paul Jr, onto the world stage of motor racing but also involved the unconditionally loyal but browbeaten youngster, who revered his father, in the shady world of high-level drug smuggling that funded their track success.

The son of a radiologist, Hans-Johan Paul was a year old when Germany invaded the Netherlands in 1940. From a very early age during the Nazi occupation, the child found himself having to hustle for enough food to stay alive by collecting discarded cigarette butts and trading them on the black market. His family emigrated to the United States in 1956 and settled in Muncie, Indiana, where he soon changed his name to John Lee Paul. Having attended Ball State University, he won a scholarship to Harvard where he washed dishes for 60 cents an hour to make ends meet on his way to achieving a master's degree in business. When aged only 20, in 1959, he married 16-year-old Joyce, a girl from Muncie, and a year later they had a son whom they also named John.

After graduating, Paul Sr joined Putnam Management in Boston and became a successful mutual fund manager by putting his ability in mathematics to good use. His contribution helped the funds grow in value from $600 million to $4 billion and his continued success as a Wall Street investor meant that he was a millionaire by the age of 30. His earnings as a fund manager enabled him to go motor racing and he first competed in a Dodge Challenger bought from Sam Posey and then an AC Cobra that he used to win races at Lime Rock and Bridgehampton as well as a minor SCCA regional championship in 1968. Over the next three seasons, occasional outings followed in a Chevrolet Corvette, including a run to ninth place in the 1969 Watkins Glen Six Hours, a round of the World Sports Car Championship.

Paul Sr's world imploded around him in 1971: Wall Street went into a slump that ruined the mutual fund market; Joyce left him, taking John Jr and two younger siblings with her back to Muncie; and he developed an ulcer. He sold all his possessions and bought a 37-foot sailing boat. A skilled yachtsman, he made two solo crossings of the Atlantic and spent time in the Caribbean, where he made some money dealing in real estate. By the time he returned to the US two years later, his son had reached the age at which he needed paternal influence and decided that life would be more comfortable and exciting if he lived with his father. John Jr was to be proved right on both counts but the insecure boy ended up with rather more than he bargained for because his father proved to be a far-from-ideal role model.

By his own admission, John Jr was not an academically minded child and, unlike his father, no good at mathematics. But for his father's wealth, he later said, he would have ended up working in a 'gas station or an auto parts store or as a tyre fitter'. After Paul Sr started to race once more in 1977, John Jr began working for his JLP Racing team as a 'gofer' following graduation from Delta High School in Muncie. The gangly adolescent, tall and thin with long dark hair, diligently carried out any chore, however menial, without complaint. Quiet, well-mannered and humble, he would jump, like the rest of the JLP crew, the moment his father barked an instruction, as happened frequently. At first John Jr learned about mechanical work and team management, but after an incident when the car he was working on fell off its jacks, damaging the suspension, he was told by crew chief Stan Loftin that he was no use as a mechanic and had better become a driver instead.

Paul Sr duly enrolled his son at the Skip Barber Racing School where the principal, endorsed by his father, told him he was a hopeless driver because he couldn't master the heel-and-toe technique. Despite this, Paul Sr bought him an old Formula Ford to race. In 1979, having learned his way around the circuits, he achieved enough success to encourage him to try some outings in quicker and more powerful Formula Super Vee and Formula Atlantic single-seaters.

As for Paul Sr's motorsport, he returned to action in IMSA sportscar racing with a Porsche 911 Carrera RSR at the 1977 Daytona 24 Hours before going on to contest most of that season. Into 1978, he ran the same car at Daytona and Sebring, finishing fourth in both events and winning his GTO class at the latter. Then he transferred to a Corvette and ended the year a creditable sixth in the GTO points standings. That same year also saw him compete at Le Mans for the first time with Dick Barbour Racing, partnering the team owner and Brian Redman in a Porsche 935 that they brought home to fifth place and first in the IMSA GTX class. For 1979, Paul Sr bought his own 935 for more IMSA racing but also turned to the SCCA's Trans-Am championship, winning six races *en route* to the title.

By this time JLP Racing was operating from workshops in Lawrenceville, Georgia, ostensibly chosen because of proximity to an international airport and to the Road Atlanta circuit, which was useful for testing purposes. More important, the team's base was also off the beaten track and therefore well hidden from prying eyes and unwanted visitors, something that would become a priority. In 1980, Paul Sr brought his 20-year-old son onto the team's driving strength, starting in May at Lime Rock Park. It was not only John Jr's first professional event but also his first race in a 935. Remarkably, they managed to win, making them the first father-and-son pairing to claim an IMSA victory. That same day, on the circuit's infield, Paul Sr married for the second time, to Chalice Alford, with his son acting as best man.

For rest of the 1980 season, JLP Racing mostly campaigned a more developed Kremer version of the Porsche 935 that the team termed JLP-2. The new car brought a string of shared podium finishes, including another win at Road America, all of which boosted Paul Sr's points tally so strongly that he finished runner-up in the IMSA championship. In a season that marked the peak of his personal achievements in the sport, he had also managed to win the FIA World Challenge for Endurance Drivers, which comprised five races on the IMSA schedule and five events in Europe, just beating renowned British driver John Fitzpatrick (see Chapter 18) by the slim margin of four points. Father and son also finished ninth overall and second in the IMSA class at Le Mans sharing another Porsche 935 with Britain's Guy Edwards. In a meteoric rise, John Jr had gone from competing in domestic Formula Ford to the Le Mans 24 Hours in just one year and had finished fourth in the IMSA standings. After uncertain beginnings, he had clearly become a precocious talent.

For the 1981 IMSA season, Paul Sr commissioned an even more special

935 with a tubular chassis and called it JLP-3. The team claimed to have used a rusty 911 bought in a Georgia scrapyard for $1,000 as the basis and put together the entire car for half the cost of a new 935 from Stuttgart. This 'home-built' 935 faced some stiff challengers, notably from Brian Redman's new Chevrolet-powered Lola T600, which had much better handling. While Paul Sr responded by buying the first customer version of the Lola, JLP-3 wasn't discarded and by the end of the year it had been developed into a winning machine. Over the course of the season, it became obvious that John Jr was now the faster driver, despite his relatively limited experience, so his father decided to step down for the shorter races, but they still competed together in the endurance events and were able to win a rain-shortened round at Pocono. During the season the youngster qualified on pole position nine times and led each of the 18 IMSA races he entered, but inexperience and youthful exuberance brought two crashes and he lost out in the championship to Redman.

In a textbook start to the 1982 season, father and son achieved astonishing back-to-back wins in America's two classic endurance races, the Daytona 24 Hours, where German Rolf Stommelen partnered them, and the Sebring 12 Hours. John Jr also won the next two rounds driving on his own, at Road Atlanta with the Porsche and Laguna Seca in the Lola, before reuniting with his father again and winning two more endurance races, at Charlotte and Mosport. Together the Pauls won five races in addition to John Jr's score of nine solo victories. The last race together for the father-and-son combination, at Pocono, brought second place, and by this time the talented 22-year-old had already clinched the title to become IMSA's youngest-ever champion.

Another 1982 novelty was that JLP Racing commissioned one final hybrid 935, JLP-4, to take on the prototypes now being admitted to IMSA's new GTP class, following on from the Lola T600. When this ultimate 935 appeared mid-season for use in IMSA's sprint races, it proved quicker than its predecessor by some five seconds per lap, and John Jr won his first two races with the car, at Brainerd and Portland. As before, the Lee Dykstra-designed JLP-4 loosely resembled the silhouette of a 935 but featured some even more radical ideas below the surface, most notably ground-effect aerodynamics with sliding skirts.

In what would be the last hurrah for JLP Racing, Paul Sr independently won the Camel Endurance Championship title of 1982 for his performance in races of six hours or more. His track record proved that he was undoubtedly a good driver even if he wasn't as naturally gifted as his son. While not the

Domineering father and naïve son: John Paul Sr and Jr were very able
racing drivers, the son even more so than the father, and achieved plenty
of success together in the early 1980s, including victory in the Daytona
24 Hours of 1982, partnered by Rolf Stommelen (centre).

John Paul Jr, pictured at the outset of his career when
competing in Formula Ford, returned to racing after his
prison sentence but his father soon vanished, suspected
of further crimes and never to be seen again.

out-and-out fastest, the father certainly possessed both the consistency and determination required in long-distance racing. However, realising that he was past his peak abilities, he announced his retirement as a driver after the final race of 1982 with the intention of channelling his energies into managing his racing team.

John Paul Sr was known in racing circles as 'The Old Pirate'. Unlike his son, he was an unlikely-looking racing driver with his short, slightly overweight build, scruffy appearance with unkempt beard, and thick-lensed spectacles. A pugnacious individual, he was unpopular with other competitors and known for his quick and often irrational temper that could explode into violent outbursts, a trait that his son judged to be linked to something that had happened to him during his Dutch childhood. The JLP Racing transporter was entirely black, which matched the temperament of a constantly angry man who rarely smiled and regularly created trouble in the race paddocks. His racing cars, on the other hand, wore the curiously garish but unattractive colour combination of baby blue with splashes of yellow, apparently because he was colour-blind.

Stories of his uncontrollable temper are legion. When Don Whittington overtook him by mistake under caution flags, he sought out the errant driver afterwards and hit him so hard that he broke his own arm. Wrongly believing that he and his son had been denied a race victory, he hurled his briefcase and even tables and chairs across a press room. He deliberately crashed into Bob Akin on a slowing-down lap in retaliation for his perception that Akin had blocked John Jr on the track earlier in the race. Many people were genuinely scared of him, with one IMSA official who observed his rants for several seasons describing him as 'the most terrifying man I have ever met' and 'more than frightening'. Unsurprisingly, everyone steered well clear of him whenever possible.

John Jr rather sadly admitted, 'He was never easy to be with and it was hard to know when he was pleased with me. People talk about walking on eggs. That was me around my dad. Eggs everywhere and my big feet always smashing them.' It seems that even the man himself acknowledged his poor behaviour when he said, 'Maybe I'm a little too tough at times but I grew up in a tough world.'

By 1982, John Jr began to realise that JLP Racing was spending vast amounts of money that weren't sustainable without major sponsorship, although the team had picked up some commercial backing from the Atlanta distributor of Miller beers, leading to JLR-4 at first being turned out in white and red rather than the usual blue and yellow. In terms of equipment, the team was never short of anything, although there was no unnecessary expenditure on extras such as team uniforms, the untidy appearance of its motley group of personnel reflecting that of its owner. The reason why there had been little need to worry too much about money was because the funding had come from Paul Sr's marijuana smuggling.

John Jr stated that his first experience of smoking weed came at the age of nine when he was given some by a babysitter. He was used to seeing his father and friends regularly smoking it at around the same time, not long before his parents separated. The son stumbled on his father's illicit business as a teenager when he saw stacks of marijuana hidden in the garage at home and at that point Paul Sr told him all about it. In Sylvia Wilkins's book *50/50*, John Jr stated, 'I was too young and naive to be shocked by finding out my dad was a smuggler. It was just what my dad did and I was supposed to help him. I kind of halfway knew then if we were going to have nice cars to go fast in, then we were going to have to do the marijuana thing.' He made no excuses for what he did and went on to say, 'I didn't think very deeply about it at the time. I was too young to understand because I just wanted to go racing.'

Having been drawn into assisting his father, the teenager's role was to unload big, heavy bales of contraband from boats and transfer them to trucks that he would then drive to his father's storage facility. In January 1979, he and one of his father's associates, Christopher Schill, were caught loading a consignment onto a pick-up truck on the bank of a canal in Louisiana. His father was later arrested on his boat *Lady Royale*, where customs officers discovered marijuana residue and $10,000 cash. The police also found a van parked nearby that Paul Sr had rented and into which they had loaded 1,565 pounds of marijuana. At the subsequent court hearing, all three pleaded guilty to possession of marijuana but received remarkably lenient punishment, comprising three years' probation with suspended sentences and fines totalling $32,500.

For John Jr, the conviction marked the end of any further involvement in his father's 'business' but he would continue to live with the ever-present fear of a 'knock on the door' — and, indeed, nightmarish repercussions were to come back to haunt him in later years. For Paul Sr, however, the conviction was just a brief setback and he soon returned to his wrongdoing, which in due course came to the notice of the federal authorities. By the spring of 1983, they had spent almost a year methodically building up a case against him, and now had a key witness, Stephen Carson, a former associate who had been given immunity from prosecution in his own drug-trafficking case.

Knowing he was cornered, Paul Sr persuaded Carson to meet him at a marina in Crescent Beach, Florida, on the evening of 19th April 1983 after a fishing trip. He told Carson to get into the back of his car but at that point his old associate tried to run away. Paul Sr fired five times with a .38 revolver but failed to kill Carson, who was hit in the chest, abdomen and leg. The gunman fled the scene after Carson's companion raised the alarm but was soon arrested and charged with trying to obstruct the grand jury's drug investigation by the attempted murder of a federal witness. It's hard to fathom why Carson even agreed to meet his assailant because he had told the police that he was terrified of him and would never have blown the whistle on him or identified him as a marijuana trafficker. 'I knew he'd kill anyone who said anything about what he was doing,' said Carson. 'But he got the wrong guy. I was too afraid of him to say anything, but I guess he thought it was me anyway.'

After 10 days in jail, Paul Sr was released on bail bond of $500,000 but failed to appear for his scheduled trial at St Augustine, Florida, in December 1983. An arrest warrant was issued and a worldwide hunt triggered, with FBI agents working through Interpol, the international police agency. Thirteen months later, in January 1985, Paul Sr was apprehended wearing a disguise outside a bank in Switzerland, where he had been living under an assumed name. He served a six-month sentence in that country for using a false passport before being extradited back to the US in March 1986. There he pleaded guilty to attempted first-degree murder and received a sentence of 20 years, later increased to 25 years after he was also tried and convicted of tax evasion and drug-smuggling offences in 1987. Additional charges related to the allegations that between 1975 and 1981 he had been the 'organiser, supervisor and manager' of a network that smuggled 50 tons of marijuana from Colombia into America. He was charged not only with drug trafficking but also racketeering together with the attempted bribery of a grand jury witness. In a highly organised operation, the consignments of marijuana were alleged to have been moved via the Bahamas using a variety of boats, including his own yacht, before being offloaded in Florida and Louisiana and transferred to various storage facilities.

Back in 1982, according to the indictment, Paul Sr had been making ambitious plans to abandon his Colombian sources and expand operations on home soil. Some of the 17 charges levelled against him, together with Christopher Schill, related to the excavation of a huge underground bunker

One of the finest racing moments for the John Pauls came when they won
the 1982 Daytona 24 Hours in their special lightweight Porsche 935.

at a 600-acre farm he had bought in the name of John Drew near Corinth,
Georgia. Here Paul Sr and Schill intended to cultivate marijuana plants on
an industrial scale in an artificial subterranean plantation measuring 200ft
by 40ft with access through a 25ft reinforced steel shaft beneath an old
barn. They were thought to have spent more than $300,000 constructing
this cavern, which incorporated artificial growing lamps powered by diesel
generators fuelled from tanks buried beneath the complex. The authorities
estimated that marijuana valued at $4 million could have been grown there
each year. They also believed that Paul Sr had used the facility as a hiding
place for some of the time that he was being sought after jumping bail.

Other than his racing in Formula Ford, Formula Atlantic and Formula
Super Vee, plus a failed attempt to qualify for the 1982 Indianapolis
500 that ended with a crash, John Jr's open-wheel experience was still very
limited when Wysard Racing asked him to race an Indycar at Road America
in September 1982. Although Wysard's March wasn't a front-running car,
he managed to qualify an impressive eighth but the engine failed in the race.

A full season of Indycar was planned for 1983 and JLP Racing's Lola
T600 was sold to help fund the $400,000 cost of a seat with wealthy Belgian
brewing magnate Count van der Straten's VDS Racing, an established team
that was turning to Indycar for the first time. Two days before his father's

attempted murder of Stephen Carson, the 23-year-old rookie débuted his year-old Penske PC10 on the high-banked oval at Atlanta and finished an impressive third. A month later at Indianapolis, however, he was devastated to crash again, this time breaking his left leg. He returned to the cockpit as soon as he could, at Cleveland on the first weekend of July, but a blown engine put paid to his chances that day. From there, VDS Racing headed to Michigan, which, like Indianapolis, is a super-fast oval.

Still barely able to walk and with his leg in a plaster cast, John Jr became an overnight sensation by bravely overcoming his physical discomfort to overtake works Penske driver Rick Mears on the last lap and win on only his fourth ever Indycar start. Post-race, the lanky youngster proclaimed: 'I'd like to say hey to my Dad. I love you, Dad.' Of course, his father was by now a fugitive wanted by the FBI and wasn't there to witness his son's biggest victory, although he was seen at the season finale in Las Vegas where the rising young star took pole position and scored an excellent second place behind 1978 F1 World Champion Mario Andretti. Combined with two other podiums, John Jr finished a respectable eighth in the points standings at the end of his first season. Although only $200,000 had been paid to VDS Racing, the rookie had earned the team $260,000 in prize money and the Count was happy.

Although John Jr initially continued with VDS Racing in 1984, the team didn't stay the course and for the rest of the season he raced intermittently for other outfits of varying quality, recording a best finish of third place at the final round in Las Vegas. Sporadic outings in sportscars included impressive second places at Le Mans (in Preston Henn's Porsche 956) and Watkins Glen (in Bruce Leven's Porsche 962). Demonstrating his versatility, he also managed to win first time out in Trans-Am, at Trois Rivières in Canada driving a Chevrolet Camaro.

By now, John Jr's world was beginning to unravel due to his father's notoriety. A first sign of this had come swiftly after his father's arrest for attempted murder, news that had prompted Ford to withdraw its interest in having him drive a Mustang GTP prototype in the IMSA series. Inevitably, the problems got worse in January 1985 when John Jr was himself arrested on new charges. The timing of his indictment, just three days after his father's arrest in Switzerland, was widely believed to be significant, in order to persuade Paul Sr to waive extradition and return to the US willingly in order to help clear his son.

Very honourably, John Jr offered to withdraw from the two contracts that had already been signed. Doug Shierson, owner of one of the top

Indycar teams, immediately accepted his driver's resignation, but Phil Conte, who already ran John Jr in IMSA, wouldn't hear of it. An ex-marine, he proclaimed: 'I never deserted my country and I'll never desert a friend. Normally in this country, a person is innocent until proven guilty.' John Bishop, President of IMSA, expressed similar feelings and was happy to have John Jr continue to compete in his series.

As court proceedings weren't due to take place until the end of 1985, John Jr knew there was nothing to stop him driving for the whole season and he was determined to repay the loyalty shown to him by Conte. Indeed, when he had to spend three days in jail in Jacksonville, Conte even posted bail of $12,500 in cash and signed a bond for the remaining $112,500 in order to free his driver. At the start of the season and just two days after his release, John Jr took pole position at Daytona with a time two seconds faster than any other driver but unfortunately that was a high point in what otherwise was to be disastrous campaign, for Conte's Buick-powered March 85G proved woefully unreliable and didn't finish any of its 11 races. John Jr also managed to pick up occasional Indycar drives but crashed his March 85C at Indianapolis and only finished one other race.

When the Pauls' case eventually came to trial in June 1986, it wasn't just father and son who appeared in court but, remarkably, a third generation of the family too. Lee Paul, Sr's father, was one of five other Florida men who were also named in the indictment on charges of racketeering. It was alleged that John Jr had been engaged in a conspiracy with his father to launder the profits from drug trafficking and four charges were made against him specifically, involving crimes in 1979 and 1981. Two of the charges related to the earlier marijuana offences for which both father and son had been convicted in a Louisiana court and put on three years' probation. A third charge involved conspiracy — being employed by and associated with the marijuana enterprise — and the fourth related to accepting delivery of a truck allegedly loaded with marijuana.

John Jr said at the time: 'I've never been caught with any pot. Not even in '79. The IRS and everyone else says that they're not really interested in me; they're trying to pressure my dad more than anything else. I think they're also just trying to get me to incriminate the others, to firm up their case against them.' As he stressed: 'I'd been out of it totally since then [1979] but some of the people we'd been involved with continued to do it. They got caught and implicated us.' John Jr pleaded guilty to a charge of racketeering in exchange for which the Federal Government dropped four drugs-related charges against him and part of the plea deal that was reached ensured that he wouldn't have to testify against his father, something that he had resolutely refused to do. His attorney, John Nuckolls, remarked: 'Theirs is the strangest relationship I've ever seen.' John Jr was unequivocal in his loyalty and affection for his father, pointing out: 'I wouldn't be racing if it weren't for my Dad. He put 150 percent into the operation, and in return for his support I was expected to do what I was told. I'm willing to bet that most people would have done the same.'

The young racer's career was suddenly and dramatically halted when he was sentenced to five years in prison in a minimum-security facility in Montgomery, Alabama. One of his Conte Racing team-mates, John Morton, was among many competitors and entrants who wrote to the judge to plead for a lenient sentence and stated: '[He] was just a kid caught up in something that his father created, a very domineering father, that no child could have bucked. Everyone in racing knew what his father was like. Junior never made excuses even though he hadn't touched a bale of marijuana since he was a teenager, he took his punishment and it took his promising career.'

John Jr served 28 months and was released in October 1988.

Soon after John Paul Sr began his prison sentence in Baker County, Florida, his ruthless character revealed itself again when, in March 1987, he and another prisoner made a clumsy attempt to escape by spraying a stinging mixture of cleaning disinfectant and chili sauce in a jailer's face. Although they managed to scale a 12-foot fence and were making their way to a stolen pick-up truck that had been left for them, they were forced to surrender because the guard, who had been wearing glasses, recovered quickly enough to be able to fire two warning shots. Paul Sr's behaviour must have improved after that because he was paroled in July 1999 after serving 13 years of his 25-year sentence.

Early in 2000, he met Colleen Wood, a 52-year-old divorcee who had recently moved from Ohio to Florida and worked as an office manager at the Lighthouse Point Marina in Fort Lauderdale. He had advertised for a first mate on his boat, a 55-foot schooner named *Island Girl*, in preparation for a five-year round-the-world voyage — a venture that would have violated the terms of his parole. The two were soon involved in what seemed to be a whirlwind romance. Although Colleen told friends that she thought her new boyfriend had a drinking problem and could be angry when drunk, she didn't appear to be unduly concerned about his behaviour. She did surprise them, however, when she gave up her job to join him in redecorating and furnishing the boat in preparation for the trip, and then also sold her condominium and entrusted the proceeds to him to invest.

Early in December 2000, Colleen called her two sons to say that she and Paul Sr would be setting sail a couple of weeks later and that she would contact them again before departure. Ten days later she accepted a friend's invitation to her former company's Christmas party. She didn't go to the party and she didn't call her sons. Neither could they contact her, because her cell phone account had been closed. Now suspicious about her new boyfriend, they searched the internet to find out more about him and were shocked to learn about his criminal history. They felt sure their mother was unaware of it. They did manage to get hold of Paul Sr by phone and he told them that he and their mother had argued about money and that she'd stormed off before returning with another boyfriend to fetch her belongings.

The sons informed the police about their mother's disappearance. Detectives established that she had last used her cell phone on 15th or 16th December. Checking credit-card transactions, they found that between December 2000 and February 2001 more than $40,000 in cash had been withdrawn from an ATM in Fort Lauderdale. Surveillance images of withdrawals showed that they were made by two women, neither of whom was Colleen. There were also credit-card payments dated December 2000 for two local newspaper advertisements, one offering a job for a first mate aboard a boat, the other in the personal section from a male seeking a female. Detectives found Paul Sr cooperative when they first interviewed him at the marina, but when they returned a week later with a warrant to search his boat, it had gone. Witnesses said that he had sailed the day after being questioned.

Meanwhile, Paul Sr also came to be considered a suspect in the mysterious disappearance of Chalice, his bride at Lime Rock in 1980. She had vanished without trace the following summer after last being seen with him. After that, Paul Sr had travelled to Haiti to divorce her *in absentia* so that he could marry Hope Haywood, sister of three-time Le Mans winner Hurley Haywood, but their relationship didn't last long.

Colleen Wood's case remains unsolved and Paul Sr remains the only suspect. Her disappearance became the subject of an investigative television programme, *Unsolved Mysteries*, in 2002 and subsequently there were several claimed sightings of him in ports in Jamaica, Fiji and Thailand between 2004 and 2009. However, the authorities have never been able to catch up with him and leads have dried up.

U pon John Jr's release, most of the racing community welcomed him back warmly, feeling that he'd done his time and paid his debt. Many felt that his father had bullied him into the drug-trafficking operations against his will when he was still an impressionable teenager. Despite the convictions, which made him undesirable to some of the image-conscious team owners and sponsors, his formidable talent meant that he was still recognised as one of America's very best drivers.

Against the odds, he was able to resume his interrupted racing career — at the age of 29 and after almost three seasons out of the sport — and go on to take seven more IMSA victories. However, having spent his formative years living with his mother about 40 miles from Indianapolis, and despite his successes in sportscars and GTs, his remaining ambitions lay in single-seater Indycars and specifically the Indy 500. In 1985, he had achieved his lifelong dream and finally taken part in America's greatest race, and in the years following his release he competed at Indy six more times, albeit relegated to driving with smaller teams. After landing a full-time drive in the Indy Racing League with Byrd-Cunningham Racing in 1998, he won at Texas Motor Speedway and also claimed a record for the longest gap between Indycar victories, at 15 years.

John Jr's story is a sad case of what might have been. As a character, he was the polar opposite of his intimidating, unpredictable, disreputable and dishonest father, a dutiful young man who paid the penalty for his loyalty and recognised it when he stated: 'What I did hurt the sport, which was the last thing I wanted to do.'

With an effortless driving style, John Jr was one of the most versatile racers of his era. He won more than 20 sportscar races, mostly in IMSA when it was at its peak. He claimed victories in two different Indycar series, won in Trans-Am and even tried NASCAR. His skills were in such demand that, apart from the family-run JLP Racing, he drove for 40 entrants including 15 Indycar teams.

John Jr retired from professional driving in 2001 after being diagnosed with the debilitating Huntington's disease. In the years that followed, he struggled with increasing physical disability, which affected how he walked and talked, but continued to fight a courageous and protracted battle against the genetic disorder that had claimed the lives of his grandmother, mother, aunt and sister. He was part of a clinical study at UCLA's Department of Neurology to find treatment to halt the effects of the disease and his contributions to the study and fundraising have greatly increased the number of clinical drug trials, bringing doctors closer to finding a cure. He died on 29th December 2020, aged 60.

NELSON PIQUET JR

Race of disgrace

Although not universally popular, team orders are a widely accepted practice and have endured in motor racing for as long as the sport has existed. Rarely, however, have boundaries been crossed by going to the extraordinary lengths of conspiring to fix the results of a race by instructing a driver to endanger his life by deliberately crashing his car.

A s the son of one of Brazil's most successful racing drivers and a three-time Formula 1 World Champion, Nelson Piquet Junior had impeccable pedigree as he sought to add to his family history in the sport, helped by his father's wealth. After retiring from the sport, Nelson Piquet Senior had enlarged his existing fortune by founding an extremely lucrative business called Autotrac, which uses advanced technology and telemetry to monitor fleets of cars for clients in transportation and logistics businesses.

After racing karts for seven years, Piquet Jr made the move into cars by jumping into Formula 3 and winning the South American championship in 2002. Then he followed the well-trodden path taken by so many Brazilian hopefuls and continued his career in England with his own team. The youngster was immediately competitive in British Formula 3, winning six races in 2003 and finishing third in the championship, then going on to win it the following year with a further six wins. The 2005 season saw him score victories in A1 Grand Prix, in which he represented Brazil, and also in the international GP2 Series, where he won at Spa-Francorchamps.

His career maintained its momentum in 2006 when he finished second in the GP2 Series to Lewis Hamilton after a season-long battle for honours. By this time, he was on the radar of Formula 1 team managers and had already tested for Williams and BAR-Honda when team boss Flavio Briatore hired him as official test and reserve driver for the Renault team for 2007.

Piquet Jr was promoted to a race seat for 2008 alongside the mercurial Spaniard Fernando Alonso, who was returning to the team after an unhappy and controversial season at McLaren (see Chapter 49). Even in the double World Champion's hands, the Renault R28 lacked pace and Piquet Jr's struggles to get to grips with the difficult car weren't helped by the pressures piled upon him by the team, particularly by Briatore. By mid-season, the rookie had retired from six of nine Grands Prix and his lack of self-belief was exacerbated by persistent rumours that he was going to be dropped at the end of the season, and maybe even earlier. The gossip and innuendo didn't stop even after he scored a somewhat lucky second place in the German Grand Prix at Hockenheim when, on a one-stop strategy, he fortuitously pitted for fuel just before deployment of the safety car.

Seven weeks later, the collapse of Lehman Brothers, the fourth-biggest investment bank in the US, triggered a financial crisis that sent shockwaves around the world, making it suddenly seem a much less certain place. Almost overnight, concerns grew within Formula 1 that consumers would stop buying new cars and precipitate the withdrawal of manufacturers from the sport, as indeed duly happened with Honda. Renault was already on hard times before the credit crunch and Briatore was acutely aware that he also needed to deliver results for the board of the parent company as well as for the team's title sponsor, the ING bank.

At that stage of the season, Alonso still hadn't scored a podium finish let alone won a race, although he had been a much more regular points scorer than his inexperienced team-mate. This paucity of results added to the pressure on Briatore, who was concerned that the R28's limitations might dissuade his star driver from staying on for another season.

Two weeks after Lehman Brothers filed for bankruptcy, the inaugural Singapore Grand Prix took place at the Marina Bay street circuit. The R28 showed great speed in practice with Alonso quickest in two of the three practice sessions but a problem in the second qualifying session left him stranded on the circuit. That meant he would start the race from a lowly 15th place on the grid, only one slot ahead of Piquet Jr, at a circuit where overtaking was extremely difficult. 'Starting from there,' said Alonso, 'I'm

Renault team principal Flavio Briatore poses with Nelson Piquet Jr at the
Paris launch of Renault's new Formula 1 challenger for 2008.

Nelson Piquet Jr deliberately crashed his Renault R28 into the wall on the
14th lap of the 2008 Singapore Grand Prix.

going to need a miracle.' Thanks to his team's scheming, that's exactly what he got.

Pat Symonds, the team's highly respected director of engineering, instructed the pit crew to fuel Alonso's car extremely light in a strategy that could only work if a safety car came out and neutralised the race. He then foolishly plotted with Briatore to create the perfect scenario by instructing the team's number two driver to crash at the appropriate time into one of the walls bordering the track. As this street circuit had no run-off areas, a crashed car would have to be recovered, guaranteeing use of the safety car. Alonso's lightweight R28 passed three cars in the opening laps before stopping for fuel and new tyres after just 12 laps of the 61-lap race. This dropped him to the back of the field, but only two laps later the safety car was deployed due to his team-mate's 'accident'.

Rashly, the naïve youngster did as he had been told, on cue, and smashed his Renault into the retaining wall at Turn 17 in a spectacular impact that was severe enough to tear off the right-rear corner of the car and shower the track with debris and shards of carbon-fibre. Through luck rather than judgement, no other drivers were involved and no spectators or marshals were injured. By the time the race resumed, the rest of the field had taken advantage of the situation and made pitstops, conveniently allowing Alonso to make up place after place and put himself into a lead that he didn't relinquish. According to plan, he recorded the team's first victory of the season, which at the time was heralded as an opportunistic and tactically astute win.

Eyebrows were raised in certain parts of the media but most of the comment was directed at Piquet Jr, with his apparent incompetence used as further evidence that he wasn't worthy of his seat in a leading Formula 1 team. In the paddock, there were certainly suspicions that events had been a bit too coincidental but no one truly believed that a team would go to such extremes to manipulate the outcome of a race. In the absence of hard evidence of anything untoward, the FIA took no action.

Ashamed about what he had done, the inexperienced driver confided in his furious father, who in turn told FIA race director Charlie Whiting (see Chapter 62) what had happened during an off-the-record conversation at the end-of-season Brazilian Grand Prix. Whiting, Piquet Sr's former mechanic at Brabham, was placed in an invidious position but, in the absence of a formal protest, felt that he couldn't take any action. Only a few days later, Piquet Jr was duly rewarded for his part in the subterfuge when his place in the team was confirmed for 2009.

FLAVIO BRIATORE
Rags to riches

Flavio Briatore's colourful background includes two prison sentences handed to him in the 1980s, the second for fraud and conspiracy in his role with a group of conmen who established rigged gambling games using fake playing cards, but he avoided serving time by becoming a fugitive in the Virgin Islands and only returned to Italy after both convictions were extinguished by amnesty. While in the Virgin Islands, he drew upon an established relationship with Luciano Benetton, whom he had met in 1974 while working on the Italian stock exchange in Milan, and opened some Benetton clothing stores. After his return to Italy, Briatore played a significant part in Benetton's expansion through franchise agreements to the point where the group had 800 stores. He was already a wealthy man when he attended his first Formula 1 race in Australia in 1988.

Although he has claimed that he wasn't a great motorsport fan, Briatore took over management of Benetton's Formula 1 team in 1990. Despite his inexperience, he soon transformed it into a championship-winning squad helped by the talents of Michael Schumacher (see Chapter 22). However, controversy followed during 1994 when the team was accused of cheating, resulting in fines and a two-race ban for its driver. After winning back-to-back World Championship titles, Schumacher departed for Ferrari in 1996 and other key staff — notably Ross Brawn and Rory Byrne — duly followed, triggering decline at Benetton that led to Briatore's dismissal in 1997.

After Renault's purchase of the team in 2000, the flamboyant Italian returned as team principal but was forced to resign after receiving a lifetime ban from all FIA-sanctioned events following his involvement in the 'Crashgate' incident, although he vehemently denied all allegations and the ban was subsequently overturned by the French Tribunal de Grande Instance.

Outside the sport, Briatore continued to generate controversy when his luxury 63-metre superyacht *Force Blue* was seized in 2010 due to alleged evasion of €3.6 million in VAT and €800,000 of fuel duties. He received a prison sentence of 23 months in 2015 but this was reduced on appeal in February 2018 to 18 months and after a further appeal he was definitively acquitted in January 2022, by which time the vessel had long since been sold by the authorities at auction for far less than its true value. The purchaser was his friend Bernie Ecclestone.

That might have drawn a line under the whole affair but for Briatore's decision to sack Piquet Jr halfway through the 2009 season, by invoking a performance clause in the young driver's contract that he needed to have scored at least 40 percent of the points accumulated by his team-mate at the halfway point of the season. The split wasn't an amicable one and Piquet Jr was sufficiently angry to go public on his website about his team boss, who was also his personal manager. The disaffected driver stated: 'I always believed that having a manager was being part of a team and having a partner. A manager is supposed to encourage you, support you, and provide you with opportunities. In my case it was the opposite. Flavio Briatore was my executioner.'

Piquet Sr decided to become whistleblower about the race-fixing at the Singapore Grand Prix. At a 90-minute hearing in Paris on 21st September 2009, the FIA's World Motorsports Council banned Briatore, who denied involvement, from any further involvement in the sport and handed Symonds, who admitted his part in the plan, a five-year suspension from working in Formula 1. As FIA President Max Mosley wrote in his autobiography, 'Flavio challenged this decision in the French courts and won a partial victory. The court did not like our procedures and set the penalties aside. But it made no finding of innocence and did not exonerate Flavio or Pat.'

Mindful of the fact that the sport could ill-afford to lose yet another team, after Honda's defection the previous winter and BMW's recent announcement that it too would be pulling out, the FIA issued Renault with what seemed to be a lenient penalty. As *Autocourse* reported, the team was given 'a permanent exclusion from the F1 business but that this would be suspended for two years and would only be activated in the (unlikely) event that their team transgressed in a similarly serious manner during that period.' While this outcome was widely considered to be at odds with the $100 million fine handed to McLaren (see Chapter 49) for a far lesser crime two years earlier, the Renault team didn't come out of the case completely unscathed as its two main sponsors, ING and Mutua Madrileña, withdrew with immediate effect.

As for Nelson Piquet Jr, he came to be seen as 'damaged goods' and never raced again in Formula 1, partly due to the inadvertent impact that his father's actions had had on his career.

The Piquets, father and son, may have had their revenge but neither they nor anyone else involved in 'Crashgate' came out of it well. The episode has gone down as one of the worst examples of blatant cheating ever seen in any sport and certainly the most damaging scandal in Formula 1 history.

CYRIL DE ROUVRE

Formula fraud

Obsession with motor racing saw Cyril de Rouvre squander his family's fortune through misguided investments in two underperforming French Formula 1 teams and eventually landed him in financial hot water with the authorities.

Cyril de Rouvre was born into extremely wealthy surroundings as the great-grandson of sugar magnate Charles Bourlon de Rouvre, who had married into one of France's richest families. He was educated at elite schools in France, England (The Oratory School in Berkshire) and Switzerland before graduating from the Sorbonne University in Paris as an aerospace engineer. After a spell working for Electricité de France (EDF) followed by compulsory military service, he joined the family business and inherited it at the age of 33, after his father Evrard had tragically been stabbed to death by his butler in 1979. The empire comprised real-estate interests and a network of 30 companies including the sugar refinery that Cyril modernised and expanded. More acquisitions were made in property and he also diversified into publishing, transport and aviation before turning to the film industry by producing movies as well as buying an archive of 650 titles.

A huge car enthusiast and great fan of motorsport, he took part in some of the early rally raids in the 1970s with Paris–Dakar founder Thierry

Sabine, including the Abidjan–Nice event in which he drove a Range Rover. His success in business was such that he was able to indulge his passion even further in 1989 by buying a majority shareholding in the struggling French Formula 1 team AGS (Automobiles Gonfaronnaises Sportives) from its founder Henri Julien. Although de Rouvre threw money at the venture by hiring more staff and building a new factory at Le Luc, the increased resources didn't lead to better results for the perennial backmarkers, especially as this was a period of exploding costs in Formula 1 with big motor manufacturers becoming involved.

Despite sponsorship revenue from electrical company Faure and fashion brand Ted Lapidus, the AGS team consumed $18 million of de Rouvre's money in the space of just two years. To keep the underperforming outfit afloat, as well as needing to fund new ambitions for a political career in his Haute-Marne *Département*, he had to start selling some of the companies in his portfolio, including Transair (an air charter operation) and the sugar refinery. Having got to the point where he was unwilling to spend any more on AGS, he allowed the team to go into administration early in 1991. During de Rouvre's two-year tenure, the team's only points-scoring result was sixth place for Gabriele Tarquini in the 1989 Mexican Grand Prix, but most of the time its drivers were unable to pre-qualify let alone get through to qualifying proper and win places on the starting grids. Although the team was briefly resurrected by Italians Gabriele Rafanelli and Patrizio Cantù, it wasn't long before it went under for good.

In 1992, de Rouvre was tempted back into Formula 1 and bought 21 percent of Ligier, another underperforming French team but at least one that had a distinguished history and appeared to have all the right ingredients in place to succeed again. The team's founder, Guy Ligier, had used his considerable political connections to secure generous backing from state-owned concerns, including Elf (oil), Gitanes (cigarettes) and LOTO (the national lottery company), and, most importantly, had negotiated supply of the powerful Renault V10 engine that was to be used to such good effect that year by Nigel Mansell in becoming a dominant World Champion with Williams.

However, while Mansell walked away with imperious victories in the first five World Championship races of 1992, Ligier's drivers, Thierry Boutsen and Erik Comas, struggled and logged only a few lowly finishes amidst many retirements. At the sixth race, the Monaco Grand Prix, Ligier got so upset about his cars being booed by fans that he decided to think about pastures new. At the end of the season he sold a further 69 percent to de

Cyril de Rouvre's brief involvement with the Ligier Formula 1 team as majority shareholder ended when he defaulted on a payment due as part of his purchase arrangements and spent two months in prison while his affairs were investigated.

Rouvre for $30 million before going on to make another fortune for himself in natural fertilisers.

With two talented British drivers, Martin Brundle and Mark Blundell, on board for 1993, the prospects looked good and under de Rouvre's one-year stewardship the Ligier-Renault JS39s accumulated ten points-scoring finishes, including three on the podium, to give the team fifth place in the constructors' championship, its best result for seven years.

Meanwhile, de Rouvre's world was collapsing. To pay for his majority shareholding in Ligier, he had organised a loan from his film business, Cofragec, at the same time as the company was being merged with its much bigger rival, UGC (Union Générale Cinématographique), in a deal whereby he took UGC shares instead of cash. Under the arrangement, he agreed to repay the loan from Cofragec to UGC through the sale of his newly acquired UGC shares, which he estimated were worth the requisite $30 million. Unfortunately, de Rouvre got caught out because UGC's share price plummeted. Although he held off selling the shares in the hope of a bounce in price, UGC lost patience and filed a complaint against him for fraud after discovering a hole of 172 million francs in Cofragec's accounts. He eventually sold the shares in May 1993 for half the amount that he had originally anticipated, leaving him unable to repay the remaining $15 million.

When the case came to court that December, the judge decided that there was sufficient evidence of impropriety for more investigation to be needed. One irregularity was Cofragec's purchase of 21 cars for eight million francs from Paradise Automobiles, whose main shareholder was de Rouvre. Of much more concern was the acquisition by Cofragec, mere days before the deal with UGC was signed, of shares costing 20 million francs in a Luxembourg-based company that de Rouvre also controlled. All the same, it still came as a considerable surprise when judge Eva Joly decided to send him to prison pending the investigation and he spent an uncomfortable two months in the Fleury-Mergois jail on the outskirts of Paris.

Wanting access to the Ligier team's supply of Renault engines, Benetton's Flavio Briatore (see Chapter 46) bought the team from de Rouvre, who then disappeared as his brief dalliance with Formula 1 came to an end. His troubles weren't over, however, as the investigations into his affairs rumbled on. On his 54th birthday in December 1999, he was convicted of various charges related to the fraud and given a suspended sentence of 18 months.

TOMAS SCHECKTER

Too close to the kerb

Son of Jody Scheckter, who became Formula 1 World Champion for Ferrari in 1979, the South African youngster's single-seater racing career was also heading towards Formula 1 until it took a nosedive after a brush with the law in the UK.

After a promising start to his career in his native South Africa, Tomas Scheckter moved to the UK as a 17-year-old and in 1998 finished third in the British Formula Vauxhall Junior Championship in his rookie season. The following year saw him progress to the Formula Opel Euroseries and he won this in dominant fashion, breaking previous records by taking eight pole positions and eight wins in 20 races. This led to him being offered a drive for the last two races of that season's Formula Nissan Championship in which Fernando Alonso had reigned supreme. Despite his lack of experience in the team and of the rather more powerful car, Scheckter put in remarkable performances by starting both races from pole, winning one and placing second in the other.

A move into the ultra-competitive British Formula 3 Championship in 2000 netted him runner-up spot at his first attempt and he also finished third at the prestigious Masters Formula 3 event at Zandvoort in the Netherlands. His season concluded with four races driving a Lola in the International Formula 3000 Championship, the feeder series into Formula 1

Jaguar appointed Tomas Scheckter as Formula 1 test driver in 2001, putting his dreams within reach until it all went wrong one night in Northampton.

that staged rounds at most of the Grands Prix held at European circuits. On only his second start, at Hockenheim prior to the German Grand Prix, he finished a fine second. As a result of these impressive performances, his chances of breaking into Formula 1 increased dramatically when the Milton Keynes-based Jaguar team signed him as test driver for the 2001 season, supporting the efforts of regular drivers Eddie Irvine (see Chapter 52) and Pedro de la Rosa (see Chapter 49).

All this momentum, however, came to an abrupt halt in February that year when he was arrested after being caught with, in the words of the *Northampton Chronicle & Echo*, 'a known prostitute in a partial state of undress'. When the 20-year-old appeared at Northampton Crown Court in April, he pleaded guilty to the charge of 'kerb crawling' — soliciting a prostitute — in the town. He was fined £200 and ordered to pay £50 in costs. He told the court: 'I've made a big mistake and it will never happen again.'

Sadly for him, Jaguar, like all prestigious brands whether in the automotive world or any other sphere, was extremely protective of its global image and reputation. Understandably, his new employer felt obliged to distance itself from any association with the young driver almost before it had started and he was dismissed from his role with immediate effect. A statement released by the racing team said: 'Mr Scheckter, who was sub-contracted to work for the team in the role of development driver, recently appeared in court and it is to matters concerning this appearance that the team and the Jaguar Racing board is left with no alternative but to terminate the relationship.'

Fortunately, the youngster was able to continue his career in single-seaters and moved to the United States, where he got into the Indy Racing League and became a regular competitor and recorded two race wins, at Michigan International Speedway in 2002 and Texas Motor Speedway in 2005.

He had come tantalisingly close to reaching the top echelons of the sport but his mistake one evening in Northampton cost him the opportunity of getting into Formula 1 and the possibility of emulating his father.

JODY SCHECKTER
Nice punch-up

Tomas Scheckter's illustrious father Jody had his own tangle with the law soon after his retirement from racing. Jody's Formula 1 career peaked when he joined Ferrari for the 1979 season, during which he took three wins on his way to becoming World Champion, appropriately wrapping up the title on the team's home ground at Monza. However, the following season with Ferrari was the worst of his career and at the end of it he decided to leave the sport at the age of just 30.

On 10th December 1980, only nine weeks after his last Grand Prix, he was involved in an altercation with another motorist not far from his home in Monaco when his Ferrari hit a car belonging to Jean-Pierre Risgalla in a traffic jam on La Promenade des Anglais in Nice. Both drivers got out of their vehicles and after an exchange of blows Risgalla needed hospital treatment for facial injuries while Scheckter spent the night in jail. The UPI news agency reported that when the case went to court the following month, Scheckter claimed that the accident had been caused by the actions of an overtaking cyclist and that the other motorist had struck the first blow. However, it was ruled that the former racing driver had carried out the assault 'with premeditation' and he was given a two-month suspended sentence and fined $2,222. He was able to keep his driving licence after his lawyer successfully argued that its loss would be 'unbearable for him'.

CHAPTER 49
NIGEL STEPNEY
'Spygate'

An embittered Ferrari employee's collusion with an old friend and ex-colleague at arch-rival McLaren led to the biggest and most public scandal in the history of Formula 1. 'Spygate' is the most blatant example of a team obtaining intellectual property and inside information about another team's design on a scale never seen before or since. It finished with McLaren being disqualified from the constructors' championship in 2007 and fined an unprecedented $100 million for being in possession of Ferrari's entire design dossier for its F2007 challenger.

Nigel Stepney made his first steps in motorsport when he joined Ralph Broad's Broadspeed racing team as an apprentice mechanic aged 17 working on Triumph Dolomite Sprints, Jaguar XJ12 coupés and Ford Capris competing in the European Touring Car Championship. When Broadspeed fell into financial difficulties in 1977, he joined the Shadow Formula 1 team at the age of 21 to start what was to be a lengthy career in Formula 1 that saw him move first to Lotus and then to Benetton.

In 1993, Stepney arrived at Scuderia Ferrari, where he became chief mechanic and later the race and test team technical manager. By the time team principal Jean Todt had assembled the triumvirate of Michael Schumacher, Rory Byrne and Ross Brawn — collectively the architects of the team's most dominant and successful era to date — Stepney had scaled the ranks and was in charge of the race mechanics. His passion for motorsport was backed by organisational skills and a tough work ethic that contributed a great deal to the team's record of reliability. He was able to instil structure and discipline that had previously been lacking in the chaos that was historically a feature of Ferrari's pit work. He built up a good working relationship with Brawn and became one of the technical director's most loyal and trusted lieutenants.

Although not part of the inner circle, Stepney held a key position within the group that helped the team capture five consecutive World Championships between 2000 and 2004 and was regarded as a major contributor, specifically when it came to the remarkable build quality of the cars and their excellent finishing record. Italy is a country where Ferrari is almost a religion in itself, with a following second only in importance to the Pope and the Vatican, so the British-born mechanic became a minor celebrity, at least in the environs of Ferrari's home town of Maranello. By 2006, he was also very highly paid and earning over £750,000 a year (including generous success bonuses), which reflected the importance of his role and the esteem in which he was held. However, at the end of that season, Schumacher decided to retire (temporarily) and Brawn judged that it would be an opportune time to recharge his own batteries and take a sabbatical.

Stepney naively believed that he was suitably qualified to take over as technical director, even though he was a skilled mechanic rather than a formally trained engineer. He had been one of three right-hand men to Brawn, the others being Mario Almondo and Aldo Costa, and it was Almondo who got the job. The Englishman was furious. He didn't believe that Almondo, who came from Ferrari's human resources department and had previously served as head of 'industrial development of racing', possessed sufficient technical knowledge to lead the team's overall car development and felt very strongly that he had been overlooked.

Angry and bitter, Stepney became an increasingly loose cannon. Ill-advisedly, he even went public with his grievances, telling *Autosport* magazine in February 2007: 'I'm looking at spending a year away from Ferrari. I'm not currently happy within the team. I really want to move forward with my career, and that's something that's not happening right now.'

In an act of pique, he asked to be given a factory-based job, saying that he felt his presence at races would be detrimental to the team's performance. In taking this stance, he compromised his position and in effect allowed himself to be moved sideways. It's possible that he thought his outburst might provoke his employer into dismissing him and that he might at least secure a favourable financial settlement, knowing how Alain Prost had been fired before the end of the 1991 season for daring to compare his car's handling to a truck. However, Ferrari didn't even comment on Stepney's lack of integrity and loyalty. Without the support and protection of Brawn as his mentor and ally, he simply made life more difficult for himself by alienating his peers. As he told *The Independent* newspaper: 'I began to feel like I was some sort of traitor. People became scared to talk to me... the situation was unbearable.'

In June 2007, just after the United States Grand Prix, the Formula 1 community was shocked to learn that Stepney was to be the subject of a criminal investigation for sabotage, the result of which led to his dismissal a few days later. This came only a few months after two other employees, Angelo Santini and Mauro Iacconi, had been caught passing aerodynamic information to the rival Toyota Formula 1 team. In Stepney's case, the barely credible accusation was that he had tried to contaminate the fuel system of Kimi Räikkönen's F2007 car ahead of the Monaco Grand Prix, causing Ferrari to make a formal complaint, with supporting documentation, to the Modena district attorney, who launched a criminal inquiry.

Closed-circuit television at the factory had apparently shown Stepney paying unusually close attention to the refuelling tank just before some suspicious white powder was discovered nearby. Police raided Stepney's home and discovered more powder that matched the residue found both in the apparatus and some of his trouser pockets. In his denial of all the allegations, Stepney claimed to have been the victim of a 'dirty-tricks campaign' by Ferrari in retaliation for his outspoken criticism of the company. However, only a few weeks later team principal Stefano Domenicali received a strange but concerning email from a photocopying shop in Surrey, which he knew to be McLaren territory, with information that led him and the company's senior management to realise that the discovery of powder might be the least of their concerns and that there was evidence of a far greater crime with much more serious ramifications.

As the rift between Ferrari and its employee widened, the situation became uglier. It was soon very clear that Stepney had not only stolen highly confidential data, including some of Ferrari's innermost secrets, but had also leaked it directly to Ferrari's long-standing rival, McLaren, which was in the process of dominating the Formula 1 season and had built up a healthy lead in the constructors' championship.

Mike Coughlan was McLaren's highly paid chief designer. A maverick, he had been at McLaren for five years and had known Stepney for over 20 as they had worked together at various stages at Lotus, Benetton and Ferrari. According to former McLaren and Ferrari designer John Barnard,

Nigel Stepney (left), pictured with Ross Brawn, became disaffected at Ferrari after believing he should have become Brawn's successor as technical director; embittered, he offered the design dossier for the Ferrari F2007 Formula 1 car to his friend Mike Coughlan at McLaren.

the pair, who had become close friends over the years on the road, enjoyed partying hard and were like-minded 'tough, durable characters having both been brought up in racing from their teens'. And it was to his ebullient friend that Stepney first reached out when he felt he had been betrayed by Ferrari.

During a phone call at the beginning of March 2007, Coughlan lent a sympathetic ear as Stepney expressed his frustration and reservations about Ferrari's new technical director. However, he was more interested when, in a succession of emails later that month, Stepney suggested that certain features of the Ferrari didn't comply with the FIA's technical regulations. Stepney made specific references to a spring-loaded device that moved the floor to improve aerodynamic performance once the car reached a certain speed and also to a rear-wing flap separator that he judged to be illegal. Not only was the Ferrari man offering inside information but he also had proof, as evidenced by drawings that he emailed to Coughlan.

Coughlan confided in McLaren's managing director, Jonathan Neale, who was sufficiently concerned to instruct the team's IT department to block any further emails between the pair. Coughlan then flew to Barcelona to meet Stepney, ostensibly, he claimed, to tell him to stop communicating with him. In fact, the meeting presented an ideal opportunity to solicit further inside information, this time in the form of diagrams for Ferrari's brake-balance assembly, and Stepney offered him a 780-page dossier of confidential Ferrari documents. In a subsequent affidavit leaked to the press, Coughlan stated: 'My engineering curiosity got the better of me, and I foolishly took the documents from him... I kept hold of the documents and took them home with me.' While it wasn't clear who else he may have shared them with, Coughlan briefly showed Neale some of the images that had illicitly fallen into his hands and was immediately told to destroy them. Unwisely, he chose not to.

Coughlan gave his wife Trudy the dossier and asked her to have the pages scanned onto a disc drive at a local photocopying shop. As they lived quite close to the state-of-the-art McLaren Technology Centre in Woking, Surrey, the shop was in the heart of McLaren country, but its manager happened to be an observant and passionate Ferrari fan and it didn't escape his notice that each page had the company's 'Prancing Horse' emblem in the corner. While he didn't know or recognise his customer, by the time she returned to collect the disc and papers the next day, he had searched her name online and discovered her husband's identity. Further searching produced contact details for Stefano Domenicali.

Police raided Stepney's home a second time. After analysing his laptop, investigators established that he had indeed printed out the 780-page dossier, which contained comprehensive technical documents for the design and build of Ferrari's 2007 challenger, including schematic drawings, technical reports, photographs and much more. The Modena district attorney's criminal inquiry widened.

Meanwhile, Coughlan had been suspended by McLaren and made a brief appearance at the High Court in London on 10th July. This was curtailed after he agreed to provide a sworn affidavit (sections of which were later seen by *The Guardian* newspaper) and to cooperate with Ferrari's investigations in return for which the company agreed to withdraw the application it had made against him to the district attorney in Modena.

As soon as lawyers were engaged, McLaren announced its own internal investigation and hired Kroll, a leading private security firm, to carry out an audit of its computer systems. Two instances were found of Coughlan receiving Ferrari information but the team was able to provide evidence suggesting that none of it went any further into the organisation. When McLaren appeared in front of the World Motor Sport Council on 26th

July, it was able to provide the necessary evidence to prove that none of the information taken from Ferrari was used by the team in the design of its own car. Consequently, the World Motor Sport Council took the pragmatic decision not to punish McLaren for the action of one rogue individual, although the team was found to have been in breach of the sporting code. Not surprisingly, this outcome provoked fury from Ferrari, whose only consolation lay in the fact that the FIA left the door open for further hearings to take place should new evidence come to light. Meanwhile, Todt vowed to appeal against the verdict.

That would probably have been the end of the matter between the two feuding teams but for the animosity that had been brewing all season between McLaren's intensely competitive drivers, Fernando Alonso and Lewis Hamilton, and that now got out of hand.

Alonso had joined the team at the start of 2007 as a double World Champion confidently expecting to rack up another title. Although it wasn't written into his contract, he had arrived with the reasonable expectation that he would be accorded the status of number one driver, which he felt his success and seniority demanded, especially as Hamilton was a novice in his first year of Formula 1. No one could have predicted that Alonso was now paired with a phenomenal talent, a man who would go on to become the most successful driver of all time by winning more Grands Prix than anyone else in history and breaking almost every other record too.

During a long, tense summer, the advantage swung back and forth between the two drivers but the Hungarian Grand Prix in August marked a flashpoint. A breakdown in communication during qualifying led to a strategic error by the team that left both drivers extremely unhappy and feeling that their chances of winning pole position had been compromised. Although Alonso had been marginally quicker than his team-mate, the FIA stewards decided that he had deliberately impeded Hamilton in the pit-lane, even though this incident had arisen because Hamilton hadn't stuck to team policy. They docked the Spaniard five places on the grid for thwarting his team-mate's chances of getting out before the end of the final session and potentially setting a faster time. This meant that Hamilton would now start on pole position for a race that he would go on to win, thereby extending his lead in the World Championship.

McLaren team principal Ron Dennis had previously experienced the challenges of managing intra-team disputes from the halcyon days when he had paired Alain Prost and Ayrton Senna almost 20 years earlier. This time he not only had to try to repair the toxic relationship between his two petulant superstars but also maintain the integrity of his team and the McLaren name in the wake of the recent accusations of espionage. This paled into insignificance when, in a row with Dennis on race morning about his treatment by the team, a highly charged and still aggrieved Alonso threatened to reveal to the FIA that Coughlan had in fact been passing information from the Ferrari documents to the team's Spanish test driver, Pedro de la Rosa, who in turn had shared some details with his compatriot.

As McLaren had been adamant that no one in its organisation other than Coughlan had had access to the documents, this bombshell suggested that detailed information had gone much deeper into the company and implied major deceit on the team's part. While Dennis refused to believe his driver and continued to maintain his team's innocence in the affair, he felt compelled — in an act of damage limitation that ultimately backfired on him — to report this development to FIA President Max Mosley. After demanding that the three McLaren drivers hand over any confidential Ferrari technical information they might have received, Mosley reopened the investigation based on the explosive new evidence.

After the Italian Grand Prix, in which McLaren soundly beat Ferrari on home ground, Jean Todt made it clear that Ferrari hadn't accepted the FIA's original verdict and that if McLaren were to be exonerated his team would move into the civil courts to pursue its claim that its rivals had benefited from its intellectual property. On the Thursday following Ferrari's defeat at Monza, lawyers and principals from both teams were called to a meeting at the FIA's Paris headquarters in Place de la Concorde. The FIA now had in its possession records of 288 text messages, 35 phone calls and 23 emails between Coughlan and Stepney, provided by the Italian police, together with a series of incriminating emails that included detailed dialogue between Coughlan and Stepney as well as between the designer and two of the drivers. Some of this email traffic was later divulged and one particularly damning message from de la Rosa to Alonso read as follows: 'All the information from Ferrari is very reliable. It comes from Nigel Stepney, their former chief mechanic — I don't know what post he holds now. He's the same person who told us in Australia that Kimi [Ferrari driver Kimi Räikkönen] was stopping in lap 18. He's very friendly with Mike Coughlan, our Chief Designer, and told him that.'

The information that de la Rosa had received from Coughlan and in turn passed on to Alonso included details of the Ferrari's weight distribution, braking system, type of gas used for tyre inflation, flexible

The 'Spygate' affair unravelled after McLaren chief designer Mike Coughlan unwisely asked his wife to have the Ferrari design dossier scanned in a local copying shop, where the eagle-eyed manager realised that something was amiss.

rear wing and pitstop strategy deployed at the first race in Australia. This wealth of new evidence led the FIA to draw fresh conclusions that confidential Ferrari information had in fact reached further into McLaren than previously realised, leaving no choice but to overturn the previous ruling. While it couldn't be proved that any of this information had been used to improve McLaren's car, the World Motor Sport Council took the view that the evidence given by de la Rosa showed that there had been no reluctance to use and test the Ferrari information for potential benefit. The FIA restated its view that Coughlin was a single rogue employee but this time judged that article 151(c) had been breached and that a penalty was the only course of action.

The intense rivalry between the Ferrari and McLaren teams has its roots as far back as 1976. That was a thrilling season that saw James Hunt narrowly win the World Championship from Niki Lauda and is mainly remembered for Lauda's heroic return to the track after receiving horrific burns in a fiery crash at the Nürburgring in Germany. Less widely recalled are two highly controversial protests by Ferrari that led to McLaren's disqualification from two race victories, although one was subsequently reinstated.

For many years, Formula 1 insiders — including the teams themselves — often quipped that FIA stood for 'Ferrari International Assistance' on the basis that the team's uniquely rich heritage ensures it retains an elevated level of political clout. Over the years there have been several examples of FIA bias in favour of Ferrari over various rivals, not just McLaren, that have dared to challenge the sport's oldest and most celebrated racing team.

With 'Spygate', however, the scandal had been slowly tearing the sport apart and soiling Formula 1's public image, so any action taken by the FIA needed to demonstrate the governing body's authority with clarity so that a line could be drawn under the sorry affair. Consequently, any punishment was likely to be extremely severe in order to reflect the long-term damage that had been inflicted on the sport.

McLaren's worst fears were realised on 13th September 2007 when Max Mosley delivered the verdict of the reconvened hearing. The team was stripped of all points for the season and disqualified from the constructors' championship, which it had been leading, although the drivers were allowed to retain their championship points in return for their cooperation. Furthermore, McLaren was handed a fine of $100 million, a staggeringly large and unprecedented penalty that remains the biggest ever in the history of all sport. Finally, and humiliatingly, there was a ruling that a technical delegation would be dispatched to inspect McLaren's 2008 challenger in order to ascertain whether any Ferrari information had been incorporated into its design and manufacture.

Ron Dennis was unbowed in stating that the penalty was unjust: 'We have never denied that the information from Ferrari was in the personal possession of one of our employees but was this information used by McLaren? This has not been proven.' While the World Motor Sport Council admitted that it had no firm evidence that McLaren had used the information, it felt that Coughlan hadn't needed to copy a complete Ferrari design for his employers to have benefited from the knowledge he had gained illegally. Despite Formula 1 supremo Bernie Ecclestone asserting that 'Everyone cheats in Formula 1… the trick is not to get caught', Mosley was determined to clean up that element of the sport and he justified the magnitude of the fine by saying that 'the sum of money is less than the difference between McLaren's budget and those of teams like Williams or

Renault so it's a very minor punishment. All we're doing is bringing his [Ron Dennis's] budget down to the level of some of the other top teams'. Mosley went on to suggest that McLaren was extremely lucky not to have been suspended from the 2008 World Championship as well.

Mosley's lack of sympathy for Dennis was shared by Ecclestone, who made a typically facetious joke in stating that the magnitude of the fine was based on '$5 million for the actual offence and $95 million for Ron being a twat'. Over the years, the relationship between Mosley and Dennis had certainly been frosty but the FIA President was quick to dispel any suggestion of a personal vendetta against the McLaren boss, whose achievements in rising from humble mechanic to team owner he grudgingly admired. In an unconvincing display of reconciliation, the two men posed for a staged photo in which they both looked extremely uncomfortable shaking hands.

Despite being excluded from the constructors' championship, McLaren was at least able to take some solace from the high likelihood of being able to salvage some honour from its tumultuous year. When the FIA delivered its punishment, the McLaren drivers headed the standings, with Hamilton two points ahead of Alonso, and between them were the strong favourites to win the drivers' title. Come the last race, in Brazil, they were still at the top of the table, now with Hamilton ahead by four points. However, fate delivered a cruel blow: Hamilton's car developed gearbox problems, which dropped him below the crucial fifth place that would have guaranteed him the title, while Alonso could only manage third place, which wasn't enough for him to claim the crown either. The outsider, Ferrari's Kimi Räikkönen, won the race and with it the World Championship by a single point from the warring McLaren team-mates who were tied in second place.

This outcome was inevitably seen by Ferrari as revenge and poetic justice. Ferrari president Luca di Montezemolo even dedicated the success to 'our fans who believe in the fairness of sport' and referred to the 'English gentleman' — the original whistle-blower at the photocopying shop in McLaren's back yard — who had recognised the stolen documents. 'Without him,' said Montezemolo, 'it would have never been possible to shine the light onto one of the worst pages in the history of motorsport.'

Under persistent pressure from forces within Formula 1, Martin Whitmarsh, Chief Operating Officer at McLaren, issued an apology for the team's role in the scandal in a letter dated 5th December. In it he expressed embarrassment that some information from the secret Ferrari documents handed to McLaren's disgraced chief designer had been distributed more widely through the team than originally thought. Two days later, incidentally, the World Motor Sport Council declared that Renault was guilty of having McLaren intellectual property in its possession but in this case chose not to issue any penalty.

Mike Coughlan received a substantial personal fine as did several other McLaren employees. He was also banned by the FIA from taking part in Formula 1 for two years after which he returned for a spell as technical director at Williams in 2011 following a public expression of remorse for his role in the scandal. Keen to put previous events behind him, he stated: 'I'd like to take this opportunity to apologise to everyone affected by my conduct, in particular the people at McLaren and Ferrari and the teams' fans. I sincerely regret my actions and I fully accepted the penalty given to me by the FIA. I can only hope I can earn back everyone's respect. It was life-changing because it made me reflect upon myself and my actions. All I can do now is work hard and try to earn my place back in F1.'

Nigel Stepney continued to protest his innocence, insisting that the legitimate reason to have the papers in his possession was because he needed them for his work in Ferrari's racing simulator. He also claimed that after the discovery of the papers and the powder, he had been spied upon and harassed, and even added that he and family members had been put in danger with 'high-speed [car] chases' involved. He maintained that Ferrari was trying to discredit him because he knew all of the company's secrets. Specifically, he stated: 'Ferrari is terrified that what I have in my mind is valuable. I guess I know where the bodies are buried from the last 10 years, and there were a lot of controversies at that time.'

After Stepney falsely claimed in a conference call with British journalists that he had no idea how Coughlan got hold of the papers, anything else he said subsequently was treated with disbelief. He was convicted in Italy of sabotage, industrial espionage and sporting fraud in 2010 and sentenced to 20 months in prison, although he didn't serve any time behind bars.

An autobiography, imaginatively entitled *Red Mist*, planned to encompass his entire career as well as shed light on his involvement in the spying affair that marred the sport, but publication was abandoned only days after the pre-launch announcement in October 2007. It was said that pressure had been brought to bear by an 'unnamed party' although Ferrari was quick to make it clear that it wasn't involved.

Although Nigel Stepney never worked in Formula 1 again, he did return to motorsport and helped Daventry-based JRM Racing win the 2011 FIA GT1 World Championship with its Nissan cars.

In the early hours of the morning of 2nd May 2014, he died in a road traffic accident having apparently thrown himself in front of an articulated goods lorry on the London-bound carriageway of the M20 motorway in Kent. He had been driving home from Belgium to Colchester, Essex when he parked his silver VW van on the hard shoulder, switched off its lights, got out and locked the doors. The Dutch lorry driver said: 'All of a sudden I saw the figure of a person dive out from the left. His arm was stretched out above his head. It was almost as if he'd been crouching down in front of the van and thrown himself into the path of my vehicle.' The police report confirmed the HGV was being driven within the 56mph speed limit and said damage to the front of the lorry showed Stepney was 'not standing upright' when he was hit and was 'moving from left to right'. He was killed instantly but despite the chilling evidence that suggested he had committed suicide, the coroner said she couldn't be certain he had intended to take his own life and recorded an open verdict.

This led to inevitable conspiracy theories as to whether he had jumped or been 'pushed'. As the inquest had heard, the 56-year-old had asked a friend, Karen Day, to witness the signing of some documents but when she met him she had been shocked to find he actually wanted her to be the trustee of two life-insurance policies that he had recently changed. She had signed the papers on 29th April, only three days before his death, which suggests that foul play was unlikely, even if it couldn't be ruled out.

BRETT STEVENS

Dragging the sport into disrepute

A three-time national champion, Brett Stevens was for many years one of Australia's most decorated and top drag racers and an iconic figure who had a remarkable career in the sport. As such he was well-practised at taking chances but it was the risks the much-celebrated former star took when away from the track that led to his downfall.

The rise of Brett Stevens from apprentice mechanic to the pinnacle of drag racing, a largely blue-collar branch of motorsport, was legendary. He became arguably its biggest name by uniquely winning three ANDRA (Australian National Drag Racing Association) titles in completely different categories over the course of an 18-year career that started in 1990 after he travelled to the US and returned home with his first Nitro Harley Top Fuel motorcycle bought from Jim McClure. The Jack Daniel's whiskey brand began giving him financial support in 1993 and remained with him until the end of his career 15 years later.

The 2004 Top Doorslammer Championship was the first title Stevens won. Top Doorslammer specifies full-bodied cars with shapes typically based on Australian or US front-engined production coupés, saloons, estate cars and even 'utes' (utility vehicles). As the name suggests, these fearsome-looking and highly modified machines must retain operational doors. The class specifies the use of 8.5-litre V8 engines that are supercharged and fuelled by methanol to produce immense power, measured in thousands of bhp rather than mere hundreds, and propelling them down quarter-mile drag strips in little more than the blink of an eye.

Stevens soon showed his great versatility by winning two other championships in different disciplines, namely Top Bike (2005) and Top Alcohol (2008), the latter for so-called 'Funny Cars'. This made him the first person ever to win a hat-trick of Group One National championship titles in three separate categories. In summing up these achievements, Jon Van Daal wrote in his book *The Boss: The Brett Stevens Story*: 'This would be akin to Craig Lowndes winning a race in his V8 Supercar and then climbing into an Indy Champ Car and winning with that and then turning around and climbing on a MotoGP bike to go and out win again.'

Some of Stevens's sensational performances led to several world and national track records and one of his many achievements was to become the fastest Top Doorslammer driver in history with a speed of 252.66mph (406.62kph) at the end of the quarter mile. In September 2008 he bettered even that in qualifying for the Winternationals at the Willowbank Raceway in Queensland when he officially reset the ANDRA speed record in his Funny Car at 260.27mph (418.86kph). This was in front of a near-capacity crowd for the largest drag racing event outside North America.

In 29 national championships contested during an illustrious career, Stevens never finished outside the top six, scoring three titles, eight runner-up positions, seven third places, six fourths, three fifths and two sixths. He also made an incredible 70 final-round appearances.

Not only did Stevens compete himself with three vastly different machines but at the same time he also managed his drag racing team, which was the biggest and most dominant in the sport and numbered as many as 40 personnel running 10 Group One machines. This included five drivers and riders who competed in four separate ANDRA classes, most of which carried heavily promoted allegiance to Jack Daniel's together with a portfolio of other backers. One of the team drivers was his wife Kath who at the age of 27 became the first woman to compete in the Top Doorslammer series and achieved a speed of 241.54mph (388.72kph). A former truck driver who had competed and won in minor rallying events, she had met her future husband as a fan when he signed a poster for her at a racetrack.

Stevens's on-track presence guaranteed him almost cult-like status and he was incredibly popular with race fans. He excelled in playing to the crowd and almost single-handedly changed the face of the sport with new levels of showmanship and his professionalism off the track. He would regularly demonstrate a Falcon 'ute' that produced 2,500bhp, the equivalent of three Indy Champ Cars or four V8 Supercars. He had had this spectacular machine built specifically to lay down rubber on the start line and create wreaths of tyre smoke simply to please the fans.

By 2008, Stevens seemed to be at the top of his game both on and off the track. In addition to his competition commitments, he also had a contract for a reality TV show and juggled an A$14 million property folio and a business empire with interests in boat charters, cement haulage, earth moving, manufacture of car parts and even a tattoo shop. However, in December that year the drag-racing world was shocked when he announced that he was hanging up his helmet and retiring with immediate effect. For someone who was justifiably proud of all that he had achieved with such passion and enthusiasm, it was evidently a very difficult decision.

The 44-year-old's bombshell initially seemed to be a pragmatic move to depart from the sport before age caught up with him and perhaps blunted his skills. However, the content of his press release hinted at something more ominous: 'Over many years I have also been the subject of many malicious and false rumours and innuendo, including personal attacks and threats on myself, my family, employees and sponsors which are taking an unprecedented toll on both my personal and professional wellbeing.'

Things soon became clearer. By the time of his last national championship in 2008, his business interests were struggling. With debts mounting, together with accumulated overdue tax demands, he was running into severe cash-flow problems.

Stevens had got to know a Serbian-born man whom he had met when competing at Willowbank Raceway. This individual, a key figure in Sydney's criminal underworld, loaned him A$200,000 to pay the Australian tax authorities — but there were strings attached. In taking up this solution to his financial difficulties, Stevens became a key part of a substantial drugs operation.

His involvement led to his arrest in February 2009, along with 120 others, as part of a two-year police investigation called 'Farus', which tracked several syndicates linked to Queensland's drugs scene. He deliberately tried to distance himself from illicit activities, speaking in code on the phone and purposely only meeting associates in public, knowing that he was under police surveillance. His arrest followed an electronic surveillance operation involving phone intercepts and video footage, and detectives collated 800 recorded interactions that inextricably linked Stevens to the ring. For nearly two years, he was involved in the production and sale of as many as 100,000

Brett Stevens, pictured in his 'Doorslammer', was one of Australia's top drag-racing stars but fell from grace when convicted of making and trafficking vast quantities of Ecstasy tablets.

ecstasy pills every week as the mastermind behind a pill-pressing operation in a series of rented houses across Brisbane.

While on bail, Stevens desperately tried to revive his business career, which included a quarry venture under the name 'Defwom', an acronym for 'Don't Ever Fuck With Our Money'. This failed after a dispute with the landowner, as did his other attempts at careers in mining and transport. His star later waned even further to the point where he was being employed as a demolition worker. By the time he eventually appeared in court, in November 2015, police had seized more than A$6 million worth of property including 11 of his prized dragsters, comprising six cars and five motorcycles.

Despite incontrovertible evidence to the contrary, Stevens maintained his innocence to the end and even resorted to social media to solicit contributions to his legal fees when he ran out of money. How much he actually made from ecstasy pills is unclear but an associate, despite having received threats from Stevens, claimed in his own testimony to have cleared A$600,000 in just six months at a cut of 50 cents per pill, and Justice Peter Lyons decided that Stevens's margin would have been at least as much. Another indication of the magnitude of his trading was the sizeable quantities of cash seized by police from his associates and employees, ranging from A$99,000 to

EVAN KNOLL
Fuelled by greed

In 1995 Evan Knoll founded Torco Racing Fuels in Decatur, Illinois to supply high-quality fuel and additives for use in motorsport, particularly drag racing. An avid fan of this branch of the sport, he became a significant sponsor and by 2005 was estimated to have either owned or helped fund as many as 50 different teams and to have spent $40 million on this in a 24-month period.

Knoll was so highly respected that in 2007 the multi-national accountancy firm Ernst & Young even presented him with an 'Entrepreneur of the Year' award in the 'Automotive & Transportation' category, recognising 'outstanding business owners who are building and leading dynamic enterprises'. That same year, however, numerous teams began to find their contracted sponsorship payments drying up as Knoll and his company ran into trouble with the Inland Revenue Service.

In the court proceedings that followed, the IRS proved that for ten years Knoll had falsely claimed that the vast quantities of fuel he bought from distributors had been sold on as racing fuel, which was tax exempt, and by this means he had been able to fraudulently claim tax rebates at 18.3 cents per gallon. This had added up to a total of $86.7 million that he had used as collateral to secure loans of a further $13 million from banks.

In July 2012 he pleaded guilty to eight charges of making false claims against the government and one count of bank fraud, and he took full responsibility for lying to his employees, his lawyers and accountants and, of course, the government. He was duly sentenced by US District Court Judge Robert J. Jonker to 14 years in prison followed by five years of supervised release and ordered to pay restitution of $100 million to the US Treasury and the banks. While the authorities had taken the precaution of seizing his assets, which included a Learjet and several homes, they refused to be drawn on exactly how much of the debt would ever be recovered.

His largesse had unsurprisingly made him extremely popular within the racing community although they perhaps didn't fully comprehend that, as taxpayers, he had actually been stealing from them.

A\$200,000. The judge also noted evidence by a police forensic accountant that Stevens had A\$1.2 million in unexplained income.

After a six-week hearing at Brisbane's Supreme Court, the jury found the former drag racer guilty of producing and trafficking (but not supplying) MDMA, also known as ecstasy, between 2007 and 2009. No doubt mindful of his high-profile and minor celebrity status, as well as his unwillingness to cooperate, the judge showed no mercy and sentenced him to a hefty 13 years in jail. He was also convicted of a serious violent offence, meaning that he would have to serve a minimum of 10 years of his sentence before being eligible for parole.

There was one more element in Stevens's fall from grace. Cementing his place in drag racing history, he had been awarded the Australian Sports Medal for his contribution to motorsport and made an inaugural inductee into the Australian Motorcycle Hall of Fame. To the fury of his many fans, who didn't feel that his off-track activities had any bearing on his successes on it, ANDRA, the governing body, controversially and unanimously voted that his achievements would no longer be recognised and that his name and titles would be erased from the record books.

CHAPTER 51
SULAIMAN AL-KEHAIMI
The Fake Sheikh

Beirut-born Sulaiman Al-Kehaimi was the son
of a former Saudi Arabian ambassador who had
a big ego and delusions of grandeur. He wanted
to be known as a prince and fêted like one, so he
masqueraded as a member of the Saudi royal
family and duped a string of celebrities and
business partners into believing he was fabulously
wealthy. In fact he was just an extremely
accomplished confidence trickster.

Business F1 magazine related that one of Sulaiman Al-Kehaimi's earlier
failed business ventures involved attracting investment from Crown
Prince Khalid of Saudi Arabia that he used to buy an elderly Boeing 707
and then customised it. While using the aircraft, which he claimed to own,
he posed as a colonel in the Saudi Arabian air force in order to get quicker
flight clearance. He offered lifts free of charge to a succession of people he
considered to be important and wealthy, including pop stars and Middle
Eastern royalty, and once they were temporarily captive on the aircraft he
would pitch deals to them. One tactic appeared to be to ensnare targets
by offering the in-flight services of call girls as an incentive to invest with
him but this soon backfired because Crown Prince Khalid learned of it
and terminated the arrangement. No deals were ever done and the aircraft
was impounded in 1996 at Stansted airport after wages and fuel bills had
gone unpaid.

Attracted by the glamour of Hollywood, he posed as a film producer
looking to finance the next blockbuster film. He had met the singer Cher

Among his various attempted cons, one of the most audacious perpetrated by
Sulaiman Al-Kehaimi involved the Tyrrell Formula 1 team and the singer Cher.
The 'Fake Sheikh' is pictured in 1995 with Ukyo Katayama in his Tyrrell 023.

in 1995 at a restaurant there and she was deceived by his apparent wealth
and made to believe that he would finance a film project of hers. He told
her that he was a big wheel in Formula 1 and, choosing the best backdrop
for the image he was trying to create, took her to the Monaco Grand Prix
in 1996. Ken Tyrrell's beleaguered outfit was desperately short of funds and
he targeted the long-established and very successful team owner as the one
who might be most open to his approach as a potential future sponsor.

He told two of Tyrrell's senior staff, Bob Tyrrell and Rupert Manwaring,
that he would be bringing his 'girlfriend' Cher to the race and would be
hosting a post-race 50th birthday party for her with 500 guests at 'his'
$30 million château in Cap d'Ail. After he duly arrived in the paddock
with the celebrity on his arm, the team took the bait and over the course of
the weekend Al-Kehaimi and his associates announced a deal to buy a 51
per cent majority stake in the ailing team for $12 million. To celebrate, he
invited members of the team to join him and Cher at the party. However,
the château wasn't his and he wasn't even renting it. According to *Business*

F1, he had viewed it a few weeks previously with an estate agent who was marketing it for sale. During the viewing, an associate had managed to take the keys to the property to a locksmith and quickly had copies cut before returning the keys to the house. This accomplice had also memorised the gate entry and alarm codes while watching the agent tap them in.

Video footage of the party showed assembled guests referring to the host as 'your Excellency' and 'the Sheikh'. At the lavish event, Al-Kehaimi's party piece was to give the embarrassed Cher her 'birthday present', the keys to a lime-green Lamborghini Diablo that was parked outside the château wrapped in a huge red ribbon. The car wasn't his either as he had simply borrowed it for a test drive from a local dealer. Although he promised to have it shipped back to America for Cher, she never saw it again.

Al-Kehaimi was arrested in 1998 after allegedly trying to fraudulently obtain money from a woman by telling her he could influence the release of her brother, who had been in jail for 10 years in Dubai without trial, if she paid him sums totalling £83,700. He was found living in a cheap rented semi-detached house in Henley-on-Thames, not far from London, and charged with six counts of theft and deception totalling $500,000 between November 1995 and March 1997. It was alleged that he had woven a web of lies to perpetrate the frauds, the charges including one of attempting to obtain property by deception and another of defrauding the Tyrrell team of $100,000 in expenses. Mr Brown, prosecuting, told Oxford Crown Court in November 1999: 'He was extremely convincing and pretended to be a man of immense wealth' but also 'All that was pretence, fantasy, a fairy story'. The prosecutor described Al-Kehaimi as 'a prince among confidence tricksters'.

The virtually penniless 39-year-old maintained that the money given to him was for legitimate business transactions and that he had every intention of paying back his creditors. Astonishingly, the jury believed him and he was cleared of five charges while the judge directed that he be acquitted of the sixth.

ADRIAN SUTIL

Over the limit

A contemporary of future multiple
World Champion Lewis Hamilton
and also his Formula 3 team-mate
one year, Adrian Sutil enjoyed a
promising career in Formula 1
until it fizzled out after a well-
publicised altercation with a team
owner in a nightclub that led to
his conviction for assault.

Born in Gräfelfing near Munich on 11th January 1983, Adrian Sutil is the son of a German mother and a Uruguayan father who was a concert violinist. Nurtured by his father's passion for music, the boy spent his formative years engrossed in the study of the piano but by the time he had reached the age of 14 his interests lay elsewhere and he started racing karts. He progressed into cars and dominated the Swiss Formula Ford Championship in 2002 by winning all 10 races from pole position and also scored five wins in the Formula Masters Austria series. He graduated to the German Formula BMW Championship the following year and then moved on to the Formula 3 Euroseries in 2004 driving for Team Kolles.

In his second season in the Formula 3 Euroseries, he partnered Lewis Hamilton in the ASM squad. While Hamilton romped to the title with 15 wins in 20 races, Sutil managed two wins and seven second places to finish runner-up in the standings. In 2006, he travelled east to race for the TOM'S team in the All-Japan Formula 3 Championship with a Toyota-powered Dallara in which he won five races and the title.

By now Formula 1 had beckoned thanks to his mentor Colin Kolles, team manager at Midland F1, who took him on as test driver, a role that led to three appearances in Friday practice sessions during 2006. When the team evolved into Spyker in 2007, Sutil became a regular driver and scored a best result of eighth place. After another change of identity in 2008, the team became Force India and employed Sutil for four more seasons. In all that time, his stand-out performance was the 2009 Italian Grand Prix at Monza, where he started from the front row next to Hamilton on pole position and finished the race in fourth place. He never managed to achieve a podium finish.

On 17th April 2011, Sutil attended a private party hosted by the McLaren team at the M1NT nightclub in Shanghai to celebrate his friend Lewis Hamilton's victory in the Chinese Grand Prix. One of the other guests was Eric Lux, chief executive of Genii Capital, which was part-owner of the Lotus Renault GP team. During the evening, Lux accused Sutil of striking him in the neck with a broken champagne glass although the 28-year-old immediately apologised and said it was an accident.

Vijay Mallya, Sutil's boss at Force India, initially supported his driver by refusing to suspend or punish him unless a further investigation was carried out, but when this duly occurred Lux, whose wound had required 24 stitches, pressed charges and filed a criminal complaint for physical assault and grievous bodily harm. German prosecutors were put in charge of the investigation and on 13th January 2012 it was decided Sutil would have to stand trial. In Munich District Court, the driver admitted 'unintentionally injuring' Lux. As reported by Fox News, Sutil told the court: 'He threatened me with "destroying" me and ensuring that I go to prison for a long time.'

When convicted later that month, Sutil received an 18-month suspended prison sentence and a fine of €200,000 (£166,000) that had to be donated to a charity 'of the court's choosing'. His lawyers had hoped that Hamilton would act as a defence witness in the trial but the World Champion declined to do so, leading to unjustified and harsh words from both Sutil and his father. The previously close relationship between the former Formula 3 team-mates never recovered.

Despite bearing a sizeable scar on his neck, Lux subsequently told *Bild* newspaper that he forgave Sutil and added: 'I would even be happy for him if he came back to race and had a job to do. For me, everything is past; I don't have emotions about it anymore. Whether the penalty was too much

EDDIE IRVINE
A racy life

Like Adrian Sutil, Eddie Irvine found himself in trouble after an incident in a nightclub, although in Irvine's case it occurred long after he had hung up his helmet.

Known for his jet-setting lifestyle almost as much as his skill on track, Irvine had a successful Formula 1 career. Two full seasons with Jordan were followed by four years at Ferrari, where he was content to play well-paid second fiddle to Michael Schumacher. His first win, in Australia in 1999, was the prelude for his best season in which he took on the mantle of team leader after Schumacher broke a leg and won another three races on his way to a career-best second place in the World Championship. After three fruitless years at Jaguar, he retired in 2002.

Six years later Irvine came to blows in a Milan nightclub with the playboy son of the city's former mayor in a dispute over the man's ex-girlfriend. In a case that dragged on for over three years, each of the two parties reported the other to the authorities and pressed charges for assault and battery, both accusing the other of using a glass as a weapon. The BBC reported that both were found guilty of 'mutual injury' and sentenced to six months in jail although neither man served any time behind bars due to the vagaries of Italy's legal system. The irony of the situation wasn't lost on fans who recalled Irvine's début with Jordan at the 1993 Japanese Grand Prix when Ayrton Senna swung a few punches at him for showing a lack of respect by having the temerity to unlap himself.

This wasn't Irvine's first brush with the law. Like fellow former Jordan Formula 1 driver, Bertrand Gachot (see Chapter 22), he had fallen foul of police on roads surrounding London's Hyde Park, for exceeding the speed limit on a scooter in 2003 without either a valid driving licence or insurance. Once the facts had been established by a court hearing in his absence, he was summoned to appear at Bow Street Court but failed to turn up, prompting a warrant for his arrest. He claimed that the court summons had been delivered to one of his homes in Northern Ireland that he hadn't visited for more than a year and told a newspaper that the first he knew of the matter was when he saw the story on TV.

or not enough is not up to me, but if it had been one centimetre different, he would be spending the next 20 years in prison in China.'

Prior to the court hearing, Mallya decided to drop Sutil from the Force India team for the 2012 season but gave him another chance in 2013, a season that brought a best result of fifth place in Monaco. Sutil had one more year in Formula with Sauber in 2014 but results were hopeless and his driving career fizzled out. Since then, he has maintained strong automotive interests and become a prolific collector of high-powered supercars.

CALISTO TANZI

Milking the cash cow

An Italian 'Big Cheese', he plunged his family's dairy empire into insolvency through dishonest business practices after bringing it to international recognition with long-time and high-profile sponsorship of Niki Lauda and the Brabham team in Formula 1. It all ended with a lengthy prison sentence but he didn't live long enough to serve it.

For years, the name Parmalat — an Italian dairy business — was synonymous with the Brabham Formula 1 team. The company's association was a huge success and its branding prominently adorned the flanks of a range of innovative and invariably beautiful racing cars created by South African designer Gordon Murray and his British colleague David North at the team's base in Chessington, Surrey. Parmalat also had a long-standing association with Niki Lauda that began in 1976, when he was the reigning World Champion, and continued long after his retirement from the sport.

A year before its arrival in Formula 1, in 1975, Parmalat had dabbled in sports sponsorship by backing the World Cup downhill skiing event in Val Gardena, after which Lauda introduced the company to motor racing. Having sealed his first World Championship title with Ferrari in fine style in front of the *tifosi* at Monza in September 1975, Lauda capitalised on his success and increased market value the following year by adding Parmalat to his portfolio of personal backers who were keen to benefit from

Calisto Tanzi developed Parmalat from a small grocery business into
a multi-national purveyor of dairy products but despite his business
success he still felt the need to conduct fraud on a massive scale.

his rapidly growing fame, although the Italian company could never have anticipated quite how quickly its investment would be repaid or how long the arrangement would last.

In 1976, Lauda was on target for a second consecutive World Championship title until the awful accident at the Nürburgring during the German Grand Prix that left his life hanging in the balance with devastating burns and severe lung damage from inhalation of smoke and toxins. His return to racing just six weeks after being administered the last rites by a priest is the bravest comeback ever achieved by any sportsman and is quite rightly a famous and memorable story. When he reappeared at Monza for the Italian Grand Prix, with scarred scalp and burned ear, he was the focus of world-wide media attention and innumerable photos were published showing him in his bright red race suit with a massive Parmalat logo across his chest. In 1977, when Lauda became World Champion again with Ferrari, his distinctive red helmet carried a prominent Parmalat motif on each side, and the following year he took to wearing a Parmalat-branded baseball cap. As he chose never to have cosmetic surgery, his disfigured appearance always made him a magnet for photographers and for the next

A big part of Parmalat's marketing visibility derived from its fruitful partnership with the Brabham Formula 1 team from 1978 to 1984, a period that saw Nelson Piquet deliver two World Championship titles.

25 years that trademark cap was almost always on his head.

Disenchanted with Ferrari, Lauda transferred to Bernie Ecclestone's Brabham team for the 1978 season, lured by the encouraging prospect of a new Murray-designed car powered by an Alfa Romeo flat-12 engine. Moving with him, Parmalat made a significantly larger funding commitment and replaced Martini as the team's title sponsor. The first season of the partnership yielded only two wins for Lauda, both rather contentious, while the second — now with a troublesome new Alfa Romeo V12 engine — was even less successful, prompting him to lose interest and announce his immediate retirement midway through practice for the Canadian Grand Prix, saying that he was tired of 'the silliness of driving around in circles'.

Lauda's timing was perhaps ill-judged. That race saw Brabham revert to Ford Cosworth V8 engines, which quickly brought improved reliability and gradually returned the team to success. Nelson Piquet, Brabham's young Brazilian driver, won his first World Championship title in Parmalat colours in 1981 and followed up with a second one in 1983, this time powered by a BMW turbo engine. Although the Italian dairy company terminated its sponsorship of Brabham at the end of 1984, it continued its interest in Formula 1 through Lauda, who had returned to the sport with McLaren, and also through associations with a string of lesser teams via its Brazilian subsidiary's backing of Pedro Diniz, the son of a national supermarket magnate who was Parmalat's biggest global customer. Over the course of 25 years it was estimated that the company spent $200 million sponsoring cars, teams and drivers.

For several decades Parmalat was one of the great business success stories of modern Italy. Its founder, Calisto Tanzi, was a 22-year-old university student when his father, who owned a grocer's shop in the village of Collecchio, near Parma, died suddenly in 1961. As the eldest son, Calisto immediately dropped out of college to look after his family's affairs. The grocery business that he inherited specialised in selling Parma ham and making tomato purée but he decided to diversify into dairy products and constructed a small pasteurising plant in the town. He named the enlarged business Parmalat. Concentrating at first on producing long-life milk by means of ultra-high-temperature (UHT) processing, the company saw rapid growth, helped by an active advertising campaign. When Parmalat expanded into cheese and desserts, sales exploded and the company quickly moved into international markets. Although retaining the values of an Italian family firm, Tanzi succeeded in transforming Parmalat into a modern and aggressively expansive dairy business.

The Italian economy during the 1970s and 1980s proliferated with family companies, more than anywhere else in Western Europe, but for years Tanzi managed the seemingly impossible by attracting external financing without surrendering any control of what continued to be a private company. In 1990, Parmalat's profile soared even higher as the food giant became publicly listed when it was floated on the Milan stock exchange. This helped it to borrow more money with which to fund acquisitions throughout the Americas over the next decade but even then the Tanzi family still retained majority control of their multinational business.

However, profits were hit hard at the turn of the new millennium by sharp economic downturns in many of the Latin American markets where Parmalat had indulged its buying spree. With huge bank borrowings, which amounted to eight times more than the lending declared in the company's accounts, Parmalat became heavily exposed and problems were compounded by the impending bankruptcy of the family travel company, Parmatour, managed by Tanzi's daughter Francesca. To ensure that creditors were prepared to continue lending money, Tanzi began to systematically falsify Parmalat's financial statements.

He ordered two of the firm's chief financial officers to create a complex web of 200 subsidiary companies and to open bank accounts based in offshore tax havens, designed to create the illusion of prosperity and the impression that they were holding billions of euros in credits from other Parmalat markets. However, many of the accounts that showed seemingly healthy credit balances were non-existent and the subsidiaries, by using sophisticated financial derivatives, were able to exaggerate their assets and conceal the increasing mountain of debt.

Alarm bells first rang in early 2003 when the company, which now employed 36,000 people in 30 countries, announced that it was unexpectedly selling €300 million worth of bonds to raise cash. Concerns escalated when auditors questioned some of Parmalat's transactions and within weeks Tanzi was forced to resign as chief executive. When investigating authorities discovered records on his computer showing €8 billion of hidden transactions, he was arrested.

Soon afterwards, Parmalat was unable to meet a €150 million bond payment, despite supposedly being awash with cash, so the Italian government moved quickly to declare the company insolvent and it was put into administration in December 2003. Until that point, the conglomerate had been valued at €3.7 billion and claimed to be generating €8 billion in annual revenue but the true financial position was a gaping hole of €14 billion in the company's accounts. Some of the hardest-hit victims of the collapse were more than 135,000 small investors, including company employees and pensioners, who lost their life savings after buying bonds in the company believing them to be a safe investment.

In 2008, Calisto Tanzi was sentenced to 18 years in prison for his part in what the US Securities and Exchange Commission described as 'one of the largest and most brazen corporate frauds in history'. Although he appealed against the verdict, it was upheld in 2010 and a year later he was sentenced to a further nine years for the bankruptcy of Parmatour, which he had propped up by illicitly siphoning €500 million from Parmalat. He had committed fraud on an industrial scale and was found guilty of embezzlement of €800 million.

To add insult to injury, Italian police found a stash of paintings secreted in three Parma apartments belonging to Tanzi. Estimated to be worth €120 million, the paintings had been bought with funds siphoned off from Parmalat and among them were works by some of the world's most famous artists, including Van Gogh, Picasso, Monet, Matisse, Cézanne and Degas. A man of wide-ranging interests, Tanzi was regarded as the 'King of Parma' who had been a popular benefactor for many local interests. He had bought the under-performing football team, Parma, and invested enough money to ensure its promotion into Serie A, Italy's premier league, with many successes that included winning the UEFA Cup. He promoted the city's Verdi Festival, in honour of the region's famous composer. As a devout Catholic, he paid for the uncovering and restoration of frescoes in the city's cathedral. His fall from grace was completed with the final and ultimate humiliation of being stripped of two honours bestowed upon him, *Cavaliere del Lavoro* ('Knight of Labour') and *Cavaliere di Gran Croce Ordine al Merito della Repubblica Italiana* ('Knight Grand Cross of the Order of Merit of the Italian Republic'). He went to prison briefly but was allowed to serve out his sentence under house arrest at his villa outside Parma where he died of pneumonia aged 83 on New Year's Day in 2022.

For Formula 1 fans of a certain age and oblivious to the scandal, however, Tanzi's creation of Parmalat will remain inextricably linked with the sleek World Championship-winning Brabhams driven by Nelson Piquet and the iconic bright red baseball cap worn for so many years by Niki Lauda.

LORD ALEXANDER HESKETH
A sour taste

An intriguing adjunct to the Parmalat story emerged in 2021 from Lord Alexander Hesketh when speaking about his eponymous and entirely self-funded Formula 1 team. Hesketh revealed that he had been in negotiation with the dairy products conglomerate to become his team's title sponsor in 1975 with the offer of £1.5 million on the understanding that one of the drivers had to be Italian. However, in an early attempt at corporate embezzlement, it transpired that the actual sum received would only be £750,000 because the company representatives insisted that the balance be paid back directly to the 'shareholders' — the Tanzi family.

CHAPTER 54
DAVID THIEME
Essex man

David Thieme was impossible to miss in the Formula 1 paddock.
His goatee beard and square-rimmed glasses were topped
off with a black fedora, giving him a strong resemblance to
the fictional character Zorro. A self-publicising extrovert, he
appeared from nowhere as a sponsor with seemingly limitless
resources, simultaneously backing top teams in Formula 1,
sports cars and Indycars through his Essex oil company. After
his arrest for fraud in April 1981, he disappeared from the scene,
seemingly without trace, just as swiftly as he had arrived.

Colin Chapman of Lotus was a motorsport innovator in many aspects of design and engineering but there was another area in which he led the way. His deal with the Imperial Tobacco Company for the 1968 season, when his cars changed from traditional British Racing Green and yellow to the stylish red, white and gold livery of Gold Leaf cigarettes, brought the first overt commercial sponsorship to Formula 1. While purists railed against the idea of racing cars being 'dressed up to look like fag packets', Chapman once again stole a march over his competitors and, with permission from the ruling body, pioneered yet another new concept that other team owners could only admire. Two World Championships were won in Gold Leaf colours, for Graham Hill in 1968 with the Lotus 49 and Jochen Rindt (posthumously) in 1970 with the Lotus 72.

For 1972, the sponsor decided to promote a different brand name from its portfolio and the Lotus 72s appeared in the bold and even more striking black-and-gold colours of John Player Special. This became one of the most recognised, admired and iconic liveries in the history of the sport and the cars themselves were even officially renamed 'John Player Specials'. In its first year of JPS branding, Team Lotus won yet another title with Emerson Fittipaldi, and one more followed for Mario Andretti in 1978 with the ground-breaking and dominant Lotus 79 'ground-effect' car. And with that, Imperial's Chairman, Geoffrey Kent, decided to pull out, job done.

After such a successful ten-year partnership, Chapman was hugely disappointed to lose his long-term and loyal title sponsor, and was left with a gaping hole in his operating budget. Fortunately, as multiple World Champions, Team Lotus was obviously an attractive proposition and the Martini & Rossi drinks company stepped into the breach for the 1979 season. Soon afterwards, another fortuitous and extremely welcome source of funding arrived. This sponsor was to prove an unusually eye-catching one, quite unlike any other.

David Thieme was born in 1942 in Minneapolis, Minnesota. His father was the chief engineer of the Northwestern Aeronautical Corporation, which manufactured and developed derivative versions of the Waco glider aircraft that he had designed and that were used in large numbers by the US Army in the Second World War, specifically in D-Day operations. The Thieme family moved to New York, where David gained a place at the Pratt Institute in Brooklyn to study industrial design. After graduating, he started his own company specialising in the design of interiors of executive aircraft for the likes of Learjet. Helped by his father's aviation connections, the business proved to be extremely successful, leading Thieme also to work with car manufacturers and oil companies on their corporate aircraft.

It was during this period that he first became interested in motor racing as a big fan of American racing legend Parnelli Jones. By the late 1960s, he was already a millionaire when he started to invest exponential amounts of his company's profits by dabbling in oil trading. He soon found that he was extremely good at it and within a couple of years was making so much money that in 1973 he closed his design business and turned all his attention to global oil markets. Aged 30, he moved to the tax haven of Monaco (once famously described by the author Somerset Maugham as 'a sunny place for shady people') and gave his new venture the rather grandiose name Essex Overseas Petroleum Corporation.

His timing may have been more luck than judgement but either way it was very good: the oil crisis began in October 1973 when the Organization of Arab Petroleum Exporting Countries (OAPEC) imposed an embargo on countries that had supported Israel in the Yom Kippur War. The embargo lasted until March 1974, by which time the even larger Organization of Petroleum Exporting Countries (OPEC) — representing oil producers world-wide — had orchestrated a four-fold increase in the price of oil, to $12 a barrel, intensifying the economic shock waves around the world. The wild price fluctuations of this period provided perfect trading conditions for someone as skilled as Thieme in reading market movements. As an independent trader of oil futures with minimal overheads, he was able to offer much more favourable terms to governments than were available from the multinational corporations, and there were huge profits to be made. In an interview with the *International Herald Tribune*, he boasted that he could make or lose a million dollars in a single supertanker shipment. Indeed, by 1977 his reputation was such that the Swiss banking giant, Credit Suisse, was happy to make additional funds available to him, enabling him to pursue ever-bigger trades and leverage some hugely profitable deals. In 1979 alone, Thieme was rumoured to have made $70 million.

Thieme's wealth enabled him to indulge his passion for motor racing. His involvement began with François Mazet, a French former racing driver who had turned to business, operating as a sponsorship agent. With a background in single-seaters, culminating in a one-off appearance in his home Grand Prix at Paul Ricard in 1971 with a March 701 rented from his friend Jo Siffert, Mazet was well-connected in motor racing and rather more successful in his commercial endeavours than he had been behind the wheel. Enabling his new client to plunge in at the deep end, Mazet brokered an agreement for Essex to sponsor both Porsche and Lotus during 1979.

The Porsche sponsorship centred on a two-car team at the Le Mans 24 Hours. Porsche hadn't originally planned to compete in any sports car races that year because it was focused on developing an Indycar engine but Thieme's offer was too lucrative to turn down. As a result, two of the previous year's 936 prototype models were dusted off in time for a lavish launch party in early May at the Ritz Hotel in Paris, where just getting a car manoeuvred into the building was a major exercise in engineering, quickly followed by a single-car entry in the Silverstone Six Hours as a shakedown before the big race. Although both Porsches, driven by the star pairings of Jacky Ickx/Brian Redman and Bob Wollek/Hurley Haywood, started on the front row of the grid at Le Mans, neither reached the finish, but Essex made an impact by setting new standards of trackside hospitality.

The previous year, over dinner at the Restaurant Septime in Monte Carlo, Mazet had introduced Thieme to Colin Chapman. A prestigious association with Lotus in Formula 1 promised to be the perfect platform for feeding

Thieme's ego and Chapman for his part was captivated by the enigmatic American's air of mystery. Although the Lotus boss may not have fully understood exactly what Thieme did, he was most impressed that his new acquaintance was apparently able to generate massive wealth by buying and selling tanker loads of crude oil while they were in transit at sea, without ever seeing the cargo or having to take physical delivery of it on dry land. Chapman and Thieme were remarkably similar characters and a friendship blossomed.

The initial arrangement was for Essex identity to appear on the sidepods of Lotus's Martini-liveried cars as secondary sponsor for most of 1979, starting at the South African Grand Prix in March. After Mario Andretti's championship-winning success the previous year with the Lotus 79, however, it proved to be a disappointing season in which neither Andretti nor his new Argentine team-mate Carlos Reutemann managed to win a race. Meanwhile, Chapman fell completely under Thieme's spell as his new friend introduced him to the high life with all its attendant very expensive tastes. As team manager Peter Warr noted, on their travels Chapman abandoned the modest family-run hotels where the rest of the team traditionally stayed in favour of highly exclusive establishments. Gérard 'Jabby' Crombac, the noted French journalist who was close to Chapman, observed that the Lotus boss, after meeting Thieme, never travelled anywhere without a copy of the *Guide des Relais et Châteaux* in his briefcase.

By the end of the 1979 season, Chapman had become so mesmerised by his new sponsor that he pulled out of Lotus's existing deal with Martini and instead reached an agreement that Essex would become title sponsor for 1980 for a rumoured $4 million as part of a promised longer-term deal. As everything with Thieme was done to excess, it was entirely in keeping that the new partnership, Essex Team Lotus, was formally launched in December 1979 at a hugely extravagant party at the historic Paradis Latin, the exclusive cabaret theatre in Paris. In comparison with most racing car launches, which generally took place in a trackside garage or at a team's factory, this marked a dramatic departure. At the time, the unveiling of a new Formula 1 car at somewhere bland like a Heathrow Post House conference room over tea and biscuits would have been considered the height of luxury.

For the occasion, the Paradis Latin was decked out from floor to ceiling in rich red velvet. Scantily dressed glamour girls served copious amounts of champagne as the press corps assembled. Over dinner at tables positioned around the dimly lit dance floor, Filet de Charolais was served with

David Thieme was hard to miss when he arrived in Formula 1 as Lotus's flamboyant new sponsor with pockets of seemingly limitless depth.

Money can't buy everything and the Essex-sponsored Lotus 81 of 1980 proved so unsuccessful that star driver Mario Andretti, pictured at Monaco, left the team at the end of the season.

Château Beychevelle 1973 while the guests watched feather-clad dancers perform. After this prolonged build-up, the new Lotus 81 was eventually revealed in its striking new blue, red and silver livery. When the car was lowered from the ceiling, bottom first, one of the guests, Mike Lawrence, remarked that this approach seemed rather appropriate, 'given some of the antics in the preceding floor show'. As the car descended, a rather nervous-looking and doubtless embarrassed Andretti could be seen seated in the cockpit, wearing a dinner jacket and waving. Loud music accompanied the car's faltering progress towards the ground, complete with a rendition of the *Marseillaise*. The cacophony continued through interviews with team personnel and nothing they said could be heard, but in any case the extent of the revelry had been such that few journalists were sober enough by this time to write anything down and accurately record details of the evening. Fortunately for those who had to report back to their editors, press releases had been distributed and confirmed that Andretti would be joined by the debonair and gifted Italian Elio de Angelis, who had been bought out of his contract with Shadow, and that British hopeful Nigel Mansell was pencilled in to make a handful of appearances in a third car later in the season.

Not content with this staggering display of opulence, Thieme contracted CSS Promotions — a leading sports sponsorship consultancy run by Barrie Gill and Andrew Marriott — to arrange an even grander event in London in February 1980. This was held in the Royal Albert Hall, no less, with the cavernous concert hall transformed into a huge dining room. Dinner for the many hundreds of guests was prepared in the kitchen facilities at the Dorchester Hotel by Roger Vergé, celebrated Michelin-starred chef from the Moulin de Mougins near Cannes. The focus on this occasion was the announcement of Lotus's new supercar, the Esprit Turbo, the first 100 of which were to share the garish colour scheme of the Essex-branded racing cars. When the time came to reveal the new road car, it rose from the stage in clouds of carbonised snow flanked by Lotus's latest Formula 1 contender and the Essex-sponsored Penske PC9/80 that Andretti was due to drive at the Indianapolis 500 in May. Afterwards, guests were entertained by Shirley Bassey.

After all that fanfare, the 1980 Formula 1 season proved disastrous, even if it began with some promise. The first two races in South America yielded better qualifying performances than the Martini-backed cars had managed most of the previous season, and de Angelis achieved a fine second place in Brazil, but thereafter neither he nor Andretti came close to equalling that result, slipping ever further down the grid. Andretti, indeed, scored only a solitary point, with sixth place in the end-of-season United States Grand Prix, his home race. With that, he left the team, having not won a single race since his championship-winning 1978 season and tiring of continual trans-Atlantic commuting by Concorde for little reward.

While Essex Team Lotus — or 'Thieme Lotus' as some dubbed it — may not have achieved much during 1980, the flamboyant sponsor's appetite for flaunting his significant wealth remained unabated and he continued to provide hospitality of unprecedented lavishness. His guests at Grands Prix, mostly from the top echelons of the oil industry, flew in to join the team from all over the world. They were entertained in a specially commissioned, custom-built, three-storey bus in which all seating was upholstered in the best-quality Connolly leather. Catering was again provided by Roger Vergé and served on the top deck, which afforded fine views of the racing.

Hoping for better things in 1981, Thieme pushed the boat out further still with an even more spectacular CSS-organised launch party at the Royal Albert Hall, where British Prime Minister Margaret Thatcher was among the 900 guests. To decorate the entire venue in the 'Riviera' theme that his favoured chef had requested, Thieme chartered a Boeing cargo aircraft to fly in the necessary quantity of mimosa from the South of France. This time he hired Ray Charles as the headline act, supported by Scottish singer Barbara Dickson. The vast Essex hospitality unit was parked outside with the host's Essex-liveried Bell Jet Ranger helicopter perched on top of it, having been lowered into position by crane. Each guest was given a lottery ticket for the chance to win an Essex-branded Esprit Turbo. The total cost of the extravaganza was put at around $1 million.

Even by the standards of the earlier events, motor racing had never seen a launch anything like this. By now, some of the more perceptive people in Formula 1 were beginning to feel distinctly uneasy about Thieme, whose excesses inevitably grated. In a portent of things to come, CSS's Andrew Marriott was dismayed that his company didn't get paid for the launch champagne, for which he still has the unsettled invoice for £20,000, after the enigmatic sponsor's last-minute decision to change the brand to the significantly more expensive Dom Pérignon.

In what was essentially a game of smoke and mirrors, David Thieme created the illusion that the Essex Overseas Petroleum Corporation was a huge multinational company with vast assets but in reality it was a fairly small operation with fewer than 100 significant clients. The impression that he had infinitely deep pockets became well and truly planted in the subconscious of many of those who either saw or experienced his largesse, including several VIPs from within the oil industry who were taken in by a charade that was soon to unravel.

As the 1981 season got underway, rumours began to circulate in the paddock when, unusually, Thieme failed to appear for the first three Grands Prix, although he let it be known that he was intending to attend the fourth race, the San Marino Grand Prix at Imola. Three weeks before it, however, the 41-year-old's jet-set lifestyle came to a sudden halt. He was arrested in Switzerland on 14th April after landing in his executive jet at Zürich airport. The city's district attorney had issued an arrest warrant for him at the request of Credit Suisse for alleged 'economic crimes', namely fraud amounting to $7.6 million with the suggestion that documents of security for his multi-million-dollar borrowings from the bank had been found to be either inadequate or false. Officials immediately impounded his Dassault Mystère executive jet and police in Basel later confiscated his beloved Team Essex Lotus hospitality bus, which was valued at $761,000, as it entered Switzerland *en route* to Imola. Thieme spent the next 13 days in jail before he was released on $150,000 bail, which was apparently paid by Akram Ojjeh, whose son, also Akram, who would play an important part in funding the Williams and McLaren teams in later years.

The catalyst for Thieme's downfall was the oil-price fluctuation that had delivered his wealth in the first place. The Iranian Revolution of 1979 and the Iran–Iraq War that began the following year brought disruption to oil production in those countries. Bouts of panic in the oil market led to abrupt changes in price, including big rises as well as sharp falls. When one price drop occurred at the end of 1980, it seems that Thieme may have got on the wrong side of the ever-bigger trades he was making on borrowed money from Credit Suisse. Any trader in the commodities or financial markets will recognise that it only takes one big bet too many to go the wrong way and end up in serious difficulty. As Nick Leeson discovered to his cost in 1995 in the case that led to the collapse of Barings Bank, trading beyond agreed credit limits in an attempt to cover losses while market prices continue to move adversely becomes a vicious cycle that can spiral out of control. For Thieme, trying to recover from losses and with no one else to answer to, it's highly likely he went beyond agreed credit limits with either insufficient or falsified collateral. Whether by design or default, the actions of the Swiss bank were not only an exercise in damage limitation but also effectively closed Thieme's business overnight to make sure that he couldn't exacerbate the situation still further.

Thieme's problems meant that the Monaco Grand Prix at the end of May was the last time Lotus ran its cars in Essex colours. Fortunately for the team, John Player Special was persuaded to return as title sponsor three weeks later at the Spanish Grand Prix, with the Lotus 87s turned out in the familiar black and gold. Essex logos were retained for most of the season in the forlorn hope that the team could claw back some of the several million dollars of unpaid sponsorship fees. It was another year of desperately poor performances, with Nigel Mansell's third place in Monaco the best result.

In the end, the fickle Chapman's short-lived and warm friendship with his benefactor seemed almost to become a distraction. After the many years of almost relentless success, right back to the first World Championship with Jim Clark in 1963, Chapman's involvement with Thieme marked the beginning of a stark downturn for Team Lotus and inevitably led to conjecture that the boss was getting his priorities upside-down. It may just have been coincidence, but the Essex years brought very little pride or achievement. Indeed, apart from Elio de Angelis's out-of-the-blue victory in the 1982 Austrian Grand Prix, Team Lotus remained in the doldrums at the time of Chapman's sudden death from a heart attack in December 1982.

Despite almost seven months of investigation into Thieme's activities after his arrest, no formal charges were ever confirmed. Although a lengthy legal battle ensued between the Essex Overseas Petroleum Corporation and Credit Suisse, enough seeds of doubt had been sown and in the world of oil trading, where reputation is everything, Thieme's business didn't survive. His 'empire', it transpired, was exposed as just a one-man trading operation run from a room in the exclusive Hôtel de Paris in Monte Carlo.

There's no doubt that for a while Thieme was spectacularly successful but, as he had demonstrated, in his line of business fortunes could be made or lost in the space of a day. It's highly likely that he was guilty of some sort of financial malpractice and got caught out in a big way, but due to the opaque nature of the Swiss banking regulations it will probably never be known precisely what he did wrong. Whatever the truth behind the allegations, sufficient seeds of doubt had been sown and in the sometimes shady, mysterious and rarefied world of oil trading, where credit and reputation are everything, even the slightest element of doubt meant that there could be no way back. His career was finished.

David Thieme effectively vanished, his desire to be in the limelight suddenly replaced by an even stronger urge to remain completely out of sight, like a chameleon. The showman became a recluse.

CHAPTER 55

MICKEY THOMPSON

Life of speed and a violent death

Once known as 'The fastest man on wheels' and a household name in American motorsport in the 1960s, Mickey Thompson achieved hundreds of speed and endurance records and built a wide variety of innovative cars, including Indy 500 racers, dragsters and off-road desert machines. One of his business ventures, as a highly successful promoter of a popular and lucrative stadium racing series, led to a falling out with a former partner and resulted in his brutal execution-style murder in a case that took an astonishing 18 years to solve.

Christened Marian Lee but always known as 'Mickey', Thompson was the son of an officer in the local police department and was born in 1928 in Alhambra, California. He was addicted to both speed and engineering from the age of seven, when he cannibalised an old washing machine for the parts he needed to create a soapbox kart. As a teenager he would tinker with cars that had been destined for the scrapyard and relished the challenge of getting them to run again and then seeing how fast he could make them go.

His hobby turned into a passion fed by the rapid rise in popularity of drag racing in the early 1950s, where impromptu quarter-mile strips often popped up on straight pieces of tarmac on the outskirts of town. This presented affordable competition with no rules or restrictions and even on a meagre budget it was possible to turn a street-legal car with a large-block engine into a roaring 'muscle car'. As the sport developed, the street-legal cars gave way to custom-built machines whose only purpose was to travel the quarter-mile distance in the shortest possible time, and this played to

Mickey's ingenuity. He not only recognised and understood the black art of tyre technology but also that additional grip and traction could be gained by placing the driver as far back as possible behind the rear axle and engine. He pioneered this concept and his design became known as the 'slingshot' dragster, which transformed that branch of the sport in 1954 and resulted in competitors regularly achieving new speed records. Mickey led the way from the outset by becoming the first to reach 120mph in 1955, a record that he smashed later in the year by hitting 150mph, and three years later he shattered that with a speed of 198mph.

By the time he was 25, he was racing professionally. But while the speeds of drag racing had hooked him, he found that the quarter-mile 'strips' were limiting his creative flair and he became more interested in establishing how fast a person could travel on land. Others had been experimenting with using jet engines and rocket propulsion but to him that was essentially flying on the ground and the challenge he saw was to see how fast a man could travel in a car propelled by conventional piston power, which was where his expertise lay. He had been captivated and inspired by the land speed records set by Englishman John Cobb after his father had first taken him as a nine-year-old to the Bonneville Salt Flats in Utah. His own early forays there were with a flathead-powered 1936 Ford Coupe and he kept returning to the place throughout his career. In 1959 alone he set no fewer than four new international speed records at Bonneville driving his self-built four-wheel-drive *Challenger 1*, which was powered by four supercharged Pontiac engines. The following year he used the car to clock a speed in one direction of 406.6mph, which put him in sight of a world record provided that he could achieve a similar figure on the return run, due to the regulations stipulating that a record comprised the average of the speeds achieved over two runs in opposite directions. Sadly, his efforts were thwarted on the return run when one of the Pontiac engines blew up and the car broke a driveshaft. He may not have been able to claim the official land speed record but he was at least unofficially the fastest man on earth.

Having accomplished part of his dream, Thompson moved onto another realm of the sport that had always intrigued him: the Indianapolis 500. Until 1961, when pioneering English constructor John Cooper took his rear-engine Cooper-Climax T54 to the 'Brickyard', all the contenders had had their Offenhauser engines placed at the front. However, Mickey was an early adopter of Cooper's approach and built his own car for the 1962 race around a chassis designed by John Crosthwaite, powered by a modified production Buick V8 engine. After qualifying eighth, Dan Gurney retired from the race, but Thompson's team did win the Mechanical Achievement Award.

Although his efforts at the 'Brickyard' didn't live up to expectations in that first season, he went on promoting his ideas and stretching the boundaries of conventional engineering over the course of six Indy 500s with innovations that included titanium chassis and four-wheel steering. Always demonstrating his versatility and ingenuity, Thompson went on to race everything from stock cars to off-road vehicles, even returning to Bonneville to try to obtain the elusive world record.

His obsession with speed also led to an accident in a high-powered drag boat that paralysed him from the waist down and left doctors fearful that he might never walk again. Despite being in a body cast from his hips to his toes, he ignored medical advice and discharged himself from hospital, to be taken home lying in a makeshift bed in the back of a station wagon. Undeterred, he proceeded to design his own rehabilitation equipment and, remarkably, went on to make a complete recovery.

Meanwhile, his business career was going from strength to strength. He had established Mickey Thompson Enterprises in 1960 and within a few years this umbrella organisation embraced a portfolio of subsidiary companies ranging from engineering to aftermarket performance accessories. Mickey Thompson Performance Tires was added in 1963 and initially developed racing tyres for Indianapolis competitors before diversifying into road tyres, and it continues to trade today. In 1963, he formed SCORE International (Southern California Off Road Enthusiasts), which sanctions the famous Baja 1000 race and other off-road events across North America.

In 1979, when he was winding down his driving career, he started an entertainment venture called MTEG (Mickey Thompson Entertainment Group), which devised and staged indoor events across the US for off-road racers. This novel concept proved immensely popular because the events were held in easily accessible sports stadiums, bringing a new type of motorsport to big audiences in heavily populated urban areas in a format that enabled spectators to see all of the action, which added to the spectacle and excitement. The setting up of one of these events involved covering the floor of a stadium with vast quantities of dirt to protect it, a labour-intensive and costly exercise, but Mickey's reputation not only brought in the crowds but also inspired confidence in the stadium operators that their venues would be returned to them in immaculate condition. Aside from NASCAR and Indianapolis, the events attracted bigger crowds than any other form of motorsport, and they proved to be immensely profitable.

By 1983, Mickey's wife Trudy was experiencing some health difficulties, so the couple began to think of ways of slowing down. Selling MTEG, however, proved to be impractical because so much of it was centred on Mickey's celebrity status and required his continued involvement.

Several other promoters observed Mickey Thompson's entertainment business and one who became a direct rival was Michael Goodwin, who had previously been involved in organising and promoting rock concerts with the likes of Jimi Hendrix, The Rolling Stones and Janis Joplin. Goodwin had developed a similar model to Thompson's but focused on motorcycles and a formula that he called Super Motocross. The appetite for motorcycles had grown into a craze due to the influx and affordability of Japanese brands like Honda, Kawasaki, Suzuki and Yamaha, and Goodwin's events were so popular that they were able to fill the Los Angeles Coliseum with more spectators than attended regular football games.

Whereas Thompson's exemplary reputation ensured that he didn't have to continually lodge large sums of money for security deposits with the stadiums, Goodwin didn't enjoy that privilege and harboured resentment about it. When some of stadium operators highlighted the synergies and potential economies of scale between the two entities, pointing out that if they staged their respective events on consecutive days, combining resources seemed the beneficial and logical way forward for all parties. A formal collaboration between Thompson and Goodwin was the outcome.

Because of Trudy's health problems, Thompson's plan was to relieve her of the burden of running their business on a day-to-day basis and for Goodwin to take the lead in this role, with Mickey's contribution being the use of his name to publicise the events and provide the operators with the confidence that they would be paid. The partnership was structured with Goodwin owning 70 percent of the equity and taking a $300,000 annual salary while Thompson would have 30 percent and take a much smaller income because it suited him to have less responsibility for the business decisions. Profits would be divided according to the shareholding and, crucially, so would any capital outlay for events.

Despite his success, Mickey remained a humble and hard-working man whereas Goodwin was an individual of excess with a huge ego. What might have been the perfect marriage of two equally determined and commercially minded men sharing costs and dividing the profits of their newly merged ventures quickly went wrong and the partnership was dissolved almost immediately. Among various areas of dispute, Thompson discovered that

Pictured in 1962, Mickey Thompson checks clearances on a Pontiac V8 engine, using his engineering mastery as ever to make the best of his machinery.

the hundreds of thousands of dollars requested from him by his new partner for event deposits actually represented the entire sums required, contrary to their 30/70 agreement, and Goodwin was investing absolutely nothing.

Despite no longer having access to the accounts, Thompson was also shocked to learn that invoices hadn't been settled and that the joint venture was already posting significant losses. As a man of his word, Thompson believed that, irrespective of whether an event had made a profit, its costs had to be honoured. To preserve his good name and reputation, he paid $515,000 out of his own pocket to settle invoices and sought reimbursement from Goodwin. It wasn't forthcoming and Goodwin's retort was that Mickey was responsible for any losses incurred by the car events, although this wasn't something that was stated in their documented partnership contract. What followed was a succession of protracted and incredibly acrimonious legal actions collectively costing millions of dollars in fees. Each time a court order was made in Thompson's favour, Goodwin would appeal against it. After the courts had added interest payments, the amount owing to Mickey had grown to $800,000, and to avoid paying it Goodwin separately declared both business and personal bankruptcy.

Away from the courtroom, the acrimony continued between the two intensely competitive individuals, neither of whom was prepared to lose to the other. Mickey managed to secure exclusive agreements for racing events at two stadiums, one of which was the biggest revenue earner for his former partner, who in retaliation went on a campaign with advertisements proclaiming that the events had been cancelled. By March 1988, Thompson had won every single legal judgment against the increasingly bitter Goodwin, who remained resolute in his wish to hurt his rival. Knowing that he was unable to damage Mickey's good name and that any physical possessions were replaceable, Goodwin devised a plan that would inflict the ultimate pain and suffering in the most cold-blooded way imaginable.

Early on Tuesday 16th March 1988, Mickey and Trudy were getting ready for work and preparing to leave their home in the bucolic setting of Bradbury, California. This is an affluent rural community from where they would make their daily commute to Anaheim near Los Angeles to the office they maintained at the stadium from which they ran their business. The famous couple disliked flaunting their wealth and for this journey they always used a humble Toyota minivan rather than their prestigious Lincoln Continental. After Trudy reversed the Toyota out of their garage, Mickey pressed the remote-control switch to lower the door and walked outside to join his wife. As he did so, there was a loud popping noise and he fell to the ground having been shot in the legs. Then, said eyewitnesses, the sound of another shot came from the direction of the Toyota, which had rolled down the steep drive and into a wall, its windows shattered. Lying injured on the ground facing the car, Mickey would have seen Trudy jump out of the driver's door and run from one of two hooded gunman before she too was shot. As she tried to crawl towards the road, the gunman stood over her, held his weapon to her head and shot her dead in full view of her devastated husband. As Mickey tried to haul himself up off the ground and go to her aid, the second gunman fired two shots at him and, to ensure he was dead, pointed his 9mm automatic pistol next to Mickey's head and squeezed the trigger twice more.

Between them, the murdered couple were wearing watches and jewellery worth $70,000 and carried $10,000 in cash, none of which was stolen. As the killers also made no attempt to gain access to the house, police were confident from the outset that this was a professional killing and that robbery wasn't a motive. The planning of the murders was made easier as the Thompsons were creatures of habit who always left home at the same time each day, just after 6am, which was also such an early hour that few if any eyewitnesses would be up and about. After completing their wicked assignment, therefore, the only remaining challenge for the two assailants — described as two young African-American males — was to find an unobtrusive escape route. As there was only one road that led away from the murder scene and police would have blocked it as soon as they were alerted by distressed neighbours, the chosen method of escape for the gunmen was by bicycle along small paths, and eyewitnesses saw them make their escape in this way. As Ronald Bowers, a former Senior Prosecutor at Los Angeles County District Attorney's Office, stated in his book *Killing of a Legend*, 'Within minutes they could meet up with a getaway vehicle, throw their bikes in the back and drive off on the 210 Freeway where they would blend in with the thousands of commuters on their way to work.' Although this couldn't be proved, police assumed that it was how the assassins, who have never been identified, managed to get away.

Knowing that he would be at the top of the list of suspects, Goodwin made sure that he had a solid alibi at the time of the murders and was exercising in his local gym. In the process of his research, Bowers discovered that in the days surrounding the murders Goodwin and his wife Diane had sold their Laguna Beach house and moved their assets — all of which were the subject of his bankruptcy orders — to offshore banks. Other investments were put into Diane's name and sold, with the proceeds used to buy quantities of gold Krugerrands that could be exchanged for local currency in any country. They then bought a 57-foot Wellington Motor Sailor yacht for $400,000, financed through a Maryland bank in Diane's name, despite failing to disclose their true financial situation. Within weeks they had illegally sold their assets, obtained a sizeable bank loan under false pretences and left for the Caribbean, where they lived as fugitives on the run for the next two years until they broke up, after which Goodwin continued island-hopping on his own.

When the Maryland bank, having received no repayments on the loan, began to suspect that it had been defrauded, it hired private detectives to track down the boat. Although Goodwin had taken the precaution of changing its name, he was traced to a port in Guatemala and the bank repossessed the boat. Now without the boat to live on and without Diane and access to the money in her bank accounts, he was forced to return to the US, where he maintained a low profile and moved in with a new girlfriend

After the murder of Mickey Thompson and his wife Trudy in 1988, his sister Collene Campbell campaigned tirelessly to get to the truth.

in a mountain retreat in the Aspen ski resort. There he made the mistake of repeatedly showing her a video of an episode of the *Unsolved Mysteries* television programme about the Thompson murders and admitting to her that he was responsible for hiring the two teenage killers and boasting how he'd got away with the crime.

At the end of 1992, Goodwin's girlfriend was hospitalised with injuries that he had inflicted on her. Although she didn't press charges against him, the incident was brought to the attention of the police, who now knew exactly where to find him. By 1995, he and his estranged wife were in court and indicted on 13 counts of making false statements on bank applications to finance their business and to buy the yacht. They were each sentenced to 30 months in prison for defrauding financial institutions.

Goodwin remained the prime suspect in the murders of Mickey and Trudy Thompson but without any firm evidence the trail had gone cold. However, Mickey's sister, Collene Campbell, vowed to see justice done for her much-loved brother and sister-in-law. Her own 27-year-old son, Scott, had met a gruesome death when thrown into the sea from a private aircraft by associates in a drug deal that had gone terribly wrong and it was through her efforts that his killers were brought to justice. As a result, she became an advocate for victims' rights and involved in support groups, which, combined with a role in local politics, gave her the ideal platform from which to pressure the authorities to continue their efforts in unsolved murder cases. In particular, she worked tirelessly to have the Thompson case reopened.

Mickey had told his sister of death threats he had received and his very real concern that Goodwin would try to harm him or, worse still, Trudy. After the police had filed the deaths as a 'cold case', Collene paid private detectives to reinvestigate every shred of evidence that could possibly link the man she was convinced had orchestrated the double murder. Over the course of several years, her detectives obtained statements from colleagues, employees, friends and even police officers, all of whom were prepared to testify in court that they had witnessed Goodwin expressing his deep hatred of Mickey and repeatedly making clear his intention to kill him or have him killed. They also had the confession that he made to the ex-girlfriend in Aspen to use against him, together with statements from neighbours in Bradbury who had seen a man believed to have been Goodwin checking out the area around the Thompsons' home two days before the murders. Although 13 years had elapsed, neighbours were able to identify Goodwin in a line-up and this all combined to add weight to the case for the prosecution.

Goodwin was 59 — the same age as Mickey when he had been gunned down — when the Los Angeles District Attorney eventually filed charges against him, in June 2004. After preliminary hearings, the court case began in October 2006 and despite limited physical evidence or DNA to incriminate him, it was clear enough that Mickey's bitter former business partner had a motive to hire assassins and have him killed. When the jury returned to court after the Christmas holidays in January 2007, they decided that the circumstantial evidence was overwhelming and reached a unanimous verdict that the embittered Goodwin had orchestrated the murders 18 years previously and he was found guilty on both counts of first-degree murder. Sentencing in March was a formality as he was given life without the possibility of parole and the convictions were upheld at an appeal in 2015.

Mickey Thompson left behind an outstanding legacy that included setting possibly more speed and endurance records than anyone else in automotive history. His gruesome death instantly immortalised him as one of the most colourful and diversely talented all-round motorsport superstars, although the vitriolic battle with Michael Goodwin was sadly one contest that he didn't win.

CHAPTER 56

GERARD
TOTH
Time for crime

This French engineer was over-promoted by
Renault and briefly reached senior management
heights in 1984 when given the job of running
the manufacturer's Formula 1 team, despite
being regarded with disdain in parts of the
paddock and seeming ill-suited to the task. What
wasn't known at the time was that some of his
efforts went into lining his own pockets and
ultimately landed him in jail.

Gérard Toth was an engineer who first started working at Renault in 1976 and rose through the ranks of research and development to become quality control director in 1982. When Gérard Larrousse left the Renault Formula 1 team at the end of 1984 to join the rival Ligier outfit, he took designer Michel Tetu with him. Toth was not only named as Larrousse's replacement as team principal but at the same time was also made the new managing director of Renault Sport, meaning that he was put in charge of all competition programmes from Formula 1 down to the junior categories.

Toth may have had plenty of engineering knowledge but it had been obtained entirely with the production-car side of Renault and he had never been involved in motorsport, with Renault or anywhere else. He certainly wasn't ideally equipped to handle the wide-ranging responsibilities suddenly placed upon him and it was probably no coincidence that his appointment marked the beginning of a sharp decline in the Renault team's fortunes.

Renault had been the pioneer of turbocharging in Formula 1, débuting at the 1977 British Grand Prix at Silverstone with Jean-Pierre Jabouille at the wheel of its singleton entry. The first win came, fittingly, for Jabouille at Dijon in 1979, marking a historic achievement for a French driver in a French car with a French engine in the French Grand Prix, even if the race is remembered most of all for the incredible wheel-banging duel for second place between René Arnoux's sister Renault and Gilles Villeneuve's Ferrari. There followed a four-year period of considerable success that brought 14 more Grand Prix victories, nine of them for Alain Prost, although a championship title always eluded the team. It came closest in 1983, when Prost won more races than anyone else, four, but lost out to Nelson Piquet by two points in the quest to become World Champion, with the constructors' title also ending with the runner-up position for Renault.

By 1985, with Toth now in charge, Renault was not only operating its own works team but also stretching its resources by supplying engines to Lotus, Ligier and Tyrrell. The factory retained the services of both Derek Warwick and Patrick Tambay as drivers from the previous year, which hadn't produced any race wins but plenty of podium positions, but the RE60 cars weren't very competitive. Although the revised RE60B design was rushed through by the middle of the season in the absence of the man who had started to design it, Tetu, it was overweight and even less competitive than the model it replaced. Lotus, as a customer team, embarrassed its engine supplier by doing a far better job, with Ayrton Senna and Elio de Angelis winning three races between them.

After such a disastrous year under Toth's command and persistent rumours about Renault's intentions, it came as little surprise when, before the end of the season, chief executive Georges Besse confirmed that the team would pull the plug on its Formula 1 project, although he promised that the company would honour its contracts as engine supplier to the three customer teams until the end of 1986.

In *Autosport* magazine's review of the season, Nigel Roebuck was damning in his condemnation of Toth's stewardship and his unsettling effect on the team: 'From the start Toth gave the impression that Grand Prix racing was rather a silly little world and one somewhat beneath him. At early constructors' meetings he displayed arrogance so rampant that other constructors noticed. And through the season he demonstrated what amounted to a genius for getting himself disliked. The other team principals held him in contempt.'

Georges Besse had been recruited to take charge of state-owned, loss-making Renault at the beginning of 1985 with a brief to return it to profitability. He orchestrated a remarkable turnaround in the company's fortunes not only by cutting out extraneous costs, such as motorsport, but also by closing several manufacturing plants across France with the loss of 21,000 jobs.

Tragically, Besse was murdered on 17th November 1986. Two assassins appeared on a motorcycle outside his home in the 14th Arrondissement in Paris at 8.30pm and as the 58-year-old emerged from his chauffeur-driven car they shot him several times in the head and chest. He died where he fell on the pavement. Three months later, the militant anti-capitalist group *Action Directe* claimed responsibility for the killing in retaliation for the massive lay-offs that he had instigated. Two women affiliated with the group were arrested and although they denied responsibility during their trial, the courts returned a guilty verdict in March 1987 and they each received life sentences.

Meanwhile, the unpopular Toth had also been arrested, accused of diverting payments by Tyrrell for the supply of turbo engines into his own Swiss bank account. He was found guilty and jailed for embezzlement in a sorry ending to Renault's original foray into modern-day Formula 1. His name was never mentioned again.

CHAPTER 57
SCOTT TUCKER
Late starter

Level 5 Motorsports was a highly successful, no-expense-spared American sports car racing team belonging to Scott Tucker, who was supposedly reclusive but liked to flaunt his extreme wealth. As an amateur racing driver, he was flattered by the abilities of far more talented co-drivers whom he paid well to help him achieve race wins and championship titles. He was also a convicted racketeer and accumulated his riches as a 'payday' loan shark, building his business empire upon desperate people's debts using illegal and contemptible methods.

Born in 1962, Scott Tucker was brought up in Kansas City, Missouri and was a very late starter in motor racing at the age of 44, when he joined the ranks of wealthy amateurs in sports car competition. He founded a team in 2006 and named it Level 5 Motorsports, inspired by a term used in a financial self-help book that he had recently read. With no previous competition experience, he began racing a Ferrari in the one-make North American Challenge series for identical F430 models. He wasn't a naturally gifted racing driver and initially had to work very hard to acquire better skills through intensive coaching, but his improvement over time brought some success that fuelled his ambition.

Within a year, Tucker and his team had progressed to the Rolex Sports Car Series and the IMSA GT3 Cup Challenge while continuing to participate in one-make series for Porsches and Ferraris. By 2009, Level 5 had moved even further up the ladder to compete in the top category of the Rolex championship and the team was now campaigning sports prototypes with the cars invariably wearing the preferred race numbers 5, 55 and 555 in deference to their entrant. Over the next few seasons, the team evolved into a serious contender for honours and became one of the most successful privateer sports car outfits of recent memory. There were numerous class wins and some significant results in the classic endurance races, including third overall in the Rolex 24 at Daytona with a Riley Mk XI in 2010 and fourth overall in the Mobil 1 Twelve Hours of Sebring with an HPD ARX-03 in 2012, while Tucker's four visits to the Le Mans 24 Hours yielded a best result of 10th overall in 2011.

As the archetypal gentleman driver, Tucker did everything he could to guarantee success and no expense was spared in hiring a roster of top professional co-drivers who included former Le Mans winner Christophe Bouchut and brothers Marino and Dario Franchitti. As Tucker paid his employees well above market rates, he was also able to recruit the most talented mechanics and engineers as well as ensuring that the team had the best cars and equipment that money could buy, irrespective of the millions of dollars that it all cost. Level 5's entry into the American Le Mans Series (ALMS) in 2010 came in the Prototype (LMP) category for which the team bought and raced a pair of French-built Oreca FLM 09s. The team's graduation to LMP2 in 2011 was another example of money-no-object spending when three Lola P2 prototypes were added to the stable, each costing over half a million dollars.

Tucker appeared to be an enigmatic character. On the one hand he gave the impression that he was shy and retiring, preferring to stay out of the limelight, but on the other he seemed to go out of his way to draw attention to himself. He claimed to have no interest in fame and yet from the outset of his racing career he employed a dedicated reporter to follow him around race paddocks before posting interviews on YouTube and he also commissioned a documentary about himself. This suggested that he was extremely image-conscious and had a sizeable ego that needed to be fed.

Many of the professional sports car teams in America by this time used their vast transporters with awnings surrounding them as mobile workshops and had sizeable mobile homes as bases for their drivers and guests. However, as journalist Marshall Pruett stated: 'He [Tucker] competed in the American Le Mans Series and Grand-Am against teams owned by fellow billionaire Roger Penske, famed entrant Chip Ganassi, and others whose businesses were incredibly successful. Yet Tucker was the only one who went out of his way to distance himself from being part of the sport's communal framework. Where the Penskes and Ganassis made themselves available to fans and the media, Tucker walled himself off from the paddock.'

Tucker's excessive spending habits were such that his operation was provided with an extraordinarily ostentatious and opulent custom-built 'stronghold' erected at each race that combined to accommodate both the racing team and hospitality unit for guests and wouldn't have been out of place in a current Formula 1 paddock. In order to ensure the utmost privacy, this compound was manned around the clock by security guards, making it both sinister and unwelcoming to outsiders. People had always questioned where Tucker's fortune came from, which may have contributed to his insecurities and bunker-like mentality, but his display of brash extravagance, which served to alienate him from other teams, the media and spectators, was a peculiar and unsubtle way of maintaining a low profile. Pruett said that even in a paddock filled with million-dollar machines, his spending habits were breathtaking, and the journalist debated whether they represented an outward display of strength or simply a strange form of insecurity.

This dichotomy was exemplified in 2013 when FIA World Endurance Championship contenders — including factory entries from global automotive giants Toyota and Audi — combined with ALMS entrants at the Circuit of the Americas in Texas. Both of these manufacturers allocated massive racing budgets for their LMP1 operations, more than $100 million per year, yet they were happy to allow unguarded access to their incredibly valuable machinery on display in the paddock. Level 5 Motorsports, of course, hid within its usual impenetrable mobile fortress.

After studying business administration at Kansas State University, Scott Tucker became involved in investing in various different enterprises including real estate, hotels and restaurants, but those that really captivated him combined internet technology with financial services. These businesses, which offered short-term loans to individual people and small companies with low credit ratings, would not only earn him a fortune but eventually bring him down. Indeed, as far back as 1991, he had been convicted of three felony charges, including making false statements to a bank and mail fraud. One of the charges related to a phoney lending company that he ran under the name of Chase, Morgan, Stearns & Lloyd and charged businesses upfront fees for loans that were never actually delivered. For this he received a one-year jail sentence that he served at the US Penitentiary in Leavenworth, Kansas.

When Tucker embarked on his racing career in 2006, he was chairman of Westfund, a private-equity firm whose name was emblazoned on the flanks of one of his Ferraris. Rumour and speculation as to how he had

Despite seeming to be shy and retiring, racketeer Scott Tucker went to some trouble to cultivate his image, as is evident from this carefully posed portrait.

accumulated such enormous wealth were rife from the start of his participation in the sport although his entry on LinkedIn was designed to leave no doubt as to his business credentials by displaying a glowing profile: 'In the 1990s, Sentient Founder and CEO, Scott Tucker pioneered the concept of web-based intelligent bank interfaces, online lending platforms, high-volume payment processing, and loan origination and decision engines. The US Patent office recognized his work in 2006. Today, leading and emerging companies, interfacing with the world's largest banks, rely on this software to run smoothly and operate efficiently. Sentient Technologies and its predecessor organizations have been in business for nearly two decades. As one of the world's leading providers of global loan origination, decisioning [sic], payment-processing technologies, market research, insight and analysis, Sentient publishes dozens of research and analyst briefings annually.' Needless to say, other aspects of his career were omitted.

Strangely, especially for a businessman who was so reclusive and keen on privacy, Tucker's self-congratulatory LinkedIn entry also listed what appeared to be a truly impressive résumé of his successes in motor racing. His reputation was further enhanced by an extremely flattering article in the *Wall Street Journal* orchestrated by the supposedly publicity-shy businessman and portraying him as a highly successful technology entrepreneur, which, on paper, he was. However, suspicions persisted about the true source of his wealth and were confirmed when Level 5 Motorsports abruptly ceased operations in 2014.

The paradigm shift that had led to take-off for Tucker's business was the arrival of the internet in day-to-day life. In 2001, he founded AMG Services to offer short-term payday loans online, at very high interest rates, to tide over borrowers until they were next paid. According to the Consumer Federation of America, 18 US states, plus Washington DC, either prohibit this type of lending or impose rate caps that effectively outlaw the practice. This didn't deter Tucker, who brazenly flouted the widespread restrictions and designed his business model specifically to take advantage of the poorest and most financially vulnerable people in society by offering loans to those whose credit ratings were so bad that they couldn't borrow from anywhere else.

The internet increased accessibility to the sort of customers who were typically struggling for small amounts, which averaged $300, and were attracted by misleading advertising that suggested a loan of this size could be obtained for a single additional payment of $90. However, the small print stated that the loan would be automatically renewed unless the customer took proactive steps to opt out. So complicated and opaque was the language used in the terms and conditions of the contracts that enormous numbers of people became unwittingly trapped in a cycle of debt and often had to resort to paying lawyers, even though they could ill-afford to do so, to unravel the true details of the charging structure. Unauthorised payments were automatically taken directly from the bank accounts of 'defaulting' borrowers so that those who were caught out often ended up paying as much as $975 in renewal fees, finance and interest charges while the original $300 still remained unpaid and outstanding.

This odious enterprise, which at one stage had as many as 1,200 employees, traded under a host of other names including Ameriloan, Cash Advance, Mister Money and One Click Cash. These entities had attracted the attention of the Federal Trade Commission (FTC) for years but state prosecutors, despite their concerted efforts to stop Tucker's illegal operations, had to prove that he was actually the owner of the companies committing the predatory lending. This was hampered by the fact that his lawyers maintained that Ameriloan, whose branding was carried on some of his racing cars, and eight subsidiary companies under the Ameriloan umbrella, were in fact owned and operated by Native American tribes, including the

Modoc Tribe of Oklahoma, the Santee Sioux Tribe of Nebraska and the Miami Tribe of Oklahoma.

Because the tribes were legally able to exploit their 'sovereign immunity' and couldn't be sued by state government, they were able to receive payments with impunity. What appeared from the outside to be a group of conventional businesses was a complete façade set up by Tucker to deliberately circumvent state lending laws. When customers phoned the call centres, they spoke to employees who had been trained to deceive them into believing that they were representing tribes and based in Oklahoma or Nebraska when in truth they were actually in Kansas. The trickery operated on an industrial scale, with Tucker's organisation taking 99 percent of the profits and paying a commission of just one percent to the tribe for posing as the business owner.

Despite documentation to the contrary, federal investigators were eventually able to persuade the Miamis into reaching a deal whereby the tribe admitted that Tucker had in fact approached them to become business partners for the enterprise in order to shield him from state investigations. The tribe agreed to give up $48 million in payday revenue in return for federal officials agreeing not to prosecute individual tribe members. In 2012, the FTC filed a lawsuit claiming that Tucker and his companies were engaging in 'unfair or deceptive acts or practices in or affecting commerce'.

By early 2014, the net was closing in. In January, Tucker competed in his last race, the Rolex 24 at Daytona, in a Ferrari 458 Italia, achieving a class win with four co-drivers. In February, Level 5 Motorsports ceased operations. In March, one of Tucker's two brothers, Blaine, who had been heavily involved in running the business and was a co-defendant in the lawsuit, commited suicide. However, it wasn't until February 2016 that Tucker was finally arrested and indicted on federal criminal charges filed in the Southern District of New York of the US Federal Court System in relation to his ownership and controlling role in various payday-lending operations. These were alleged to have charged illegal interest rates in violation of the Racketeer Influenced and Corrupt Organisations Act (RICO) and the Truth in Lending Act (TILA), both of which are statutes designed to protect consumers.

Speaking in 2016, FBI assistant director Diego Rodriguez described how Tucker (55) and Tim Muir (46), his lawyer, right-hand man and co-defendant, deliberately preyed on more than 4.5 million working people to enter into payday loans with massive interest rates ranging from 400 to 700 percent. The case for the defence argued that this was 'justifiable business enterprise' that was 'satisfying demand'. The jury at the Manhattan federal court took a different view, that this was a predatory scheme to take callous advantage of vulnerable workers who were living from hand to mouth, and took less than a day of deliberation to reach its verdict and find both men guilty of all 14 criminal counts against them. Although some of the charges each carried maximum sentences of 20 years in prison, the pair were fortunate that in early 2018 they were given lesser sentences of 16 years eight months (Tucker) and seven years (Muir) for convictions that included racketeering, wire fraud and money laundering.

It was calculated that between 2008 and 2013, Tucker's incredibly lucrative businesses made more than five million payday loans that accrued more than $2 billion in deceptive charges. In addition to the custodial sentences, an unprecedented $1.3 billion litigated judgment awarded against them was the largest that the FTC had ever obtained. Federal authorities determined that a Learjet 60, six Ferraris, four Porsches and an $8 million holiday home in Aspen, Colorado were all bought from the proceeds of crime and these were among a range of assets that were confiscated to meet a small part of the judgment and compensate victims. Numerous bank accounts controlled by Tucker and his wife Kim were also frozen.

There was a postscript. Tucker's lawyers filed an appeal that questioned the authority of the FTC to force a company like AMG Services to pay restitution of the $1.3 billion. Their argument was that 'it was as an administrative shortcut that was improperly wielded to capture and return the $1.3 billion in question'. The initial appeal was rejected by the Ninth Circuit Court but the Supreme Court decided otherwise and in April 2021 absolved Tucker and AMG from the $1.3 billion debt repayment.

Tucker, the unscrupulous amateur racing driver, had made himself rich beyond belief by fleecing the poor with predatory lending tactics that created misery for millions of victims. These were predominantly struggling everyday people who were illegally charged exorbitant interest rates in such a way that was designed to mislead and deceive.

Jeff Braun, technical director at Level 5 Motorsports, said that Tucker had run the world's most expensive amateur racing team. Whether or not that was the case, it was estimated that by the time the team was wound up in 2014, its owner had accumulated two dozen sports prototype racing cars, enough to fill a grid and form his own race series. However, within weeks of his incarceration, the team's assets were auctioned and its fleet of prototypes sold without reserve. It marked the sorry end of a high-profile racing team that was best known for all the wrong reasons.

CHAPTER 58

JEAN-PIERRE VAN ROSSEM
Wheels of fortune

A highly eccentric and contradictory figure, Jean-Pierre Van Rossem was a self-proclaimed stock-market guru. Despite being a Marxist sympathiser and avowed anarchist, he became a multi-millionaire whose fortune at one point included ownership of innumerable Ferrari road cars, two private jets, a superyacht and, briefly, a Formula 1 racing team. He was also a convicted fraudster, heroin addict, novelist and arguably the most colourful figure in the history of Belgian politics after founding a party expressly to avoid another jail sentence.

Like so many other racing teams over the decades, Onyx Race Engineering decided to step up to Formula 1 after many years in lower categories and embarked on the 1989 season with the experienced Stefan Johansson as lead driver and rising star Bertrand Gachot (see Chapter 22) in a second car. The budget was precarious for the fledgling Formula 1 operation until Gachot introduced Mike Earle, the team principal, to a potential Belgian sponsor.

'I went to Brussels and Bertie [Gachot] warned me not to be too shocked by what I found,' said Earle. 'Well, I walked into Jean-Pierre Van Rossem's office and I *was* shocked! There was this man behind a huge desk with long white hair down to his waist, a beard to match, and wearing what would become his trademark red racing boots on his feet. This was the man who invented Moneytron, a system that he claimed to predict the money markets, and he'd made a fortune. By the time I was back at the factory he'd sent over his first payment.'

This was Earle's strangest experience yet in a long career in motor racing that went back to the 1960s. Having put his own driving ambitions to one side, he worked for Church Farm Racing in Sussex running Derek Bell and Peter Gethin in their early days. He branched out to set up his own Formula 2 team in 1972, partnering with Greg Field to run another Sussex man, David Purley, in Formula Atlantic, Formula 2 and Formula 5000 under the LEC Racing banner. They had a short-lived foray into Formula 1 that ended when Purley was seriously injured in a massive crash during pre-qualifying for the 1977 British Grand Prix at Silverstone. In 1979, Earle and Field founded Onyx Race Engineering and the new team tackled Formula 2 for three seasons before attempting Formula 1 in 1982, this time with Emilio de Villota in a March, but the Spaniard was unable to qualify in five attempts. More Formula 2 followed, this time running March's outsourced works programme until the end of 1984, when Formula 3000 took over as the main feeder category into Formula 1. Still with March's support, Onyx driver Emanuele Pirro finished third in the International Formula 3000 Championship in both 1985 and 1986, followed by the team's biggest success of all with Stefano Modena becoming champion in 1987.

Having finally won a championship, Earle decided to test his credentials once again in Formula 1 in 1988. After that attempt fell through, Onyx found itself back in Formula 3000 for one more season, a disappointing one that saw Volker Weidler in the team's March outclassed by Ralt and Reynard opposition. Meanwhile, Earle hired Alan Jenkins, formerly of McLaren, to design Onyx's own Formula 1 car, the neat ORE-1, with a customer Cosworth DFR V8 engine and six-speed transverse gearbox. Now rebranded as Onyx Grand Prix, the experienced team went into the 1989 season with cautious optimism, although money, as ever, was tight — until the arrival of the strange new sponsor provided the vital financial lifeline.

After weeks of sleepless nights at Onyx Grand Prix's Littlehampton factory in West Sussex, one car was completed just in time for a Van Rossem-orchestrated pre-season launch at London's Hippodrome. After an inauspicious start to the proceedings, when the ORE-1 was clamped by an overzealous traffic warden outside the venue, the car was placed on a lift beneath the stage ready for the 'reveal', which involved it rising amidst a cloud of dry ice sporting its garish blue-and-pink livery. Journalist Nigel Roebuck wrote that it was the most tasteless Formula 1 launch he had ever attended.

With the project running behind schedule, Onyx did well simply to get to the first race, in Brazil, although the team's personnel were still completing build of the cars in the paddock and had to resort to the incongruous setting of a local go-kart circuit for the first shakedown runs. As Formula 1 had become over-subscribed in this period, with 20 teams and 39

With backing from Jean-Pierre Van Rossem's Moneytron operation, a fraudulent pyramid investment scheme, the Onyx Formula 1 team achieved a best result of third place for Stefan Johansson in the 1989 Portuguese Grand Prix.

drivers registered for the 1989 World Championship, Onyx faced a brutal environment in which its two cars were amongst a dozen that had to fight to 'pre-qualify' on Friday morning for only four places in the official qualifying session, and in Brazil, unsurprisingly, neither of the team's cars cleared that hurdle. Without the benefit of any testing, this pattern continued in the early races as the team struggled to find its feet and unlock the potential of what Johansson described as 'an incredibly good car' that was 'nimble, easy to drive and to dial in, and with a good operating window'. Johansson finally made the grid at the fourth round, in Mexico City, after which he qualified for four races in succession. In France, where Van Rossem had a fleet of his personal Ferraris in the paddock for his guests to use, Gachot was finally able to put the second Onyx on the grid for his Grand Prix début and outqualified his experienced team-mate in an impressive 11th position, but it was Johansson who did better in the race by scoring the team's first World Championship points with fifth place.

Van Rossem had been gradually buying into Onyx Grand Prix by acquiring equity from Paul Shakespeare, who had made the initial investment to fund the team's expansion into Formula 1. Soon the eccentric Belgian became the team's majority shareholder as well as prime sponsor. His displays of lavish lifestyle and extravagant spending continued unabated and included the purchase of several more Ferraris and the acquisition of a $20 million Gulfstream IV business jet. He had also extended Moneytron sponsorship to the Belgian KTR Formula 3 team and even backed a pair of Ferrari Mondials racing with none other than ex-World Champion Keke Rosberg on the driving strength. Of all the illustrious Ferrari models he could have attempted to turn into a racing car, the underpowered and overweight four-seater Mondial was the least suitable.

After the points-scoring result in France, the ambitions of the team's patron started to stretch reality. Tensions arose with Onyx's management who were unable to prevent him making bold pronouncements to anybody who would listen. He was quoted in the press as saying that he intended to make the team one of the biggest in Formula 1 to match the likes of McLaren and Ferrari and to be winning within two years. This was accompanied by suggestions that he planned to provide the team with a wind tunnel near its factory and its own test track in the South of France.

Flights of fancy aside, however, an interesting possibility arose with Porsche. After a meeting at the company's headquarters in Stuttgart, Earle and Van Rossem reached a verbal understanding that Porsche would consider supplying Onyx with purpose-designed V12 engines for the 1990 season in return for an investment of $40–50 million in the project. This understanding was subject to a strict confidentiality clause, partly to give Porsche time to satisfy itself about the source of the funds. Earle, therefore, was very surprised to learn from Gachot's manager, Pierre van Vliet, that Van Rossem had talked about the potential engine deal during a television interview. Porsche ceased negotiations as a result and decided to partner with the safer option of the Arrows team. On hearing of Porsche's decision, the reaction of the wild Belgian was to set fire to one of his own Porsches in an attempt to insult the company that he felt had slighted him.

Although Van Rossem's bombastic statements continued to raise the public profile of Onyx, the team didn't always make the news for the right reasons. The reality was that he was beginning to realise the true costs of running a team and becoming reluctant to pay its spiralling bills. Years later, in an interview with Simon Taylor for *Motor Sport*, Johansson said: 'The team was right on the edge with money. Funds would always appear just in time to get to the next race, but I couldn't get paid. My retainer was a serious amount to me, close to $1 million, and race followed race without a sniff. Before the last race at Suzuka, Van Rossem called and asked me to meet him in a hotel in Tokyo. I went to his room, he opened a suitcase and it was crammed full of cash, my entire salary for the year. I walked out of the hotel with a couple of bulging plastic bags. I didn't know what to do with it. I called a friend from my racing days in Japan and we managed to pay it into a bank. Then I wired it to my account in Europe!'

Gachot also struggled to receive his much more modest salary, although he did have use of a Ferrari Testarossa from Van Rossem's collection. In the end, the oddball sponsor reportedly offered Gachot a deal whereby, in return for foregoing any payment in 1989, he would receive $1 million the following year. Soon after he declined that offer, Gachot was as surprised as anyone to hear that he had been fired on the incorrect premise that he had issued a press release criticising the team and its owner for the lack of testing. Gachot, who had been responsible for introducing Van Rossem to the team in the first place, had to resort to threatening Onyx with an injunction until the erratic owner was persuaded to give him a letter promising severance pay, although the money never arrived.

Following Gachot's dismissal after the Italian Grand Prix, Marlboro-backed Finn JJ Lehto (see Chapter 59) replaced him for the next race, in Portugal, but failed to pre-qualify. However, it was here that Johansson made an opportunistic and inspired call to stay out on worn tyres towards the end of the race and, helped by a collision between Nigel Mansell and Ayrton Senna, found himself in a remarkable third place, which he managed to hang on to despite crossing the finishing line out of fuel and with the tyres worn down to their carcasses. This podium finish behind winner Gerhard Berger and second-placed Alain Prost was a fairy-tale result for a team that had had to spend much of its first season fighting its way through pre-qualifying. Everyone in the team, from Van Rossem downwards, was ecstatic about this stunning result. Sadly, however, there would be no more championship points.

Jean-Pierre Van Rossem was born on 29th May 1945 in the Belgian city of Bruges into a conservative, royalist Roman Catholic family with a bourgeois lifestyle that he claimed to have despised from an early age. He said that when his favourite pet rabbit died, his authoritarian father, a railway office manager, forced him to eat it. Into adulthood, he became estranged from his father and described him as having 'a mouth full of vinegar and slime'.

Maintaining that he never felt intellectually understood by his parents, he left home when he was 17 with little money to try to make his own way in the world. He won a place to study Economics at the University of Ghent, where his final term's thesis ('The velocity of money: Theoretical approach to understanding and practical applications in Belgium') won a prize called the International Scholarship of Flanders that enabled him to continue post-graduate studies. He spent two years in America at the University of Pennsylvania's Wharton School studying econometrics — the branch of economics concerned with the use of mathematical methods in describing economic systems — under Nobel Prize winner Lawrence Klein. Van Rossem seems not to have made a great impression on Klein, who, when asked in 1990 by the *Wall Street Journal* about memories of his student, replied that the name meant nothing to him.

During his student years, Van Rossem developed an interest in the theories of Karl Marx and became a strong advocate of Marxism. Having obtained a PhD, he began writing papers and books on economics, and started a private teaching business. He developed a drug addiction and when his business went bankrupt he was found to have been writing unsecured cheques. As a result, in December 1973, when aged 28, he was sentenced to four years in prison for fraud. While behind bars, he claimed to have developed a mathematical model that could anticipate and predict stock-market movements.

Once back in Europe, he resumed his teaching career and attracted many students from wealthy Flemish families who would become useful sources of investment capital in future years. After a short-lived first marriage when living in America, he married Nicole Annys in 1978. His new wife's shopping excesses, he said, led him to further develop his financial modelling to the point where his algorithm could not only predict and beat market trends but also yield previously unheard-of returns. Presenting himself as an expert on global financial markets, the convicted fraudster started an investment company employing a research team with the aim of predicting macro-economic trends. After a reputed 1.6 million man-hours of work involving groups of mathematicians and economists, Van Rossem claimed to be able to predict share values, currency rates and commodity prices by taking into account hundreds of economic and political variables. He named the company Moneytron after the supercomputer that supposedly contained all the accumulated data but no one was ever permitted to see. It was said to be housed in a secure room behind his office but a cleaner later confirmed that this room was actually just a broom cupboard.

The first investors were the parents of students to whom he was giving night classes in economics. It wasn't long before word of mouth ensured that the reports of staggering returns spread around the world and investors, now restricted to those with 'High Net Worth' status, were falling over

As well as being a crook, Jean-Pierre Van Rossem was a man of unusual appearance and unsavoury habits who ended up being banned from Formula 1 paddocks for ill-advised remarks about the powers-that-be.

themselves to channel funds in his direction. The exclusivity accorded in only allowing the ultra-wealthy to invest, starting with a minimum of $50 million, was clever marketing that became self-fulfilling. Such was the greed and fear of missing out, it simply accelerated demand from people who were dazzled by the notion of sophisticated scientific methodology and happy to entrust funds to this apparent investment magician without carrying out any due diligence or asking too many questions. Certain high-profile investors were paid handsome dividends and their returns made public, resulting in valuable press coverage that in turn enticed others to join the queue to invest. Despite Van Rossem's explicit distaste for monarchy, his clients even included members of the Belgian royal family.

According to the *Financial Times*, by 1989 Van Rossem had attracted $7 billion to 'manage' on behalf of clients and, helped by the hefty five percent commission he charged, was said to have accumulated a personal fortune of $860 million. At the peak of his success, he claimed to own not only the Onyx Grand Prix team but also a castle, a $4 million yacht (*The Destiny*), two Falcon 900 aircraft and 108 Ferraris — all of which was rather at odds with his Marxist values. He also had an expensive drug habit.

At the peak of his supposed fortune in the 1980s, Van Rossem was probably the most famous personality in Belgium after the country's king. Unimpressed by this, Bernie Ecclestone made it clear that while his money was welcome in Formula 1, his presence was not. As Stefan Johansson said, 'It's easy to forget that he spent barely a year in Formula 1 because everybody remembers him.'

Formula 1 wasn't Jean-Pierre Van Rossem's only foray into 'motorsport' sponsorship. Like the man, another venture at much the same time was unconventional, involving professional slot-car racing. As the American magazine *AutoWeek* put it in 1988, 'Just as Formula One has FISA and Bernie Ecclestone, slot racing has its own sanctioning body — the International Micro Car Association (IMCA) — and czar — Dr. J.P. Van Rossem, a wealthy, eccentric 44-year-old Belgian who still sports '60s length hair and publishes *EuroSlot*, one of the sport's many magazines.' Van Rossem used to sponsor championship events all over the world and would even cover the cost of flying top-ranked racers to his events to compete for prize funds worth thousands of dollars. Indeed, it wasn't uncommon for the winner of a very big contest to receive a real car, which on one occasion was a Ferrari 328.

Van Rossem was a bizarre-looking figure in the Grand Prix pitlanes and paddocks of the world. He had made a lot of money out of his company Moneytron and had no interest in what people thought about his unconventional and unkempt appearance. Very overweight, he had long white hair and a greasy beard that reached nearly to his waist, and always wore bright red racing boots. *Autosport* magazine described him as 'an out-of-shape Sumo wrestler' while another press report likened him to a rather sweaty Father Christmas, albeit one with food stains down his shirt front. A chain smoker, he claimed never to brush his teeth or wash his long and sometimes pony-tailed hair. He was invariably accompanied by an entourage of scantily clad young models and several bodyguards who were obviously armed. On one occasion, recalled Mike Earle, the attention-seeking team owner wanted to rent a bazooka, fill it with banknotes and fire them into the grandstands.

Van Rossem's lack of judgement was also destructive. Over the course of the 1989 season, he became an increasingly outspoken critic of anyone and everyone in Formula 1, endearing himself to no one and causing embarrassment for his team. His controversial remarks about how the sport was run included highly personal verbal attacks that were quoted in newspapers during the Belgian Grand Prix weekend and incurred the wrath of the two most influential and powerful men in motorsport at the time. Formula 1 commercial rights holder Bernie Ecclestone (see Chapter 25) didn't appreciate being described as a 'mafia boss and a shark' while FIA President Jean-Marie Balestre (see Chapter 7) took great exception to being called a Nazi sympathiser because of his membership of the pro-Nazi Vichy French military during the Second World War. Besides being ill-advised and offensive to the powers that be, Van Rossem's remarks reflected badly on the team. In the end, everyone at Onyx Grand Prix must have been relieved that his continual indiscretions led to him being prohibited from attending any more Grands Prix, and he faded from the scene just as quickly as he had arrived.

Even without the ban, Van Rossem's absence would have occurred soon enough. In reality, the overt and exuberant displays of wealth associated with ownership of a Formula 1 team were a classic case of 'fake it until you make it' and simply a diversionary tactic designed to reassure the world at large, and his trusting investors in particular, that Moneytron was flourishing and in robust financial health. In a sad ending for a team that had shown so much early promise and established a solid foundation on which to build, things quickly began to unravel.

Onyx Grand Prix was sold at the end of the 1989 season and another eccentric and unappealing character, Peter Monteverdi, a small-scale Swiss car manufacturer, museum owner and one-time racing driver, acquired 50 percent of the equity. After a turbulent winter that saw most of the team's experienced staff move on, including Earle, Onyx did at least make the grid for the new season, initially still with Johansson and Lehto driving the previous year's cars. After two races, Gregor Foitek, son of shareholder Karl Foitek, took Johansson's seat, by which time two new ORE-2 cars had been built. Although Foitek's seventh place in the Monaco Grand Prix provided a flash of hope, results were woeful, with the team's reputation not helped by Monteverdi's choice of a decrepit London double-decker bus as the team's motorhome and hospitality unit. After Monteverdi moved the team to his home country in July, standards of preparation plummeted, with worrying reports of broken suspension parts being welded back together rather than replaced. When Karl Foitek withdrew his funding and refused to let his son drive what he regarded as a dangerous car, the team folded without completing the season.

Moneytron had worked so well for Van Rossem while it lasted and allowed him to spend lavishly. In reality, the investment model, which may well have started out as genuine statistical methodology, turned out to be nothing more than a smoke-and-mirrors pyramid scheme whereby returns for early investors were paid out of funds supplied by new ones. The returns paid to investors were in reality few and far between.

The seeds of Van Rossem's downfall lay in the stock-market crash of 1987. A rapid and severe downturn occurred in the US stock market over several days of October, with the 22nd of the month, when the Dow Jones Index fell 22.6 percent, becoming known as Black Monday. Over the course of the next 18 months, Moneytron's clients became extremely cautious and fresh investment dried up. Then, when markets started to show signs of recovery, some clients decided they wanted to withdraw their capital. In due course, with little or no new investment coming in, it became impossible to meet the gathering number of requests for repayment. Van Rossem's problems were exacerbated by his claim that an unnamed US broker had failed to repay $362 million from a futures deal of which he said $200 million belonged to clients. Whether or not that was true, the snowball effect of redemptions meant that Moneytron collapsed entirely during 1990 as the truth behind the Ponzi scheme became increasingly evident to investors.

In his book *Rise and Fall of a Financial Straw Man*, Ludwig Verduyn quoted Van Rossem as stating that he had made more than 10,000 transactions with Moneytron since 1986. However, the judicial investigation, which involved a multitude of searches, found no evidence of any trading at all, but simply a mass of counterfeit contracts from the American brokerage house Prudential Bache and a series of unsecured cheques.

At the end of 1989, as his brief tenure as team owner drew to a close, Van Rossem's troubles were compounded when his heavy-drinking wife Nicole was discovered by their son to have drowned in her bath, although her husband was convinced that she had been murdered. In a bizarre twist, he bought Europe's first refrigerated coffin in which to store her body, in the hope that one day medical science would be able to revive her, so that, in his words, 'I can see her again before I die.' He was prevented from installing the coffin in the graveyard by the local community, who thought the noise of its electric motor was excessive, so instead he used the services of a cryogenics company until he was no longer able to afford the ongoing maintenance costs and literally 'pulled the plug'.

Less than a year after he had disposed of his interest in Onyx Grand Prix, Van Rossem married his third wife but spent part of his honeymoon in prison on charges of forgery and, once again, writing bad cheques. Even as the net closed around him, he had continued to flaunt the illusion of great wealth by driving around the nightlife districts of Bruges in one of his fleet of Ferraris, throwing quantities of 1,000-franc notes into the cafés and restaurants on the Eiermarkt, in gestures reminiscent of Robin Hood stealing from the rich and giving to the poor. By 1991, he was facing more fraud charges relating to the collapse of Moneytron, including the printing of fake share certificates and siphoning funds off to Swiss bank accounts, for which he received a five-year sentence and was ordered to pay back $30 million to creditors. However, with astonishing gall, he managed to temporarily evade prison by entering politics, which gave him a period of immunity.

He founded his own libertarian political protest party called *Radicale Omvormers en Sociale Strijders voor een Eerlijker Maatschappij,* or *ROSSEM* for short, the title meaning 'Radical Reformers and Social Warriors for a Fairer Society'. The party's manifesto pledges included the privatisation of Belgium's social-security system, direct elections for police officers and the abolition of the monarchy. Although this charade was met with widespread derision, the party still managed to win 200,000 votes (3.2 percent) in national elections held in November 1991. Under the system of proportional representation, that was sufficient to win three seats in the Belgian Federal Parliament, one of which Van Rossem himself held until May 1995. He repaid the faith of those who had cast their votes in his favour by admitting that he was a 'crook and a gangster' and cynically telling an interviewer, 'If 200,000 people are voting for such a person who was in jail it is because they feel that the other candidates are even more corrupt. The people here must be hopeless to vote for a nutcase like me.' In 1993 he further vented his anti-monarchist opinions when he interrupted the coronation of King Albert II by bellowing '*Vive la république d'Europe, vive Lahaut*' during the oath-taking ceremony; this was a reference to Julien Lahaut, who had also shouted '*Vive la république*' at the coronation of King Baudouin of Belgium in 1950.

Once his parliamentary immunity expired with the loss of his seat at the next elections, Van Rossem returned to jail to serve the rest of his sentence. While inside, he put his time to good use by writing a diary of his day-to-day experiences that was later published and went on to become a bestseller. He was the author of several other books, one of which gained him even more notoriety. This was a Michelin-style guide to more than 1,000 of the country's brothels, illustrated with symbols to signify certain attributes:

condoms showed good hygiene, wallets indicated value for money, beds represented comfort and smiley faces ranked good performance.

Separately, he chronicled his own sexual fantasies in a series of cartoon strips, showing him being stretched by nuns on a rack and then saved by blonde maidens in castles. These were sold to fund his continuing political ambitions, which led him to go back to the electorate in 2014 with his party *ROSSEM 2*, although this time he obtained only a fraction of the votes he had attracted in 1991. In the meantime, his celebrity status grew as he seemingly continued to court controversy at every opportunity. His background and controversial views ensured that he remained in demand as a guest on television chat shows and on one of his appearances in 2004 he famously offended the Dutch Prime Minister, Jan Peter Balkenende, by calling him a 'dick'.

He remained in the limelight until his final days, campaigning for euthanasia and the right to voluntarily end his life while he struggled with pulmonary complications. Towards the end, when he needed to be taken to hospital, the fire brigade had to remove him from his rented apartment in a Brussels suburb. Only a month before he died, he received his fourth custodial sentence of two years for forgery, money laundering, tax evasion and fraud, but was too unwell to go to prison. The authorities confiscated his last remaining assets of €390,000 (£350,000) and so when he died — on 14th December 2018 at the age of 73 — he was destitute, despite his years of unimaginable wealth. The transformation from colourful extrovert to tragic figure was complete.

CHAPTER 59

JOS VERSTAPPEN

Wrong side of the track

Best known as father of and mentor to Max Verstappen, the most prodigiously talented Formula 1 driver of his generation, Jos Verstappen is also a former Grand Prix driver, although he never came near achieving his son's level of success despite getting an enviable break by making his début in the sport's top echelon as team-mate to Michael Schumacher at Benetton. Outside the cockpit, however, he had a dark side and a volatile temperament that regularly got him in trouble with the law and led to a succession of criminal convictions.

Born on 4th March 1972 in Montfort in Holland, Jos Verstappen began karting at the age of 10. Despite being hospitalised following a bad crash in his very first race, he became Dutch junior champion in 1984 and went on to compete successfully elsewhere in Europe. Enthusiasm from Dutch sponsors helped his transition into cars and for the 1992 season he joined highly respected Van Amersfoort Racing for a season of Formula Opel Lotus and won the championship at his first attempt. Staying with Van Amersfoort for 1993, he moved up to Formula 3 and won that year's prestigious Marlboro Masters event at Zandvoort as well as scoring eight victories in the German championship. When invited to test the Formula 1 Footwork Arrows at Estoril later that year, he demonstrated his raw speed by setting a time that would have put him tenth on the grid at the previous weekend's Portuguese Grand Prix.

With his name now on the radar of several Formula 1 teams, he was snapped up by Flavio Briatore as test driver for Benetton in 1994 on condition that he also signed a personal management contract. This was to prove an unwise move as it meant losing his independence and made him reliant on Briatore for his future. Benetton's number one driver that year was the mercurial Michael Schumacher with JJ Lehto as number two, but when Lehto was incapacitated through injury in pre-season testing Verstappen was called up to replace him for the first two races. There was no doubting the Dutchman's speed but his début in the Brazilian Grand Prix ended in controversy when Eddie Irvine's Jordan hit him, triggering a four-car accident in which the Benetton was launched into a series of somersaults, fortunately without injury to Verstappen or the other drivers involved.

When Lehto returned, his performances were disappointing and he was 'rested' after four races, making way for Verstappen once again. Another spectacular incident followed in the German Grand Prix when a refuelling hose leaked onto Verstappen's car, engulfing the driver in flames, but he escaped almost unscathed with only minor burns. Despite being overshadowed by Schumacher, who was on his way to his first World Championship title, Verstappen did well in the next few races, finishing in points-scoring positions three times, twice with third places, which turned out to be the only podium finishes of his career. In an unsuccessful bid to win the constructors' championship, the ruthless Briatore replaced him for the last two races with the more experienced Johnny Herbert and subsequently signed the Englishman for the following season, leaving Verstappen out in the cold after a truncated season that was to prove the highpoint of his intermittent Formula 1 career at the age of just 23.

After the bitter disappointment of being dropped from the team but still under contract to Briatore, he was loaned out to the uncompetitive Simtek team for 1995 but it collapsed midway through the season, leaving him out of a drive again. Despite his natural talent, he now found himself more attractive to teams because of his Dutch backers and the next two seasons saw the hard-charging driver employed by Footwork Arrows and Tyrrell, where his efforts to make up for uncompetitive and under-developed equipment made him better known for crashing than for driving skill.

A lifeline arrived halfway through 1998 when Jackie Stewart recruited him to replace Jan Magnussen but he was outclassed by team leader Rubens Barrichello and was left without a drive once more. A year of testing for the still-born Honda team opened the door for a return to Arrows with his group of loyal Dutch sponsors but two seasons in the team's hopelessly unreliable and off-the-pace cars brought little reward. The 2002 season saw him sitting on the sidelines again but somehow he managed to scrape together enough money to pay for a drive with Paul Stoddart's tiny Minardi

After his own Formula 1 career, the volatile Jos Verstappen devoted himself
to nurturing son Max's prospects, as pictured here with the 12-year-old
during his first season of international karting.

team the following year. This became his swansong season and his Formula
1 career ended at the age of 30 after competing in 107 Grands Prix.

Having failed to find an environment in which he could develop his raw
talent, his largely unfulfilled career at the top level of the sport fizzled out,
although he did obtain berths here and there. After racing in the A1GP
series for Team Netherlands in 2005–06, he had a few opportunities in
sports cars. A campaign in a privately entered Porsche Spyder in 2008
brought class victories at Le Mans, Barcelona and Spa and culminated in
winning the LMP2 championship.

The explosive temperament of 'Jos the Boss', as his adoring Dutch
fans nicknamed him, led him to develop a habit of falling out with
a succession of team bosses, including Flavio Briatore, Tom Walkinshaw,
Jackie Stewart and Jan Lammers, and did nothing to enhance his career
prospects. His relationships away from the track were no better and
reflected a troubled and controversial personal life.

In 1998 he became embroiled in a serious fight at a karting track in
Lanaken, Belgium in a dispute with rival competitors that arose because
he and a group of friends wanted sole use of the circuit. Accused of

grievous bodily harm, he was alleged to have punched a 45-year-old man who suffered a fractured skull and life-threatening injuries that left him hospitalised for several months. When the case came to court in October 2000, Verstappen and his 53-year-old father, Frans, were found guilty of assault and both were given five-year sentences that were suspended after an out-of-court settlement was reached with the unfortunate victim and the public prosecutor, ensuring that neither assailant went to jail.

Ironically, several years later 'Jos the Boss' was in trouble again for physical violence, *Der Telegraaf* reporting that this time he had assaulted his father. Stating that Frans Verstappen had filed a complaint with the police, the newspaper commented: 'We've seen before that Jos has loose hands but this was the limit.' Frans, showing multiple wounds and bruises on his body and head, was quoted as saying, 'Jos is very bad.' However, any charges were dropped and no case ever went to court.

His marriage to Sophie Kumpen, a Dutch woman who had been a karting ace, began to break down when their son Max was seven years old and their separation was fraught with drama and played out in public view. In December 2008, the estranged husband found himself in court in Tongeren in Belgium charged with physically attacking her. Although he wasn't convicted of assault, he was found guilty of threatening his estranged wife in text messages, causing criminal damage to her car and violating a previous restraining order. Potentially he faced eight months in prison but got away with a three-month suspended sentence.

His next reported misdemeanour occurred when he drove his car at his 24-year-old ex-girlfriend after an argument near his home, leaving her with, according to *Der Standaard*, 'heavy bruises and abrasions'. The unnamed woman told RTL television: 'It's definitely not the first time he does this, I think now I need to go and hide. I don't know what to expect now when he is released.' He fled the scene but later turned himself into the police. After his arrest in January 2012, the 39-year-old was imprisoned for aggravated assault and attempted manslaughter but was released after 15 days following an appeal by his lawyers.

He was in trouble again in April 2017 when he got into a fight with another customer at a beach club in Roermond and refused to leave when security guards asked him to. When police arrived, they arrested him and took him into custody.

The successful career of his prodigiously talented and good-natured son appears to have given Jos Verstappen a mission in life that perhaps had been lacking since his own career faded and has latterly kept him out of the news.

JJ LEHTO
A bridge too far

The driver whose injury presented the opportunity for Jos Verstappen to make his Formula 1 début alongside Michael Schumacher was JJ Lehto. Over the course of his 20-year career, he competed in 62 Grands Prix for several teams, including Benetton, Sauber and Onyx, and twice won the Le Mans 24 Hours, with McLaren in 1995 and Audi in 2005. Following his retirement from the sport, Lehto also found himself in serious trouble with the law.

On the night of 17th June 2010, he was travelling in a speedboat on a narrow canal in Raasepori, southern Finland, his home country, when it collided with a pillar supporting a bridge, tragically killing the other occupant, a close friend, and leaving him unconscious with serious head injuries, broken ribs and multiple fractures. A blood test proved that Lehto had been intoxicated at the time of the accident and he was duly charged with negligent homicide. The Lansi-Uudenmaan district court heard that the boat had been travelling at almost 80kph in an area in Raasepori where the speed limit was only 5kph.

The former driver said that he had no memory of the early-morning accident. Despite the absence of any recollection of the tragedy, he denied that he had been steering the boat when it crashed and claimed that he had been sitting in the back. Nonetheless, he was convicted in December 2011 and sentenced to two years and four months in prison, but his lawyers duly appealed and the following year he was cleared of all charges. Steering a boat drunk or allowing a drunk person to control it are both crimes, but as there was uncertainty about which of the two Lehto had committed, he couldn't be sentenced for either offence. Investigators later disputed this and stated that Lehto's injuries had been consistent with those of someone who had been in the driving seat of the boat.

CHAPTER 60

DONALD WALKER

Circuitous dreamer

The one-off Dallas Grand Prix of 1984 will be remembered by Formula 1 fans for all the wrong reasons, including the practice crash that put Tyrrell driver Martin Brundle out of action for the rest of the season with broken ankles and feet. Behind the scenes, meanwhile, the former accountant who had instigated and organised the event was soon to find that the luxury existence he and his wife enjoyed was about to evaporate because he had been putting his hand in the till and forgetting to pay his taxes.

Formula 1 supremo Bernie Ecclestone had always recognised the commercial importance of staging a Grand Prix in the United States. After the demise of the popular races in Long Beach, California (1976–83), due to a disagreement with promoter Chris Pook about the pricing of admission tickets, followed by the farcical Caesars Palace events in a Las Vegas parking lot (1981–82) and the disappointing start to Detroit's efforts (from 1982), Ecclestone would have welcomed 41-year-old Donald Walker's initiative to stage a Grand Prix in the streets of Dallas, Texas in 1984.

Oklahoma-born Walker was an accountant turned property developer and investor who had only recently become involved with motor racing. He ran a company called Dallas Motorsports Inc. through which he had briefly rescued the struggling Can-Am series for the 1984 season by taking over its lease and introducing CRC Chemicals as title sponsor. Walker and his socially ambitious wife Carol appeared to have come into great wealth only a few years previously and his interest in cars had started with occasional forays in historic events in 1982. For someone who dreamt big,

NGUYEN DUC CHUNG
Bending the rules

Formula 1 had grand plans to launch a Grand Prix in Vietnam with a 10-year deal whereby the government would pay $60 million each year to host the race in the hope that the glamour of the sport would reshape the image of Hanoi, the country's capital. A semi-permanent circuit was constructed on the outskirts of Hanoi but the first race, due to be held in April 2020, had to be cancelled because of the Covid-19 pandemic.

A key figure in launching the proposed event was 53-year-old Nguyen Duc Chung, a former director of Hanoi's police department and also the city's mayor. Just a few months after the abandoned race, he was arrested on charges of fraud and sentenced to five years in prison for misappropriating state secrets and misusing assets. *Business F1* magazine reported that his misdemeanours came to light after auditors were called in to assess the impact of the pandemic on the event and to agree a new budget for future races, but instead they discovered financial irregularities.

At the time of writing, it remains uncertain whether a Vietnam Grand Prix will ever take place.

it was appropriate that one of his successes had been winning a race at the annual 'Walter Mitty' event at Road Atlanta, and he had also built up a collection of almost 50 exotic cars in a short space of time. These were mainly Porsches and Ferraris, and included an ex-Clay Regazzoni Formula 1 car and a Ferrari 250 GTO.

As journalist Joe Saward wrote: 'Although not an outgoing individual, he lived an extravagant life, owning a $6 million French-styled mansion in North Dallas, employing a butler and flitting around other residences, including an 800-acre woodland ranch in Terrell, Texas; a ski lodge in Crested Butte, Colorado; a house near the sea in Carmel, California; and another on the Atlantic coast, near Jacksonville, Florida. There was also a yacht in Florida and a house in the Cayman Islands.'

The Walkers were an extravagant couple who spent money without compunction and travelled the world by private jet. The race in Dallas provided an ideal and glamorous route through which Carol could inveigle herself into local society, something that she craved, as well as hopefully making money for Walker and his business syndicate.

Although Walker had signed a five-year contract to stage races, only one Dallas Grand Prix ever took place, on 8th July 1984, which was an ill-advised choice of date. In sweltering 40-degree heat at the peak of the Texan summer, track temperatures rose as high as 66 degrees and caused the makeshift circuit to crumble during the race, making the surface so treacherous that 14 of the cars retired as a result of hitting retaining walls. Only eight of the 26 starters reached the finish, led by Keke Rosberg, who took his only win of the season driving a Williams-Honda FW09.

One reason why there was never another Dallas Grand Prix was that a key member of the race organisation absconded with some of the takings. Early in 1985, Walker's co-investors accused him of a host of irregularities, and a few weeks later the holding company, Dallas Grand Prix of Texas Inc., filed for Chapter 11 bankruptcy.

At the same time, Walker's own business, DRW Investments, became the target of concurrent investigations by the FBI and the US Securities and Exchange Commission amidst allegations from investors that he had embezzled funds from some of the 92 syndication projects in which he was a partner. Included in the charges against him was the secret sale of three apartment complexes without the legally required approval of his partners, after which he deposited $400,000 of the profits into his own money-market accounts.

By the following March, Walker had filed for personal bankruptcy due to a $17 million dispute with the Internal Revenue Service, which claimed that in the period 1981–84 he had understated his tax liabilities in property-development projects by a massive $165 million. He and his wife were charged with owing $85 million in back taxes, interest and penalties and in January 1988 he was jailed for seven years after pleading guilty to tax fraud.

KLAUS WALZ

Shot in the dark

A man of many names, this former sports car racer appeared to be the saviour that Gérard Larrousse so desperately needed for his financially beleaguered Formula 1 team. He emerged as an extremely nasty criminal and serial killer whose short-lived ownership ended when he shot himself dead after a stand-off with German police.

Gérard Larrousse's troubled Formula 1 team, Équipe Larrousse, was on the crest of a wave — relatively speaking — at the end of 1990 after finishing sixth in the constructors' championship. That marked quite a turn-around from its position at the beginning of the previous year, when Larrousse's then partner in the team's ownership, Didier Calmels (see Chapter 14), had murdered his wife, causing some elements of the British press to cruelly dub the shocked team 'Murder Racing Ltd'. However, more scandal lay ahead, to the point where it began to look like Larrousse was a man of poor judgement.

Although the team's drivers for 1991, Éric Bernard and Aguri Suzuki, were unchanged from the pairing that had delivered modest success in 1990, they now struggled and the best results of the new season were just one sixth place apiece. Part of the problem was that the cash-strapped team had lost its Lamborghini V12 engine deal to Ligier and now had to fall back on the outdated Cosworth DFR V8 engines used by various tail-end outfits. Once again the team finished the year in severe financial difficulty, owing money to the suppliers of both its chassis (Lola) and engines (Hart). When Bernard broke his ankle in qualifying at the penultimate race in Japan, a stand-in driver was needed for the final race in Australia and Larrousse judged that Bertrand Gachot was the man he needed. As the Belgian had just been released from prison after assaulting a London taxi driver (see Chapter 22), there was some irony in the fact that the first drive he was able to secure was with a team already associated with wrongdoing.

Meanwhile, Gérard Larrousse prepared his plans for the 1992 season. He did a deal with respected designer Robin Herd, formerly of March, for his design studio Fomet 1 to create a new chassis with engines once again supplied by Lamborghini. After teetering on the edge of bankruptcy for many months, the team got a new lease of life when Venturi, the small French manufacturer of road-going supercars of that name, came in to take a 65 per cent stake alongside Japanese investment house Central Park, which had already bought into the team. Renamed Central Park Venturi Larrousse, the team signed Japanese driver Ukyo Katayama and retained Gachot, who delivered the only championship point of the year with sixth place at Monaco. Funding difficulties continued until midway through the year when Venturi, which really didn't have the resources to compete in Formula 1 anyway, used the excuse that it was tired of seeing its cars run near the back and sold its shareholding to an investment group called Comstock. At that point, it seemed that the team's financial struggles might finally recede.

According to his business card, 'Rainer Walldorf' headed the Cannes-based Comstock investment group. Unknown to Gérard Larrousse, or any of his team members, the real name of this unsavoury 50-year-old German 'businessman' was Klaus Walz, who sometimes also called himself 'Peter' Walz when it suited him to do so.

He had had a short-lived international racing career, mostly in sports cars built by ToJ, a small German racing car constructor run by Jörg Obermoser. Following minor races at Monza in 1976 and at Hockenheim and Paul Ricard in 1977, Walz moved up to take part in the Interserie, a thinly supported 'allcomers' sports car championship staged mainly at German circuits. Competing in five of the six rounds in 1978, he claimed some good results, with second place at Wunstorf and third places at Colmar-Berg (Luxembourg) and Hockenheim, although the opposition was always sparse. Driving a ToJ-entered March 782, he also tried his hand in single-seaters but wasn't quick enough to qualify for either of the two European Formula 2 Championship races he entered. After a handful

By the time the name Comstock appeared in Formula 1 in 1992 on the Venturi
LC92 cars driven by Bertrand Gachot (see Chapter 22) and Ukyo Katayama,
the man behind this mysterious entity, Klaus Walz, was wanted by
police for four murders.

of lacklustre showings driving the same March in the 1979 Aurora AFX
British Formula 1 championship, which included a Formula 2 category to
bolster the numbers, he disappeared from the sport until his return as a
majority shareholder in the Larrousse team 13 years later.

With great fanfare, it was announced that Comstock would fund the
team through an 'investment bond/sponsorship' scheme. This was forecast
to produce sufficient income to support the operation and ensure that
investors would not only make a profit but also have their money paid back
in full after five years, hence giving sponsors free exposure. Even in 1992
that sounded highly implausible, although no one in the rarefied world of
Formula 1, which was quite accustomed at that time to accepting money
from dubious sources, appeared to be the slightest bit concerned.

Comstock's proprietors had named their company after a vast field of
silver ore, the Comstock Lode, that was discovered in Nevada in 1859
and generated vast fortunes for prospectors over a 15-year period. This
alluded to the fact that Walz and his colleagues were confident that their
ventures would make a great deal of money for them, if not for anyone else.
Unfortunately for the beleaguered Larrousse team, the partnership with

Comstock and its boss, 'Walldorf', proved to be even shorter than the one with Didier Calmels, who was by now out of prison and trying to repair his reputation and rebuild his business. Only a few weeks after the Larrousse announcement, Walz's brief tenure as a team owner was over, almost as soon as it had started.

His primary accomplice was a nephew, Gordon Walz, although this individual was always introduced in Formula 1 circles as a son-in-law. He usually went by the name 'Klaus Sorajowski' but sometimes used 'Patrick' or 'Peter' as his first name. Between them, 'Walldorf' and 'Sorajowski' had other companies headquartered in Cannes using various combinations of Comstock identities as well as the name L'Art Minéral. 'Walldorf' portrayed himself as a dealer in exotic and luxury cars but was in fact the mastermind behind a vast criminal network handling high-value cars stolen to order and sold to customers all over the world after suitable makeovers. The centre of this international operation seems to have been a large workshop facility in northern Italy in the town of Desio, just north of Milan and near the Monza race circuit. Here the cars had their identities changed by means of forged documents, alteration of chassis and registration numbers, tampering with mileage recorders and sometimes resprays in different colours.

After a dispute with one of the Italian mechanics who worked for them, 'Walldorf' and 'Sorajowski', together with a Canadian accomplice, murdered him on 6th December 1989 in countryside near Turate, about 20 miles from the workshops. It is believed that the victim, Antonio Tonetto, knew too much about what his employers were up to. They killed him in a particularly abominable way, by locking him in the boot of a Fiat Panda and setting fire to it, only to resort to releasing him and shooting him in order to silence his screams of agony.

By the time of the Comstock tie-up with Larrousse, police had connected 'Walldorf' with three other murders. Two of them occurred in Portugal, the victims being a Dutchman from whom 'Walldorf' was renting a coastal villa and a Swiss businessman who was visiting the Lisbon area to conclude a deal with the villain. During investigations into the mysterious disappearances of these two men, Portuguese police tore the villa apart looking for evidence and found their corpses buried under a terrace that had recently been tiled over. According to Interpol, there was a fourth murder but no details of this are known.

All this put 'Walldorf' and 'Sorajowski' high on Interpol's list of most-wanted criminals and an international arrest warrant was issued. When French police noticed the Comstock name displayed on the Venturi LC92 cars, they suspected a possible connection. 'Walldorf' owned a luxurious villa in Valbonne, a chic hamlet near Mougins, in the hills behind Nice, and when further investigations established that the criminals were in residence, the *Gendarmerie* raided the house early one morning and apprehended them.

Neither man offered any resistance but 'Walldorf', realising that he had been exposed as Klaus Walz, asked for permission to fetch important documents from a desk in his study before agreeing to his formal arrest. Incredibly, the police agreed and, instead of the paperwork, their quarry produced a live hand grenade that he threatened to detonate, blowing everybody up, unless the *gendarmes* obeyed his instructions. Using the police's own handcuffs, 'Walldorf' and 'Sorajowski' manacled all but one of the officers to large items of furniture. The exception was the chief of police, whom they took hostage before forcing him to drive with them to a remote rendezvous with an accomplice they had telephoned before leaving the house. When they arrived, they left the chief of police shackled to the steering wheel of his car, threw the hand grenade into a nearby chicken coop, and sped away with the accomplice.

Using a BMW estate car, the two fugitives drove initially towards Italy with 500,000 francs in cash but, sensing that the net was closing in around them, changed their minds and headed to Germany. Within a month, the *Bundespolizei* had tracked them down to a Munich hotel and, mindful of the ordeal experienced by their French colleagues, took steps to minimise the risks involved in arresting 'Walldorf' and 'Sorajowski', who had barricaded themselves in their hotel room. With the room surrounded, there was a nine-hour stand-off before armed officers stormed in. In the ensuing gun battle, the younger Walz gave himself up and was taken into custody to face a raft of criminal charges. The elder Walz shot himself dead.

So ended Klaus Walz's extremely short career as owner of the Formula 1 team through which he had planned to launder some of his illicit profits.

The perennially impoverished Larrousse team continued without 'Walldorf' and battled on to the end of the 1993 season, its drivers, Erik Comas and the returning Philippe Alliot, picking up a couple of points-scoring finishes. There was yet another campaign in 1994 with a variety of drivers, but plans to limp on into 1995 under new ownership faltered when suppliers refused to cooperate until invoices had been paid, and the team collapsed with Gérard Larrousse facing several lawsuits. It was a sad ending for a man of his standing as well as for his team, which had raced its cars in liveries that had sometimes been almost as colourful as the characters behind it.

NICK WHITING

Petrol in the blood

Brother of leading FIA delegate Charlie Whiting, Nick Whiting was a national saloon car champion and entrant of Britain's only female Formula 1 racing driver. Undesirable connections with the criminal underworld in the aftermath of the biggest gold-bullion heist in British history led to his brutal and callous murder, which stunned the world of club motorsport.

At West Kingsdown in Kent, just a short distance from the main entrance gates to Brands Hatch, Nick Whiting had a race-preparation and accessories business where his younger brother, Charlie, used to help out working on saloon and rally cars while still a schoolboy. After first competing in rallycross in the late 1960s, Nick switched to the circuits where his forceful style and immaculate car preparation soon led to championship success in Special Saloon and Super Saloon racing. By the mid-1970s, he had become a hero of British club racing and a crowd favourite, particularly at his local track, first in a heavily modified Ford Anglia and then in a succession of predominantly Cosworth-powered Ford Escorts, presented in the vivid bright yellow livery of his All Car Equipe (ACE) racing team. His later fire-breathing machines were immensely powerful, their 450bhp on a par with contemporary Formula 1 cars, and during this period he had some epic scraps against Gerry Marshall, fellow car dealer, nemesis and arch-rival, in similarly fearsome Vauxhalls.

In 1976, the Whiting brothers pooled their talents and resources with

After a prominent club-racing career in various high-powered saloon cars,
including this Ford Escort of 1976, Nick Whiting was kidnapped from his
All Car Equipe garage business in 1990 and his body was found four
weeks later dumped in marshes.

racing impresario John Webb of Motor Circuit Developments (MCD),
owner of Brands Hatch, to prepare and run a two-year-old ex-works
Surtees TS16 Formula 1 car for Webb's latest bright young hopeful, Divina
Galica, a skilled skier who had captained the British Women's Olympics
Ski Team in 1968 and 1972. Racing under the name ShellSport Whiting,
they concentrated on the ShellSport Championship, a British *Formule
Libre* series, with the car carrying the supposedly unlucky number 13.
While David Purley won the title convincingly, Galica finished fourth in
the standings, her best results being fourth places at Thruxton and Mallory
Park. She also entered the British Grand Prix at Brands Hatch but failed to
qualify.

Charlie, having enjoyed this experience, joined Hesketh Racing for 1977
but the glory days that Lord Hesketh's team had savoured with star driver
James Hunt were long gone and it closed its doors at the end of the year.
Charlie then moved on to Bernie Ecclestone's Brabham team, where he
stayed for 10 years and, as chief mechanic, oversaw Nelson Piquet's World
Championship titles of 1981 and 1983. After the sale of the team, in 1988,
Charlie became the FIA Formula 1 Technical Delegate at Ecclestone's
behest and this involved overseeing scrutineering and technical eligibility

in a textbook case of 'poacher turned gamekeeper'. As an experienced mechanic and engineer, he was well equipped to spot attempts to lean on the regulations. By 1997, he had become FIA Race Director and Safety Delegate, a role that involved inspecting all the circuits used in Formula 1. In a remarkable progression from humble beginnings, he later took on additional very senior roles at the top of the sport, including becoming Formula 1's Permanent Starter. As a hugely respected and much-liked figure at the top of world motorsport, his sudden death from a pulmonary embolism in a Melbourne hotel room a few days before the 2019 Australian Grand Prix at the age of just 66 came as a great shock to the motor racing community.

The Brink's-Mat robbery remains one of the most notorious and biggest gold-bullion heists ever pulled off although the thieves involved wouldn't have realised it at the time. At 6.30am on the cold, grey morning of Saturday 26th November 1983, a South London gang of six armed and masked men, headed by Brian Robinson and Micky McAvoy, broke into Unit 7 of the Heathrow International Trading Estate adjoining London's Heathrow Airport. This nondescript-looking warehouse was one of the most secure storage facilities in Britain and was occupied by Brink's-Mat, a company that specialised in shipping ultra-valuable goods around the world. Inside knowledge provided by Anthony Black, Robinson's brother-in-law and one of the company's security guards, gave the gang quick and easy access to the site, where they overpowered the guards and forced them, by dousing them with petrol and threatening to set them alight, to reveal the combination numbers to the 12 locks of the reinforced concrete vault. Black was also able to assist by disabling the array of five electronic security systems.

The gang had expected to find about £3 million in stacks of easily transportable banknotes but instead the incredulous men discovered a much more valuable prize belonging to American bank Johnson Matthey. Three tonnes of gold bullion, comprising 6,800 bars divided into 76 cases, together with a stash of hundreds of thousands of pounds' worth of cut and uncut diamonds, were destined to be transported to the Far East. The combined value of the spoils was a staggering £26 million. So huge was the haul that it caused the price of gold to shoot up on world markets and within days the gang members had unwittingly benefited even more because the value of their ill-gotten gains had increased by a further £1 million.

However, the thieves soon realised that stealing the bullion was the easy part of the job. As none of them had experience in handling gold, they had to rely on other senior underworld figures to help them turn their haul into cash. This necessitated melting down the ingots to disguise the origins of the gold, disposing of it, and then laundering the proceeds. This procedure also increased the risks because it widened the circle of people who knew about the crime. One of the first people to whom the gang turned was master criminal Kenneth Noye, who was later to be flatteringly described by one of the investigating police officers as 'a successful businessman'. An obvious choice to act as middleman, Noye was entrusted with the complexities of orchestrating the movement of the vast quantities of gold through illicit channels and then back into the legitimate market for cash.

Police were quick to suspect Black, who had been the last guard to arrive on the morning of the raid. He not only confessed to providing detailed information but also identified McAvoy and Robinson, who in December 1984 were duly handed down jail sentences of 25 years each while Black got just six years. However, many other gangsters who were involved remained at large and they all had vested interests in the millions of pounds that were flooding the underworld. Over the next few years, incidents of betrayal between them turned to violence and unleashed a tide of gangland murders from the East End of London to the Costa del Sol in Spain.

The first death related to the crime occurred in 1985, when Noye, who was under police surveillance, killed undercover detective John Fordham after finding him hiding in the garden of his luxurious home in Kent. At the ensuing trial, Noye was found not guilty of murder even though he had stabbed the officer nine times, the jury determining that he had acted in self-defence. Noye found himself back in court the following year after police discovered 11 gold bars at his home and this time he received a 14-year sentence plus two more years for non-payment of a fine, a requirement that he had been unable to meet because his assets had been confiscated. In 1996, two years after his release, he stabbed and killed 21-year-old Stephen Cameron in a road-rage attack on a slip road of the M25 motorway and fled the country. Eventually he was caught and at his trial in April 2000 he was sentenced to life imprisonment, although he was released on parole in 2019.

In his book, *The Curse of Brink's-Mat*, author and crime journalist Wensley Clarkson listed no fewer than 19 people connected with the crime who met violent deaths between 1987 and 2003. They included a former policeman found with an axe embedded in his head, an underworld figure gunned down on his yacht off Corfu, and an enforcer who's now believed to be part of the foundations of the O2 Arena in London. One of the other victims was Nick Whiting.

In April 1990, Charlie Wilson, one of the Great Train Robbers (see Chapter 29), was gunned down on the doorstep of his Marbella home after £3 million of Brink's-Mat proceeds went missing in a drugs deal. Not long afterwards, on 7th June, Whiting, who had expanded his All Car Equipe business into car sales, was kidnapped from his showroom in Wrotham, Kent, by an armed gang who also stole five cars from the premises. The cars — a Jaguar E-type, an Audi quattro, a VW Golf GTi, a Ford Escort RS Turbo and a BMW — were recovered within days but detectives believed that their theft was just cover for an underworld hit. A few weeks later, a tip-off led police to a remote spot on Rainham Marshes in Essex where, on 2nd July, they found the badly decomposed body of the 43-year-old former racing driver hidden in a shallow grave in undergrowth. He had been beaten, tied up and gagged before being stabbed nine times and shot twice in the head with a 9mm pistol.

By the time of his death, Whiting was a millionaire living in a palatial house at Ightham, Kent, ostensibly on the proceeds from his garage interests. It was common knowledge that amongst his dangerous associates was old school friend Kenneth Noye and the inference was that, having been questioned by the police about allegations that he had played a part in laundering some of the proceeds from the robbery, Whiting had talked too much and paid the ultimate price for his indiscretion, although this was never proven. Two men were questioned about his killing but no one was ever charged, so the case remains unsolved.

As for the stolen gold, most of it has never been recovered, and would be worth over £500 million at today's prices.

FRANZ DUBOIS
Murder in the fast lane

Nathalie Maillet was born in Verdun, France in 1970 into a family of motor racing enthusiasts. Her father was an amateur racing driver and two of her uncles were involved in circuit management. As a youngster, she yearned to race but her family couldn't afford to help fund her aspirations. Having earned a degree in architecture at the University of East London, she founded an architecture practice in Luxembourg in 2000 and four years later was able to take part in her first motor race.

Despite being a successful architect, in 2016 she became a high-ranking official in motor racing by following both her genes and dreams by taking up the position of general manager and chief executive of the world-famous Spa-Francorchamps circuit in Belgium. During her five-year tenure, she transformed the circuit's management and was the driving force behind plans to modernise the iconic but ageing venue, which was in the middle of a $100 million revamp. She was also responsible for a large increase in the number of events held there.

Her Belgian husband of 17 years, amateur racing driver and driver coach Franz Dubois, was co-founder of the VW Fun Cup (see Chapter 17), a one-make racing series that became extremely popular because of the relatively low cost of taking part. There are several national series, all of which culminate each year at Spa for a 25-hour endurance event. Nathalie competed in seven such events, beating a field of 152 cars to win the 2006 race.

On the night of 14th August 2021, two weeks before her circuit hosted the Belgian Grand Prix, 51-year-old Nathalie was one of three people found dead at her home on the Rue de Houffalize in Gouvy, Luxembourg, 20 miles from the track. Echoing a statement released by the local public prosecutor, *Le Républicain Lorrain* newspaper reported that Dubois had discovered her in bed with her alleged mistress, Ann Lawrence Durviaux, an eminent law professor at the University of Liège, and had produced a gun and shot them both dead before turning the weapon on himself after first calling the police. It was Ann's birthday and less than a month after she had first experienced the Spa circuit when Nathalie had driven her around for five laps in a Fun Cup car.

DON AND BILL WHITTINGTON

Wings and wheels

Don, Bill and Dale Whittington had the distinction of being the only family of three brothers ever to have qualified for the same Indianapolis 500, in 1982. Relative latecomers to motorsport, Don and Bill also won the Le Mans 24 Hours despite little experience at that level and they remain the only siblings ever to have won the race together. But after an intense and short-lived foray into the sport, it was off the track that the outwardly respectable and successful businessmen became notorious for making history in an entirely different way.

Sons of occasional 1950s USAC racing driver Don Whittington, Reginald Donald ('Don') was born in 1946 and William Marvin ('Bill') in 1949 in Lubbock, Texas. By their teenage years, the family had moved to Fort Lauderdale, Florida, where Don and Bill attended Stranahan High School. From there, both pursued their formative passion for flying and became sufficiently accomplished that by their early 20s they had progressed to air racing. From 1976 they were regular competitors at the Reno Air Races over a 20-year period and Don's early successes included setting a qualifying record of 438mph in a Mustang P-51 named 'Precious Metal'. They became deeply involved in the restoration and preservation of World War II military aircraft — known in America as 'warbirds' — that they not only raced but also frequently displayed and demonstrated at air shows.

In their constant quest for adrenaline, there was almost an inevitability about their transition to motor racing, especially with their father's background. They burst onto the IMSA sportscar racing scene in 1978 when Don finished 24th in the Sebring 12 Hours driving a Porsche 934/5.

They were soon entering their own Porsche 935s in the sprint races and co-driving the cars in longer events. No one in the paddock knew much about them, but they were quick to learn and did very well throughout the 1979 IMSA season, with Bill finishing second in the points and Don fourth.

Meanwhile, they also decided to try their hand at Le Mans that year and bought drives for $20,000 each with the renowned team owned by German brothers Erwin and Manfred Kremer to share a well-developed and very competitive Porsche 935 K3. When they arrived at the circuit, they were displeased to learn that the Kremers would be making the decision about the running order of their drivers. On discovering that Klaus Ludwig, the team's highly talented professional driver, was going to start the race, they decided they weren't prepared to be dictated to. Their contention was that they had paid a great deal of money for the privilege of racing there and if Ludwig damaged the car before either of them had a chance to drive it, they would have lost $40,000 with nothing to show for it. When they asked Erwin Kremer what it would take for one of them to start the race, they received the light-hearted response that it could only happen if they were to buy the car outright. He quoted the grossly inflated price of $200,000, far more than the price at which the car had previously been advertised, but they agreed to that straight away. To his amazement, they produced the exact sum in cash from a duffle bag in their caravan.

Even in a year when the field contained relatively few of the faster bespoke sports prototype entries, not even a scriptwriter would have dreamt up a story line of two virtual unknowns winning the world's oldest and most prestigious endurance race. Through the torrential rain that made this Le Mans the slowest for over 20 years, the Kremer entry emerged to claim victory. In doing so, the Whittington brothers completely overshadowed the real Hollywood story provided by the participation of movie superstar Paul Newman in the second-placed 935 entered by Dick Barbour Racing. Although the victory probably wouldn't have been possible without the vastly experienced Ludwig's pace, the brothers nevertheless did their fair share of the driving and were no slouches, as proved by the fact that they beat 13 other 935s. Their miraculous and unlikely victory was a major upset and notable for the fact that it marked the last Le Mans success for a true production-based car.

Team manager Achim Stroth remembered both as being good drivers, with Bill the quicker of the two and Don the more technical, so it was fortunate that it was Don in the car when it broke and he had to jury-rig a

For drug-smuggling brothers Don and Bill Whittington, their finest hour
in racing came when they won the Le Mans 24 Hours in 1979 driving
a Kremer-entered Porsche 935.

fix at the trackside in order to get it back to the pits. Their win led to the
Kremer outfit being bombarded with orders for 935 K3s, including from
the Whittington brothers, who now decided, after being propelled into
sporting stardom, that they would like a couple more of the cars. Legend
has it that they paid for the two further K3s with more cash from the duffle
bag. Although their success encouraged them to enter Le Mans again in
both 1980 and 1981, they didn't come anywhere near the same level of
achievement and failed to finish both times.

Revelling in their success, the pair returned to the US and variously
embarked on race schedules that included the International Race of
Champions and a handful of NASCAR events, with Don taking part in
ten such races and Bill in two, neither with any real success. In sportscars,
however, they continued to make their mark with their bright yellow 935s,
now joined by youngest brother Dale. They scored a good few wins and
podium finishes although some of these successes were called into question

years later when it was discovered that concealed nitrous oxide bottles had been illegally fitted to their 935s during qualifying and connected to modified fuel filler necks. By boosting power output from the normal 750bhp to over 1,000, they had been able to set blisteringly quick laps in qualifying before the bottles were removed for pre-race technical inspections. For 1984, the brothers teamed up with Randy Lanier (see Chapter 34) to form Blue Thunder Racing, which achieved huge success in IMSA with its pair of Chevrolet-powered March cars, Lanier taking the title and Bill finishing runner-up.

Don and Bill also competed sporadically in Indycars, each starting the Indianapolis 500 five times between 1980 and 1985, with the best finish between them being Don's sixth place in 1982. This was the year in which all three brothers qualified for the race, an unprecedented and unique feat in Indy history and a significant achievement for 22-year-old Dale in particular. Much younger than his brothers, by 13 and 10 years, Dale had done far less racing, especially on oval circuits. Unfortunately for him, he was unable to take the start from his 23rd position on the grid after getting caught up in an accident on the final pace car lap precipitated by Kevin Cogan crashing into A.J. Foyt and Mario Andretti at the front of the pack, and he never appeared in the big race again.

S upported by what appeared to be inexhaustible amounts of money, the brothers' racing ambitions appeared to know no boundaries. Although rumours abounded and eyebrows were raised, very few questions were ever asked about the source of funding for their extravagant lifestyle. Illicit enterprise was strongly suspected but without hard evidence people in both racing and aviation circles could only look the other way. Whereas most drivers at that level went out of their way to generate publicity for their sponsors, the publicity-shy Whittingtons had no interest in promoting themselves and, like their friend Randy Lanier, were notably reticent interviewees.

Although their cars were usually devoid of any genuine corporate advertising or signwriting other than the drivers' names on the cockpits, the brothers were conscious of the need to create the illusion that funding for their excesses was coming from legitimate sources, so they occasionally promoted non-existent goods and services for fictitious companies whose names would adorn the flanks of the cars. On one occasion they even went to the lengths of hiring models to spray perfume over race fans under the pretext of it being a new product from one of their fake 'sponsors'. Despite taking a low profile when it came to PR, the brothers did draw attention to themselves by continuing to pay large bills in cash. One day at the March factory at Bicester, Ian Phillips recalls being asked to take the brothers out to lunch at a local pub while Robin Herd counted large stacks of banknotes in payment for three Indycars.

Don and Bill also owned a well-known race circuit, Road Atlanta in Georgia, which they had bought in 1979. It became the base for their businesses and their valuable collection of World War II fighter planes, including a Grumman Bearcat and their matching pair of P-51 Mustangs used for racing. As Mark Raffauf of IMSA recalled, 'At race weekends the brothers would often make a grand entrance by shutting down all track activity in the middle of the day so they could buzz the field in their Mustangs and then land on the back stretch. Once on the ground, the fighter planes would taxi up the hill, underneath the bridge leading onto the front straight, down the other side of the hill and into the pit area on the outside of the track.'

As we have seen, the Whittingtons were no strangers to bending the rules in motorsport, and the same applied in business. The secluded back section at Road Atlanta included a particularly long straight and this doubled as an ideal runway. Aircraft that landed on it were often engaged in the more sinister activity of flying in marijuana that was then hidden in a variety of usefully located buildings before onward distribution. An added attraction was that with thousands of fans paying for entry tickets, refreshments and goods in cash, the race circuit also provided ideal cover for the laundering of money. There were reports of several hundred thousand dollars of receipts being deposited at banks from low-profile 'club' meetings.

Eventually, the brothers' wealth attracted attention from both the Internal Revenue Service (IRS) and the Drug Enforcement Agency (DEA), whose investigations revealed that they had been running a lucrative business smuggling drugs from Colombia. It was alleged that they had established an aircraft rental company and at night-time would run two flights. One would be 'official', with a logged flight plan to a recognised airport, while the other would go unnoticed to Colombia and bring back its illicit cargo.

At the 1985 Indianapolis 500, both brothers qualified well. Don was an impressive sixth fastest, not far behind two-time winner Emerson Fittipaldi and ahead of four-time winner Al Unser, while Bill lined up 12th. Neither finished the race — and neither competed at Indy again. By the time of the 1986 event, where their former Blue Thunder Racing team-mate Randy

Lanier was named 'Rookie of the Year', the two older Whittingtons had been arrested and indicted in a federal court on charges of conspiracy to import marijuana, tax fraud and income tax evasion. Although Lanier was engaged in the same area of illegality, he had operated independently, and when everything blew up both sides claimed ignorance of each other's activities.

'Bill had nothing to do with any of my smuggling,' Lanier said later. 'Whatever he did, he did on his own.' When the entirely innocent Frank Arciero, who at one stage was unwittingly harbouring both Bill Whittington and Randy Lanier in his 1985 Indycar team, asked Whittington about being indicted, the response was, 'Ah, it's a bunch of bullshit, I make my money selling mobile homes.' On a previous occasion when the concerned team owner had questioned Lanier about rumours surrounding Whittington, he had also denied any involvement, saying he was 'totally against any drug habit'.

When the Whittingtons' empire came crashing down, the DEA disclosed that the enterprise had netted them as much as $73 million a year, income that unsurprisingly they omitted to declare to the tax authorities. The prosecution included the accusation that the proceeds from their crimes had been used to finance their racing and further links with drug smuggling were made by an article in the *Sun Sentinel* newspaper stating that their entries in the 1980 Indy 500 had been supported by 'Sun System', a name that was often seen on their Porsche 935s. This was merely a front company, the proprietor of which was one C.W. Cobb, supposedly a Fort Lauderdale suntan lotion distributor, who in a federal investigation codenamed 'Operation Sunburn' was later convicted of running a $300 million marijuana import operation with connections to Pablo Escobar (see Chapter 38).

Investigators determined that Dale Whittington, the youngest of the three brothers, wasn't involved and he was never charged with any crimes. Bill was sentenced to 15 years in prison in 1986 when he admitted to heading up the operation and pleaded guilty to tax evasion and conspiracy charges, abruptly ending a racing career that had seen so much success, including ten IMSA victories. Don was also indicted for drug smuggling but after his brother's plea those charges were dropped and his 18-month sentence was for money laundering and investing the illicit profits in legitimate businesses. As part of the plea deal, the brothers had to forfeit substantial assets of $7 million in restitution to the government, a settlement that included the sale of their prized P-51 Mustangs as well as clones of their Le Mans-winning Porsche 935.

Following their release, Bill's in 1990 after serving only four years, they returned to their first love of aviation and founded an aeroplane sales and leasing company called World Jet based in Fort Lauderdale, Florida. In 2013, World Jet was investigated by federal agents for allegedly running drugs by plane. The possibility that Don and Bill continued to inhabit a murky world received further attention in a February 2014 report in the *Miami New Times* that stated:

> On September 24, 2007, a turbo jet laden with nearly four tons of cocaine crashed in the Yucatán. Flight logs reportedly showed the plane had flown years earlier from Washington, D.C., to Guantánamo. That revelation incited speculation that, in addition to smuggling drugs, the plane had also been used in the rendition of suspected terrorists.
>
> The aircraft's owner was a shell company called Donna Blue. According to the Miami DEA affidavit targeting the Whittington brothers, the firm was being used for 'Operation Mayan Jaguar', a clandestine program run by U.S. Immigration and Customs Enforcement. The Whittingtons, the affidavit alleges, were 'implicated' in selling the turbo jet to the undercover operation.
>
> One of the jet's pilots was Gregory Dean Smith, a Fort Lauderdale man who today is a 'target for trafficking cocaine from South America to Central America', the Miami DEA affidavit alleges. Stranger still, the investigative website Narco News alleges Smith, who today pilots for the Whittingtons, has worked for numerous U.S. intelligence operations.
>
> Around the same time, the Austrian Parliament claimed two planes owned by the Whittingtons had stopped at Guantánamo Bay likely on missions for the CIA, according to Austrian government documents. The planes were listed by their tail numbers, N229WJ and N252WJ. The documents raise the possibility that the CIA employed the Whittingtons in the War on Terror despite the brothers' well-known rap sheets for trafficking — and at a time when the DEA now says the two were back in the drug business.

Bill moved to Colorado where his two daughters, Nerissa Whittington and Keely Reyes, had bought the Pagosa Springs Resort and Spa, and turned it into an opulent hotel complex. He focused on helping them manage the

The Whittington brothers, Don (left) and Bill (centre), chat before Le Mans in 1979 with movie star Paul Newman, who was one of the drivers of the second-placed car.

business but old habits proved difficult to kick and his 'creative accounting' led him, according to a press release issued by the U.S. Department of Justice, to under-report his income received in the form of 'personal expense' from the hotel complex by more than $900,000 and to fail to pay more than $360,000 in taxes. Separately, the U.S. District Court in Colorado had issued a warrant to search World Jet on the request of the DEA, which, together with the FBI, raided the company's offices in a hunt for records of financial transactions between Don and Bill. In an apparent reversal of roles, the damning allegation supporting the search warrant was that Don was tapping into his old network of drug smugglers all over South America and supplying aircraft to cocaine cartels at inflated prices while this time it was Bill who was helping to launder the proceeds through the family-owned hotel business in Colorado. The affidavit suggested that the DEA had been monitoring two offshore bank accounts in Liechtenstein controlled by Bill that generated about $9.7 million in investment income in the period 2003–12 on which he paid no tax. The combined effect of these improprieties was a loss of at least $1.8 million in taxes owed to the IRS. In October 2018, the 68-year-old pleaded guilty in the U.S. District Court in Durango, Colorado, to fraudulently under-reporting his income and filing a false tax form in 2010. In a plea deal he agreed to pay approximately $1.8 million in restitution to the IRS and was sentenced to 18 months in prison.

Upon his release, Bill's name and World Jet were once again in the news. As the COVID-19 pandemic took hold in the spring of 2020, World Jet was awarded nearly $20 million in purchase orders from the state of Oklahoma to provide personal protection equipment (PPE), but when it failed to deliver the orders were cancelled.

On 23rd April 2021, only a few days after being reunited with old friend and team-mate Randy Lanier for the first time in 34 years, 71-year-old Bill Whittington's tumultuous life came to an end. He had taken an aviation enthusiast friend who was suffering from terminal cancer, and had lost his pilot's licence, for a flight in his Merlin aeroplane and crashed in the Arizona desert, killing both of them.

Having avoided the drugs scandals that embroiled his siblings, Dale Whittington went into endurance racing, competing in the IMSA American Le Mans Series and the Daytona 24 Hours in 1999 and 2000. He also competed in Grand Am in 2001, often racing with his eldest brother Don, with whom he also worked at World Jet. Tragically, the 44-year-old was found dead at home in Fort Lauderdale by his eldest son on 14th June 2003, which was Father's Day. The Broward County Coroner's report listed a drug overdose as the cause of death.

Don Whittington courted further controversy when he sued the Hall of Fame Museum at the Indianapolis Motor Speedway over ownership of the famous 1979 Le Mans-winning Porsche 935 K3. The car had been on long-term display there for at least 20 years when, in 2004, Don demanded its return, claiming that he and Bill had merely loaned it rather than donated it. In 2010, the U.S. Court of Appeals ruled in favour of the museum in the absence of any documentation concerning prior ownership.

CHAPTER 64

CHRISTOPHER WILDER

In the tracks of a serial killer

An occasional IMSA driver in 1983–84, this exceedingly
unpleasant individual killed eight women in a seven-week
nationwide rampage of violent sexual crime. The man dubbed
the 'Beauty Queen Killer' was briefly on the FBI's 'Ten Most
Wanted' list and the subject of its biggest-ever manhunt before
he was finally caught, at which point he took the cowardly way
out and killed himself. None of his racing acquaintances had
ever been aware that this outwardly amiable man was
a monster with violent and psychotic tendencies.

Born in 1945 in Sydney, Australia, Christopher Bernard Wilder was the oldest child of an American father, a naval officer, and an Australian mother. According to the *Encyclopedia of Serial Killers*, he was so close to death immediately after his birth that a priest performed the last rites on him. A sickly child, he nearly drowned in a swimming pool when aged two and his formative years were troubled.

After a marriage in 1968 that lasted less than a week before his wife fled from him, the 23-year-old left his home country and arrived in Boynton Beach, Florida, a little way up the coast from Miami. There he established the Sawtel Construction Company and capitalised on a building boom before branching out to become a successful property developer. By 1982, he was making enough money to indulge in his new-found interest of motor racing and started competing in amateur events. He also paid for various girlfriends to attend track experience days at racing schools.

Wilder stepped up a gear in 1983 and made his IMSA début in the GTU class for smaller-engined cars in the Sebring 12 Hours co-driving Jack

Rynerson's Porsche 911 with Van McDonald and the car's owner to finish 27th overall and 10th in class. Wilder partnered Rynerson in two other events that season, at Road Atlanta and the end-of-year finale at Daytona, after which the car owner retired from racing. Striking out on his own in 1984, Wilder entered his sinister-looking black Porsche 911 in February's blue-riband season opener, the Daytona 24 Hours, with two other Florida-based drivers, Buz McCall and Dennis DeFranceschi. Other competitors in this race included some of motorsport's biggest names: past and future Indy 500 champions A.J. Foyt, Mario Andretti and Bobby Rahal, and sports car legends Derek Bell, Bob Wollek, Al Holbert, Hurley Haywood and David Hobbs. Having qualified 66th in a field of 82 cars, the three amateurs retired after completing 212 laps, leaving them 52nd in the overall classification and 14th in the GTU class. Three weeks later, the next event on the IMSA calendar was the Budweiser Grand Prix on the streets of Miami, where the GTU race, a short single-driver contest, saw Wilder finish 17th.

Friends, team-mates and fellow competitors all described the Australian bachelor as a likeable and personable character who was generous to a fault. Indeed, the archetypal 'gentleman racer' behaved like a perfect gentleman off the track too and was noted for impeccable manners, including giving up his seat to women and holding doors open for them. He was even described by fellow racer Vicki Smith as: 'The type of guy you bring home to your parents.'

Wilder's next entry was the Sebring 12 Hours four weeks later. The #51 black Porsche showed up but only McDonald and DeFranceschi were present to race it.

Christopher Wilder's first brush with the law came at the age of 17 when he and other youths were convicted of the gang rape of a girl on a Sydney beach. He pleaded guilty and escaped with a sentence of one year's probation, counselling and electro-shock therapy. All of this was unknown to his young bride six years later but their marriage ended after only a few days because she discovered some dark sexual tendencies.

In 1971, and now living in the US, he was reported to the police in Florida and fined for trying to coerce women into posing for nude photographs. Another arrest for sexual assault soon followed, this time involving a young high school girl, but the only action taken at his trial was a recommendation from the doctor and psychiatrist who evaluated him that he should receive more supervised treatment. Three years later, he posed as a magazine photographer named David Pierce and, in what had become his *modus operandi*, lured a schoolgirl out of a shopping centre on the false promise of

After a seven-week murder spree in 1984, occasional IMSA driver Christopher Wilder — the 'Beauty Queen Killer' — was shot dead by police.

a modelling contract, then drugged and raped her. After she reported him to the police, he was again arrested but this time he claimed that he suffered from blackouts during which he wasn't accountable for his actions and negotiated a plea bargain whereby the penalty was probation with therapy. On a trip back to Australia to visit his parents, he kidnapped two teenage girls from a beach and after tying them up forced them to pose for a series of pornographic photographs. Once again he was arrested but his parents put up the necessary bail and he was allowed to return to Florida until his trial, which was repeatedly postponed, and he never did return to his home country to face justice.

It's thought that Wilder began his nationwide killing spree on 26th February 1984, the day he competed in the Budweiser Grand Prix in Miami. As this circuit was quite short and tightly confined, each of the three IMSA categories — GTU, GTO and GTP — had its own race, starting with the one in which Wilder competed. Afterwards, he recognised 20-year-old model Rosario Gonzalez, whom he had photographed two years earlier and was working at the race. Witnesses saw him talking to her late in the afternoon but she disappeared without ever collecting her earnings for the day and her body has never been found.

On Monday 5th March he kidnapped an ex-girlfriend, 23-year-old Elizabeth Kenyon, a former finalist in the 'Miss Florida' beauty competition with whom he had remained friends although she was dating someone else. Days before her disappearance, she had told her parents that Wilder had claimed he would be able to get her work as 'Miss Budweiser' at the Miami Grand Prix. She too has never been found but her parents hired a private detective who strongly linked her case, and Gonzalez's, to Wilder and alerted the authorities. The *Miami Herald* newspaper reported that police were investigating a racing driver in connection with the disappearances but didn't mention him by name, although Wilder now would have known that the net was closing in because police had visited his office to question him.

On Sunday 18th March, and now on the run, Wilder killed 21-year-old Terry Ferguson in Merritt Island, Florida. Two days later, on Tuesday 20th March, he kidnapped 19-year-old Linda Grover after offering her $25 to pose as a model for him and took her to a motel in Georgia where he tortured her with electric shocks, superglued her eyes shut and raped her, before she managed to escape. He moved on to Beaumont, Texas and on Friday 23rd March repeatedly stabbed to death 24-year-old Terry Walden, a wife, mother and student nurse, after she refused his requests to pose as a model and then dumped her body in a canal before escaping in her yellow Mercury Cougar. On the same day, charges were filed against him in Georgia for Grover's abduction and the FBI, which now also linked him to the disappearances of Gonzalez and Kenyon, began an urgent manhunt.

In a bizarre scenario, the killer owner's racing team competed at Sebring the next day, Saturday 24th March, its personnel initially unaware as to why Wilder hadn't appeared at the racetrack. Instead of taking up his entry, he was over 1,000 miles away in Oklahoma City, where on Monday 26th March he kidnapped 21-year-old Suzanne Logan and drove her 180 miles north to Newton, Kansas, where he tortured and raped her before stabbing her to death. On Thursday 29th March he abducted 18-year-old Sheryl Bonaventura in Colorado and is believed to have killed her in Utah within two days by both shooting and stabbing her, although her body wasn't found for almost five weeks.

The FBI felt that his movements towards the West Coast suggested that he might be tempted to visit a racetrack, specifically the upcoming Long Beach Grand Prix, the first round of the CART PPG Indy Car World Series, but while agents swarmed over the event, Wilder remained elsewhere. On the day of the race, Saturday 31st March, he kidnapped and killed 17-year-old aspiring model Michelle Korfman in Las Vegas, Nevada and dumped her body in southern California where she lay undiscovered for several weeks.

Wilder then attacked and kidnapped 16-year-old Tina Marie Riscio in

Torrance, California on Wednesday 4th April. To make himself appear less threatening and enable him to attract more innocent victims, he forced her to be an accomplice and drove with her back across the country to Indiana, where he abducted another 16-year-old, Dawnette Wilt, and raped her several times before continuing to drive eastwards with her as well. In Penn Yan, New York, he tried to suffocate Wilt before stabbing her twice and leaving her for dead in woods, but miraculously she survived and was able to tell police that the murderer was heading for Canada. On Thursday 12th April, he forced his final victim, 33-year-old Beth Dodge, into his car in Victor, New York and after a short trip shot her in the back before dumping her body in a gravel pit. He then used her Pontiac Firebird to drive Riscio, his 16-year-old hostage, to Logan Airport in Boston where, remarkably, he showed some compassion and bought her a plane ticket back to Los Angeles.

The next day, Friday 13th April, he managed to lure 19-year-old Carol Hilbert into his car in Beverly, Massachusetts after seeing her standing at the side of the road with her broken-down car. He threatened her with a gun while driving but when traffic forced his car to a halt she managed to escape. Now on his own, he drove north towards Canada but by this time his distinctive image was displayed on posters all over the country and a video tape he had made for a dating service had been discovered and was being widely shown on TV.

After reported sightings by some vigilant truck drivers, the police were put on alert. When he stopped at a service station in Colebrook, New Hampshire, just 12 miles from the Canadian border, two state troopers recognised him. When they approached him, he retreated to his car to fetch his Colt Python .357 Magnum. A scuffle ensued and one of the officers tackled him from behind, at which point Wilder turned the revolver on himself and fired two shots. He died instantly and one of the unfortunate police officers was injured.

His seven-week rampage of unimaginable terror had finally been brought to an end.

In his car police found ammunition, handcuffs, rolls of duct tape and lengths of rope. Other items included his business partner's credit card and a book, *The Collector* by John Fowles, a novel that appears to have been the inspiration for several other killers.

Wilder's body was cremated in Florida and his substantial estate divided between the families of his victims. Apart from the eight known murders, the precise number that he actually committed is unknown but he has been subsequently linked as prime suspect to at least 10 more, together with several other cases of rape in Australia and the US.

L.W. WRIGHT

On the wrong side of NASCAR

A completely unknown and still-unidentified swindler managed to take part in a top-level NASCAR race — his one and only recorded race appearance — by being able to talk faster than he drove. To live his dream, he duped NASCAR itself as well as race organisers, sponsors, media, trade suppliers and fellow drivers. No one ever discovered who the mystery driver really was, where he had come from or indeed where he went after the race.

During America's Prohibition Era of 1920–33, when alcohol was banned, bootleggers used specially developed cars to transport illegal whiskey — otherwise known as 'moonshine' because it was made under the light of the moon in the hope that no one would see the smoke rising from secret stills — on back roads in the middle of the night. These cars may have looked understated and ordinary from the outside to avoid unwanted attention but were stripped out inside and had strengthened suspension so that they could carry as much illicit cargo as possible. They were also fitted with significantly more powerful engines that made them fast enough to evade police.

Even before Prohibition was repealed, making the cars redundant, owners would congregate to race them, having honed their driving skills by outrunning the authorities after dark and often with their headlights turned off. It was Bill France who brought together owners, drivers and mechanics and developed unified rules and regulations for the racers based on 'stock' cars (standard showroom models). Thus, the National Association for Stock

This is the start of the Winston 500 NASCAR race at the Talladega Speedway in Alabama on 2nd May 1982. While eventual winner Darrell Waltrip leads the field as it roars away, the mysterious 'L.W. Wright' is somewhere at the back.

Car Auto Racing (NASCAR) was born at the end of 1947 with its first race staged two months later. Since then, NASCAR has evolved into the biggest branch of motorsport in the US and produced numerous national heroes such as Richard Petty, Dale Earnhardt and Jimmie Johnson. Sometimes it has also been an arena for complete unknowns like 'L.W. Wright'.

The first anyone heard of that name in the context of motorsport was in April 1982 when a man who called himself William Dunaway from Hendersonville, Tennessee contacted a newspaper in Nashville — 'Music City' — claiming to represent a promising driver who had lodged an entry under the name Music City Racing for the following week's prestigious Winston 500 at the Talladega Speedway in Alabama. To take part in the race, 'L.W. Wright' had paid NASCAR $115 for a competition licence and $100 for the entry fee and submitted requests for permits for the Music City Racing crew. Although NASCAR officials were suspicious about the new driver's background, 'Wright' claimed to have taken part many years earlier in 43 'Grand National' races and in any case Alabama's 'Right to Work' legislation, incredible as it may seem, allowed him to compete.

Music Row in Nashville is home to radio stations, record labels and recording studios where icons such as Elvis Presley have recorded hits. Somehow 'Wright' managed to tap into the industry by sweet-talking Space Age Marketing's Bernie Terrell, who had little knowledge of or interest in motor racing but could see the PR opportunities, to give him $30,000 plus $7,000 in expenses to fund his alleged race team. Terrell's goodwill enabled 'Wright' to acquire a black-and-gold 1981 Chevrolet Monte Carlo for $20,700 from Sterling Marlin, an up-and-coming NASCAR racer who accepted payment as $17,000 in cash and the balance by cheque. Impressed by his new customer's big spending, Marlin also offered to recruit mechanics and put his own skills and experience to good use by acting as crew chief for the big race. 'Wright' also bought a sizeable transporter.

By calling his team Music City Racing, 'Wright' generated a lot of publicity, especially when he claimed to have additional financial backing from high-profile country music artists Merle Haggard and T.G. Sheppard — which would have been very impressive had it been true. However, Sheppard himself happened to read a newspaper interview with the driver and denied any knowledge of him, to which 'Wright' responded that his announcement of sponsorship had been a little 'premature'. Deep suspicions were already awakening among other drivers on the grid because they had never heard of him either and they had certainly never raced against him. On further questioning, the pretender changed his story to admit that he had only participated in NASCAR's lower-ranking 'Sportsman' class races that took place at 'Grand National' tracks, but not in any 'Grand National' race. But this wasn't true either.

By the time the race weekend arrived, Marlin was also having big doubts about the driver. 'Wright' was clearly way out of his depth and asked peculiar and naive questions that a driver of his so-called experience would never have raised. During qualifying, which was notable for Benny Parsons lapping at 200mph for the first time in NASCAR's history, 'Wright' crashed after two flying laps. However, the car was repairable and somehow he was allowed to start the race, 36th of 40 starters with one of his two laps timed at 187.37mph.

Come race day, 2nd May, David Simko's crash after only four laps brought out caution flags and a safety car for the next six laps. Once the race was running again, it took only three laps of the 2.66-mile tri-oval before 'Wright' was lapped by the best of the star-studded field. At that point, to everyone's relief, officials showed him the black flag, ordering him off the track for being too slow. This led to the only mention of his participation by ESPN television commentator Larry Nuber: 'The black flag [is] coming out for one of the backmarkers. Perhaps a little bit of inexperience showing for the young driver.'

Every starter in NASCAR receives prize money and for his 39th place in the final classification 'Wright' was awarded $1,545, which he made sure he collected after abandoning his car in the pitlane. By the time race winner Darrell Waltrip was soaking up the congratulations in Victory Lane, the pretender had disappeared, leaving behind not just the racing car but also his pit crew and all the equipment he had acquired at other people's expense. To no one's great surprise and confirming the fears of everyone involved, all the swindler's cheques bounced and among those that weren't honoured were payments to Goodyear for tyres, South Central Bell for his phone bill and the landlord of his apartment for rent. Marlin and Terrell, without whose largesse the extraordinary deception might never have got off the ground, were both left significantly out of pocket.

Although NASCAR had warrants issued for the imposter's arrest and Terrell hired a private investigator to try to track him down, four decades passed without anyone ever knowing the true identity of the man who conned his way into taking part in one of the biggest and most prestigious races in American motorsport. However, on the 40th anniversary of the race — 2nd May 2022 — long-time NASCAR journalist Rick Houston released an interview on his Scene Vault Podcast with a man in poor health whom he believed to be 'Wright' after spending 12 months searching for him.

CHAPTER 66
CHARLES ZWOLSMAN SR
Tracked down

Although Charles Zwolsman and his son of the same name never shared driving duties in a racing car, they did emulate the John Pauls (see Chapter 45), another father-and-son partnership of Dutch heritage, with a racing habit allegedly funded by large-scale drug trafficking.

Charles 'Sjarrel' Zwolsman was born in Oostzaan in the Netherlands in 1955. He wasn't an academically gifted child and spent as much time as possible developing a self-built go-kart. At the age of 18 he married a local girl who had become pregnant by him and his parents decided to help the young father-to-be by buying him a flower stall. Within only a few years, Zwolsman had developed from being a simple florist into running a large wholesaling business that was successful enough to enable him to pursue his passion of motor racing, starting with local events at Zandvoort.

As his business prospered, he was able to move up the ranks of GT and sports car racing to the point where, by 1990, he was competing in the World Sports-Prototype Championship (WS-PC) for Group C cars in a Spice SE89C run by Chamberlain Engineering and usually partnered with British driver Nick Adams. For 1991, he set up his own team, Euro Racing, and did another season in the same championship, now renamed the Sportscar World Championship (SWC) and invited fellow Dutchman Cor Euser to share his Spice SE90C. Ambitiously competing against manufacturer-backed teams from Jaguar, Mercedes, Peugeot, Porsche and Toyota, the pair impressively scored four fourth places — at Suzuka, Monza, Magny-Cours and Mexico City — and Zwolsman managed to end up sixth in the drivers' standings.

He had another crack at the series in 1992, this time fielding a Lola T92/10, but persistent transmission problems meant that he only saw the chequered flag once during the entire season. The highlight of his season came at the Le Mans 24 Hours where, with a late addition to the squad, he teamed up with Heinz-Harald Frentzen, who had been dropped by the Mercedes young-driver programme and was seriously considering getting out of racing. However, Frentzen's strong performance in the race led directly to a drive in Japanese Formula 3000 and in turn to his Formula 1 début with the Sauber team a year later, following which he went on to score three Grand Prix victories, one with Williams and two with Jordan. Zwolsman is rightly credited with resurrecting Frentzen's career.

Two of Zwolsman's sons, Ross and Charles, followed their father into motor racing and Charles Sr oversaw Charles Jr's career. After winning his second kart race in 1990, the youngster competed against the likes of Jenson Button and Kimi Räikkönen over a period of eight years. This was followed by progress through a traditional route of Formula Ford and Formula Renault, where he won a few races, before moving on to race in European Formula 3. He competed for both Colin Kolles and Manor Motorsport, where he was Lewis Hamilton's team-mate in 2004 but only finished 17th in the standings. After an unremarkable career up to this point, Zwolsman Jr moved to America in a last-minute deal for 2005 where the unknown 25-year-old quickly made an impression and won three races on his way to sealing the Toyota Formula Atlantic crown. This success led to the opportunity to race Indycars, first with Team Australia and then with the Mijack Conquest team with which he ended up 13th in the 2006 standings after eight finishes in the top ten.

By the time Charles Zwolsman Sr was 30, his business had gone bankrupt, his marriage had broken up and his motor racing was consuming increasingly large amounts of money. It didn't take long before he decided to capitalise on his knowledge of international logistics, learned from his experience of flower wholesaling and the convenient location of the Netherlands. He became involved in drug trafficking.

On one of his earliest forays to England, he was arrested while in possession of 2,000kg of hashish and received a two-year prison sentence,

By 1991, world championship sports car driver Charles Zwolsman Sr, pictured (right) with his Spice SE90C and the famous Hawaiian Tropic girls before that year's Le Mans 24 Hours, had become an international drug baron.

although it wasn't until 1992 that he ended up behind bars. Meanwhile, he had started a car dealership, Investment Cars BV, specialising in high-priced prestige marques that were bought for cash. Through this company, with its Dutch, Danish and American offices, he was able to launder the vast sums of money that he was making from smuggling 'product' from Morocco and Spain. He lived in a substantial villa in Blaricum, not far from Amsterdam, and also had a 45-metre yacht called *Maxime Z*, named after his daughter with girlfriend Sylvia, moored near St Tropez in the south of France.

By 1991, the former florist was not only racing at an international level but had also become an international drug baron of considerable stature in that world. The murder of notorious former drug lord Klaas Bruinsma, who had been gunned down in June that year in front of the Amsterdam Hilton by Martin Hoogland, an ex-policeman turned associate, provided him with the opportunity to expand his business even further. Bruinsma had become the largest drug dealer in Europe and his organisation had been generating as much as $500,000 a day at the time of his death so with this rival out of the way Zwolsman Sr was able to expand still further. He now headed a sophisticated criminal organisation that numbered 60 people who cultivated and sold drugs on a massive scale before laundering the proceeds. Even when he was eventually imprisoned in Leeuwarden in 1992, he continued to conduct business through phone calls and notes smuggled out to gang members by his girlfriend.

Dutch police threw resources at breaking up his ring and set up a 50-strong taskforce named 'Formula' in deference to their quarry's interests. Two days before his release date in September 1993, 'Formula' officers pounced. As well as arresting Zwolsman Sr in prison, they raided several locations around the world, arresting 66 people and seizing nearly 50 high-value cars. After some of his former employees provided incriminating evidence, Zwolsman Sr received a new sentence of four years. When he appealed, the term was increased to five years.

Upon his release at the end of 1997, he went back to trading cars, specialising in Porsches through his company Cool Cars Porsches, but he also started dealing in drugs again. After just three years of freedom, he was arrested and imprisoned again for involvement in a large drug cartel exporting hashish. Once out again, he continued to be arrested on a regular basis for more drug-dealing and related offences but managed to avoid conviction. That changed in 2009 with an arrest on charges dating back to 2006 that included possession of 2,000kg of hashish, 60kg of amphetamines, four firearms and the management of three cannabis farms in Barneveld and Lunteren. Sentenced in 2010 to three years in prison in Nieuwegein, he was found dead in his cell the following year. The cause of the 55-year-old's death has never been disclosed.

Charles Zwolsman Jr's most significant race appearance came at Le Mans in 2009 when he reunited with Colin Kolles's team to drive an Audi R10 with André Lotterer and the pair finished seventh overall. However, this was also the year of his father's final arrest and that had to significant ramifications for him.

Evidence that more than €1 million had been paid from bank accounts in Luxembourg to a racing team in the US led to allegations that his racing had been entirely funded by the proceeds of his father's crimes. At the end of 2011, he was charged with involvement in money laundering, which he denied. In court, the prosecution requested a 15-month suspended jail sentence, a fine and 240 hours of community service but he continued to fight the allegations and was eventually cleared of all charges in 2016. Since then, he has unsurprisingly kept a low profile but maintains an interest in the sport by making a legitimate living as a driver coach.

GLOSSARY

AAA	American Automobile Association	CIA	Central Intelligence Agency (USA)
ACM	Automobile Club de Monaco	CNC	Computer Numerical Control
ACO	Automobile Club de l'Ouest	CPS	Crown Prosecution Service
ADAC	Allgemeiner Deutscher Automobil-Club	CSI	Commission Sportive Internationale
AIB	Allied Irish Bank	DEA	Drug Enforcement Agency (USA)
ALMS	American Le Mans Series	DFV	Double Four Valve
ANDRA	Australian National Drag Racing Association	DNF	Did Not Finish
ARCA	Automobile Racing Club of America	DNS	Did Not Start
		DNQ	Did Not Qualify
ATA	Air Transport Auxiliary	DNPQ	Did Not Pre-Qualify
ATM	Automated Teller Machine	ETCC	European Touring Car Championship
BARC	British Automobile Racing Club		
		ELMS	European Le Mans Series
BDA	Belt Drive, A series	EU	European Union
BDG	Belt Drive, G series	FBI	Federal Bureau of Investigation (USA)
BHP	Brake Horse Power		
BLB	Bayerische Landesbank	FFSA	Fédération Francaise du Sport Automobile
BRCA	Bureau Central de Renseignements et d'Action		
		FIA	Fédération Internationale de l'Automobile
BRM	British Racing Motors		
BRDC	British Racing Drivers' Club	FIFA	Fédération Internationale de Football Association
BRSCC	British Racing & Sports Car Club		
		FISA	Fédération Internationale de Sport Automobile
BTCC	British Touring Car Championship		
		FOA	Formula One Administration
CART	Championship Auto Racing Teams (USA)	FOCA	Formula One Constructors' Association (formerly FICA)
CCJ	County Court Judgment		
CCRC	Criminal Cases Review Commission	FOM	Formula One Management
		FTC	Federal Trade Commission

FTSE	Financial Times Stock Exchange		NHRA	National Hot Rod Association (USA)
FVA	Four Valve, A series		NSC	National Saloon Car Championship
GBH	Grievous Bodily Harm			
GLAS	González Luna Associates		OPEC	Organisation of the Petroleum Exporting Countries
GPDA	Grand Prix Drivers' Association			
GRP	Glass Reinforced Plastic		PAYE	Pay As You Earn (UK)
HMRC	Her Majesty's Revenue & Customs		RAC	Royal Automobile Club
			RAF	Royal Air Force
ICSS	International Centre for Sport Security		RICO	Racketeer Influenced and Corrupt Organisations Act (USA)
IOC	International Olympic Committee			
			RUC	Royal Ulster Constabulary
IMF	International Monetary Fund		SCCA	Sports Car Club of America
IMSA	International Motor Sports Association			
			SCU	Special Crimes Unit
IRA	Irish Republican Army		SEC	Securities and Exchange Commission (USA)
IRL	Indy Racing League			
IRS	Internal Revenue Service (USA)		SFO	Serious Fraud Office
			SHKP	Sun Hung Kai Properties
ISC	Interactive Sportscar Championship		SS	Schutzstaffel
			TILA	Truth in Lending Act (USA)
ITA	International Touring Association		TPR	The Pensions Regulator
			UCLA	University of California, Los Angeles
LMP	Le Mans Prototype			
MCD	Motor Circuit Developments		UPI	United Press Agency
			USAC	United States Auto Club
MRD	Motor Racing Developments		USAR	United Speed Alliance Racing (USA)
MDMA	Methylenedioxy-methamphetamine			
			VAT	Value Added Tax
MSV	Motorsport Vision		WEC	World Endurance Championship
NART	North American Racing Team			
			WFMS	World Federation of Motor Sport
NASCAR	National Association for Stock Car Auto Racing		WMSC	World Motor Sport Council
NCAP	New Car Assessment Programme		WSCC	World Sports Car Championship

REFERENCES

Akira Akagi *How to Build a Car* by Adrian Newey, *Le Soir*, *Motor Sport*

Kankamol Albon *Formula 1: The Knowledge* by David Hayhoe, *East Anglian Daily Times*, *Daily Mail*, *Motor Sport*, BBC News, Reuters

Giovanna Amati *Autosport*, *Motor Sport*, Joe Saward

Franco Ambrosio *Autosport*, *Motor Sport*, *Autocourse*

Simon Atkinson *Watford Advertiser*, *Accountancy Daily*

Trevor Baines *Daily Mail*, *The Independent*, *The Times*, *Daily Telegraph*, *Daily Express*, *Isle of Man News*, Press Association, BBC, *Motor Sport*

Jean-Marie Balestre *The Guardian*, *Autoweek*, *Business F1*, Joe Saward

Ted Ball *The Independent*, *Accountancy Age*, *Motor Sport*

John Bartlett *Chequered Justice* by John Bartlett

David Blakely *The Times*, *Daily Telegraph*, *Sheffield Daily Telegraph*, *Daily Mirror*

Bob Boston *The Charlotte Observer*, Jim Utter, Blake Hanson, Jared Paben, Cox Media Group

Lord Charles Brocket *Call me Charlie* by Charles Brocket, *Daily Express*, *The Independent*, *Spokesman Review*, Courthouse News Service

Ian Burgess *Cooper Cars* by Doug Nye, *Grand Prix Who's Who* by Steve Small, *Daily Mail*, *The Guardian*, *Autocourse*, Gordon Cruickshank, 500 Owners' Association

Didier Calmels *Le Soir*, *Autocourse*, *Autosport*, *Jour de Course*

Colin Chapman *The DeLorean Story: The Car, the People the Scandal* by Nick Sutton, *Team Lotus: My View From The Pit Wall* by Peter Warr, *Colin Chapman: The Man and his Cars* by Gérard 'Jabby' Crombac, *Colin Chapman: Wayward Genius* by Mike Lawrence, *Jochen Rindt: Uncrowned King of Formula 1* by David Tremayne, *Jochen Rindt: A Man of Hidden Depths* by Erich Glavitza, *Mario Andretti* by Nigel Roebuck, *Motor Sport* (Paul Fearnley), *The New York Times*

Dominic Chappell *The Guardian*, *The Sunday Times*, *Daily Mail*, *The Sun*, *Scottish Daily Mail*, *Retail Gazette*, Sky News, Jaya Narain, Christopher Tate, Martin Braybrook

Jack Cottle *Daily Mail*, *The Guardian*, *The Sunday Times*, *The Irish Times*, *Irish Independent*, *The Argus*, *Autosport*

Jerry Dominelli *Captain Money and the Golden Girl* by Donald C. Bauder, *MoneyWeek*, *The San Diego Union-Tribune*, *San Diego Reader*, *The New York Times*, *Time*, *Los Angeles Times*, *Motor Sport*, Michael Cotton

Juan Manuel Fangio *Fangio: The Life Behind The Legend* by Gerald Donaldson, *Fangio: My Racing Life* by Juan Manuel Fangio with Roberto Carozzo, *On Four Wheels*, Joe Saward, Laurence Edmondson

Luis Fontés *The Times*, *The Autocar*, *Motor Sport*, Mick Walsh

Jonathan France *Racecar Engineering*, *Autoweek*, *Yorkshire Post*, *Shropshire Star*, *Yorkshire Business*, *Yorkshire Evening Post*, *Batley & Birstall News*, *Pontefract & Castleford Express*, *Yorkshire Live*, www.gov.uk

REFERENCES

Bertrand Gachot *Eddie Jordan: The biography* by Timothy Collins, *Eddie Jordan: An Independent Man* by Eddie Jordan, *Motor Sport*, *Autosport*, *Daily Telegraph*, *Sunday Independent* (Dublin), *Le Soir*, *Evening Standard*, *Irish Times*, Sky News, Ian Phillips, Joe Saward, Leigh O'Gorman

Elmer George *Grand Prix Who's Who* by Steve Small, *Washington Morning Star*, *The Nashua Telegraph*, *The New York Times*, *The Indianapolis Star*, *Autocourse*, *Shell Motorsport Profile*, ESPN, Jeff Olson

Fernando González Luna *Autosprint*, *Autosport*, *Motoring News*, Joe Saward, Jeremy Clarkson

Gerhard Gribkowsky *No Angel: The Secret Life of Bernie Ecclestone* by Tom Bower, *Bernie's Game* by Terry Lovell, *Bernie: The Biography of Bernie Ecclestone* by Susan Watkins, *BILD*, *The Guardian*, *Business F1*, BBC News, Christian Sylt

André Guelfi *Formula One: The Knowledge* by David Hayhoe, *The Guardian*, *Wall Street Journal*, *The Washington Post*, *Malta Today*, *Times of Malta*, *Le Monde*

Gene Haas *The New York Times*, *Toronto Star*, *Ventura County Star*, *USA Today*, *Autoweek*, *Autosport*, ESPN

Angela Harkness *Associated Press*, *Vail Daily*, *Taiwan News*, *Car and Driver*

Roy James *Pedals and Pistons* by Peter Procter, *Motor Sport*, *Autosport*, Joe Saward

Michael Jones *Daily Mail*, *Accountancy Daily*

Achilleas Kallakis *Survive, Drive, Win* by Nick Fry, *The Guardian* (Nick Mathiason), *Property Week*, *The Irish Times*, *The Times*, BBC News, Peter Bill, Simon Bowers

Jonathan Kern *Autocar*, *New Haven Register*, *The Guardian* (Julia Harley Brewer), *The Independent*, *Unsolved Mysteries* (TV series), Jonathan Palmer

Russell King *Jersey Evening Post*, *Business Insider*, *The Guardian*, *Sonntagszeitung*, *Autosport*, *Business F1*, BBC

Randy Lanier *Sports Illustrated*, *Sun Sentinel*, *Rolling Stone*, *Miami Herald*, Damon Tabor, Jason Henry, Will Higgins

Vic Lee *Touring Car Racing 1958–2018* by Matt James, *Daily Mail*, *Newcastle Journal*, *Yorkshire Post*, *Scottish Herald*, *Sunday Mercury*, Steve Soper, Vic Lee, William Kimberley

Colin Lees *The Bankrupt, the Conman, the Mafia and the Irish Connection* by Chris Moore, *Hidden Glory: The Story of the Crosslé Car Company* by Alan Tyndall, *The Irish Times*, *The Irish Independent*, *Belfast Telegraph*, *The Herald* (Scotland), *The Guardian*, *The Times*, *Liverpool Echo*

Greg Loles *Road & Track*, *Autoweek*, *New Haven Register*, *Connecticut Post*, *GreekNews*, *Sports Car Racing News*, Marshall Pruett

Ricardo Londoño *El Tiempo*, Mike Doodson

Joachim Lüthi *Bernie's Game* by Terry Lovell, *Autocourse*, *Autosport*, *Motor Sport*

Malik Ado Ibrahim *Motor Sport*

Sid Miller *Paying for the Past* by Geoff Green, *The Times*, *The Argus*, *Daily Express*, *The Scotsman*, Geoff Green, Wil Arif, Bob Constanduros, Joe Saward

Max Mosley *Formula One and Beyond* by Max Mosley, *Autosport*, Joe Saward

James Munroe *News and Star*, *Motor Trader*, *Road & Track*, *Daily Express*, *Accountancy Age*, John & Ann Swift, Richard Smeeton, Chris Goodwin, Calum Lockie

471

REFERENCES

Don Nichols *From Drawing Board to Chequered Flag* by Tony Southgate, *Arrows* by Jonathan Nash, *Shadow: The Magnificent Machines of a Man of Mystery* by Pete Lyons, *Autosport*, www.vice.com

John Paul Sr & Jr *50/50* by Sylvia Wilkinson, *The New York Times*, *Los Angeles Times*, *Chicago Tribune*, *Autoweek*, Robin Miller

Nelson Piquet Jr *Total Competition* by Ross Brawn and Adam Parr, *Formula One and Beyond* by Max Mosley, *Survive, Drive, Win* by Nick Fry, Nigel Roebuck, Adam Cooper

Cyril de Rouvre *L'Express*, Joe Saward

Tomas Scheckter *Autosport*, *The Times*

Nigel Stepney *Total Competition* by Ross Brawn and Adam Parr, *Formula One and Beyond* by Max Mosley, *The Independent*, *Autocourse*, *Autosport*, *Motor Sport*, David Tremayne, Mark Hughes, Joe Saward, Alan Henry, Mike Lawrence

Brett Stevens *The Boss: The Brett Stevens Story* by John Van Daal, *The Guardian*, *Brisbane Times*, *The Courier Mail*, *Autoweek*, ABC News Australia

Sulaiman Al-Kehaimi *The Guardian*, *The Independent*, *Oxford Mail*, *Business F1*

Adrian Sutil *Formula One: The Knowledge* by David Hayhoe, *Grand Prix Who's Who* by Steve Small

Calisto Tanzi *Money Week*, *The Florentine*, *The New York Times*

David Thieme *Team Lotus: My View from the Pit Wall* by Peter Warr, *Colin Chapman: The Man and his Cars* by Gérard 'Jabby' Crombac, *Colin Chapman: Wayward Genius* by Mike Lawrence

Mickey Thompson *Mickey Thompson: The fast life and tragic death of a racing legend* by Eric Arenson, *Killing of a Legend* by Ronald E. Bowers, *Los Angeles Times*, *Muscle Machines*

Gérard Toth Joe Saward

Scott Tucker *Reuters*, *Daily Mail*, *Wall Street Journal*, *The Kansas City Star*, Marshall Pruett, Netflix

Jean-Pierre Van Rossem *The Independent*, *Daily Telegraph*, *AP News*, *Krant Van West-Vlaanderen*, *Autosport*, *Autoweek*, *Motor Sport*, *Autocourse*, Rob Widdows, Paul Fearnley, Simon Taylor

Jos Verstappen *Business F1*, *Autosport*, *Daily Mirror*, *The Sun*

Donald Walker *Bernie's Game* by Terry Lovell, *Business F1*, Joe Saward

Klaus Walz *Autosport*, *Autocourse*, *Le Soir*

Nick Whiting *The Curse of Brink's-Mat* by Wensley Clarkson, *The Sun*, *Autosport*, *Motor Sport*, *Business F1*, Joe Saward, Simon Arron

Don & Bill Whittington *The Indianapolis Star*, *Sun Sentinel*, *Miami New Times*, *Autoweek*, John Ficarra, Will Higgins, Terrence McCoy, Marshall Pruett, Mark Raffauf

Christopher Wilder *The Beauty Queen Killer* (Serial Killer Documentary, YouTube)

L.W. Wright *The Tennessean*, Larry Woody

Charles Zwolsman Sr *The Hunt for Octopus* by Henk Schutten, *On Life and Death* by Gerlof Leistra, Adam Cooper

INDEX

INDEX

THE AUTHOR

Crispian Besley is a first-time author with a life-long interest in cars and a passion for motor racing. Inspired by James Hunt's Formula 1 exploits with Hesketh and having become friends with the World Champion's youngest brother at school, he competed in Formula Ford during the late 1970s against future Grand Prix stars, including Nigel Mansell, Jonathan Palmer, Kenny Acheson, Tommy Byrne and Mike Thackwell, but had to face the reality that lack of finance and his results were not going to earn him a place in Formula 1. Under increasing pressure from his parents to get a 'proper' job, he embarked on a 30-year career in the city. Later he returned to racing as an enthusiastic amateur, firstly in Ferraris but mainly in historic single-seaters, which have included a Formula 1 Cooper car as well as Surtees TS15 and Brabham BT38 Formula 2 cars. His main focus has been historic Formula Junior, in which he has competed all over Europe, in New Zealand and America in a variety of cars including Gemini, Lotus, OSCA, Elva and Cooper. An enthusiastic collector of classic cars, he lives in a 16th century manor house in Northamptonshire, conveniently close to Silverstone.